Praise for *Nothing Less Than War*

"*Nothing Less Than War* is a thoughtful look at America's entry into World War I. Based on impressive research, it carries the reader back to a very different time, reassesses the wide-ranging debate over the war in Europe, and provides a stimulating reexamination of the strengths and weaknesses of Woodrow Wilson's leadership."
—Charles E. Neu, coeditor of *Artists of Power: Theodore Roosevelt, Woodrow Wilson, and Their Enduring Impact on U.S. Foreign Policy*

"Justus Doenecke has written a model of judicious scholarship. Historians and nonhistorians alike will profit from reading his informed and insightful account of a pivotal period in American diplomatic history."
—George H. Nash, author of *The Life of Herbert Hoover: The Humanitarian, 1914–1917*

"Justus Doenecke has written a fine, authoritative study of America's flawed struggle for neutrality in the First World War—and the first comprehensive reexamination of the subject in more than a generation."
—Thomas J. Knock, author of *To End All Wars: Woodrow Wilson and the Quest for a New World Order*

"Thorough, thoughtful, pointed, and wise, this sprightly, sometimes wry account covers familiar material with fresh insight and commendably a sense of irony. A splendid read for anyone with an interest in Wilson and the war."
—Mark T. Gilderhus, author of *Pan American Visions: Woodrow Wilson in the Western Hemisphere, 1913–1921*

"Justus Doenecke's impressive new study of President Woodrow Wilson's attempt to keep the United States out of the Great War by maintaining American neutrality from 1914 to 1917 is a substantial contribution to historical scholarship. It offers three major contributions: first, an excellent depiction of public opinion during these years as expressed by the press and by leaders in Congress and various national organizations; second, a comprehensive review of historical scholarship, which is integrated into the narrative throughout the chapters; and third, a clear assessment of Wilson's leadership within this framework."
—Lloyd Ambrosius, author of *Wilsonianism: Woodrow Wilson and His Legacy in American Foreign Relations*

Nothing Less Than War

Nothing Less Than War

A New History of America's Entry into World War I

Justus D. Doenecke

THE UNIVERSITY PRESS OF KENTUCKY

Copyright © 2011 by The University Press of Kentucky
Scholarly publisher for the Commonwealth,
serving Bellarmine University, Berea College, Centre
College of Kentucky, Eastern Kentucky University,
The Filson Historical Society, Georgetown College,
Kentucky Historical Society, Kentucky State University,
Morehead State University, Murray State University,
Northern Kentucky University, Transylvania University,
University of Kentucky, University of Louisville,
and Western Kentucky University.
All rights reserved.

Editorial and Sales Offices: The University Press of Kentucky
663 South Limestone Street, Lexington, Kentucky 40508–4008
www.kentuckypress.com

15 14 13 12 11   5 4 3 2 1

Library of Congress Cataloging-in-Publication Data
Doenecke, Justus D.
    Nothing less than war : a new history of America's entry into World
War I / Justus D. Doenecke.
       p.   cm.
    Includes bibliographical references and index.
    ISBN 978-0-8131-3002-6 (hardcover : acid-free paper) —
    ISBN 978-0-8131-3003-3 (ebook)
    1. World War, 1914–1918—United States. 2. United States—Politics
and government—1913–1921. 3. Wilson, Woodrow, 1856–1924. 4. World
War, 1914–1918—Diplomatic history. 5. World War, 1914–1918—Public
opinion. I. Title.

    D619.D64 2010
    940.3'73—dc22   2010045039

This book is printed on acid-free recycled paper meeting
the requirements of the American National Standard
for Permanence in Paper for Printed Library Materials.

Manufactured in the United States of America.

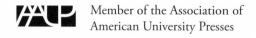

Member of the Association of
American University Presses

This book is dedicated to my fellow historians
John Belohlavek
Irwin Gellman
David Trask

and to New College librarians
the late Holly Barone
Barbara Dubreuil
Ed Foster
Gail Novak
Caroline Reed

I advise that the Congress declare the recent course of the Imperial German Government to be in fact nothing less than war against the Government and people of the United States.

—President Woodrow Wilson, War Message to Congress, April 2, 1917

Contents

Preface

Some years ago I was privileged to participate in a seminar on the presidency of Woodrow Wilson conducted by Arthur S. Link, the world's foremost scholar on America's twenty-eighth president. My doctoral dissertation, however, though written under Link's direction, centered on U.S.–Far Eastern relations in the early 1930s. Since then I have worked primarily in the presidencies of Herbert Hoover and Franklin Delano Roosevelt, with a side excursion to the those of James A. Garfield and Chester Alan Arthur. Yet, despite what has long been the main focus of my research, Wilson's leadership has never ceased to fascinate me, in particular his foreign policy during World War I and its aftermath. I began this book in part with the aim of self-education, hoping to share with both general reader and advanced scholar my extensive investigation in the secondary literature and published primary sources.

Since 1965, when Link's multivolume biography reached the age of American belligerency, and since 1983, when Link's edition of the Wilson papers approached the time when the president signed the war resolution, many studies have appeared, often drawing upon Link's work. Even within the past decade, scholars have produced a host of specialized accounts. Included are major works that concentrate on Wilson's neutrality policy, compare the president's view with those of Americans of pacifist and "Atlanticist" persuasions, cover women's activism and citizen diplomacy, and examine submarine strikes against American ships just before the United States entered the conflict. We have also garnered fresh biographies of Colonel Edward Mandell House, William Jennings Bryan, William Randolph Hearst, Theodore Roosevelt, and Wilson himself. Certain neglected monographs, articles, and doctoral dissertations—some dating back several decades—

should be integrated into a general narrative. In order to make my work of synthesis complete and to recognize that the study of history involves a never-ending dialogue among its practitioners, I have included the views of leading scholars on controversial matters.

Much of my research over the years has focused upon opponents of American foreign policy during the initial years of World War II and the cold war, and this work continues somewhat in that vein. In examining the debates over Wilsonian foreign policy toward Europe in the years 1914–17, I have sought to scrutinize the events of the period from several vantage points. The published Wilson papers, the *New York Times,* and the *Congressional Record* remain indispensable. Certain vehicles of opinion have proven particularly helpful: the *Nation,* pro-Wilson but harboring pacifist leanings; the *New Republic,* a progressive weekly that articulated its own brand of Realpolitik; the *Outlook,* which combined Protestant moralism with Rooseveltian stridency; the fervently pro-German *Fatherland;* and Hearst's *New York American,* a daily that linked the most aggressive form of militarism with a neutralist posture toward the European war.

In an effort to keep my references in manageable shape, I have usually limited endnotes to direct quotations, diplomatic documents, and the contemporary press. For readers who seek to ascertain my sources for sheer narrative, such as the sinking of merchant ships or the military course of the war in Europe, I have provided an extensive bibliographical essay.

This book could never have been written without the aid of others. Particularly meticulous readings have been given by John Belohlavek, Irwin Gellman, and David Trask. For all three no book dedication is truly adequate. Perceptive comments have also been offered on the entire draft by John Milton Cooper Jr., John A. Thompson, Laszlo Deme, Scott Perry, Thomas Jackson, and June and Elliot Benowitz. Lloyd Ambrosius kindly read introductory material and my conclusion. The entire library staff of the New College of Florida have extended themselves far beyond any reasonable call of duty, and I must single out those to whom I have also dedicated this work: Gail Novak, Caroline Reed, Barbara Dubreuil, Ed Foster, and the late Holly Barone. The college generously awarded me a research grant in the summer of 2005. Ben Proctor expedited my research in the Hearst press. As an editor Steve Wrinn has been all one could ever hope for. No one could extend more friendship nor offer more encouragement. As always, my wife Carol has been my most rigorous critic and closest collaborator.

1

Setting the Stage

"WE ARE WALKING ON quicksand," wrote Woodrow Wilson to a cousin in September 1915. For over a year the president had sought to steer a neutral course during a conflict first known as the Great War, then as World War I. Costing 30 million casualties and 8 million dead, the event was sufficiently cataclysmic for diplomat and historian George Frost Kennan to designate it "*the* great seminal conflict of this century."[1] During the past few months, one major power had confiscated huge amounts of American goods being shipped to Imperial Germany. Another leading belligerent had sunk the world's largest ocean liner, in the process killing well over one hundred U.S. citizens.

That autumn the situation showed itself increasingly precarious. On one side of the massive struggle were the Central Powers, in August 1914 an alliance of Germany and Austria-Hungary but soon extending to the Ottoman Empire and close to a year later to Bulgaria. On the other side were the Allies, also known as the Entente, a coalition of Britain, France, and Russia. Japan joined the Allies in late August 1914, Italy in May 1915, and Rumania in August 1916. At the time Wilson voiced his apprehension, the French were about to begin a futile offensive between Rheims and the Argonne forest, the Italians were in the midst of a series of inconclusive battles on the Isonzo River, and the Russians had just lost all of Poland, Lithuania, and Courland, a duchy located in western Latvia.

During the entire period of American neutrality, Wilson's term "quicksand" was a most apt one. To the chief executive the conflict appeared as if it would never end. Possibilities of American ensnarement seemed most real, particularly given the crises created by Germany's submarine warfare against merchant and passenger ships.

1

The United States remained the world's strongest neutral power from August 1914, when the conflict erupted, until April 1917, when it entered the struggle. During this time, Americans fiercely debated every facet of administration policy, ranging from how best to sustain traditional commercial rights to providing the most effective means of maintaining the country's security.

Obviously Wilson was American's foremost policymaker. Before he became chief executive in 1913, he had held various professorships and had served as president of Princeton University and governor of New Jersey. His voluminous writings concentrated on American history and government, not on European diplomacy and global rivalries, though he demonstrated genuine familiarity with Western political institutions. A major work, *The State* (1889), traced the evolution of governmental forms from classical antiquity to contemporary western Europe. At Princeton he had taught courses in international law. After 1902, when he was chosen to lead the university, he occasionally wrote essays on government and politics but henceforth engaged in little serious reading.

Years before he entered the White House, he developed distinctive views of America's role in the world community. Although critical of his nation's actions in the Mexican war ("ruthless aggrandizement") and the Hawaiian revolution of 1893 ("mischievous work"), he perceived the Spanish-American War as rooted in "an impulse of humane indignation and pity." In general, the United States had been founded to serve humanity, bringing "liberty to mankind." By sheer moral example, America could offer such virtues as self-government, "enlightened systems of law," and "a temperate justice" to a backward world. Conversely, if the nation acted irresponsibly abroad, it would compromise its democratic values. In his first Fourth of July address as president, he remarked: "America has lifted high the light which will shine unto all generations and guide the feet of mankind to the goal of justice and liberty and peace."[2]

In fulfilling the American mission, Wilson's religion played a crucial function. The son, grandson, and nephew of Presbyterian ministers, in 1905 he defined his nation's "mighty task" as making "the United States a mighty Christian Nation," a country that would in turn "Christianize the world."[3] Care should be taken, however, in describing Wilson's supposed messianism. Admittedly, much of his self-assurance was grounded in the belief that he could serve as a chosen instrument of an omniscient deity, but he also thought every individual, not he alone, could assume such responsibilities. Both individuals and nations lay subject to a divine moral law that they could not transgress without peril. He even perceived God's will in his personal defeats.

In 1904 the future president spoke of sharing America's global calling with the British Empire: "The Anglo-Saxon people have undertaken to reconstruct the affairs of the world, and it would be a shame upon them to withdraw their hand." Wilson harbored strong English ties. His mother was born in the British Isles, as were both paternal grandparents. He greatly admired English culture and institutions, esteeming the practices of Parliament and revering such figures as Edmund Burke, William E. Gladstone, and political theorist Walter Bagehot. In 1900 he praised Secretary of State John Hay for confirming "our happy alliance of sentiment and purpose with Great Britain."[4] Before assuming the presidency, he had visited the British Isles several times, particularly enjoying long walks in the Lake District, but had crossed the Channel only once to visit the Continent.

Like the British, Wilson believed in overseas expansion. He was the first prominent scholar to endorse the thesis of historian Frederick Jackson Turner, a personal friend, who argued that the frontier had forged American nationalism and democracy. The closing of the nation's hinterland, Wilson wrote at the turn of the century, necessitated venturing into new territory: "Our interests must march forward, altruists though we are; other nations must see to it they stand off, and do not seek to stay us." Convinced that the nation must retain its gains of the Spanish-American War, he expressed thanks that America, not Germany or Russia, had acquired the Philippines, even alleging that his country represented "the light of day" and the two rivals "the night of darkness." By 1913, however, during a major crisis with Mexico, he pledged that "the United States will never again seek an additional foot of territory by conquest."[5]

Economic penetration supplemented territorial growth. Wilson championed a form of what later was called "globalization," seeking a world economy based on low tariffs, prohibition of monopolies, extensive financial investments overseas, and an Open Door—equal access to foreign commerce. As the American manufacturer insisted on "having the world as a market," Wilson noted in 1907, "the doors of nations which are closed against him must be battered down."[6] Nevertheless, he focused far more on his nation's moral responsibility abroad than on lucrative trade. Conversely, Wilson was indifferent to military and naval strategy, hostile to power politics, and impervious to the part force played in international relations.

Just before he assumed the presidency, Wilson told an old friend: "It would be an irony of fate if my administration had to deal chiefly with foreign problems, for all my preparation has been in domestic matters." Though he sought an anti-imperialistic foreign policy and attacked the "dollar diplomacy" of his predecessor, William Howard Taft, his 1913 inaugural address made no reference to overseas matters. Certainly until World War I broke out, the president's priorities lay at home. He concentrated on his domestic program, which was called the "New Freedom" and which consisted of tariff reduction, regulation of business, and reorganization of the banking system. If in December 1915 he hoped that the European war would permit the nation to engage in the "peaceful conquest of the world," he did not find exports crucial to America's prosperity.[7]

In many ways, Wilson was one of the most gifted chief executives in American history, achieving an impressive string of legislative successes. A superb party leader who staunchly believed in a strong presidency, Wilson exercised almost matchless control over Congress. He studied bills carefully, conferred continually with legislators, and was unafraid to use the patronage whip against recalcitrant Democrats. Using his superior intelligence to assimilate material quickly, he soon reached the heart of any problem. He was an excellent public speaker, though at times his eloquence could backfire, as when he spoke of being "too proud to fight" or making the world "safe for democracy."

Just as important, Wilson possessed an uncanny ability to articulate the fears and aspirations of his people. "No other public figure of the time," writes historian Robert W. Tucker, "mirrored the nation's mood; none voiced the nation's hopes and fears as did the president." Yet one must be careful. His brother-in-law Stockton Axson noted that the president lacked "faith in the supreme wisdom of the people." Rather, he believed "in the capacity of the people to be led right by those whom they elect and constitute their leaders."[8] When the public was uncertain or deeply divided, Wilson could exercise a decisive influence.

On crucial matters of foreign policy, Wilson often made major decisions alone. In his *Constitutional Government in the United States* (1908), he discerned the presidential initiative in foreign affairs as unlimited; the chief executive possessed "virtually the power to control them absolutely." Although acknowledging that the president could not conclude a treaty without senatorial consent, he believed that the chief executive could dominate every step of the diplomatic process. In keeping with this outlook, Wilson examined diplomatic documents, wrote dispatches on his own typewriter, and frequently acted without the State Department's knowledge. At times he kept his secretaries of state ignorant of important negotiations. The department's staff equaled the size of a second-rate power, the chief executive making meager use of its scant resources and preferring backdoor contacts to formal channels. As historian Patrick Devlin writes, "The President might almost have been running a parish with the help of his wife and a curate and a portable typewriter."[9]

Similarly, Wilson sought to insulate himself from journalists. As early as December 1914, he stopped reading press accounts of the war, seeking "to hold excitement at arm's length." Believing that opponents controlled many of the nation's newspapers and magazines, he read relatively few, relying instead on letters, telegrams, petitions, and meetings with congressional leaders. A month before, the president told his closest adviser, Edward Mandell House, that he had no qualms about lying to the press concerning foreign policy matters.[10] From July 1915, as the *Lusitania* crisis unfolded, until late in 1916, he did not hold a single press conference.

In regard to foreign affairs, Wilson tended to listen to those who either agreed with him or who showed strong admiration. He confided in his two wives and trusted House to an extraordinary degree, although "the colonel" always approached him with deference. Wilson was far from facetious when he told a Princeton critic that he felt sorry for those who differed with him—"Because I know they are wrong."[11] From the time he was a university president, Wilson could view opposition as an attack on his very person. Admittedly, he at times exercised caution, consulting Secretary of State William Jennings Bryan and, on the eve of entering the war, his cabinet. He met with prominent peace leaders, including acknowledged Socialists, though he was out of sympathy with their immediate agendas.

For several years, Colonel House remained Wilson's sole intimate adviser. A man of considerable means, he was the son of an Englishman who had made his fortune in the Lone Star State when it still belonged to Mexico. An adviser to several Texas governors, House became an honorary colonel in the Texas militia in 1892, a reward for organizing the successful reelection campaign of James Hogg. During the 1912 presidential race, he became so close to Wilson that by election time he could have chosen any cabinet position he desired. The colonel demurred, in part because of his fragile constitution, but he spoke of seeking "a roving commission," particularly in matters of foreign policy. Secretary of State Robert Lansing, Secretary of Agriculture

David F. Houston, Secretary of the Interior Franklin K. Lane, Postmaster General Albert S. Burleson, and ambassador to Britain Walter Hines Page received their appointments in large part through House's intervention.

Often operating from his apartment in Manhattan, House appeared so self-effacing that he was called "the Texas Sphinx." He exhibited a sense of confidentiality and sympathy to all he encountered, while playing the role of "operator" in a way that left Wilson untainted. Behind this diffident demeanor lay shameless flattery, a burning ambition, an overreaching ego, and a penchant for intrigue. The colonel was so skillful in this regard that Johann von Bernstorff, the German ambassador to the United States, never detected House's strong pro-Allied bias, maintaining in his memoirs that the colonel had always been genuinely neutral.[12]

If one believes House's account of the president's sentiments, the colonel served as the chief executive's "second personality," his "independent self." "His thoughts and mine are one," Wilson supposedly said, adding: "If I were in his place I would do just as he suggested." Historian Robert W. Tucker describes the confidant as a combination of chief of staff, national security adviser, and chief diplomatic agent.[13] Given House's length of service and the importance of his missions, he may well have been the most important informal executive agent in American history. In the winter of 1915–16, when Wilson sent House to Europe, he bestowed unique diplomatic authority on the colonel.

Yet there is danger of exaggerating House's influence. By spring 1915, the colonel ceased being the president's closest intimate; he was replaced by Edith Bolling Galt, who soon became Wilson's wife. That summer Galt, who harbored misgivings about House, conveyed to Wilson a vague suspicion of the colonel's character. The president responded that House was "capable of utter self-forgetfulness and loyalty and devotion. And he is wise. He can give prudent and far-seeing counsel." Wilson did share her view that intellectually House was "not a great man." His mind was "not of the first class. He is a counselor, not a statesman."[14]

From the outset of the war, the president's confidant favored an Allied victory but not one that would allow Russia to gain additional territory. By the summer of 1915, House had decided that American entry into the war was inevitable, though he subsequently questioned this judgment. As time passed, the colonel increasingly played a perilous and destructive role, undermining Wilson at crucial junctures while displaying a false fealty. A son of Wilson's secretary of the navy remarked: "He was an intimate man even when he was cutting a throat."[15] In negotiating with British and French leaders in February 1916, the colonel ignored Wilson's instructions to avoid discussing concrete peace terms, seeking to transform what Wilson envisioned as a mediation bid into a commitment to enter the war. He naively assumed that European leaders were anxious for American diplomatic intervention, ignoring their explicit denials that negotiation was then possible. Not until the Paris Peace Conference of 1919, however, when House appeared to undercut Wilson's liberal agenda, did the president abruptly sever personal relations.

Upon becoming president, Wilson chose William Jennings Bryan as secretary of state. "The Great Commoner" had served as Democratic standard-bearer in three presidential elections. His influence among the party rank and file, particularly in the South and the West, was second to Wilson's alone; as a man he was even more beloved. Although not responsible for Wilson's nomination in the Baltimore convention of 1912, he played a major supporting role. The president was originally reluctant to make the appointment, having little respect for the Nebraskan's judgment, fearing possible conflict over party matters, and knowing that his choice was ignorant concerning foreign affairs. Wilson ultimately selected Bryan as a reward for party service and as a means of retaining allegiance of a man who, if alienated, could be a troublesome opponent. Besides, the chief executive anticipated few international crises that he could not personally handle.

Almost immediately, Bryan received much criticism, though it often involved matters of style, not substance, and centered on such concerns as his obesity, pietism, untidy dress, and sanguine optimism. The secretary's reputation suffered from surreptitious sniping from such influential figures as Colonel House. Wilson could tolerate Bryan's banning of alcohol at diplomatic functions and frequent lectures on the Chautauqua circuit, where he could share the platform with the likes of Tyrolian yodelers. Less acceptable was his replacing lower-ranking personnel at the ministerial level, individuals who had risen through the merit system, with "deserving" but incompetent Democrats.

In some ways, Bryan proved a pleasant surprise. Intensely loyal to Wilson, who thought of him as "my elder son," the secretary shared much of the president's moralistic approach to statecraft. To Bryan international relations centered on the spreading of democracy and of divinely ordained moral principles. If the president once referred to him as "a spoilsman to the core" and "the worst judge of character I ever knew," he gave him a free hand in conducting many Latin American affairs. He permitted Bryan to negotiate some thirty "cooling-off" treaties that pledged the signers, if confronted with a major dispute, to conduct an impartial investigation for a year before taking up arms. Bryan expressed delight when, late in August 1914, Britain signed such a treaty with the United States, not finding the slightest incongruity in the fact that it had declared war upon Germany just weeks earlier. Though neither Germany nor Austria-Hungary ever entered into such a pact, the secretary convinced himself that Germany backed the arrangement "in principle." Wilson, too, believed in the efficacy of such agreements, declaring in 1919 that had they been in effect in 1914, they might have prevented the world conflagration.[16] Until the United States entered the world war, Bryan treated the agreements as capable of resolving wartime tensions. None of these treaties was ever invoked.

When, in 1914, the European conflict erupted, Bryan refused to allocate blame, much less examine strategic or economic implications of the conflict. Historian John Milton Cooper Jr. conveys his attitude: "America would act like Bryan the fundamentalist by avoiding sin and like Bryan the evangelist by preaching to the unredeemed." In November 1916, though out of office, he offered to visit Europe and personally mediate the conflict. Speaking of the Continent's leaders, he said: "They are all Christians and not pagans, and I could talk to them in a christianlike way and I am sure they would heed."[17] The secretary focused exclusively on maintaining rigid neutrality and stopping the fighting. He never became adept at deciding the timing of peace proposals, developing the substance of possible negotiating terms, or grasping the complexity of diplomatic maneuver.

Within a year, Bryan showed himself temperamentally unsuited and intellectually incompetent to handle European matters. There was hardly a problem that he did not oversimplify. In his public pronouncements and his monthly magazine, the *Commoner,* he reduced tangled legal issues to matters of sheer right-versus-wrong and complicated issues of force and military credibility to simple "truths." The secretary loved to tell fellow diplomats, "Nothing is final between friends," implying that the United States' interest simply lay in preserving its neutrality. Personal sentiment substituted for viable policy.

Wilson recognized his secretary's limitations, keeping crucial matters either in his own hands or, at times, those of Colonel House. When Bryan resigned in June 1915, however, the president lost the sole powerful voice in his administration that warned against intervention. Future restraint would have to come from Wilson himself.

Bryan's successor, too, lacked the president's ear. Robert Lansing, who became counselor of the State Department in 1914, possessed impressive credentials. The son-in-law of Benjamin Harrison's secretary of state, John Watson Foster, Lansing was one of the nation's most respected authorities in international law, representing the United States in more arbitration cases than any other living American. In some ways he was the very opposite of Bryan, projecting the popular image of a diplomat: handsome, urbane, formal, and well educated, a man whom historian Cooper calls "a theater director's idea of a secretary of state." Though his mind was slow and his diplomatic notes sometimes bordered on pedantry, he could master complex legal matters and remained at ease during subtle negotiations. To Lansing any "missionary diplomacy" based on the Golden Rule and evangelical Christianity appeared totally alien. "Force," he once imparted, was the "great underlying actuality in all history."[18]

Unlike Wilson and Bryan, the new secretary became so ardently pro-Entente that he sought to enter the conflict long before April 1917. In his own way as simplistic as Bryan, he viewed the European war as centering on freedom versus absolutism, democracy against autocracy, conveniently ignoring the fact that one of the Allies, Russia, remained an archdespotism. Certainly he never considered how damaging total defeat of the Central Powers could be upon Europe's balance of power. Admittedly, he made legalistic demands on both Germany and Britain and did not openly voice interventionist sentiments, believing the United States could act only when its public itself desired war. In his war memoirs he confessed, "There was always in my mind the conviction that we would ultimately become an ally of Great Britain and that it would not do, therefore, to let our controversies reach a point where diplomatic correspondence gave place to action. . . . Everything was submerged in verbosity. It was done with deliberate purpose."[19]

Although Lansing raised morale within the department, doing so in the wake of Bryan's irresponsible use of patronage, Wilson treated him like a glorified clerk. Being marginalized made the secretary so resentful that he undermined his commander in chief. At one crucial point he jeopardized House's sensitive negotiations in Europe. Another time he imperiled Wilson's effort to initiate peace talks. On the eve of American entry into the struggle, Wilson complained to House that Lansing was "the most unsatisfactory Secretary in his Cabinet." The man "had no imagination, no constructive ability, and but little real ability of any kind."[20] Although the president did not fire his insubordinate underling, he remained convinced he must be his own secretary of state.

The chief executive was hardly served better by two major ambassadors. Walter Hines Page, Wilson's emissary to Britain, was a leading editor and publisher, affiliated with *Forum,* the *Atlantic Monthly,* the *World's Work,* and his own firm of Doubleday, Page. He expressed strong enthusiasm for Wilson's presidency, engaging in strategy sessions as early as February 1911. Though finding the English people arrogant and their government undemocratic, Page soon became, in the words of the president, "more British than the British." Perceiving the war as a great struggle against German militarism, he wrote a friend in 1916 that America and Britain must "work together and stand together to keep the predatory nations in order." Germany, he informed a close acquaintance, would eventually attack the United States, the Panama Canal, and South America.[21]

The ambassador met with the British foreign secretary, Sir Edward Grey, almost daily and became well acquainted with other British leaders, including Prime Minister Herbert Asquith. Grey reported an incident in which Page, after delivering a communiqué of his government, said to him: "I do not agree with it; let us consider how it should be answered."[22] By the end of 1915, Wilson ignored his representative's dispatches, which he deemed hysterical. By March 1917 the president considered removing Page, but he did not act. Like many other presidents, he tolerated unreliable subordinates, possibly fearing the political consequences of any firing.

If anything, James Watson Gerard, Wilson's ambassador to Germany, proved even more unsatisfactory: in the words of historian Arthur S. Link, "an authentic international catastrophe."[23] A wealthy New York attorney affiliated with the Tammany Hall machine, Gerard had chaired the Democratic National Campaign Committee and was serving as an elected justice of his state's supreme court. Totally unprepared for a position demanding the utmost judgment and tact, Gerard possessed a fierce temper, was given to snap judgments, and made no secret of his hostility toward a regime he branded as "Kaiserdom." Both American and German officials soon ignored his advice. Instead they relied upon Joseph C. Grew, the urbane embassy secretary and at times chargé d'affaires, who in July 1916 assumed the newly adopted rank of counselor.

Heading the War Department was Lindley M. Garrison, a leading New Jersey corporation lawyer and former vice chancellor of his state. Wilson had originally considered federal regulator Franklin K. Lane and Pennsylvania politician A. Mitchell Palmer for the post. He soon believed that Lane was needed at the Interior Department, and Palmer belonged to the Society of Friends, or Quakers, a denomination that officially espoused pacifism. Garrison, whom Wilson aide Joseph Tumulty suggested, at first balked, claiming that he knew little of military matters and lacked a political temperament. Nonetheless, despite his novice status, Garrison was a most able administrator, winning the confidence of the military brass. But his overbearing personality bode ill for long-term relations with a president who never really knew him personally.

Josephus Daniels, Wilson's secretary of the navy, began his tenure as ignorant of ships as Garrison was of armies, though as editor of the *Raleigh News and Observer,* he had endorsed the robust naval policy of President Taft. During the 1912 presidential campaign, Daniels directed Democratic publicity. He was first considered for postmaster general, but Colonel House, so often responsible for filling major positions, thought that someone with greater influence in Congress was needed for the postal slot. Daniels experienced frequent ridicule for his rustic demeanor, his own assistant secretary, Franklin Delano Roosevelt, at best patronizing him. Yet he proved himself a genuine reformer, stressing naval education, requiring sea duty for promotion, and successfully fending off the armor-plate lobby. Aside from Lincoln's secretary of the navy, Gideon Welles, no one served as long in this post. Under his administration the U.S. Navy underwent unprecedented expansion.

A totally different framework for decision making existed in Imperial Germany. At the apex of the Reich stood Wilhelm II, who headed his nation's civil administration and was not limited by parliamentary restrictions. The Kaiser possessed a mercurial and indolent personality, approaching all questions, as one scholar noted, with "an open mouth."[24] Upon him lay the responsibility of harmonizing military and political advisers so as to create a united national policy. As long as the power of both sets of counselors remained equal, he could exercise some influence. In wartime the task increasingly exceeded his ability. Until January 1917 Wilhelm possessed sufficient power to back his civilian leaders, who, challenging major elements among the military, opposed the use of U-boats against American shipping.

Under the Kaiser stood the chancellor, who served at the emperor's pleasure. From 1909 to July 1917, Theobald von Bethmann Hollweg held the office. Bethmann possessed a melancholy self-doubt akin to Hamlet's; his personal warmth and Stoic ethos failed to compensate for political ineptitude, diplomatic inexperience, and mediocre intelligence. He enjoyed support from his foreign secretary, Gottlieb von Jagow, who, in November 1916, was replaced by Arthur Zimmermann, a diplomat who manifested more energy but far less judgment. Zimmermann, a hawkish policymaker, supported submarine warfare upon the Atlantic. He suffered from poor health and lacked parliamentary skills.

At first glance, Johann Heinrich Count von Bernstorff, ambassador to the United States, seemed most suitable for the position; his father had been foreign minister of Prussia and he himself had served in such far-flung posts as Constantinople, Belgrade, St. Petersburg, London, and Cairo. Intelligent, elegant, and charming and married to an American, the suave Bernstorff appeared the quintessential diplomat and, until war erupted in Europe, was quite popular in the United States. Believing in a compromise settlement between the Allies and the Central Powers, at times he exceeded his instructions in the hopes of maintaining peace with America. Yet the count's stiff bearing disturbed Wilson, making personal contact difficult.

Germany possessed a parliament, but its powers were extremely limited. The lower house, the Reichstag, by no means possessed the prerogatives held by the American Congress, the British House of Commons, or the French Chamber of Deputies. It did exercise one crucial function, for it had the sole authority to vote military allocations.

In Germany the military played a far more crucial role than in the United States. The Kaiser bore the title of supreme war lord and legally commanded the armed forces, but once war began, the general staff increasingly wielded decisive power. In mid-1916 Wilhelm complained that he had become a mere shadow, relegated to the sidelines. When Germany entered the war, its first chief of staff was General Helmuth von Moltke ("the younger"), but after his defeat in September 1914 at the battle of the Marne, Wilhelm replaced him with Erich von Falkenhayn. Falkenhayn suffered major failure in Verdun and eastern Europe, thereby giving way late in August 1916 to Paul von Hindenburg. By then the real authority lay in the hands of quartermaster general Erich Ludendorff. Army leaders at first exercised caution, but by the fall of 1916 they endorsed massive use of U-boats, a policy that ultimately drew the United States into the conflict.

Certain admirals exercised strong influence. Grand Admiral Alfred von Tirpitz, state secretary of the navy office, began the conflict as his nation's foremost naval leader. By February 1915 he ardently supported U-boat warfare. His faulty analysis of British strategy alienated Wilhelm, who forced his resignation in March 1916. Tirpitz's replacement, Eduard von Capelle, long remained opposed to unrestricted submarine use but finally bowed to the wishes of his fellow officers. Georg Alexander von Müller, chief of the imperial naval cabinet, possessed great influence; he often voiced caution in confronting the United States. Henning von Holtzendorff, chosen to head the Admiralty staff in the spring of 1915, initially wavered on U-boat use but in December 1916 presented convincing arguments in support of this policy.

If Germany had one bitter foe among the Americans, it was Theodore Roosevelt. Among critics of Wilson's diplomacy, none was as prominent. The former president endorsed an "intimate association" with the British Empire and adhered to the notion that the English-speaking peoples were superior to all others. Recently defeated for the presidency on the Progressive or Bull Moose ticket, TR had almost abandoned domestic reform by the end of 1914 in order to concentrate on foreign policy. In late August, though apprehensive concerning Japan and Russia, he privately voiced the fear that a victorious Germany would soon engage the United States. Within a year Roosevelt condemned Germany's invasion of Belgium, endorsed universal military training, and called for a league of nations that would "put force back of righteousness." Given such views, as well as his desire to recover his party's fortunes, he sharply criticized the Wilson administration. No major American leader expressed himself with such venom. In August 1915 he wrote to his son Kermit that the president was an "abject coward."[25] In public he was almost equally abusive. In the 1914 congressional elections, the Roosevelt Progressives were decimated, retaining only one Senate seat, but the volatile ex-president still enjoyed considerable popularity among Americans.

TR's views on Europe lacked coherence. Though he frequently indicted Germany, praised the Allies, and advocated policies that would invariably lead to war, he never publicly endorsed outright intervention. Indeed, he asserted that a show of force would keep America at peace. "The worst policy for the United States," he wrote soon after war began, "is to combine the unbridled tongue with the unsteady hand." A woefully weak America could have perceived wisdom in this view, but, as the *Nation* magazine observed: "he pleads his cause with such heat and so little moderation that his words fail to be impressive." The *New York Times* added: "He warns, he denounces, he glares, he shrieks."[26] Nevertheless, he drew such popular support that had he lived in 1920, he might well have been the Republican presidential candidate.

Roosevelt gained strong support from senators Elihu Root (R-N.Y.) and Henry Cabot Lodge (R-Mass.) as well as from Congressman Augustus P. Gardner (R-Mass.). Root had been secretary of war under presidents McKinley and Roosevelt, then became TR's secretary of state. Far more of a standpatter on domestic policy than TR, in 1912 Root supported the reelection of President William Howard Taft, thereby "betraying" his close friend Roosevelt. Nevertheless, when a German U-boat sank the British liner *Lusitania* in May 1915, Root privately maintained that the United States should enter the conflict. In February 1916 he publicly accused Wilson of "threatening words without deeds."[27]

Lodge, the ranking Republican on the Foreign Relations Committee, was even more strident. Just slightly less conservative than Root on domestic matters, he supported Wilson on certain specific measures, such as permitting arms traffic with the belligerents and defending the right of Americans to travel on their passenger ships. Like Roosevelt, Lodge considered Wilson far too timid, even unpatriotic, and also like TR, he harbored a personal animosity, finding the president downright dishonest. Lodge wrote TR in 1915: "I never expected to hate anyone in politics with the hatred I feel towards Wilson."[28] His son-in-law, the highly powerful and visible "Gussie" Gardner, was a Spanish-American War veteran who spearheaded the preparedness movement in the House of Representatives.

Wilson's foreign policy triggered strong opposition from congressional leaders of his own party and from Bryan's followers in particular. Senator William J. Stone of Missouri, chairman of the Foreign Relations Committee, fought the president on such matters as arming American merchant ships in 1917; he voted against war with Germany. The committee's second-ranking Democratic member, Gilbert M. Hitchcock of Nebraska, shared many of Stone's sentiments, though, in times of crisis, he upheld the president out of loyalty. In the House, Claude Kitchin of North Carolina, majority leader and chairman of the Ways and Means Committee, took the lead in fighting military appropriations. Like Stone, in April 1917 he opposed the president's war message.

Wilson also received sharp criticism from certain midwestern Republicans, who believed him far too pro-British. Senator Robert M. La Follette stood foremost in their ranks. Using the monthly *La Follette's Magazine* as his forum, the Wisconsin Republican espied Wall Street greed behind most U.S. actions overseas, whether the matter was intervention in Latin America or loans to the Allies. Whereas Bryan stressed "cooling-off" treaties to preserve American neutrality, La Follette emphasized an advisory war referendum by which the American public could directly express its views on entering the conflict.

Debate in the Congress spilled over to the world of journalism. Certain weeklies offered particularly articulate perspectives. Oswald Garrison Villard's *Nation,* an affiliate of the *New York Evening Post,* manifested a Wilsonian perspective. Publisher Villard usually limited his own comments to matters concerning preparedness and the activities of German Americans; Rollo Ogden, a former Presbyterian minister, wrote most of the editorials. The *Outlook,* edited by Congregationalist clergyman Lyman Abbott, espoused Theodore Roosevelt's brand of interventionism, although TR had resigned as its contributing editor in July 1914. The *New Republic* began as a voice for Bull Moose progressivism and a mild version of Rooseveltian foreign policy. Its editors, Herbert Croly, Walter Weyl, and Walter Lippmann, supported the Allies, Lippmann being the most intense advocate. By March 1916, finding TR lacking in positive alternatives to Wilsonian diplomacy, it veered toward the president. Early in 1917 Croly and Lippmann became close to Colonel House, a circumstance that confirmed the journal's increasing reputation as the semiofficial Wilsonian organ.

The newspaper chain of William Randolph Hearst, which reached 4 million readers daily, stood in a class by itself. Hearst was unsuccessful in frequent bids to secure public office, including the presidency, but nonetheless exercised greater influence over the public than many members of Congress. His holdings included a movie studio, a newsreel firm, and a company supplying syndicated features. His wire agency, International News Service, served several hundred newspapers. By 1914 the flamboyant publisher owned newspapers in San Francisco, Los Angeles, Chicago, and Boston, though he took particular pride in his *New York American,* which boasted the highest circulation in the nation and which drew upon eighty correspondents in covering the war. Though denounced as a mouthpiece for Imperial Germany, the *American* gave far more space to pro-Entente articles than to those inclined to the Central Powers; it featured such prominent British contributors as H.G. Wells, Rudyard Kipling, and George Bernard Shaw. Hearst was a progressive in domestic politics but trumpeted a strident foreign policy, pressing for major rearmament, warning against a "predatory" Japan, and seeking the annexation of Mexico. Mutual animosity marked the relationship between Hearst and Wilson, reflecting in part the publisher's desire for a far more rigid neutrality in the European war than the president envisioned.

No community backed Hearst's European policy more than the German Americans. In 1914 this group comprised a markedly distinct element in American society, preserving its own identity and asserting itself with vigor whenever its ancestral land came under attack. According to the 1910 census, well over 8 million people of the nation's nearly 92 million either had been born in Germany or had a German parent. In 1916 the National German-American Alliance (the *Nationalbund*), a federation of various societies, boasted 3 million members, though it was largely a paper organization consisting primarily of people who belonged to local societies or clubs. Such cities as New York, Chicago, Cincinnati, Milwaukee, and St. Louis possessed German American neighborhoods distinct enough, in some cases, to be nicknamed *Kleines Deutschland*. About five hundred German-language newspapers existed, possessing a total circulation of 1.75 million. One daily, Herman Ridder's *New Yorker Staats-Zeitung*, which received payments from Berlin, attracted seventy thousand readers.

Such journals were often more extreme than rank-and-file German Americans. Take, for example, the weekly English-language magazine the *Fatherland*, launched within two weeks after war began. Costing a mere nickel, it became the Reich's most outspoken propaganda vehicle in America. Within a month circulation peaked at over one hundred thousand. The poet George Sylvester Viereck, who edited the journal, combined flamboyance and bombast to such a degree that he often hindered his cause more than helped it. In the maiden issue of the journal, he contributed a poem, "Wilhelm II, Prince of Peace." The cover of the 1915 Christmas issue portrayed a tree bedecked with ornaments depicting the locale of German victories; at its base, gifts included a U-boat and a Big Bertha cannon.[29] Beginning in June 1915, Viereck received subsidies from the German government.

In addition, certain highly respected scholars, who in many cases had received their graduate training in Germany, backed the Central Powers. Several were of British stock. Some Lutheran and Roman Catholic communities articulated the German case, as did various organizations and legislators representing German American constituencies. On January 30, 1915, the National German-American League was formed in Washington, D.C. It passed a series of resolutions, introduced by Dr. C.J. Hexamer, president of the *Nationalbund*. The group called for the construction of an American transatlantic cable because the British had cut German cables and thereby controlled dispatches from Europe. It also demanded an arms embargo, an American merchant marine, and, taking a slap at the British blockade, "a free and open sea for the commerce of the United States and unrestricted traffic in non-contraband goods as defined by international law." It supported politicians who placed "American interests above those of any other country."[30]

Be the matter the conduct of German troops in Belgium or the necessity of unrestricted submarine warfare, German Americans soon became an irritant to the Wilson administration, not to mention the bane of those Americans who were sufficiently pro-British to deem such defenders of the Reich as Viereck abject traitors. Hexamer did little to help matters, declaring: "We have never yet had such a miserable, weakkneed government as now."[31] At times crude, at times subtle, pro-German propaganda was nevertheless so extensive that, in the judgment of historians Arthur S. Link and David Wayne Hirst, it could well have preserved peace between the two countries.[32]

Various Irish American spokesmen, out to avenge themselves against British rule of the Emerald Isle, allied themselves with their German counterparts. Numbering 4.5 million in 1914, the Irish were concentrated in northeastern and midwestern cities, which could well have given them more political influence than their German confederates, who were often located on midwestern prairies. Pro-Irish elements possessed a spirited English-language press, represented by such newspapers as the *Gaelic American* and the *Irish World*. They espoused the cause of Irish nationalism and thereby attracted broad American sympathy, giving them an audience that narrowly pro-German partisans could not match. Organizations included Clan-na-gael (party of the Irish), headed by Tammany judge Daniel Cohalan, and the anti-British American Truth Society, led by New York lawyer Jeremiah O'Leary. If a mere minority of Irish Americans supported the Central Powers, they expressed their sentiments vehemently. "Liberty for Ireland can only be won through the triumphs of Germany-Austria," wrote James K. McGuire, a former mayor of Syracuse, who served as a liaison between German partisans and the Irish press. At one rally in New York City, the strains of "Die Wacht am Rhein" mingled with "The Wearing of the Green."[33]

Both German and Irish Americans confronted an overwhelming fact: many Americans sympathized, in varying degrees to be sure, with Britain and France. Within this body, the greater numbers possessed a subtle outlook, discerning the causes of the war as complex and finding flaws on both sides. A minority perceived the conflict as one of good versus evil, right versus wrong, democracy and liberalism confronting an overwhelming autocracy, though one must distinguish between abstract sympathy and the desire to intervene directly. Realizing that much American sentiment was at least tacitly pro-Entente, British ambassador Sir Cecil Arthur Spring Rice counseled his government to avoid overt propagandizing.[34] Despite this warning, Sir Gilbert Parker, who directed Britain's American Ministry of Information, blanketed the nation with news releases, pamphlets, and speeches.

When, in early August 1914, war broke out in Europe, Wilson immediately realized that his decisions could vitally affect the international order. He discovered that his advisers served him poorly, either being inadequate to the task or offering counsel that was downright destructive. The Congress and the press presented a cacophony of voices, at times advancing positions that challenged the foundations of his policies. An examination of the president's leadership, how he interacted with all the players, and the judgment of historians is the subject of this book.

2

The Earliest Debates
August 1914–March 1915

ON THE AFTERNOON OF August 6, 1914, a dying woman whispered into the ear of her physician: "Promise me that you will take good care of my husband." As a downstairs clock chimed five times, her spouse asked the doctor, "Is it over?" Receiving a nod, he walked to a window and cried out: "Oh, my God, what am I to do?" Then, composing himself, he vowed: "I must not give way." Nonetheless, the man remained sitting in his chair, maintaining an isolated vigil. President Woodrow Wilson had just lost his wife Ellen to Bright's Disease, a fatal kidney ailment. He soon wrote an intimate friend: "Every night finds me exhausted,—dead in heart and body." He blamed his own ambition for her death. His brother-in-law called him "the loneliest man in the world."[1]

It took months for the excruciating grief to pass off. As late as November, the president told his most intimate friend, Colonel House, that he hoped someone would kill him. Wilson confessed that he "was not fit to be President because he did not think straight any longer, and had no heart in what he was doing."[2] The burden of work sustained him, for the chief executive found himself suddenly facing challenges that no world leader could envy.

At the very time that Wilson's inner world disintegrated, the outer one experienced calamity. Just five days before Ellen died, war in Europe erupted on an unprecedented scale. To most Americans, the outbreak of the conflict appeared as something far off, remote, even unreal. The flurry of diplomatic dispatches, the massing of huge armies, the orders of mobilization—all seemed a kind of gruesome illusion. After the assassination of the Hapsburg heir, the archduke Francis Ferdinand, and his wife Sophie in Sarajevo, Austria-Hungary threatened Serbia, a nation having the protection of Russia.

Imperial Germany backed Imperial Austria, while republican France upheld the czar. After seeing Germany suddenly pounce upon Belgium, Britain came to France's aid and on August 4, 1914, declared war on the Reich. The Great War had begun, and it soon engulfed almost all of Europe.

When the Serbian crisis first broke out, most Americans saw it as another one of Europe's chronic ailments. On July 27, the day before Austria declared war on Serbia, Wilson told the press: "The United States has never attempted to intervene in European affairs."[3] Agriculture Secretary David F. Houston queried in a memo: "What? Another little war in the Balkans? Serbia is in the Balkans, isn't it? A lot of fuss over an archduke. Calls himself Francis Ferdinand. He probably didn't amount to much; he couldn't have with a name like that."[4]

Nevertheless, Americans took events most seriously. The same David Houston remarked: "I had the feeling the end of things had come." Franklin Delano Roosevelt, assistant secretary of the navy, foresaw "the greatest war in human history." To former president William Howard Taft, the event was "a cataclysm." Novelist Henry James feared that the world had plunged into "an abyss of blood and darkness."[5] More than one journal made reference to the biblical battle of Armageddon, the conflict marking the end of human history.

More than ever, citizens expressed gratitude for their isolation. "Again and ever I thank Heaven for the Atlantic Ocean," wrote Ambassador Walter Hines Page to the president, soon adding: "How wise our no-alliance policy is."[6] A Chicago journal blessed Columbus for having discovered America, while a Buffalo newspaper remarked: "This European war suggests that the white man's burden is the white man himself."[7]

Soon, however, the citizenry began to choose sides. Although scientific polling of the wider public did not take place for another two decades, the sentiments of opinion leaders became clear. In November the weekly *Literary Digest,* which frequently surveyed the nation's press, canvassed over 350 newspapers. It noted that 49 percent of the editors expressed no sympathies for either side, while 46 percent favored the Allies. A regional breakdown indicated pro-Allied leanings in New England, the South, the West, and the Pacific coast. In the Midwest, which contained a large German American population, feelings were either neutralist or occasionally pro-German; often such views predominated where the Populist movement had drawn its strongest support. Furthermore, small towns tended to be more neutralist than urban areas. The *Digest* itself observed: "The sympathy on either side is that of the distant observer." Practically no one desired to enter the war.[8]

Historian Ernest R. May puts the issue well: "It was thought possible to be sympathetic yet completely neutral." At the same time, May notes that an American could shift easily between a desire to avoid war and the wish to defend the nation's rights by spirited diplomacy. Journalist Mark Sullivan compared the sentiment to the cheering of baseball fans sitting in the bleachers. In September a newsboy hawked a late edition, crying: "Extra! Giants and Germans lose! Extra!" Cecil Arthur Spring Rice, British ambassador to Washington, discerned that Americans regarded the conflict "as a bore, or as an immensely interesting spectacle provided for their entertainment." Either way, the diplomat deemed it "useless and misleading to depend on these people for help or for practical sympathy."[9] Certainly, the great majority assumed that no vital interests, economic or military, lay at stake. Planting crops, earning wages, selling goods, raising children—these remained the most important priorities. Moreover, the United States assumed that the Allies would win without its direct involvement.

By November 1914 a major portion of thoughtful Americans had decided upon the causes of the conflict; they did not really change their perspective during the war itself. The belligerents released various "white papers" or color books, selecting those diplomatic documents that best argued their case: white for Germany and Britain, yellow for France, red for Austria, green for Italy, orange for Russia, gray for Belgium. Though the contents of each volume were highly biased, taken together they revealed the complexity of the war's origins.

On August 4 Wilson issued a sweeping proclamation of strict neutrality, though he feared that an event might occur on the high seas to make this stance impossible. Within three weeks he released his "Appeal to the American People," calling upon his countrymen to "be neutral in fact as well as in name," "impartial in thought as well as in action." No sentiment, no transaction should indicate "a preference of one party to the struggle over another."[10]

The president was obviously aware that many fellow Americans harbored biases. Nevertheless, in their activities, he thought that they should put the interests of the United States ahead of any belligerent. In this plea he received strong support across the political spectrum, ranging from George Sylvester Viereck's militantly Teutonic *Fatherland* to the ardently pro-Allied

Outlook. The latter said: "This is not our war. Let us keep out of it." Senator Henry Cabot Lodge spoke of absolute impartiality.[11]

Almost immediately Wilson privately revealed his own proclivities. On August 19 he informed Sir Edward Grey, the British foreign secretary, that their two nations were "bound together by common principle and purpose." Conversely, the president told Ambassador Spring Rice that a German victory would force the United States to "take such measures of defence as would be fatal to our form of Government and American ideals." "Everything that I love most in the world is at stake," he asserted. He warned Colonel House on August 30 that a German victory "would change the course of our civilization and make the United States a military nation." The impact of Germany's destruction of Louvain, which had taken place late in August, wore heavily upon him, as did the German chancellor's crude justification of the attack on Belgium. That October Wilson reported to Ambassador James W. Gerard in Berlin that German bombing had created "terror and the destruction of innocent lives," making a "fatal" impression on the American public. Just before the November congressional elections, Wilson supposedly informed his aide, Joseph Tumulty, that "England is fighting our fight and you may well understand that I shall not, in the present state of world affairs, place obstacles in her way."[12]

Wilson usually expressed such sentiments at the start of the war, a time when the Allies seemed to face defeat. After September 9, when the Germans were repulsed at the Marne River, a long stalemate appeared in the offing, leading Wilson to think that the United States had avoided possible danger. By late autumn, he was becoming increasingly detached, moving toward a more impartial position. In mid-September he defined his own peace agenda, one that included restoration of Belgium, an independent Poland, the cession of Alsace (but not Lorraine) to France, the neutralization of the Dardanelles, and the formation of a Balkan federation at the expense of the Austro-Hungarian Empire.[13]

Already on September 28, Wilson advised House to tell Foreign Secretary Grey, whom the colonel already knew personally, that Britain would be most unwise to destroy Germany and Austria completely; otherwise Russia's ambitions on the Continent would remain unchecked. Early in November, the president accused the British of seeking a "complete defeat of Germany" and "to a very considerable degree a dismemberment of the German empire." Even if Germany won the war, he told a skeptical House, it would be in no condition to menace America.[14]

Later that month House told Wilson that Germany disliked America's policy, would "hold us to account," and had designs on Brazil, to which the president countered that the European conflict might have been "a Godsend to us," for otherwise "we might have been embroiled in war ourselves." Navy Secretary Josephus Daniels later recalled Wilson's comment: "Every reform we have won will be lost if we go into this war."[15]

In an off-the-record interview that took place in mid-December, the president informed *New York Times* writer Herbert Bruce Brougham that Germany might not have been solely responsible for the conflict and that the best outlook lay in a deadlock followed by a peace of reconciliation. A victory of the Allies, however, would not significantly injure American interests. He added that the German government needed profound change and that Chancellor Otto von Bismarck had been unwise to annex Alsace-Lorraine in 1871. He called for dissolution of the Austro-Hungarian Empire and noted that land-bound Russia deserved "natural outlets for its trade with the world." Wilson told his brother-in-law Stockton Axson in February 1915 that he envisioned a peace involving legal equality of small and large nations, public ownership of munition firms, the repudiation of any conquest, and an association of nations bound together against aggression.[16]

During the last days of peace, the United States offered to intercede in the conflict. On July 28, Bryan offered America's good offices to the British. Three days later, Grey thanked the secretary but, acting with polite evasion, avoided further discussion of Wilson's gesture. In the first few months of the conflict, Wilson and Bryan hoped that they might lead the belligerents to the conference table. On August 4, just two days before Ellen Wilson died, the president wrote the great powers of Europe: "I should welcome an opportunity to act in the interest of European peace, either now or at any other time that might be thought more suitable." The respondents all made excuses. As part of his neutrality proclamation of August 18, he spoke of America's readiness "to play a part of impartial mediation." In mid-November Page reported from London that Britain envisioned a protracted war.[17]

The president's overtures never had a chance. Each side thought the other completely responsible for the conflict and therefore undeserving of parlay. Furthermore, all the warring states believed that a major victory would assure their security for many generations. Both combatants advanced war aims that became increasingly ambitious and therefore less acceptable to the other side. While Britain had not yet announced specific desires, it considered major transfers of territory and population: Alsace-Lorraine to France,

Schleswig-Holstein to Denmark, South Germany to Austria, and the Austrian Slavs to Russia. Belgium would receive an indemnity. The German colonies would serve as trading pawns.[18]

The September Program of Germany's chancellor, Theobald von Bethmann Hollweg, was equally comprehensive. It would have turned France into a second-class power, subject to German economic penetration and deprived of the Briey ore region. Belgium would lose territory and accept limits to its sovereignty, becoming essentially a German province. Luxembourg would be a federal state within the Reich.[19]

To compound the problem of negotiation, the Central Powers held the advantage on both fronts. By autumn 1914 they had conquered almost all of Belgium. Although Germany occupied only a tenth of France's territory, it was an area that contained much of its major industry, four-fifths of its coal, and nine-tenths of its iron. The British did gain a foothold in northern France. They also tenaciously hung on to an exposed salient around Ypres, Belgium, the defense of which cost them fifty thousand men, about half their regular army. Germany captured territory well inside Russian Poland and took over two hundred thousand Russian prisoners in East Prussia. These successes strengthened Allied opposition to any peace settlement that would shift Europe's balance of power in Germany's direction.

Not surprisingly, Americans debated the question of war guilt. And quite predictably, the Central Powers received the most condemnation. The pro-Allied *North American Review* indicted Austria for issuing an ultimatum that triggered Russian mobilization and consequently war itself. The Hapsburg Empire had insisted that Serbia permit Austria-Hungary to join its internal investigation into the archduke's assassination. Not only would Vienna place every Serbian officer "at the mercy of foreign malice," it practically demanded that Serbia renounce "her own essential sovereignty and independence." James Montgomery Beck, a former assistant attorney general, stressed that Serbia had attempted to submit the crisis to an international tribunal at The Hague, only to be met by a humiliating forty-eight-hour ultimatum from Austria that threatened invasion if Belgrade rejected its demands. The *Nation* magazine admitted that Austria held a just grievance against Serbia but insisted that Belgrade's general compliance should have resulted in a peaceful settlement.[20]

Though believing the Hapsburg Empire had triggered the conflict, Americans usually deemed its Hollenzollern counterpart the main culprit. They conceded that Germany possessed a rich cultural heritage, an advanced system of social insurance, and a superb public school system and had achieved major scientific breakthroughs. Nonetheless, many noted that it harbored strategic ambitions in the Caribbean and had confronted the United States in Manila Bay just as the Spanish-American War ended. It competed with the United States for markets in Latin America, had recognized the despotic regime of Victoriano Huerta in Mexico, and opposed Wilson's takeover of Haiti's customhouses. Emperor Wilhelm II often exhibited such bluster as to make him an embarrassment to himself. Because the Kaiser's "blank check" to Austria-Hungary, dated July 5, promised unequivocal support to the Hapsburg Empire for any stance it took, it aroused considerable American ire. Austria, said William Howard Taft, might have formally initiated the conflict, but "I think William was behind it all the time." Harvard's former president Charles W. Eliot declared that "In Germany, all the forces of education, finance, commercial development, a pagan philosophy, and Government have been preparing for this war since 1860."[21]

The American media portrayed Berlin's war aims in sweeping terms. On August 5 the *New York World* announced, "Germany has run amuck," warning that "the map of European republicanism may well be rolled up," forcing Americans to make "a last great stand for democracy." In September Ambassador Page warned: "If German bureaucratic brute force could conquer Europe, presently it would try to conquer the United States; and we should all go back to the era of war as man's chief industry and back to the domination of kings by divine right."[22]

Germany's most severe critics pointed to an obscure work written by a sixty-five-year-old general who had previously been a cavalry corps commander. The very chapter titles of Friedrich von Bernhardi's *Germany and the Next War* (1911) conveyed a tone of immeasurable arrogance: "The Right to Make War," "The Duty to Make War," "World Power or Downfall." War, he declared, was "not merely a necessary element in the life of nations, but an indispensable factor of culture, in which a true civilized nation finds its highest expression of strength and vitality." France, he continued, must be so crushed as to nevermore threaten Germany.[23]

Just six thousand copies were printed; they made little impression on ordinary Germans. In 1912 the British translated the volume and, when war erupted, circulated it widely. Even William Randolph Hearst's *New York American* offered excerpts, calling it "The Book That Profoundly Stirred Germany's New War Spirit."[24]

Teutonic sympathizers challenged such claims. Herbert Sanborn, philosophy professor at Vanderbilt University, justified Austria's "vigorously worded" ultimatum to Serbia on the grounds that it suited "the treacherous people to whom it was sent." Indeed Balkan peoples lived "on the plane of semi-savagery." German-educated John W. Burgess, a Columbia University professor and the founder of the *Political Science Quarterly,* asked how America would react if its vice president and his wife had been assassinated in Texas in a "plot hatched in Mexico City and implicating high officials of the Mexican government." The United States would have "slapped Mexico off the face of the earth."[25]

To some defenders the Kaiser was a paragon of statesmanship, a "knight without fault or blemish," as one German American newspaper described him. He had done "all in his power to mediate between Austria and Russia," remarked the *Fatherland,* doing so at the very time both nations were secretly arming for the conflict. As for Bernhardi, the journal stressed that he had been dismissed from command. Said editor Viereck in a debate with British publicist Cecil Chesterton: "You have annexed our Bernhardi and we have annexed your Shakespeare."[26]

While defending the Central Powers, pro-German spokesmen sought to blacken the reputation of the Allies. The initial issue of the *Fatherland* described Entente war aims in one sentence: "Russia wants Constantinople, France wants revenge, and England wants Germany's commerce." Kuno Francke, director of Harvard's Germanic Museum, expressed himself similarly. England sought to cripple German trade, France desired the lost provinces, and Russia hoped to undermine German commercial influence in the Near East and eliminate Austrian power in the Balkans. Furthermore, the Anglo-Japanese alliance of 1902 and Japan's intervention in the war revealed that Britain had no qualms about betraying the Pacific interests of the United States. Conversely, Germany harbored just two goals: "the consolidation of German middle Africa from sea to sea, and a leading position in the commercial opening up of the near Orient."[27]

Such partisans emphasized Russia's prominence among the Allies. Harvard psychologist Hugo Münsterberg portrayed the issue as a struggle between two civilizations, that of German *Kultur* versus "the Cossacks with their pogroms." Simon N. Patten, an economist at the University of Pennsylvania, remarked that "assassination and bomb-throwing are zealously promoted by Servian hatred and Russian gold." Hence Austria was forced either to fight or to become "disrupted by racial discord." Similar sentiments were not limited to German sympathizers, as seen by the views of Wilson and

House. Reformist publisher Oswald Garrison Villard queried: "What shall it avail humanity if a hateful Prussian militarism be smashed only to leave in its place a more hateful and dangerous Russian militarism and an even more dominating British navalism?"[28]

The wide-sweeping debates became increasingly concentrated on one event—Germany's invasion of Belgium. In 1905 the chief of the German general staff, Alfred von Schlieffen, inadvertently produced what military historian John Keegan calls "the most important government document written in any country in the first decade of the twentieth century."[29] Realizing that Germany could never win a two-front war against both Russia and France, he devised an operational plan that went under his name. One must first defeat the French, doing so within six weeks; then one must tackle the Russians. However, as France's border was heavily fortified, one must strike through Belgium, whose neutrality the Great Powers, including both Britain and Prussia, had guaranteed in the Treaty of London signed in 1839.

On August 2, 1914, in the capital of Brussels, the German minister delivered a note to Belgium's foreign minister. "Reliable information," it stated, revealed that French forces intended to attack Germany through Belgium's Meuse Valley. Hence, out of self-defense, Germany felt itself forced to invade first. Berlin attempted to soften the news by promising to pay cash for necessities, offering an indemnity to cover damage, swearing to evacuate Belgium, and, when peace was concluded, guaranteeing its territory and independence. If Belgium resisted, Germany would be compelled to consider it an enemy. The Belgians were given twelve hours to respond. If Belgium had accepted the offer, writes historian Larry Zuckerman, it would have lain at Germany's mercy and Britain and France would have felt directly threatened. Even if the Allies won the overall conflict, Belgium could have faced Berlin's annexations as well as political and economic controls that would have compromised its independence.[30]

When Belgium rejected this ultimatum, German patrols started crossing the Belgian border, attacking at 8:00 A.M. on August 4. On that very day, Britain declared war on Germany, an act that might ultimately have determined Allied survival. In justifying the German action, Chancellor Bethmann Hollweg told the Reichstag: "Necessity knows no law." He also indicated to the British ambassador to Berlin that the 1839 guarantee was simply "a scrap of paper."[31] Though Bethmann soon averred that he had been misunderstood, the phrase haunted him the rest of his life. The Germans captured Brussels on August 20 and Namur on August 25, the same date that they began five days of brutal devastation in the university town of Louvain, known as "the Oxford of Belgium." Here the Germans destroyed over a thousand homes, a quarter of the city's building surface. That night a Zeppelin bombed Antwerp, which fell to German troops on October 9. The Germans claimed that snipers were firing on occupation troops, but they were never able to prove their allegation. After the Germans occupied Belgium, they looted it, a practice that continued throughout four years of occupation.

The invasion of Belgium offered a view of the future that most Americans wanted to avoid. In describing the entry of the Kaiser's troops, Richard Harding Davis, an internationally known war correspondent, wrote of the "uncanny, unhuman" nature of their march. "You returned to watch it, fascinated," he said; "It held the mystery and menace of fog rolling toward you across the sea." Another journalist, Will Irwin, ably captured the impersonal nature of the conflict: "We had seen three days of the German army by now; and it seemed to me . . . that the whole world had turned into a gray machine of death—earth and air and sky."[32]

More important, the German actions left an indelible impact on many Americans, who perceived that the Germans had become barbarians. Although accounts of brutality were highly exaggerated, photographs of devastated buildings in Antwerp and Louvain, together with those of the severe damage done to Rheims cathedral in France, severely injured Berlin's reputation. Germany, it appeared, had deliberately trampled on the rules of civilized warfare. To many Americans, a powerful nation had decimated a small neighbor, a peaceful country had found its neutrality violated, and a lawless power had broken an international treaty and in the process dishonored itself. The Kaiser simply added to the impression of callousness when he wrote Wilson, claiming that he had to destroy Louvain in order to protect his troops.[33]

Outrage was instantaneous. Journalist Mark Sullivan ably caught his countrymen's sentiment: "America's attitude had been fixed the hour that Germany's army projected the first goose-step of its vanguard's toe across the boundary-line of Belgium." Average citizens saw the invasion "in the simplest possible terms, a big dog pouncing on a little one." "By this action," remarked the *Nation,* "Germany has shown herself ready to lift an outlaw hand against the whole of Western Europe." The assault on Antwerp, Lansing wrote Bryan, embodied "an outrage against humanity." Mary Bryan, wife of the secretary of state, called the zeppelin bombing of the city "this cowardly way of sneaking up under cover of darkness and dropping death down upon sleeping people."[34]

Theodore Roosevelt appeared to be of two minds. Writing a British friend on August 22, he accused the Germans of having "trampled on their solemn obligations to Belgium and on Belgium's rights." Over the past forty-three years, Germany had "menaced every nation where she thought it was to her advantage to do so." TR opposed any Allied march to Berlin, however, for western Europe might need the Reich "as a bulwark against the Slav." In late September, while in the midst of a congressional campaign, he refused to pass judgment on the Germans. While conceding that Belgium was entirely innocent, he claimed that "almost all great nations" had ignored matters of "abstract right and wrong" when "matters of vital national moment" were at stake. Certainly the United States bore not "the smallest responsibility" in the matter; it should remain "entirely neutral." Probably no American action could have affected the situation.[35]

Within weeks, Roosevelt radically reversed himself. Meeting with an official Belgian delegation visiting the United States, he learned more of German atrocities than had first been conveyed through British accounts. Early in October he wrote psychologist Münsterberg, claiming that Belgium deserved reparations. In another letter, this one to the head of the German Information Service, Roosevelt accused Berlin of seeking to integrate Belgium into Imperial Germany and to retain Antwerp and other North Sea cities in the process. In December his own daughter Ethel reinforced such reports. The wife of a surgeon serving Allied soldiers in Paris, she had heard of scandalous behavior on the part of German troops.[36]

In 1914 the Commission for Relief in Belgium (CRB), a neutral organization, was established. An American mining engineer, Herbert Hoover, headed the body. It created much sympathy for that invaded land and therefore indirectly for the entire Allied cause. The CRB centered attention on ordinary Belgians, using the techniques of advertising to induce American support. It publicized pleas from King Albert, the royal family, and the highly vocal Cardinal Désiré-Joseph Mercier and circulated films portraying German behavior in most unflattering terms.

Some Americans took a more benign view, maintaining that Belgium lay naturally within the German sphere of influence. Wrote economist Simon Patten: "Everyone knows that the economic welfare of Germany and

Belgium are bound together. They form parts of one economic unit." Publisher S.S. McClure observed that the efficient occupiers had abolished contagious diseases there.[37]

Far from being a small, defenseless country, Belgium, according to John W. Burgess, possessed a population of nearly 9 million, a well-equipped army of over two hundred thousand men, and an empire of over a million square miles, not to mention benefiting from a vigorous commerce. The Columbia scholar argued that it was Prussia and the German Confederation that had signed the 1839 guarantee, not the German Empire, which was founded in 1871. Therefore, the treaty was invalid. Philosophy professor Herbert Sanborn accused France and England of violating Belgian neutrality before German troops had begun to mobilize.[38]

Some of Germany's defenders took on the matter of Louvain, maintaining that the real atrocities were those committed against the Germans. Even Belgian priests, they asserted, supplied snipers with ammunition. Viereck called the city's destruction "an act of humanity, for it will teach other noncombatants, wherever they may be, to keep their guns out of their hands." Once the Belgians acted responsibly, women, children, and art treasures would no longer be endangered. Herman Ridder of the *New Yorker Staats-Zeitung* denied reports that the Germans had destroyed the town hall and the cathedral. In justifying the bombardment of Rheims, he blamed the French for deliberately making the cathedral their military stronghold. Certain journalists in Belgium, among them the representatives from the *New York World* and the *Chicago Tribune,* challenged accounts of German atrocities. The *Fatherland* asked: "Should the Germans Drop Bon-Bons into Antwerp?" as it argued that women and children had no place in a fortified town. After all, even before France declared war, its aviators had bombed Cologne and the unfortified Nuremberg.[39]

On September 16, Wilson met with a delegation of Belgian officials, led by the Belgian minister, who presented material concerning atrocities. The president promised his "most attentive perusal" of the documents but added: "You will not expect me to say more." When the war ended, "the day of accounting will then come when I take it for granted the nations of Europe will assemble to determine a settlement." The commission distributed a well-publicized report, *The Case of Belgium in the Present War.* As the drafters had little time, they lacked hard evidence and accepted hearsay; therefore their credibility was weakened. Wilhelm protested to Wilson, alleging that the British and French used splintering dumdum bullets, supposedly discovered in large quantities at Longwy fortress, to which the chief executive responded in almost the same words as those he addressed to the Belgians.[40] The president denied a hearing to a German American delegation concerning Belgium, a move that convinced Berlin's sympathizers that Wilson was insincere and pro-British.

The Germans in turn released three recently captured documents that appeared to compromise Belgium's neutrality. In 1906 the chief of the Belgian general staff and the British military attaché in Brussels had supposedly made an agreement by which, in the event of war between France and Germany, Belgium would admit one hundred thousand British troops. A 1911 paper indicated that the British sought to attack the Lower Rhine and Westphalia through Belgium. In 1912 still another record revealed Britain's presumed intention to counter a German attack with a landing on Belgian territory, whether invited or not. Even if the documents were spurious, noted historian Roland Usher of Washington University, the fact remained that the Belgian army had disposed its forces and readied its forts on the advice of British and French generals.[41]

Supporters of Belgium replied quickly. Any such arrangements were designed solely to defend Belgium and embodied mere contingency plans relating to a possible attack. Historian Zuckerman notes that if Belgium and Britain had planned their joint operations effectively, as the operations appeared to suggest, they would have hampered the German advance.[42]

Wilson's critics attacked his failure to invoke various provisions of the Second Hague Conference, convened in 1907. According to its provisions, belligerents were forbidden to move troops or supplies across the territory of a neutral power, much less bombard undefended towns or levy tribute from conquered provinces. In November Theodore Roosevelt accused the Wilson administration of shirking its duty, claiming, "We are bound in good faith to fulfill our treaty obligations." At the very least, the United States should have investigated and put itself on record. Writing Lodge, he labeled Wilson and Bryan "the very worst of men we have ever had in their positions."[43]

The administration responded quickly. Robert Lansing, counselor to the State Department and therefore its second-ranking officer, argued that Belgium's evidence was one-sided and that no one possessed the resources to conduct an impartial investigation. The Hague stipulations were unenforceable, and neutral governments were not obligated to interfere in the action of belligerents. To President Wilson, Lansing's observations were "sound and wise."[44]

By the winter of 1914–15, western Europe was experiencing stalemate. Both sides erected trenches that stretched from the English Channel to the mountains of Switzerland. For several years countless numbers of men were lost in frontal attacks that might at best gain a few yards. In January 1915, Ambassador Page wrote Wilson:

The horror of the thing outruns all imagination. Yet somehow nobody seems to realize it—men marched into the trenches to as certain slaughter as cattle when they are driven into the killing house in a stockyard. . . . There's nothing of the old "glory" of war—the charge, the yell, the music, the clash, and the giving way of one side or of the other. That's all gone. . . . Just plain, beastly butchery of men in such numbers as were never before killed in battle in so short a time, every mollifying thing gone—use any weapon, lie in the mud wounded for twelve hours, lie dead unburied for days! And when bombs strike a farmhouse and kill a family, that's not a subject even of passing remark.[45]

Although the Central Powers made inroads on their western front, they experienced frustration on their eastern one. Germany initially pulverized the Russian invader, but the entire Austrian army experienced setbacks in Poland and Serbia. In short, as in the west, neither side could expect a rapid victory.

News of deadlock overseas conveyed little reassurance to Americans. Instead of realizing that Europe was engaged in suicidal conflict, many feared that such massive mobilization portended ill for the United States. George Harvey, editor and publisher of the *North American Review,* issued a warning:

Suppose a German Empire, rising triumphant over a ruined England, lord of the sea, hungry for markets and colonies to recoup its losses. Suppose an aroused and aggressive Asia, with the United States the sole unscathed member of the white world. Suppose, even, a firmly welded British Empire, united by successful war, militarized by the intoxication of victory, and allied to a hungry and bellicose Japan. . . . At any rate, one lesson seems to lie fair for our reading: on this day of Armageddon America should neglect nothing for the sure maintenance of her position in a quaking world.[46]

Some military figures were obsessed with fears of a German threat. At the turn of the century, American naval leaders, including the famous strategist Alfred Thayer Mahan, believed that Berlin sought to occupy territory in the Western Hemisphere and challenge the United States for the control of world markets. In 1910 Captain Bradley Fiske, who directed war planning during Taft's administration, foresaw a commercial rivalry that would eventually lead to war. In August 1914 the Navy General Board warned that a victorious Germany would covet territory "on this side of the ocean." George H. Dewey, admiral of the navy and hero of Manila Bay, chaired the Board, thereby lending his personal prestige to this finding. Taft's secretary of war, Henry L. Stimson, observed that the American coastline harbored thousands of places where an invading army could land.[47]

The German conquest of Belgium, Theodore Roosevelt argued, proved conclusively that a German victory over England would inevitably cause the Reich to invade the United States, probably in alliance with Japan. Germany would commence hostilities, first challenging American interests in the Caribbean. Unfortunately, he warned *Chicago Tribune* publisher Joseph Medill Patterson, America would have "far less chance of success *than if we joined with the powers which are now fighting her.*" In fact, he told Princeton students that he had personally seen the plans of two great warring empires to seize America's great coastal cities. In an article appearing in the *New York Times,* he warned that Germany would hold these cities for an enormous ransom. Again, though, he argued that the total defeat of Germany would be "a great calamity," leading to war between the entire world and the newly victorious Russia.[48]

Hearst's *New York American* echoed somewhat similar sentiments: "Many shrewd observers of international affairs apprehend that whatever the outcome of the European war we shall have to fight the victor." The *New York Times* noted the German book *Operations upon the Sea* (1901), in which Captain Franz von Edelsheim of the general staff proposed a German strike on America's Atlantic Coast, landing at an unexpected point and aiming guns at several of the wealthiest coastal cities. The complete conquest of the United States was unnecessary; Berlin's control of major commercial arteries would create such an unbearable state of affairs that the United States would readily sue for peace. Early in November, according to Colonel House's diary, Wilson instructed intelligence services to investigate whether German agents, preparing for invasion, were building gun foundations disguised as tennis courts.[49]

Americans genuinely feared threats to coastal defense and to the "hands off" provisions of the Monroe Doctrine, but their preoccupation with continental threats, rather than overseas involvement, reflected domestic politics as well. By ignoring any possibility of sending an expeditionary force to Europe, the Wilson administration could assuage the anxiety of a neutralist people, who opposed massive rearmament. It might also rally support from German Americans, a group far from anxious to see the United States fighting against their former homeland.

German naval leaders had long believed that Britain and the United States were tacit allies, sharing the desire to freeze Berlin out of world markets. Assuming the weakness of the American navy, they made no serious studies of American strength. In 1903 Berlin developed a contingency scheme to land forces in Canada and conduct attacks against its southern neighbor. However, Operations Plan III, as it was called, was soon deemed quixotic and was dropped three years later.[50]

Admittedly, America's armed forces were unprepared for major conflict, their numbers being only slightly larger than those of Mexico or Belgium. The regular army totaled well under one hundred thousand men, divided into thirty regiments of infantry, fifteen of cavalry, and six of field artillery. It also possessed 170 companies of coast artillery. Some units were nowhere near wartime strength. Furthermore, half of these troops were stationed overseas, spread from Tientsin (now Tianjin) to the Canal Zone. According to War Secretary Garrison, those remaining in the United States hardly doubled the police force of New York City. The army possessed only 11 airplanes and even in emergency could produce just 100 more within a year. In comparison, France possessed 1,400 planes; Germany, 1,400; Russia, 1,000; Britain, 900; Austria-Hungary, 600; Belgium, 60; Italy, 300; and Japan, 20. Certainly no major power feared one of the world's smallest land forces.

In addition, a National Guard of 120,000 existed, but this body was poorly trained and badly led. State governors controlled these troops, possessing the sole power to muster out forces. Of this militia just 67,000 had fired a gun during range practice; 38,000 never drilled as much as twenty-four hours in a given year. Summer camps, even if conscientiously administered, offered little real instruction. In 1912 the attorney general ruled that the militia could not be required to serve outside the United States. During the Spanish-American War, some state units refused to obey presidential directives.

There were some pluses in the overall picture. Almost half the officer corps of 3,450 men were West Point graduates. Many had seen field service in the Philippines and on the Mexican border. The 77,300 well-trained enlisted men possessed such superior weapons as the Springfield rifle and the three-inch gun. The army's twelve-inch guns and huge mortars protected the nation's principal seaports. The chief of army ordnance judged American field guns as good as those of any nation.

Turning to the navy, one finds it barely adequate for a world power facing two major oceans. Assistant Secretary Franklin Roosevelt claimed that target practice was infrequent, long tours in the tropics undermined morale, and the sea arm lacked a proper staff. Since 1906, most of America's thirty-one battleships had become obsolete, with few being replaced. The Atlantic fleet, stationed off the Mexican coast, had become an increasingly inferior force.[51]

Hearings of the House Committee on Naval Affairs, held in late fall 1914, created genuine debate. Rear Admiral Victor Blue, chief of the Bureau of Navigation and a hero of the Spanish-American War, pictured the navy as undermanned, short of experienced officers, and riddled with timeservers, a sentiment echoed by the *Army and Navy Journal.* Assistant Secretary Roosevelt placed his nation's force third among the great powers; over eighteen thousand additional sailors were needed to man the fleet on a wartime basis. Commander Yates Sterling, in charge of the Atlantic flotilla of submarines, claimed that only one such craft could remain underwater for more than fifteen minutes. Retired rear admiral French E. Chadwick warned that a victorious British Empire would turn upon the United States as easily as it had confronted Germany.[52]

Particularly vocal was Rear Admiral Bradley Fiske, the navy's chief planner and aide for operations to Secretary Daniels. Fiske had seen combat in the Spanish-American War and the Philippine insurrection and was a well-known inventor of electric devices. As early as 1910 he had sought a navy outmatched by none. At the end of October 1914, Fiske privately noted that he could not "get any one to bet 2 to 1 that we will not be in war in two years." Needed were war plans for "Black and Orange—Germany and Japan." In his testimony of December 17, he stressed that the navy lacked a general plan of development. Enemy aircraft launched from ships might possibly be able to bomb the United States from a distance of five hundred miles. Both the Panama Canal and New York City in particular remained exposed to such strikes.[53]

Other admirals countered such claims, thereby supporting the Wilson administration. Rear Admiral Charles J. Badger of the navy's general staff responded that ship for ship, American forces equaled any in the world, though he pleaded for a naval reserve, eight more battleships, and one hundred submarines. Admiral Dewey concurred with Badger's assessment. Frank F. Fletcher, commander in chief of the Atlantic Fleet, boasted that the United States could control the seas against any foe but Britain. He considered existing fortifications and mines sufficient to protect New York City. In addition, he maintained, American ships remained in a high state of efficiency. Although the fleet could not defend the Philippines unaided, it could wrest the seas from Japan.[54]

Josephus Daniels discerned no need to increase the number of naval personnel, much less engage in any crash program. "We should just go on as if there were no war," he said on December 10. Although the Navy General Board sought four dreadnoughts, Daniels's first annual report only recommended two. He conceded that the United States lacked any battleship capable of resisting torpedo attack, though he noted that five battleships under construction would enjoy such protection. Conversely, Germany possessed twenty fortified dreadnoughts.[55]

Augustus P. Gardner served as the preparedness movement's chief advocate in Congress. No ordinary legislator, Gardner was one of the most visible, vocal, and powerful members of the House. On October 15, having just returned from Europe, he presented a resolution advocating creation of a national security commission. Assistant Secretary Franklin Roosevelt claimed to have initiated the idea, even suggesting Gardner's wording. This body would be composed of three senators, three representatives, and three presidential appointees. Its task: to scrutinize America's military weakness. Strongly favoring the Allies, the Massachusetts congressman deemed Berlin's cause "unholy," "a menace to the principles of democracy." Although he predicted that "the God of battles will visit defeat upon the Germans," he asked his countrymen to remember that "victorious nations have proved headstrong and high-handed."[56]

Almost immediately, Gardner sought a radical increase in dreadnoughts, torpedoes, and artillery. The navy, he charged, was shrinking to fourth or fifth place. He judged the militia woefully ill trained, even being inept in riflery. Placing some of the blame upon himself, he noted: "For a dozen years I have sat here like a coward, and I have listened to men say that in time of war we could depend for our defense upon our National Guard and our Naval Militia, and I have known all the time that it is not so." Unless the United States was fully armed, Germany and Japan would threaten the Monroe Doctrine.[57]

Gardner took full advantage of the controversy over naval strength. In testifying before the House naval affairs committee, he warned that eighty vessels, including nine battleships, were not battle-ready. Furthermore, the navy possessed a mere dozen "aeroplanes." He told a New York audience: "The guns in your defense have one and a half miles less range than the dreadnoughts laid down by Great Britain." Assistant Secretary Roosevelt surreptitiously supplied Gardner data with which to attack Daniels.[58]

The American press split over Gardner's accusations. To the pacifist-leaning Oswald Garrison Villard, the legislator had ignored reports of the army and navy secretaries to rely upon congressional testimony from top brass. The *New Republic,* more Realpolitik in its perspective, supported the congressman's plea for an independent investigation, charging that the United States was unable to protect its own coasts from invasion, much less defend the Philippines, Panama, and Hawaii.[59]

Wilson patronizingly called the controversy "good mental exercise," noting that he had heard such talk since he was ten years old. After meeting with Gardner, he told the press that the representative's proposal "might create very unfavorable international impressions." Gardner responded by finding that "the scholarly surroundings which environed the President" led him to "take too kindly a view of the good intentions of foreign nations."[60] In reality the president possessed the southern progressive's usual suspicion of rearmament, discerning jingoes, high finance, and heavy industry behind any such crusade. To Wilson America's mission centered on neutrality and mediation, not preparation for war.

On December 8, the House Rules committee refused to report out Gardner's bill. Southern Democrats, who controlled the Congress, stressed frugality and entertained antimilitary sentiments. During subsequent debates over Gardner's resolution, Congressman Martin Dies Sr. (D-Tex.) asked his Bay State colleague: "Can you point to a nation of militarism that maintained the liberty of the people?" Senator Lodge, who introduced a similar resolution in the Senate, countered that "the ocean barrier which defended us in 1776 and 1812 no longer exists. Steam and electricity have destroyed it." Less than three months earlier, the Massachusetts senator had endorsed an Allied victory, warning that if Germany conquered Europe, it would seek to dominate the world.[61]

Gardner was certainly not the sole preparedness advocate. Major General Leonard Wood, physician and Rough Rider, was even more prominent. Wood had served as military governor of Cuba and of the rebellious Moro province of the Philippines. In 1914, when his term as chief of staff expired, he was appointed commander of the Department of the East, the nation's most important military post. Its headquarters, located at Governors Island in New York harbor, was an ideal spot from which to launch his crusade. In particular he stressed the need for camps to provide military training, first for college students, then for young professionals and businessmen. He conceded that he did not expect to accomplish much in the way of instruction but sought to inculcate "a sound military policy," that is, a belief that any vigorous foreign policy needed force behind it.

Wood wrote Gardner, saying: "Our people do not appreciate the suddenness with which modern war develops. . . . Our condition is one which invites attack." During the first year of the European war, the fiery general gave sixty speeches, always in uniform and always offering tacit criticism of Wilson. In mid-December he publicly attacked unnamed figures who, as he pointed out, would recommend that American troops enter the battlefield unprepared; they were "fake humanitarians . . . slayers of their people." Wilson wanted War Secretary Garrison to order a reprimand but had to be satisfied with a mild rebuke.[62]

If anything, Theodore Roosevelt was even more adamant. In a series of articles for the *New York Times,* Roosevelt attacked those pacifists who had "made and applauded our recent all-inclusive arbitration treaties, who advocate the abandonment of our policy of building battleships and the refusal to fortify the Panama Canal." Justice could only be attained, the former president insisted, by the exercise of power. Therefore, the United States must be prepared for any eventuality, including participating in an international police system.[63]

Similarly, Roosevelt warned against ratifying the so-called Bryan treaties, which provided for permanent investigating commissions and a year's "cooling-off." Such procedures, warned TR, would cause the United States to wait in idle helplessness while a potential enemy "could make a Gibraltar" of one of the West Indian islands or of Magdalena Bay off the coast of Mexico. Better, he continued, to rely on the time-tested Monroe Doctrine, which was keeping America out of the current conflict, than choose the chimera of arbitration. The former president had his followers. In case of war, asserted the military inventor Henry Wise Wood, Roosevelt alone could "remasculinize what had become an almost demasculinized America."[64]

The preparedness issue united many Old Guard Republicans with the more belligerent elements of Roosevelt's foundering Progressive Party. After all, most preparedness leaders came from Republican and Progressive ranks. Wilson suspected that the defense movement was rooted in partisanship, particularly because its adherents feared that the Republican domestic policy was too reactionary to draw popular support. At the same time, the crusade created new fissures among Bull Moose reformers, as it soon would among Wilsonian Democrats. To be sure, far more than political expediency motivated Roosevelt, for he had exhibited such militancy since the 1890s.

Even before the European war started, certain organizations had pushed the preparedness cause. Foremost was the Navy League, organized in 1902 and located in Washington, D.C. Steel and banking companies were heavily represented among its directors; the son-in-law of J.P. Morgan served as general counsel. Big business and high finance, though, played little role in determining policy. Civil War general Horace Porter was president, but Colonel Robert M. Thompson, financier and chairman of the executive committee, ran the organization. A son of Josephus Daniels wrote of Thompson: "The Navy League seemed almost as much his private property as his houseboats, his big houses, his securities or his stables." Despite attacks made by contemporary critics, League historian Armin Rappaport argues that it was motivated solely by patriotism and did not seek war.[65]

Only when the European conflict began did the League gain members and influence, boasting over fifty thousand members late in 1915. Endorsing Gardner's proposals, the League stressed the threat to "race purity" that stemmed from Oriental immigration to the Western Hemisphere. Its journal, *Seven Seas,* advocated wars of conquest, but in May 1916 an embarrassed leadership terminated publication. Its successor, *Sea Power,* was far less strident. At first advocating strict neutrality, the organization had long discerned in Germany a menace to American security and blamed the Central Powers alone for triggering the European conflict. Leonard Wood founded a similar Army League in 1913, but it exercised limited influence. As the army was far more labor-intensive than the navy, its league lacked the backing of steel companies and shipyards that the Navy League received.

A new organization soon overshadowed both groups. On December 1, 1914, the National Security League (NSL) was formed when Solomon Stanwood Menken, a prominent Manhattan lawyer, called fifty public leaders to meet at New York's Hotel Belmont. Their purpose: to make American armed forces combat-ready. Menken had personally observed the House of Commons on the day Britain entered the war; he feared that the United States would be similarly unprepared in an hour of peril. The NSL chose

Menken president but in mid-1916 gave the position to Robert Bacon, former ambassador to France and briefly secretary of state.

The base of the association lay among New York's business and social elite. Joseph H. Choate, former ambassador to Britain, was made honorary president, and former judge Alton B. Parker, Democratic presidential candidate in 1904, honorary vice-president. Other prominent leaders included Elihu Root, Henry L. Stimson, and Herbert Barry, a New York corporation lawyer. Among the various backers were corporation lawyer James M. Beck; Charles E. Lydecker, New York attorney and NSL president in 1918; and George Haven Putnam, who had enlisted in the Union army at age eighteen. At its initial meeting, Putnam warned of a German invasion through the Hudson Valley while foreign ships fired at New York City with impunity.[66] Although primarily composed of Republicans, the League was ostensibly nonpartisan and Menken was a Democrat. It never took an open stand on the war's outcome, even if such individual leaders as Bacon and Root made no secret of their desire for an Allied victory. By October 1915, it boasted fifty thousand members and seventy chapters in forty-two states. Within a year it had distributed a million pieces of literature and conducted over one hundred meetings.

In 1914 some sixty-three peace organizations existed, none matching the influence of the National Security League. The League's formation led to the creation of a counterassociation, the American League to Limit Armaments. Spearheaded by New York City's Episcopal bishop David H. Greer, it chose Nicholas Murray Butler, president of Columbia University, as permanent chairman. In the call for organization, dated December 10, it accused preparedness advocates of playing into the hands of the "Armour Plate Trust." At the very first meeting, members endorsed "strict neutrality." A host of progressive reformers backed the League, including publisher Oswald Garrison Villard, philanthropist George Foster Peabody, Socialist legislator Morris Hillquit, Congregationalist minister Charles E. Jefferson of New York City, and two leaders whose names were synonymous with urban settlement work, Jane Addams and Lillian D. Wald.[67]

Preparedness proponents drew little support from Wilson's annual message, delivered on December 8. The president devoted a third of his speech to the defense issue. In every time of national peril, he admonished, the United States must depend "not upon a standing army, nor yet upon a reserve army, but upon a citizenry trained and accustomed to arms." More than this, he added, would mean "that we had been thrown off our balance by a war with which we have nothing to do, whose causes can not touch us, whose existence affords us opportunities of friendship and disinterested service which should make us ashamed of any thought of hostility or fearful preparation for trouble." Wilson endorsed a voluntary reserve system and recommended strengthening of the National Guard. With an obvious reference to Congressman Gardner, he pledged: "We shall not alter our attitude . . . because some amongst us are nervous and excited." Speaking of the navy, he found long-term projections difficult to make, adding: "The question has not changed its aspect because the times are not normal."[68]

Though Republicans responded with tepid applause, the Democratic majority was enthusiastic. In his rejection of a strong military presence on the world scene, the president had skillfully captured the popular mood as well. Without referring directly to Wilson's address, Taft deplored the current "hysteria" over preparedness, finding that any victor would be far too exhausted to fight the United States.[69]

Secretary of War Lindley Garrison was less convinced. In his annual report he requested more troops for coastal defense along with additional artillery and ammunition and an adequate flying corps. He also sought one thousand more officers and twenty-five thousand additional enlisted men, the entire force to constitute the base of an army reserve.[70] He submitted his proposals in a series of seven bills, but the retrenchment-minded Congress ignored his agenda.

Obviously America's strength lay far more in its productive capacity than in its armed forces. By 1913 its economy had become the world's largest, producing one-third of the global industrial output. Nevertheless, the first few weeks of war created great uncertainty. Stock markets closed in every great city in Europe and the Americas. Wall Street experienced hysteria, anticipating the collapse of transatlantic trade. On July 31, as Austria, France, and Germany mobilized, the New York Stock Exchange endured its biggest losses since the Panic of 1907. Experiencing a heavy sale of English securities, a fall in the dollar's exchange value, and a run on gold, it shut its doors for over four months. Treasury Secretary William Gibbs McAdoo worked with private bankers to stave off financial panic. He permitted the use of $370 million worth of "emergency currency" to tide over matters until the newly created Federal Reserve System could react positively. Nonetheless, the Stock Exchange did not resume normal interchange until the following spring. The war, commented the *Banker's Magazine,* had fostered "a total financial disaster."[71]

Business in general was in no better shape. At the end of 1913 a severe recession had developed, causing particularly harsh unemployment in the industrial areas of the Northeast and the Midwest. If conditions were slack in July 1914, before the war began, they were prostrate in October. Over 16 percent of the labor force in New York City lacked jobs. During that winter, joblessness remained high throughout the nation, abetting Democratic losses in the midterm elections. By January 1915 mills of the massive United States Steel Corporation operated at half capacity. Concurrently railroad construction reached its lowest point in fifty years. Prices suffered their greatest decline since the Panic of 1907. The cost of wheat, essential in baking bread, reached record levels.

The disappearance of America's maritime trade compounded the downslide. During the first half of every year, the United States faced an unfavorable commercial balance, but massive exports of such crops as wheat, corn, and tobacco usually corrected this slide. With the advent of war, Germany and neighboring neutral countries were suddenly severed from American trade. Materials bound for Europe—grains, copper, meat, oil, steel manufactures—all lay idle in warehouses and freight cars. The dry goods trade suffered because it was suddenly shut off from German dyes. The copper industry was damaged, for the German Reich had formerly received 88 percent of this resource from the United States. The president of the New York Chamber of Commerce remarked: "Europe has placed an embargo on the commerce of the world."[72]

Cotton growers experienced the worst of the downturn. The base of southern prosperity, cotton production involved about 4 million people. Now some $500 million was at risk. Seventy-seven percent of Germany's cotton had come from the United States. The disruption of European markets lowered the price of cotton considerably, so much that the price of 12.5 cents a pound in July plummeted to less than 7.0 cents by mid-October. Because cotton farmers always borrowed heavily on their future earnings, in November they fell into heavy debt. Writes historian Ray Stannard Baker: "Ruin threatened the farmer, the railroads that transported his crops, the merchants that supplied him, and the banks that loaned him money."[73]

Wilson defeated any effort that would have involved price supports. He instituted "cotton loan funds," involving private banks and the Federal Reserve Board, but they failed to raise prices and therefore did not restore the desired prosperity. The fact that the South provided the political base of the president's political support made his stance even more embarrassing.

In January 1915, Governor Oscar B. Colquitt of Texas called the Wilson administration "the greatest failure in the history of the Presidency." Because, he contended, Britain's spinners robbed the American cotton farmers of half their crop's value, southern business was prostrated, credit impaired, and "thousands of its people are starving." Were he president he would send "ironclads" to protect American shipping against any blockade. Similarly, by June 1915, Senator John Sharp Williams (D-Miss.), a strong Wilson man, warned the president of a southern backlash if he did not condemn Britain.[74]

Amid such anxieties, the administration debated the extension of loans to belligerent governments. Early in August 1914, France sought a $100 million loan from J.P. Morgan & Company, the world's largest banking firm. The company stressed that the loan would benefit the American economy as a whole because the money could be used to purchase American goods.

On August 15, Bryan forbade the transaction, publicly declaring that any such deal betrayed "the true spirit of neutrality." "Money," he wrote Wilson five days earlier, "is the worst of contrabands—it commands everything else." Besides, lenders would have "pecuniary interests" in the victory of a warring party, while the more powerful investors would use their influence in the press to support one side of the conflict. In addition, foreigners might absorb so much American money that the drain could affect the nation's ability to borrow. Conversely, the American example of restraint might hasten an end to the conflict. In his personal magazine, the *Commoner,* the secretary of state asked: "The government withdraws the protection of citizenship from those who do enlist under other flags—why should it give protection to money when it enters into foreign military service?" The *Nation* concurred. Though pro-Entente, the weekly found this the "time for the United States to sit tight," not "weakening our home resources and becoming financially bound up with the fate of the warring nations."[75] At first the business press supported Bryan, warning that belligerents were poor risks.

Wilson's support for Bryan was somewhat out of character, because of the sweeping nature of Bryan's measure and the secretary's belief that in the power of example alone lay effective policy. Historian John Milton Cooper Jr. offers several reasons why Wilson might have supported the move: distractions of grief, his usual deference toward a cabinet member's prerogative, a shared fear of Wall Street power, and the hope that the ban might help create peace.[76]

Wilson's biographer Arthur S. Link finds good reasons for a *temporary* ban. The sudden advent of war put international markets in chaos. Europe's demand for gold and dollars had already demoralized the American money market. Further lending might well have drained financial resources, intensifying the domestic recession. The nation had to stop the flow of gold. Just as important, Bryan's initial move symbolized the administration's quest for genuine impartiality.[77] A *long-term* ban, however, Link judges economically unfeasible. It would have ruined the nation's foreign trade, in the process creating economic catastrophe. Only overseas sales could pull American farmers and manufacturers out of the recession. Perpetuating Bryan's proscription would have damaged the American economy, created political unrest, and aided a Germany that the public certainly distrusted.

Moreover, Link, along with fellow historians Daniel M. Smith and Kendrick A. Clements, sees a permanent ban as essentially unneutral. Highly prejudicial to the Allies, it worked against Britain, a sea power, to the advantage of Germany, a land one. Indeed, it might have caused the Entente to lose the war. As Britain and France were far more America's natural customers than was Germany, the trade-off would not have been a good one. In fairness to Bryan, this fact was as yet unclear, because none of the Allies yet needed American credits. No Allied government protested Bryan's pronouncement. Germany, the Wilson administration thought, would still maintain a lively trade in noncontraband goods. Bryan's prohibition also revealed muddled thinking. His arguments against loans, which he considered a form of contraband, could be used against exporting any kind of war material, contradicting another one of his tenets: America's right to export.[78]

By mid-October 1914, the other leading State Department officials favored loans to the warring powers. Either lift the ban, Lansing admonished Wilson, or Canada, Australia, Mexico, and Argentina would steal war orders from the United States. On October 23, in the wake of a French request for a $10 million loan, Wilson told him that he would not oppose an extension of commercial "credits," news at once relayed to the powerful National City Bank and Morgan firms; the former then extended a $10 million credit to France.[79]

In March 1915, Morgan and two other firms sought government approval for a $50 million "commercial credit" to France. In reality the transaction was a loan, but at the end of the month Bryan ruled that the State Department did not object.[80] Many businessmen supported such credits on one major assumption, the continued belief that otherwise American commerce would be paralyzed, a situation disastrous to the nation's entire economy. The administration had imposed the original proscription when it thought that the war would be brief. Now, as prolonged fighting obviously lay ahead, the belligerents desperately needed credit. If European nations could not pay for American goods, they would stop buying them. Though German sympathizers later criticized the reversal, at the time Berlin favored the change because it, too, pushed subscriptions for its cause. The United States was ceasing to be a borrower of capital; it was on its way to becoming a lender—and on a huge scale.

As early as October 1914, the American economy slowly started to rebound. Although cotton farmers remained destitute and large numbers of unemployed still pounded the pavements, Allied governments began placing massive orders for raw materials and manufactured goods. The steel industry in particular sprang into unprecedented activity. European demand for foodstuffs was virtually unlimited. Even horses and mules were sought. By the end of 1914, elements of the U.S. population became dependent on trade in war supplies, a phenomenon welcomed by a business leadership who even feared that an early peace might lead to relinquishing wartime gains.

In the long run, America had begun what one financial writer called "the most remarkable period of financial and industrial expansion that had been witnessed in history."[81] Full employment returned. In 1914 American exports to Europe exceeded imports by $500 million; in 1917 the total was $3.5 billion, a development unparalleled in the world's commercial history. Furthermore, the United States gained Asian and Latin American markets previously dominated by Europe. Despite the decline in trade with the Central Powers, within two years the economy was booming. Early in 1915 foreign purchases of cotton led to a healthy rise in prices.

To sustain the nation's recovery, the Wilson administration sought to maximize its trade with the belligerents, hoping to transport raw materials, foodstuffs, and manufactured goods to whatever nation was willing to pay. Britain sought the shipment of American goods to the Entente alone, seeking to prevent the Central Powers, and Germany in particular, from receiving U.S. imports. As British Foreign Secretary Edward Grey wrote in his memoirs: "The Allies soon became dependent for an adequate supply on the United States. If we quarreled with the United States we could not get that supply. . . . The object of diplomacy, therefore, was to secure the maximum of blockade that could be enforced without a rupture with the United States."[82]

The United States stressed that the rules for commerce in time of war lay in the Declaration of London, a document drafted in 1909 by the world's major maritime powers, among them Britain, Germany, and the United States. Summarizing the world's most advanced thought on wartime trade, the declaration provided definitions for contraband, that is, those goods shipped by a neutral power, bound ultimately to a belligerent, and legally subject to enemy confiscation. Defined were *absolute contraband,* articles used exclusively in war and ranging from uniforms to warships; *conditional contraband,* articles capable of being used in war as well as peace (e.g., grain, fodder, clothing, fuel); and *noncontraband,* articles deemed as possessing no military use whatsoever (e.g., rubber, paper, soap). Conditional contraband could be seized only if bound directly for a belligerent port. The declaration allowed great freedom for neutral trade, specifically exempting from seizure the copper ore and cotton crucial to American commerce. It was ratified by the American Senate and the British House of Commons. Ironically, Britain's House of Lords rejected it on the grounds that its contraband restrictions were too severe. Although the declaration was not binding on the English government, one could still argue that its Admiralty had tacitly endorsed the declaration, even to the extent of incorporating its provisions unchanged in its manuals.

Within a week after the fighting began, Bryan asked the leading belligerents to abide by the Declaration of London. Both Austria and Germany declared that they would honor the measure, provided their enemies did likewise. Britain hedged on the whole matter, saying on August 26 that it would adopt the declaration "subject to certain modifications and additions . . . they judge indispensable to the efficient conduct of their naval operations."[83]

Soon the British navy restricted Germany's access to copper, oil, food, and cotton. Exactly a month after the British note, Counselor Lansing triggered the first Anglo-American dispute of the war by calling the modification totally unacceptable. Yet, when the British rejected Lansing's grievance, on October 22 the United States found itself retreating to preexisting international law, a far more controversial and complicated entity.[84]

The British thought they had no choice. Grey realized that the declaration's contraband list was obsolete, as it excluded such strategic items as copper, chemicals, and cotton, the last item an ingredient of gunpowder. Furthermore, the London accord failed to recognize the doctrine of continuous voyage, which specified that it was the ultimate, and not immediate, destination that determined whether various exports were legally subject to confiscation. Goods at first slated for such neutral countries as Holland, Denmark, Sweden, and Norway might end up in German hands. Not surprisingly, most trade with Germany went through the ports of neutral nations, in particular the Netherlands.

Over two years later, in September 1916, Ambassador Page defended the Entente practice, writing to Wilson: "That Declaration would probably have given a victory to Germany if the Allies had adopted it." Historians tend to concur. Link observes: "No government that promised to concede virtual freedom of the seas could have survived for an hour at Whitehall." Ernest R. May argues: "Were Britain to accept the Declaration, she would virtually forswear the use of economic weapons."[85]

In the meantime, Britain soon made clear its intentions. On August 20, 1914, it launched what in time historian Patrick Devlin called "the starvation policy." By executive decree, called an Order in Council, it began its policy of economic strangulation, capturing neutral ships if it deemed Germany a cargo's final destination. In practice, during the first three months of war, Britain seldom interfered with neutral trade. Late in October Britain ruled such items as copper, rubber, and gasoline as absolute contraband, finding a ship guilty until proven innocent.[86]

On October 29 Britain imposed a blockade, although it never used the term. By this order, it sought to control the coasts of neutral Norway, Sweden, Denmark, and the Netherlands. Since the entire North Sea might be mined, neutral ships could enter only "at their own peril." The measure was highly illegal, for, according to international law, a blockade must not extend beyond the enemy's ports and coasts. It forced neutral vessels into the English Channel, where they needed Admiralty pilots to guide them through newly laid minefields. Obviously the announcement made it far easier for Britain to search suspected cargoes. The Admiralty deemed it necessary, however, "to adopt exceptional measures appropriate to the novel conditions under which this war is being waged."[87] The British justified the measure on the ground that Germany had laid mines outside the legal three-mile limit (directly violating the second Hague convention of 1907), used submarines in the area to torpedo cruisers and battleships, and threatened the home islands with invasion.

Given the stalemate in western Europe, Britain increasingly saw its one hope in an effort to starve the enemy. Soon its cruisers stopped neutral vessels on the high seas. These ships would cruise near enough to intercept any approaching vessel, shepherd it to a "control station," and examine it at leisure. They even seized food cargo. Vessels could be delayed for months, held up without court hearings and sometimes without notice to the owners. If British authorities judged the goods contraband, they were subject to confiscation. If they were not so judged, they could still be snatched, though in this case Britain would pay for the cargo. At times Britain would permit skilled pilots to guide "harmless" cargoes through its maze of mines.

Because such practices flagrantly violated international law, pro-Germans were not alone in believing that Britain not simply "ruled the waves but waived the rules." Even Allied sympathizer Theodore Roosevelt promised that if he were president he would never allow "the British or any other people" the right to engage in such conduct.[88]

Although the neutral nations of northern Europe protested vigorously, the United States acquiesced in the British practice. Late in September America filed an informal plea, claiming that it was "greatly disturbed," but the move was strictly for the record. Historians Thomas A. Bailey and Paul B. Ryan find the American response "astonishing," although Ernest R. May notes that relatively few American vessels sailed the North Sea and American passengers were rare. Besides, the British government sweetened the new orders by its offer to safeguard those ships that complied with its new contraband rules.[89]

After another month and a half of frequent British seizures, the State Department, acting on December 26, issued its first public protest. Accusations included inconsistent regulations, designating food as conditional contraband, seizure of cargoes without proof they were bound for an enemy, and detention of ships without prize court proceedings. "Many great industries," it asserted, suffered because they were denied long-established European markets. Producers and exporters were particularly damaged, as were steamship and insurance companies. There existed the feeling, "doubtless not entirely unjustified, that the present British policy toward American trade is responsible for the depression in certain industries which depend upon European markets." If the situation was not alleviated the friendship of the American people could be lost. The note gave the British a loophole by recognizing "the momentous nature of the present struggle" and the belligerents' "imperative necessity to protect their national safety."[90]

Editorial opinion tended to back the department. The *New Republic*, for example, expressed gratification that the United States was no longer submitting "meekly to the British exactions" but had "come to the assistance of the American merchant."[91]

The protest posed no real challenge to the British. Written in a polite, indeed friendly tone, the message repeated past entreaties and did not threaten retaliation. Emphasizing commercial details more than broad policy, it involved no frontal assault upon Britain's behavior. British foreign secretary Edward Grey and Prime Minister Herbert Asquith correctly found little threat in the note and acted accordingly. By the beginning of 1915, the British system was almost fully intact. On January 9, 1915, Wilson told Chandler P. Anderson, Page's legal adviser just returned from London, that he saw no major principles at stake; all controversies could be resolved once the war ended.[92]

Grey formally replied to Wilson on January 7, denying that the United States had any legitimate grievance because its trade losses were grounded in "the existence of a state of war." Attempting to justify the British seizures, he stressed that "under modern conditions" the right of search could only be exercised in such manner. He questioned whether American trade had really been hampered, given the radical rise in U.S. exports to Denmark, Sweden, Norway, and Italy over the past year.[93]

By and large, the American press did not accept Grey's arguments, although it expressed relief that the issue was still under negotiation.[94] This type of exchange over neutral rights, a U.S. protest and a British rejoinder, was repeated continually, sometimes more harshly than other times, almost until the time the United States entered the war.

The United States was in a quandary. If it continued to export contraband, the Allies benefited because they dominated the seas and bought most of the U.S. war supplies. If it withheld such trade, the Central Powers would be strengthened and America would weaken its own economy. Moreover, if it conceded rights of blockade to the Allies, the United States would condone what would be called a "starvation" policy. Any American action was bound to help one side at the other's expense, making most pertinent Link's claim that genuine neutrality consisted of doing things that would give the least advantage to one side or the other.[95]

One must note that neutrality is a legal status, one that brings into operation an entire series of rules regulating relations with belligerents. The neutral state possessed both duties and rights that it must exercise in a nondiscriminatory manner. At the same time, a neutral had no obligation to ensure equality of outcome, something well-nigh impossible anyhow. A belligerent, in other words, lacked grounds for complaint if the commerce of a neutral state worked to its disadvantage.

Wilson was not about to challenge the British, and his defenders offer several reasons why. First, they judge international law as both ambiguous and outmoded, the advent of the submarine alone rendering much of it obsolete. For example, international law was vague concerning the laying of mines, the Hague Conventions restricting their use but still accepting them as legitimate weapons. Wilson biographer Ray Stannard Baker calls the traditional legal order "merely a feeble and contradictory assemblage of precedents backed by no real sanctions," as useful as oxcarts in an age of airplanes.[96] Its codification, drafted at The Hague in 1907, could not bind belligerents in a war begun in 1914. Nor could precedents established at the time of the American Civil War or the Spanish-American War.

Second, even if the United States adhered to a more rigid neutrality, most of its trade, as had been the case before war had begun, would have been with the Allies, who, at any rate, needed American goods far more than did the Central Powers. Third, convenience played a role. Wilson wrote Bryan in March 1915: "We are face to face with *something they are going to do,* and are going to do it no matter what representations we make. We cannot convince them or change them." As historian Ross Gregory writes: "Wilson acquiesced in the British system because it seemed the best way of avoiding difficulty, was profitable, and seemed perfectly safe."[97] In short, why seek trouble when there was no compensating reward?

Given the argument that American trade with the Allies entwined the U.S. economy with Britain and France, one might ask: Why not embargo all foreign trade, thereby minimizing friction with any foreign power? Several problems arise here. Domestic statute code gave Americans the freedom to trade with whomever they chose. The president lacked authority to stop any transatlantic commerce. Wilson would have faced great difficulty securing Congress's authorization to halt exports, even the shipment of war goods, unless he could show convincingly that American security and world peace were at stake. In addition, to retain its legal status as a neutral power under international law, a nation faced the obligation of permitting its citizens to trade with anyone they chose.

Historian Link argues that a total embargo would have been a singularly unneutral act, threatening the entire rationale for asserting one's neutral status, which was to conduct America's legitimate war trade. Even Britain's orders of October 29, which tightened the categories of contraband, were based upon international law and practice that enjoyed legality through custom and usage. The United States had applied the doctrine of continuous voyage to Britain during its own Civil War. Could a truly neutral nation deny Britain the right to seal off materials essential to Germany's war machine? Such a policy would be "tantamount to undeclared war."[98]

Conversely, some observers argued that a general embargo could have threatened the entire American economy, maintaining that by mid-1915 the economic well-being of the United States depended upon the Allied trade. House wrote Wilson in July: "If it came to the last analysis and we placed an embargo upon munitions of war and foodstuffs to please the cotton men, our whole industrial and agricultural population would cry out against it." The loss of the $5 billion gained from Allied trade, warned journalist John Callan O'Laughlin, would precipitate "domestic cataclysm." Historian Ross Gregory argues that the nation possessed the means to survive without its European trade but at the cost of intense distress. Production, distribution, and perhaps the nation's political system itself would have required alteration. "The merchant needs the customer no less—at least little less—than the customer needs him." In a curious paradox, Gregory contends, the maturation of the American economy over the preceding quarter century had made the United States more dependent upon others, for the nation was now part of an international trade structure that left it most vulnerable to changes overseas. The United States still needed to sell goods to Europe while requiring raw materials from both Entente nations and their empires.[99]

Suppose, ask Wilson defenders, such a move had caused the Allies to lose the war. To challenge British sea power could well ruin America's friendship with the great European democracies (ignoring despotic Russia) and ensure the victory of the far more autocratic Central Powers, implacably hostile by 1917. "In short," Link affirms, "destroying the British blockade would have brought not a single compensating gain to the United States while it would, at the same time, have imperiled its own national security."[100]

Besides, the nation would sacrifice any chance of mediating the conflict. A great power, Link argues, should not simply defend traditional neutral rights; it should use its economic power to achieve particular ends, in this case ending the war. Otherwise the United States might risk everything without securing a single gain for its own people—and for humanity.[101]

Several historians have challenged such arguments. Ray Stannard Baker suggests that if Washington had "realized the immense strength of its position," it could have "played the game as cleverly as the British government." By threatening London with embargoes to enforce what it considered its legal rights, it might have kept noncontraband trade open to Germany and neutral nations. To Robert W. Tucker, Wilson's acquiescence in the Allied blockade and later his opposition to Berlin's sole means of retaliation led inevitably to one outcome: war with Germany. Even though Wilson was certainly sincere in his desire for neutrality, his actions were counterproductive. "Wilson was unneutral from the outset," claims Tucker, "and he remained so until events finally left him with no alternative but war."[102]

Legal historian John W. Coogan accuses the president of permitting, at times encouraging, "systematic British violation of American neutral rights on a scale unprecedented at the height of the Napoleonic Wars," abandoning in the process the viable system of international law created before 1914. According to Coogan, the president feared repetition of James Madison's folly in 1812: inadvertently making war against a "civilized" nation, Great Britain, while siding with a "tyrannical" one, Bonaparte's France. Unfortunately for the United States, Wilson placed the preservation of Anglo-American friendship above the defense of his nation's legal rights. He helped destroy a system that "offered the United States a realistic opportunity to maintain effective neutrality, to mitigate the horrors of war for other neutrals and for belligerent civilians, and perhaps to create a favorable position for mediation."[103]

Had Wilson ordered warships to escort American merchantmen, Coogan argues, Britain could not have retaliated, because its navy was already strained to the limit in fighting Germany. Bailey and Ryan concur, adding that London simply could not afford to fight its leading munitions supplier. Wilson did not play "this trump card" partly because his sympathies lay with the Allies, as did those of most advisers, and partly because such a course would have been unpopular with a predominantly pro-Allied public.[104] Moreover, as the American merchant fleet was extremely small, any such escort could little affect the blockade's effectiveness.

Ship incidents were not long in coming. On January 28, 1915, a German passenger ship turned auxiliary cruiser, *Prinz Eitel Friedrich,* sank an American steel clipper, the *William P. Frye,* off the Brazilian coast. Owned by Arthur P. Sewell Company of Bath, Maine, and named after a senator from that state, the *Frye* was transporting wheat, an item considered conditional contraband, from Seattle to Britain's Queenstown. The *Frye*'s crew was taken aboard the *Prinz Eitel* and then, six weeks later, safely transported to Newport News, Virginia, where the German ship sought supplies and repairs. The released passengers and crew complimented Korvettenkapitän Max Thierichens on being treated so well, but the State Department strongly protested the sinking. Because of the incident, Berlin reaffirmed the validity of a treaty that the United States had made with Prussia in 1778, which defined how limited were the immunities possessed by neutral ships in wartime. In April press reports noted that Germany agreed to pay $180,000 in damages, though the matter was never really resolved.[105]

One commercial controversy centered on an American arms embargo affecting all belligerents. In his "Contraband Circular" of October 15, 1914, Bryan issued a public statement declaring that the United States might sell any product to a warring power. The executive could not prevent such commerce.[106] The British sought to keep supplies to the Allies open while limiting American access to the Central Powers. After the battle of the Marne, they found themselves markedly deficient in artillery and high explosive shells and becoming dependent upon American supplies. When, in May 1915, David Lloyd George became Britain's minister of munitions, he sought massive shipments of American weaponry. Even U.S. factories devoted to electrical work or locomotive production accepted contracts for explosives that ran into millions of dollars.

Until the Marne battle, the Germans had been indifferent to the embargo issue; now they suddenly became quite embittered. In December 1914 Grand Admiral Alfred von Tirpitz accused the United States of prolonging the war, telling former senator Albert J. Beveridge (R-Ind.): "If America would not send any more powder, guns and food to our enemies, this war would very soon be over."[107]

Beginning on December 7, 1914, several midwestern congressmen introduced resolutions that would have given the president discretion to prohibit munitions exports. One representative, Richard Bartholdt (R-Mo.), was born in Germany. Others spoke for strong German American constituencies; included were Horace Mann Towner (R-Iowa), Charles O. Lobeck (D-Neb.), and Henry Vollmer (D-Iowa), the latter also president of the German American Central Verein of Davenport and Scott counties. By mid-February 1915, pro-embargo forces organized the American Independence Union. In time similar groups were formed—the American Neutrality League, the American Humanity League, the American Embargo Conference, the Friends of Peace, the League of American Women for Strict Neutrality. Congress was flooded with letters, telegrams, and a petition supposedly fifteen miles long and bearing a million signatures. The language was invariably harsh, the argument was repetitious, and the signers often bore German names. Of course, not every advocate was markedly pro-German; some of the pacifist inclination endorsed the strategy.

Embargo supporters advanced several arguments, at times drawing on precedent. From 1794 to 1914, the United States, maintained Vollmer, had enacted a number of arms embargoes itself. Psychologist Münsterberg recalled that in 1913 the Taft administration had embargoed weapon shipments to warring factions in Mexico. Other backers of an embargo argued that the munitions trade prolonged the conflict. Vollmer claimed that the measure could end the war within ninety days, while Bartholdt forecast a peace in which "the markets of the whole world will again be thrown open to our cotton and all other American products," something that could outweigh a hundred times temporary profits for a few manufacturers.[108]

In the late 1930, a time when postwar disillusionment was extremely high, historian Charles Callan Tansill alleged that an arms embargo might have kept America out of the war. A journalist writing at the same time, Walter Millis, insisted that Wilson missed a valuable opportunity; there was nothing whatever in international law to prohibit imposing such measures, provided they applied equally to each belligerent. Early in the conflict, an embargo would not have damaged American prosperity or the Allied war effort to the degree that it would have later. "At the time," Millis wrote, "we might have preserved a much greater share of practical neutrality at relatively small cost."[109]

Furthermore, embargo proponents asserted, the arms traffic made the United States a homicidal nation. "By permitting the export of arms and ammunition when we have the right and power to stop it," cabled Vollmer in December to a mass meeting in Boston, "we are helping part of our dear friends kill others of our dear friends." Similarly, art historian Edmund von Mach, who had served in the German army, accused Americans of committing outright murder, because they were "turning their factories over to the god of war." Representative Clyde H. Tavenner (D-Ill.), who had headed publicity for his party's national congressional committee in 1910 and 1912, attacked what he called the "war trust." His accusations were not limited to merely the exporting of armament; he accused military officers and such steel companies as Bethlehem, Midvale, and Carnegie of collaborating in a huge international combination that fleeced the "taxpayers of the world."[110] In an effort to avoid confusion and prevent increased prices, the British war and Admiralty offices designated J.P. Morgan and Company as their sole purchasing agent in America, a move that added to populist denunciations of Wall Street.

The Wilson administration quickly countered, stressing that arms trade had always been the legal right of any neutral power. In mid-October 1914 the State Department released *Neutrality and Trade in Contraband,* a document announcing that American citizens could sell any article they chose to whom they chose, unrestrained by international law, treaty provision, domestic statute, presidential authority, or congressional prerogative. The pro-administration *New York Times* cited precedent: American statesmen from Alexander Hamilton to John Hay had defended arms sales. To shift ground suddenly was in itself deemed unneutral. On December 10, Counselor Lansing wrote Wilson: "Any change in our statutes by amendment or repeal would undoubtedly benefit one or the other of the belligerents." Early in January, Secretary Bryan concurred, adding that Bartholdt's resolution deliberately aimed at assisting one side at the expense of the other. The president quickly agreed. The *New Republic* branded the embargo agitation as "nothing less than a barefaced and unscrupulous attempt to drag the United States into the European war as the ally of Germany."[111]

Moreover, as anti-embargo forces noted, the European powers never limited arms sales. Ambassador Gerard recalled that Germany had supplied Spain during its recent war with the United States, aided Britain during the Boer War, and helped Mexican general Victoriano Huerta during his conflict with America. Besides, noted Lansing, Germany sold "enormous quantities of arms and munitions" to both belligerents in the recent Russo-Japanese and Balkan wars. Admittedly, the United States had banned arms from reaching Latin American nations, but that policy was motivated only by the desire to avoid abetting the "civil strife" there.[112]

In December 1914 even German ambassador Bernstorff conceded that the United States possessed this right. Similarly, German American historian Kuno Francke warned that an embargo might drive the United States into war with England.[113]

The resolutions were quickly tabled, for the Wilson administration was not about to risk much-needed economic recovery. In November 1914 Wilson told House that any such move would "restrict our plants and, in a way, make us less prepared than we are now." Ambassador Gerard wrote: "There is no doubt, however, that a real neutrality would stop the sale, but would our people 'stand' for such a curtailment of American industry?" The *Chicago Tribune* implied that embargo advocates possessed dual loyalties; they had "gone to Congress to close down American factories and put American citizens out of work in order to benefit one of the contesting parties." Expressing itself more crassly, the *Nashville Banner* wrote: "Let 'em shoot! It makes good business for us!"[114]

Besides, embargo opponents feared Britain might retaliate. Journalist O'Laughlin, for example, warned that Britain would withhold such needed goods as rubber and wool. More important, it could finance a Japanese war on the United States. "With the British navy and troops operating upon our Atlantic seaboard, the Japanese navy and troops operating on our Pacific slope, and Canada menacing us from the north, we could be in an exceedingly dangerous situation." Although he conceded that such a contingency was remote, O'Laughlin wanted to show that Britain was far from helpless.[115]

Moreover, Germany was not perceived as being in dire straits. Horace White, who had briefly been governor of New York, noted that the Reich possessed the great Krupp works, which employed ninety thousand employees round the clock and controlled a major Belgian arms factory at Liège. The *New Republic* claimed that an embargo might stop the war but found the price too high: German retention of Belgium and the richest part of France.[116]

Bryan articulated his objection on January 20, 1915, in a letter to Senator William J. Stone, chairman of the Senate Foreign Relations Committee and Missouri's former governor. Responding to Stone's accusation that the United States pursued a markedly one-sided commercial policy, the secretary maintained that any arms embargo would violate the nation's neutrality. Bryan, whose text had been dictated by Counselor Lansing, made a wider point. "The fact that the commerce of the United States is interrupted by Great Britain is consequent upon the superiority of her navy on the high seas. History shows that whenever a country has possessed such superiority our trade has been interrupted and that few articles essential to the prosecution of the war have been allowed to reach its enemy from this country."[117] Aided by the Republican leadership, he helped keep embargo resolutions buried in committee.

An overwhelming majority of the press backed the administration. The *New Republic* found pro-embargo sentiments rooted in "the anti-Americanism of American citizens," although it did add that the asymmetrical nature of U.S. trade was grounded in "a difference of interest" that was "incapable of legal solution." Predictably, the *Fatherland* accused Bryan of subservience to Britain ("Sir Wm. Jennings," it called him), while the *New York American* saw him as lacking genuine patriotism. Americans, Hearst's paper continued, must not "bow our necks to the yoke of Great Britain."[118]

In mid-February 1915, this issue surfaced in the Senate. Gilbert M. Hitchcock sought to attach an arms embargo amendment to a major shipping bill. Duncan Fletcher (D-Fla.) effectively tabled the proposal, his motion carrying 51-36. Most Democrats and eastern Republicans supported Fletcher. Delegations from Illinois, Iowa, Michigan, Nebraska, and North Dakota backed Hitchcock. Such prominent Republican progressives as George Norris of Nebraska, John D. Works of California, William E. Borah of Idaho, and Albert B. Cummins of Iowa were pro-embargo. Robert M. La Follette spoke for many peace progressives in finding but one purpose to the munitions trade: "to sacrifice human life for private gain."[119]

A *Literary Digest* poll published in early February 1915 revealed a similar geographical lineup. Of 440 editors who responded to an inquiry concerning an arms embargo, 244, that is, over half, opposed the move; 167 favored the ban; and the remaining 29 were noncommittal. Just as revealing, many midwestern editors endorsed the prohibition, as did a considerable number of southerners. So, too, did numerous small-town newspapers throughout the entire nation.[120]

The administration cracked down on one form of armament exportation. Early in November, the State Department learned that Bethlehem Steel and the Fore River Company of Quincy, Massachusetts, had contracted to build submarines, deliverable in sections, to the British government. Wilson, acting against both Lansing and his Joint Neutrality Board, supported Bryan in finding the proposed transaction "a violation of the spirit of neutrality."[121] Bethlehem's president, Charles M. Schwab, formally retreated but circumvented the president by shipping prefabricated parts to Canada, where they were assembled at the Canadian Vickers shipyard in Montreal. By mid-1915 the yard had launched ten such submarines.

Most initial conflicts centered on British action. This circumstance soon changed because of a decision made in Berlin on February 4, 1915, that radically altered the nature of the war itself. Even the faintest hope that the war might remain something of a gentleman's conflict was about to vanish.

3

In Peril on the Sea
February–August 1915

"OUR SWORD MUST ALWAYS remain clean. We are not waging war against women and children. We wish to fight this war as gentlemen, no matter what the other side may do. Take note of that."[1] Kaiser Wilhelm II uttered these words to his admirals late in November 1914 in expressing relief that a large British liner escaped a submarine.

Just over two months later, on February 4, 1915, the German Admiralty proclaimed a submarine blockade of the British Isles. After two weeks, enemy merchant vessels would be destroyed, "even if it may not be possible always to save their crews and passengers." More important for the United States, Germany observed that "neutral vessels cannot always be prevented from suffering from the attacks intended for enemy ships." In an explanatory note issued two days later, the German Foreign Office warned that neutral merchantmen must avoid the war zone or use such designated safety areas as the Dutch coast.[2]

The chief of the German Admiralty staff, Hugo von Pohl, stressed the blockade's urgency. Although England, he observed, had a mere six or seven weeks of food supplies remaining, grain would soon arrive from Argentina. At the same time, Germany faced a dwindling food supply. Admiral Alfred von Tirpitz, state secretary of the navy office and the man who had created his nation's massive fleet, expressed himself bluntly. Although still reluctant to engage in major submarine warfare, he told an American journalist in late December: "England wants to starve us. We can play the same game. We can bottle her up and torpedo every English or allied ship which nears any harbor in Great Britain, thereby cutting off large food supplies."[3] Hopefully an isolated Britain, severed from outside supplies, would give up its blockade and consider peace.

When Wilhelm toured the Wilhelmshaven naval station, Pohl persuaded the emperor to support the case for intensive submarine warfare. Civilian leaders were confronted with a fait accompli. German economists and an enthusiastic public backed the admirals, which prevented Chancellor Bethmann from resisting the pressure. Bethmann accused England of seeking to starve 70 million people. As neutral nations had not protested against the British blockade, "they must take the consequences. We certainly are not going to die of a famine."[4]

Originally Germany envisioned submarines as a mere experimental weapon, at most an observation craft or an auxiliary arm in striking enemy dreadnoughts. It began the conflict with a mere eighteen U-boats, far fewer than Britain or France, and of these eighteen a mere third were serviceable at any one time. Not until September 1914 did the Admiralty perceive U-boats as raiders on the high seas. An attack made on a single day, the ninth, on three aged British vessels—*Cressy, Hogue,* and *Aboukir Bay*—revealed their effectiveness against enemy cruisers. Because the German High Seas Fleet had remained confined in harbor while Britain established control of the North Sea, the submarine suddenly emerged as a most appealing weapon against maritime commerce, indeed one that would hopefully ensure victory.

Berlin's gambit reflected irresponsible bluster and gross miscalculation. The German public remained unaware that the major offensive on the Marne had failed. The Reich's naval effort was sheer bluff, a mere "paper blockade." Germany could deploy only four submarines in designated waters; hence, U-boats woefully lacked the ability to sever Britain's lifeline. Because the Germans harbored an exaggerated estimate of British defenses across the Straits of Dover, they did not risk crossings through the English Channel. Instead they ordered their submarines to make a detour of fourteen hundred miles around the North Sea and Scotland, adding an extra seven days to reach the Atlantic.

Furthermore, the Royal Navy did not fear the tiny number of submarines available to Germany. In March Allied losses were relatively small, certainly in comparison to the many merchant ships that safely reached the British Isles from the Western Hemisphere. Viscount Richard Haldane, England's lord chancellor, stated accurately: "The submarine business is annoying but that is all."[5] Even when the submarines began to attack large British ocean liners, the overall military threat remained negligible. Between February and September 1915, the twenty-seven U-boats becoming available for duty sank only 21 of 5,000 ships that traveled to and from Britain.

Conversely, Germany's decision deeply antagonized the United States. Acting under the all-too-accurate assumption that the United States lacked combat-ready troops, Berlin believed that intimidation would keep American ships at home. At the moment when Washington was strongly protesting British malfeasance, the Reich's Admiralty opted for possible slaughter on the sea-lanes. "If this is not braggadocio, it is brutality," wrote the *Nation*, expressing the attitude of many countrymen.[6]

Six days after Germany proclaimed its blockade, the United States responded. On February 10, the State Department cabled Berlin, declaring that the unprecedented German announcement was hardly believable. The United States would hold the Imperial government to "a strict accountability" (Lansing's phrase) for the destruction of "an American vessel or the lives of American citizens on the high seas." It would take all steps necessary to safeguard their lives, property, and "acknowledged rights" on the oceans. Germany must respect established rules of "visit and search" and promise that no ship would be sunk without first providing for the safety of passengers and crew. To give a veneer of impartiality, the dispatch was accompanied by an innocuous protest to Britain, which had sported neutral flags on its own craft, but this missive contained no threat of retaliation.[7]

The American press strongly approved the administration's response, though partisans on both sides criticized Wilson's policy. Wrote the *Fatherland*: "If Germany does it it's a shame/If England does it it's the game." Roosevelt predicted that Wilson's government would never make good on its threats, though he asked Grey to "show every consideration to the American flag and the American position."[8]

The president had seen the need to respond strongly. The note, writes Arthur S. Link, advanced "the only position that Wilson could have taken without abandoning national rights and dignity so ignominiously as to lose all power for good in the world." Possibly, Ernest R. May suggests, the president might have considered the Germans so morally obtuse that a threat of force alone would cause Berlin to reconsider its U-boat policy. Realizing that 90 percent of the American people sympathized with the Allies, Wilson could have feared severe criticism had he failed to challenge the Central Powers.[9]

Ironically, Wilson may well have committed a serious blunder of his own. According to historians Thomas A. Bailey and Paul B. Ryan, the message might have encouraged some of Wilson's fellow citizens to book passage on British ocean liners. While the main burden of his argument centered on protecting U.S. citizens on *American* ships, his language was ambiguous. Would a pledge of security hold true if Americans traveled on ships belonging to belligerent nations? More concretely, was Germany obligated to spare an Allied ship if a single American were on board? Counselor Lansing, who had played a major role in drafting the document, obscured the matter when, in a personal letter dated February 26, he deemed the matter "open to interpretation." At any rate, as historian Robert W. Tucker points out, Wilson's response took on an unexpected life of its own.[10]

Few Americans thought that the U-boat campaign would endanger their nation's security, much less foster a German victory. Of course, the U.S. economy might be threatened, for its trade increased fourfold from 1914 to 1917. The new surge of orders caused a host of indexes to rise sharply, including the export-import flow, wheat futures, new plant construction, and overtime labor for machine-tool manufacturers. In a cable to Colonel House, Wilson branded the German policy an "extraordinary plan to destroy commerce." Yet historian John A. Thompson argues that this trade needed no protection from the U.S. government; the Allies were so dependent on American supplies that they would seek to assure safe transport across the Atlantic.[11]

Like the British Order in Council, the new German edict ran counter to conventional international law. According to time-honored practice, any warship that approached a merchant vessel must ascertain its identity, then fire a warning shot. The skipper was obligated to escort the captured cargo and crew into port, where a prize court would adjudicate the case. Only if the merchant craft resisted capture did the warship have the right to sink it. In such an event the safety of passengers and crew must be assured. Whenever possible Germany observed standard practice. The U-boat captain would surface in front of his quarry, using the single large gun on his deck to force his prey to surrender. Only after the merchant seamen took to their lifeboats would he destroy the vessel, either with gunfire or time bombs. From 1914 to 1917, most merchantmen were sunk this way.

Today it is hard to realize the primitive quality of the early submarines, which were easy game for armed merchantmen or enemy cruisers: they were light and flimsy, and they traveled slowly. Limited in size, a submarine was far too small to take on more than forty crew members. Miserable working conditions prevailed, with sailors experiencing intense heat and practically living on top of each other. Supplies were stored on top of the torpedoes. Oil and carbonic gas created a continual stench.

Because the sailors could see only through the periscope, many things obscured their vision—waves, fog, darkness, a hazy horizon, and poor light at dawn or dusk. Identifying the nationality of a strange ship, much less its passengers, cargo, and crew, was at best difficult. How could submarine captains ascertain whether their quarry had mounted a gun? And was this gun real or a dummy? Stormy weather forced U-boats to submerge, making it most difficult to launch a torpedo through mountainous waves. Shooting too close to the target might cause the shell to damage, even sink, the submarine itself. But if one fired from too great a distance, the torpedo might fizzle out. Torpedoes left a telltale trail of exhaust bubbles that, if spotted by a lookout, could permit the steamer to avoid destruction. Commanders had to husband them carefully; a U-boat could carry no more than twenty. Furthermore, the submarine operation had a limited range. Because the Irish and North seas were stormy in wintertime, U-boats remained in port during those months, not venturing forth until spring.

In response to this new threat, the British armed their steamers. At the outset of the war, First Lord of the Admiralty Winston Churchill warned that he would commission British armed merchantmen as ships of the Royal Navy, making them, in his words, "indistinguishable in status and control from men of war." By this statement, he put U-boat commanders on notice: they endangered themselves if they attempted to caution such vessels. For a submarine skipper to honor traditional rules of international war, that is, surfacing and firing a warning shot or signal, ran the risk of being sunk oneself.[12] A single well-placed British shell could end the U-boat's voyage—forever. During close-in operations, submarines risked attack by machine-gun bullets, rifle fire, and tossed grenades.

Dangers did not end at this point, because the merchantman might ram a U-boat. The British Admiralty issued secret orders to merchant ships. First, they should first try to escape. "If a submarine comes up suddenly close ahead of you with obvious hostile intention, steer straight for her at your utmost speed, altering course as necessary to keep her ahead." In brief, the captain of every British cargo ship or passenger liner possessed orders that, under certain circumstances, obligated him to crush the U-boat. International law upheld the legitimacy of ramming. On February 25, the Admiralty circulated confidential instructions stating that the besieged submarine "may not have committed a definite hostile act such as firing a gun or torpedo." Though British skippers were told that if they were captured, they were to destroy these orders, the Germans secured copies and eventually passed them to Washington.[13]

Germany issued its submarine blockade without concern for possible American reactions. When Wilson dispatched his February 10 warning, the civilian leadership in Berlin feared that the United States might enter the war. Ambassador Bernstorff cabled: *A mistake could have the most serious consequences.*[14] The admirals were far less frightened, reasoning that intimidation of neutrals was the very goal of the decree.

On February 16, Germany's foreign secretary, Gottlieb von Jagow, replied to Wilson's "strict accountability" note. He accused the British of pursuing a policy of "death by famine." Nevertheless, his nation would spare American craft if they did not carry contraband, were clearly identified, and sailed in convoys. Were a U.S. merchant ship to be sunk in an "unfortunate" accident, Germany would not accept responsibility. Berlin, he continued, could not protect American ships from mines. Jagow hinted at lifting the submarine blockade provided Britain would allow "the legitimate supply of foodstuffs and industrial raw materials." He also called attention to the "the flag question," whereby British commercial ships—including a liner christened the *Lusitania*—would sport the American flag in order to prevent capture. Two days later the German Admiralty issued orders to protect U.S. shipping, particularly if the American craft traveled in convoys and were escorted by warships.[15]

The conflict had entered a new stage, one in which each side violated America's neutral rights in order to crush the other. As Wilson wrote to a close female friend on February 14: "Together, England and Germany are likely to drive us crazy." Less than a week later, Bryan cabled Germany and Britain, asking both to abandon reckless minelaying and honor international law relating to commercial vessels. Britain should stop the misuse of neutral flags and agree to a plan that would allow German "non-combatants," not the army, to receive food imports.[16]

Already the Senate had begun to debate the wisdom of allowing American ships to enter war zones. Wesley L. Jones (R-Wash.) advised American ships to avoid them altogether or enter at one's own peril. "We may lose thirty or forty million dollars," he said, "but that is nothing to what would happen if we should get into war." Charles E. Townsend (R-Mich.) countered that the defense of traditional maritime rights best guaranteed the peace. J. Hamilton Lewis (D-Ill.) added: "Shall we decline to enforce our rights because it is inconvenient to any of those now at war? I think not."[17]

Germany's novel U-boat warfare gave Britain a cogent excuse for retaliation. By the end of February, London determined that food was contraband, that is, it contributed to the enemy's war effort, even if intended for German civilians. Besides, the British maintained that the Reich's armed forces, not noncombatants, would be the ones to receive this food. They also defied American requests to forgo the display of the Stars and Stripes on British ships, although the Germans could claim that this practice would risk the torpedoing of an American vessel.

On March 1, Britain and France issued a declaration prohibiting any trade with Germany; included were "goods of presumed enemy destination, ownership, or origin." That day, in speaking to the House of Commons, Prime Minister Asquith stated: "Germany has forfeited all rights to diplomatic terms. Nor is the alliance to be strangled in a network of judicial niceties." On March 11 an Order in Council proclaimed a de facto blockade.[18]

In a memo dated March 13, Foreign Secretary Grey declared the food blockade an appropriate retaliation for Germany's "unprecedented methods, repugnant to all law and morality." These misdeeds stretched from barbarous treatment of prisoners of war to bombardment of defenseless coastal towns. He added that Britain certainly would not bargain with Germany, a nation whose word it deemed worthless. On March 15, Britain rejected Foreign Secretary Jagow's offer of mutual concessions, a proposal by which Germany would drop its submarine blockade in return for the funneling of food and raw materials from neutrals.[19]

Washington was stymied. Wilson and Bryan sympathized with Jagow's hope that his nation might receive food. On March 24 the frustrated president wrote Bryan concerning Britain: "We are face to face with something they are going to do and they are going to do it no matter what representation we make." Within six days the United States formally criticized Allied policy, pointing out its inconsistencies, reminding Britain and France of American neutral rights, and reserving all legal rights. Yet no reprisals were threatened.[20] In reality, Washington accepted the new British blockade despite its obvious violation of international law.

The British took almost three months to reply to the American note of March 30, not responding until July 23, a time when America was experiencing great tension with Germany. They conceded nothing of substance. Grey recited certain atrocities in Belgium, upheld the legality of the blockade, and argued that Britain had merely responded to the German submarine menace. He defended the doctrine of continuous voyage, by which the *ultimate* destination of a vessel determined its liability to seizure. He noted that during the American Civil War, Union forces intercepted the British merchant ship *Springbok* on its way to Nassau because its goods had been scheduled for reshipment to Confederate ports.[21]

Historians differ over the president's tacit acquiescence. Ross A. Kennedy claims that Wilson supported Britain's illegal warfare, thereby cooperating with its military effort. Why, Kennedy asks, should Germany regard the United States as other than a de facto ally of its enemies? Other scholars find that Wilson had little choice but to recognize the British blockade. John A. Thompson sees the president appraising the situation correctly. The American people did not want to risk war with the world's leading naval power. Just six months earlier, Churchill had told an acquiescent Grey that Britain should grant no concessions, at least "until it is certain that persistence will actually and imminently bring the United States into the field against us." In 1915 Britain was not dependent upon U.S. credit; the leverage that Wilson possessed a year later was not yet available. Robert W. Tucker accuses London of harboring indifference, if not contempt, for Washington's reaction, but he opined: "Economic interest had tied the United States to the Allied cause."[22]

Such arguments did not make the American press less furious. A protest even came from the militantly pro-Entente *New York Tribune*. The *Chicago Tribune* suggested a punitive arms embargo, repeating the cry of naval hero Stephen Decatur: "Our Country! In her intercourse with foreign nations may she always be in the right; but our country, right or wrong." Hearst's *New York American* recalled that in 1812 the United States had gone to war over such matters. America faced a stark choice; either it must submit to foreign nations or "declare war against any power that molests commerce voyaging under the American flag." Senators Thomas J. Walsh (D-Mont.), speaking for his state's copper interests, and Hoke Smith (D), representing Georgia cotton growers, sought to retaliate by a total embargo.[23]

Seizures of American ships caused particular grief. On February 9, the British took command of the steamer *Wilhelmina*, which landed at Falmouth seeking refuge from a storm. Owned by the Southern Products Trading Company, the ship had set sail from Galveston to Hamburg with a cargo of foodstuffs. The German upper house, the Bundesrat, promised the American consul in Hamburg that the food would reach civilians, but Britain remained unmoved. It was later revealed that the German government had arranged the *Wilhelmina*'s sailing as a test case, conceived to expose Britain's suppression of food shipments.

Just two weeks later, on February 27, the French cruiser *Europe* seized another American steamer, the *Dacia,* near Britain's Isles of Scilly, off Land's End, and escorted it to Brest. Had the French not acted, the British were prepared to capture the ship. The *Dacia* originally belonged to the Hamburg-American line but was sold on January 4 to Edward N. Breitung, a Michigan mine operator and banker. To Breitung, this move was simply a trial run, for he later told reporters: "It was our intention to purchase many, if not all, of the interned German liners now in American harbors."[24] The *Dacia* left Galveston bound for Rotterdam with a cargo of cotton, which was then to be transported to Germany.

Even before the *Dacia* sailed, the British cabinet warned that it would impound the vessel. When Grey deemed the sailing "a distinctly unneutral and practically hostile act," Bryan responded on January 23 with a lengthy and significant cable. The United States, he stressed, would acquiesce in a moderate and limited British maritime system but would neither compromise on the *Dacia* nor block American ship purchases from other foreign owners.[25]

The *Dacia* matter became entwined with efforts of Treasury Secretary McAdoo to create a government-owned merchant marine. In large measure, this fleet would be created from the purchase of fifty-four German ships that lay idle in American ports, though it might also include similar British and French ships. Such vessels could possess the added advantage of serving in wartime as auxiliaries to the regular navy. In December the administration introduced a bill to create a national corporation that would buy, build, charter, and operate ships. The cost: $30 million.

By 1914 the United States depended upon foreign shipping. Less than 10 percent of the nation's commerce was carried in American vessels. Only six American cargo ships plied the ocean. Conversely, British merchantmen carried about 50 percent of the nation's transatlantic trade. When war broke out, many of these ships were suddenly shifted to wartime service, thereby injuring American shippers, manufacturers, and farmers. Supplies were piling up on the nation's docks, wasting or rotting. To the Entente, U.S. purchase of German merchantmen created several dangers: it would increase the income of the Central Powers, ease their access to American goods, and help the United States seize the trade of the world.

The Senate balked at McAdoo's proposal in what was the most hotly debated issue of Wilson's first term and the main item of the current session. As cots were placed in its cloakrooms, the upper house set a record for its longest session to date. In filibustering against the bill, Reed Smoot (R-Utah) spoke nonstop for eleven and a half hours, Theodore Burton (R-Ohio) for thirteen. Not only was the proposal attacked as "state socialism," it was portrayed as a measure guaranteed to involve the United States in the conflict. To Elihu Root, America was "buying, not a ship, but an international quarrel." The measure, said Henry Cabot Lodge, would neutralize British domination of the ocean lanes while replenishing the German treasury, thereby making the United States a de facto ally of the Kaiser. It would create confrontation not merely with Britain but with France, Russia, and Japan as well. No nation at war would recognize the transfer of a belligerent ship to a neutral power. Lodge wrote Theodore Roosevelt: "We shall find ourselves with Government-owned ships afloat, which the Allies regard as German ships and therefore good prize and which are liable to be fired on and sunk." The former president concurred, condemning the proposal as "a criminal act." The Republican solution to the shipping shortage: private initiative and federal subsidies. Defending the Wilson administration, William J. Stone claimed that government ownership would be the surest safeguard for American shippers; belligerents would never fire on U.S. vessels.[26]

Historians Link and Cooper claim that Wilson could have alleviated concerns by accepting a Senate amendment proposed by James O'Gorman (D-N.Y.) that forbade the purchase of any belligerent ship. The president stubbornly considered the issue as a crucial test of his leadership, a decision that produced the first major defeat of his presidency. On February 17 the House voted 215 to 122 in his favor, but the upper chamber failed to act.[27] Because the *Dacia* incident involved a German ship, its fate certainly strengthened opposition to Wilson's bill. Berlin now realized that such sales were too risky. Not until September 1916 did Wilson sign a shipping bill that contained several features of the original proposal.

By mid-February conflict had increased with the Reich. On the nineteenth, one day after its blockade went into effect, a German mine located off Borkum Island in the North Sea sank the American steamship *Evelyn*, which was carrying foodstuffs from New York to Bremen. Within three days an American steamer, the *Carib*, struck a German mine in the same area.

This ship, bound from Charleston to Bremen, transported cotton. In both cases, the goods were consigned to the Germans themselves, but the vessels had not traveled in the German-designated safety zone, much less hired a German pilot. In neither case were lives lost, and the United States did not protest. Usually, German commanders obeyed secret orders to spare ships flying the American flag, and at any rate few U.S. ships sailed the North Atlantic. Yet, during the third week in March, Leonard Wood was privately predicting that America would be fighting Germany within six months.[28]

Far more significance was attached to the U-boat sinking of a small British passenger and cargo ship, the *Falaba,* on March 28, thirty-eight miles from Milford Haven, a town on the Welsh coast. En route from Liverpool to Africa's Sierra Leone, the craft carried 242 people and several tons of cartridges. It flew no colors and bore no identification marks. The commander of *U-28* used signals and flags to stop the ship, but the *Falaba's* skipper attempted to escape and thus lost legal immunity under international law. As *U-28* stood one hundred yards from its prey, its commander gave the passengers and crew five minutes to enter lifeboats. Before they could act, his ship fired a torpedo. Of the 247 on board, 104 lost their lives. One fatality was American mining engineer Leon Thrasher, who was returning to Africa's Gold Coast.

The *U-28's* commander recorded in his logbook that several British trawlers lay nearby, one of which followed his craft for an hour. He believed that his submarine could remain safe for only twenty-three minutes and did not think the *Falaba* would sink so rapidly. Despite the German captain's rationale, the damage to his nation's reputation far outweighed any possible benefit.

On March 31, when the news reached the United States, its press expressed outrage. Writers used such terms as "assassination," "massacre," "barbarism run mad," and a "triumph of horror." "This is not war," wrote the *New York Times.* "It is murder." To the *Nation,* German "wickedness" had seldom been matched in "the history of war." Even the more neutralist *New York American* asked: "Can sober-minded Germans really believe that the advantage they gain by running amuck on the high seas will overbalance the risk they incur?" Some Americans sought an unequivocal protest to Germany, although excitement ran higher in the East than in the Midwest.[29]

Pro-German spokesmen sought to justify the action. New York's *Deutsches Journal* insisted that "war is war"; the presence of civilians on board did not confer immunity on such ships. The *Fatherland* held the *Falaba's* captain solely responsible, as he did not honor the submarine commander's signal to halt. Instead, despite repeated warnings, the craft radioed British warships to destroy *U-28*. Publisher Herman Ridder stressed upon readers of the *New Yorker Staats-Zeitung* that Britain was seeking to starve out Germany.[30]

Thrasher's death raised a crucial issue: did "strict accountability" apply to loss of life on belligerent ships or just to American ones? At first the Wilson administration was divided internally over the matter. To Bryan, it seemed incongruous to admonish American citizens to flee Mexico, then in the throes of revolution, while the United States risked war to protect thoughtless passengers voyaging on a ship belonging to warring nations. Writing the president, he warned against those whose regard for personal business unnecessarily involved their country in international complications. Lansing responded that "debating the legality to destroy life and the legality to destroy property are very different things." Even if the United States chanced conflict, it must uphold international law and demand that Germany disavow the act, punish the commander, and pay damages.[31]

Initially Wilson sided with Lansing. Acts lacking sanction in "the accepted law of nations" should not threaten the lives of American citizens. By April 28, the president realized the weakness of legal grounds for any protest. Furthermore, public sentiment soon cooled; any domestic pressure for a strong stand was lacking. Germany, Wilson assumed, would no longer attack passenger ships.[32]

The chief executive was far too optimistic. On April 29, a German plane bombed the American oil tanker *Cushing* off the Dutch coast. The unarmed ship was carrying petroleum from New York to the Netherlands and did not fly any discernible flag. There was no damage, much less loss of life.

Two days later, May 1, a more serious incident occurred: *U-30* torpedoed the American oil tanker *Gulflight* without warning fifteen miles east of the Isles of Scilly. En route from Port Arthur, Texas, to Rouen, France, and owned by the Gulf Refining Company, the ship did not sink; it was towed to Crow Sound. Submarine commander Erich Rosenberg did not discern that the *Gulflight* had raised an American flag until he had launched his torpedo. Two British patrol boats that appeared armed seemed to be escorting the ship, in his mind exposing it to legitimate attack. Three deaths occurred. The captain experienced heart failure; the wireless operator and a crew member were drowned. British trawlers rescued the rest of the crew. The three seamen remained the sole Americans killed by U-boats on one of their own ships before February 1917, when Germany again initiated unrestricted submarine warfare. On June 1, Jagow apologized for the *Gulflight* sinking and agreed to pay full compensation.

Again, many Americans were infuriated. The *Nation* accused Germany of having committed an act of war. To Roosevelt the Germans were pirates. The *Fatherland* countered that the *Gulflight* carried contraband in a war zone while bound for an enemy port. The journal added: "Before long, a large passenger ship like the *Lusitania,* carrying implements of war to Great Britain, will meet a similar fate."[33] The suggestion that U-boat commanders might attack passenger liners raised far more serious issues than those involving merchantmen, even if the victimized steamer belonged to a belligerent nation, not an American firm.

On May 1, the Imperial German Embassy published an advertisement in the shipping section of American newspapers. The text was brief, the contents simple. The notice reminded readers that a state of war existed between the Allies and the Central Powers: "Vessels flying the flag of Great Britain, or of any of her allies, are liable to destruction in those waters . . . travelers sailing in the war zone on ships of Great Britain or her allies do so at their own risk." Within the Wilson administration, reactions were predictable. An agent for Britain's Cunard Line declared that the Atlantic was free of German cruisers, that the Royal Navy was convoying all British ships in the "danger zone" of the English Channel, and that the speed of British liners was itself a form of protection. Lansing called the German announcement "insolent," though Bryan saw it as friendly in nature.[34]

The warning was placed none too soon. On May 7, 1915, an event took place that compared in popular memory much later to the attacks that occurred on December 7, 1941, and September 11, 2001. As after the Japanese attack on Pearl Harbor and the Al Qaeda strikes on New York's World Trade Center and Washington's Pentagon, many Americans remembered years later exactly what they were doing when they first heard the news. To historian John Milton Cooper Jr., the day marked the great turning point in the nation's stance toward the war, a "shock of recognition" when the European conflict touched ordinary people in a way unknown before.[35] Finally the nation had come face-to-face with the reality of total war, with civilians as well as armed forces now directly involved.

On the afternoon of May 7, passengers on the Cunard liner *Lusitania* (Latin for Portugal) were viewing the southern point of Ireland. The ship was deemed "The Empress of the Seas"; it bore the earmarks of a magnificent floating hotel, the fastest and largest steamer in the entire Atlantic. Supposedly it could outrun any submarine. Because of the German warning, its departure from New York to Liverpool had made front-page news six days earlier. The *New York American* carried an ominous headline: "Lusitania Sails; 1250 Deny Peril."[36] In sight of land, a few voyagers jested about possible U-boats in the vicinity. Suddenly, at 2:30 P.M., a tremor shook the ship, the bow began to dip, and the liner sank within fifteen minutes. The result: 1,198 lost, 726 saved. Among the victims were 124 of the 188 American passengers.

The *Lusitania*'s captain, William T. Turner, considered himself such an expert skipper that he ignored Admiralty warnings to avoid coastal areas, where he might encounter lurking U-boats. Instead he headed toward the most dangerous spots—Brow Head, Galley Head, and the Old Head of Kinsdale. Although the Admiralty ordered him to proceed at full speed when close to harbors, he dropped velocity from twenty-one knots to eighteen. The Admiralty instructed him to steer a zigzag course, but Turner steamed straight ahead. Drills had been farcical, portholes were left open, and lifeboats swung too far inboard. The ship lacked destroyer escorts, First Lord Churchill having told Parliament that the navy lacked the ability to provide them.[37]

The captain of *U-20*, Walther Schwieger, undoubtedly realized that he had engaged a passenger ship. "It was the most horrible sight I have ever seen," he later recalled.[38] Secret British Admiralty orders had given the *Lusitania* the choice of taking flight or ramming the submarine. Either option would have nullified international legal protection and, in German eyes, would have made the *Lusitania* an escaping ship, whether or not *U-20* gave a warning signal.

Moreover, though a cruise liner, the *Lusitania* also served as a blockade runner, traveling through a German-designated war zone. Although it carried relatively little cargo, the overwhelming bulk of its freight was contraband. In particular, the ship conveyed some 4,200 cases of Remington rifle cartridges and 1,250 cases of empty shrapnel shells, these manufactured by Bethlehem Steel; this matériel was bound for the British Royal Arsenal at Woolwich. The ship also carried a relatively large shipment of food, notably packages of cheese, beef, and bacon, all of which the British themselves had proscribed. Schwieger did not realize the liner carried such contraband; he only knew that he had been ordered to attack Allied ships.

The brutality of the attack created a lasting shock among Americans, who appeared to exhaust their lexicons in search of damning labels, "savage," "villainous," "barbaric," "massacre," "unspeakable," "ghastly," and "homicidal" among them. If the ship had been a cargo vessel, its destruction might be deemed detestable, the death of the crew outrageous. But, as historian Patrick Devlin notes, "the death of women and children was beyond the pale." It appeared as if "one of two pugilists had suddenly lashed out at a ringside spectator."[39] Germany's campaign to win over the American public had gone to the bottom with the *Lusitania*.

The press was irate. The *Literary Digest,* summarizing opinion, reported: "Condemnation of the act seems to be limited only by the restrictions of the England language." The *Chicago Tribune* accused Germany of engaging in "the slaughter of the innocents." To one Presbyterian journal, the event marked the "worst crime of responsible government since the crucifixion of Christ." The *Nation* commented: "It is a deed for which a Hun would blush, a Turk be ashamed, and a Barbary pirate apologize." The *Des Moines Register and Leader* ended its editorial with the sentence "The sinking of the *Lusitania* was deliberate murder." Journalist Mark Sullivan later wrote that the Iowa paper spoke for the nation as a whole.[40]

Furthermore, the incident moved some of the more militant pro-Allied partisans, primarily located in the Northeast, to openly advocate policies that would risk war with Germany. Colonel House privately predicted: "We shall be at war with Germany within a month." Two days after the *Lusitania* sinking, he wrote Wilson that American intervention would save lives, not lose them. Roosevelt sought to sever all trade with the Reich and maximize commerce with the Allies. William Howard Taft suggested a break in diplomatic relations, although he soon warned that the United States should not be rushed into the conflict. Senator Lodge called for the detention of German ships in American ports until Berlin offered apology and reparations.[41]

Voices hitherto more moderate expressed themselves similarly. "Some of these days," Belgium relief administrator Herbert Hoover wrote a friend, "the civilized world has got to fight these people to a finish." While opposing immediate entry into the war, he envisioned an alliance of neutral nations that would use its "whole military and naval strength" to punish criminal deeds and enforce international law. To the *New Republic,* the sinking revealed the commercial and political dependence of the United States upon Britain; shared common grief and indignation might unite both nations in "a common war."[42]

The German American and Irish American press usually deplored the tragedy and hoped that the United States would avoid conflict, though it argued that the *Lusitania*'s passengers had received ample warning. The *New*

Yorker Staats-Zeitung commented: "There is one way to safeguard American life, and that is by staying at home. Travel at sea is decidedly dangerous at the present time in the neighborhood of the English Channel." Viereck demanded Bryan's impeachment on the grounds that he had not warned Americans against traveling in a war zone. The *Buffalo Volksfreund* accused Britain of turning Americans into human shields, serving to guard ammunition that had been transported on what, it claimed, was in reality an auxiliary naval cruiser. Because the ship was "laden with munitions," the *Gaelic American* judged it a "floating arsenal" and the *Irish World* praised the submarine commander for performing "a patriotic duty." The pro-German physiologist Yandell Henderson of Yale University asserted that the armament aboard the ship would have "slaughtered thousands"; he claimed that the sinking saved ten times the lives lost.[43]

A contributor to Viereck's *Fatherland* commented, quite incorrectly, that the ship sported twelve six-inch guns. The weekly noted an interview with former representative Richmond Pearson Hobson, a naval hero of the Spanish-American War, who posed a series of embarrassing questions. Why, asked the Alabama Democrat, did not Cunard prescribe a safe route around the northern coast of Ireland? Why did the *Lusitania* sail so slowly in a danger zone? How could a torpedo sink a ship in just twenty minutes? And how could so many people have perished on a calm sea during a clear day?[44]

Despite their indignation, Americans expressed surprisingly little warlike sentiment. Commenting on the same day that the *Lusitania* sank, British Ambassador Spring Rice remarked concerning the conflict: "The general feeling here is that the United States Government ought to keep out of it." A compilation of about a thousand editorials, composed within three days after the sinking, revealed that just a half dozen wanted Congress to declare war, though many sought disavowal, an apology, and payment of an indemnity. Similarly, rudimentary congressional polls reported that only one senator and three representatives believed that Germany had given the United States sufficient provocation for hostilities. The rest apparently thought that Americans should avoid ships that carried contraband, though they were willing to leave the entire negotiation in Wilson's hands. Perhaps about one-half of 1 percent of the entire population wanted to enter the clash. Senator Thomas S. Martin (D-Va.) and Congressman Henry de la Warr ("Hal") Flood (D-Va.) warned the administration that Congress would not support any war resolution. Wrote General Leonard Wood in his diary: "Rotten spirit in the *Lusitania* matter. Yellow spirit everywhere in spots."[45]

Confrontation with Berlin, many believed, could lead to nothing but trouble. Boarding a belligerent ship, stated Senator Stone, meant setting foot on belligerent soil, something comparable "to being within the walls of a fortified city." The United States, contended Senator Works, had permitted a lucrative arms trade but did nothing to discourage its citizens from sailing on belligerent ships; hence, it bore moral responsibility for the sinking. Senator Hitchcock reasoned that a German reparation payment would suffice to ensure U.S. neutrality. Former congressman A. Mitchell Palmer (D-Pa.) remarked: "The *Lusitania* was flying the British flag, and carrying munitions for the support of a belligerent." Why should Americans enter "a great war," asked Ambassador Gerard, because someone wants to travel on a ship where he can have a private bathroom? Even the contentious General Wood noted: "You cannot cover 10,000 tons of ammunition with a petticoat."[46]

Full-scale belligerency would pose certain logistic problems. Because the United States lacked a credible army, the American press declared, it could not offer the Allies much aid. Citizens were already sending supplies and lending money. Given the supposed threat of a German blockade, total participation could create a serious handicap. Besides, it was feared that millions of German aliens might engage in actual uprising, thereby paralyzing the country. Indeed, a half million German and Austrian reservists supposedly lived in the United States, a number far exceeding the relatively sparse number of troops in the American army. At least some Americans assumed that these auxiliaries possessed dubious loyalty to their new homeland.

German culpability for U.S. losses on the *Lusitania* might not be as clear as it seemed at the time. Bailey and Ryan assert that American citizens had a legal right to travel on the *Lusitania,* but they could not claim immunity for the ship itself. "The Americans were somewhat like the man who died at a street crossing in his automobile while resolutely maintaining his right of way. He was right, but he was just as dead as if he had been wrong." Given Captain Turner's orders to escape or ram, a neutral adjudicatory body might well have ruled that the *Lusitania* had lost its immunity as an unarmed merchant vessel. The British government in effect owned the ship, which operated solely under Admiralty control, and could easily have turned it into a troop transport. "The German case, both legal and moral, now appears to be a strong one, although never adjudicated by an impartial tribunal." To the two historians, the sinking of the American ships *Cushing* and *Gulflight* raised more serious issues than did that of the British *Lusitania.* Had the United States, notes historian Ross Gregory, come upon this matter in less turbulent circumstances, it might have taken a less rigid position, but questions of morality, national honor, and prestige now compounded the problem.[47]

Wilson himself confused matters. Speaking in Philadelphia on May 10, he said: "There is such a thing as a nation being so right that it does not need to convince others by force that it is right. There is such a thing as a man being too proud to fight." Publisher Oswald Garrison Villard claimed to have originated the phrase "too proud to fight"; he was mistakenly perceived to be close to the chief executive. Although Wilson merely sought to stress that fighting was not always the most effective answer to provocation, his statement was easily misunderstood. Though his live audience applauded his address, his language caused him much grief, fortifying critics who branded him as close to being a coward.[48]

On the following day, Wilson sought to recoup the damage, assuring newsmen that he had simply expressed a "personal attitude." He "did not have in mind any specific thing," much less a reference to the *Lusitania*. He explained privately that he had "a bad habit of thinking out loud" and that he should have "kept it in, or developed it further, of course."[49] The president sought to remove the phrase from the printed version of his speech. Biographer John Milton Cooper Jr. stresses that from his childhood Wilson's mother had instilled in him values of patience and self-control, qualities he now hoped the public would exhibit. Moreover, the president was engaged in an intense courtship with Edith Bolling Galt, an attractive widow whom he had met that March and would marry in December. He expressed his sentiments more accurately a month later when he summarized his countrymen's opinion and his own: "I wish with all my heart I saw a way to carry out the double wish of our people, to maintain a firm front in respect of what we demand of Germany and yet do nothing that might by any possibility involve us in the war."[50]

On May 10, three days after the sinking, Germany expressed "deepest sympathy at the loss of American lives" but placed the blame squarely on the British. The illegal seizure of foodstuffs and raw materials had forced Germany to engage in "retaliatory measures." Its U-boats could not treat British merchant ships as "ordinary merchant vessels," that is, subject to traditional visit, search, and seizure, because they were "generally armed with guns" and had repeatedly tried to ram German submarines. Sadly, Berlin continued, Americans were inclined to trust English promises rather than heed German warnings.[51]

At best the note was inaccurate, at worst a blunder. At the time, the British rarely armed merchantmen and large passenger vessels. Despite the secret orders, few ramming incidents had taken place. The clumsy effort at scolding could only backfire. One Philadelphia newspaper summarized the German apology in these words: "Sorry, but I'll do it again."[52]

Five days after the *Lusitania* was sunk, Great Britain published a document titled *Report of the Committee on Alleged German Outrages,* usually called the Bryce report. In December 1914 the British government appointed a commission to investigate atrocities in Belgium. Viscount James Bryce headed this body. Bryce, whose name was familiar to Americans, had written the highly respected *American Commonwealth* (1888) and had served as British ambassador to Washington from 1907 to 1913; the other six members were respected jurists, editors, and scholars. Based upon depositions of twelve hundred Belgians, the report concluded that their homeland had been subject to "deliberate and systematically organized massacres of the civil population." Although much of the account was drawn from hearsay evidence, historian Larry Zuckerman finds that the investigators reached "many sound conclusions," even if "drowned out by the publicity hoopla and often dismissed since." The report focused on systematic terror, which certainly took place, but in the process inadvertently obscured acts of murder, arson, pillage, and deportations. American editors expressed horror and shock over Bryce's findings. The timing of the revelations, although not intended to take advantage of the sinking, strongly aided the British cause.[53]

In dealing with the *Lusitania,* Wilson could choose among several options. First, he could have let matters drift, accepting the German note of May 10 and hoping time would cool tempers. Nevertheless, he faced a public that expected action, at the very least a strong note of protest. He was no doubt aware that a presidential election was just eighteen months away. In addition, he believed, no Great Power could show signs of weakness. Second, he could have protested to London, stressing that the nationality of the ship, rather than the citizenship of the passengers, determined whether the craft was legally immune from attack. At this time, American exporters and importers were deluging the State Department with objections to a British blockade that tied up $50 million worth of goods. Nevertheless, a simultaneous reprimand might indicate to belligerents and the American public that the president was placing both parties on the same moral footing. Mutual condemnation of London's blockade and Berlin's submarine warfare would put him at odds with both sides. Could any president afford to take on two enemies at once?

There were other alternatives as well. Wilson could have waited for Britain to protest directly to Berlin, although such a move was unlikely. The two powers had broken diplomatic relations. He could simply have pressed Germany to pay an indemnity for the loss of American life and property, although such insistence tacitly meant ignoring his belief that the incident constituted a serious breach of international law.

Wilson first approved a draft by Secretary Bryan that suggested possible arbitration of the entire matter, hoping to "tip-off" the press that Germany would accept this proposal. Counselor Lansing protested that the provision would gravely weaken the note, and Wilson aide Joseph Tumulty asserted that Germany would ignore the thrust of his message. The president finally told Bryan that suggestions of a "prolonged debate" would sacrifice "all chance of bringing Germany to reason."[54]

The president also rejected a suggestion that Bryan had long made, namely that Americans should be warned not to book passage on ships carrying contraband. Lansing retorted that the secretary's stance would leave citizens at risk, receiving no protection from their government. Referring to his February note on strict accountability, Wilson wrote Bryan on May 11: "We defined our position at the outset and cannot alter it—at any rate so far as it affects the past." Three days later, the president revisited the issue, lecturing the secretary: "It is hard to turn away from any suggestion that might seem to promise safety for our travelers, but what is suggested seems to be both weak and futile. To show this sort of yielding to threat and danger would only make matters worse."[55]

Arthur S. Link believes that Wilson sympathized with Bryan's position concerning the risk taken by American passengers. The sinking of the *Lusitania,* however, "raised the issue in such a dramatic, horror-evoking way that it was difficult to deal with it sanely." Furthermore, Link contends that Germany would have been wise to limit U-boat attacks to merchant ships, thereby sparing those that carried travelers. This policy would not have compromised vital interests.[56]

On May 13, Wilson replied to the Germans in what is called the first *Lusitania* note. He reviewed the cases of the *Falaba,* the *Cushing,* and the *Gulflight,* then moved to the tragedy of May 7. In all cases, he declared, Germany acted "absolutely contrary to the rules, the practices, and the spirit of modern warfare." Holding the Germans to strict accountability, the president demanded nothing less than abandonment of U-boat warfare against both unarmed American and belligerent liners and merchantmen. "Manifestly submarines cannot be used against merchantmen, as the last few weeks have shown, without an inevitable violation of many sacred principles of justice and humanity." Berlin, he continued, must disown the sinking of the *Lusitania* and make reparation for the loss of American life. For the first time the president unequivocally endorsed the right of neutrals to travel on belligerent ships. "American citizens," he argued, "act within their indisputable rights in taking their ships and in traveling wherever their legitimate business calls them upon the high seas." Referring to the German "death notice" published in the American press on May 1, which cautioned against traveling on British vessels, he stressed that "no warning that an unlawful and inhumane act will be committed" could serve as an excuse. In short, Germany must either abandon submarine warfare or experience a break with the United States.[57]

Bryan did win a round against Lansing; he made sure the note limited the ban on U-boat attacks to *unarmed* merchantmen. In one sense, he narrowed the field of controversy, as he was conceding that a submarine had a right to attack *armed* merchant ships without warning. Nonetheless, the secretary approved Wilson's more strident position with a "heavy heart," fearing that it would encourage jingoes, alienate Germany, and make America appear to be a most biased power. At the very least, he maintained, the United States should simultaneously protest Britain's misuse of the American flag, interference with American trade with neutral powers, effort to starve German noncombatants, and exploitation of American passengers in order to immunize its shipping.[58]

By taking his position, Cooper notes, Wilson initiated something resembling "a tennis game in extreme slow motion—first, the United States would send a diplomatic note; next, after a time, Germany would reply; then the United States would volley again. While this was going on, debate and conflict would wax and wane on each side over the latest move in these exchanges, often heightened by events on the battlefield or on the seas."[59]

Most of the public stood firmly behind Wilson's communiqué. The magazine *Current Opinion* asserted that no state paper ever received more widespread approval. Though not every legislator went as far as Senator Key Pittman (D-Nev.), who claimed that it constituted the greatest declaration of American rights since the Monroe Doctrine, the document received strong legislative support. Outspoken Allied sympathizers, including Elihu Root and Augustus P. Gardner, backed the president. Publisher Herman Ridder represented many German Americans in saying the communication "must compel the support of the entire American people." Ridder hoped that wider mediation might follow, aimed at ending the war.[60]

Some dissent remained. The *Vital Issue,* an extreme pro-German journal, blasted the administration. To insist that U-boat warfare be lifted upon British ships importing ammunition embodied "the most extraordinary demand which has ever been made by one nation of another." Conversely, while saying nothing publicly, Theodore Roosevelt told his son Archibald that Wilson was a man of "abject cowardice and weakness."[61]

Historians have long debated this note. Gregory suggests it deftly combined firmness with conciliation. Wilson asked Germany to change course, but neither presented an ultimatum nor threatened a diplomatic rift. Thompson argues that the president skillfully occupied the middle ground between Bryan's pacifist leanings and TR's belligerency.[62]

Some scholars are more critical. Tucker writes: "The man and nation that were too proud to fight were also too proud to relinquish 'rights' that in the end could only be vindicated by fighting." Devlin claims that the president made demands "from which he would almost certainly have to recede." Bailey and Ryan accuse Wilson of issuing "an unneutral ultimatum." The chief executive insisted that Germany must cease U-boat warfare because its submarines were unable to follow rules made in the days of the sailing ship. Besides, the president sought to exact "a degree of immunity that British subjects sailing in the same vessels, if offensively armed or resisting, could not claim for themselves." He also failed to make necessary distinctions between controversies concerning such American ships as the *Gulflight* and those that involved the British-owned *Lusitania.*[63]

Although Germany ignored the issue of its attacks on Allied vessels, it sought to assure neutral powers that it would not allow such incidents as the *Gulflight* to be repeated. On May 9, the Wilhelmstrasse claimed that both submarines and aircraft had been given "the most definite instructions" to avoid striking neutral ships. Should such an event occur, Berlin would pay damages.[64] Early in June the Admiralty forbade U-boat commanders to attack any craft of uncertain nationality. The Kaiser bucked his own admirals, who warned that Germany was losing its major weapon against England.

On June 6 Wilhelm banned the torpedoing of large passengers liners, even if they belonged to enemy nations. Because the Reich did not want to show weakness, these orders were kept secret. Even Ambassador Bernstorff remained uninformed. Such silence had its drawbacks, depriving Bryan of leverage in his struggle with Lansing and Germany of favorable publicity. Wilson had gained a victory of which he was unaware.

During the entire spring and summer of 1915, stalemate remained in western Europe. The British failed to achieve breakthroughs at Neuve Chapelle and Loos. The Germans gained ground at Ypres, but despite their introduction of chlorine gas, they were unable to continue. In September they repulsed the major offensives of General Joseph Joffre, the French commander, in the Champagne.

The Allies were equally unsuccessful on other fronts. In April forces primarily from the British Empire launched an assault in the Dardanelles to gain the Turkish Straits for the Russians but suffered incredible slaughter. In May Italy entered the war on the side of the Entente, but it gained at most twelve miles against the Austrians. By September Russia had lost Poland, Lithuania, and Courland, sacrificing the larger portion of a million men in the process.

Nonetheless, Germany was stymied at sea, its U-boats failing to meet expectations. Because Berlin possessed so few submarines, success could not be measured by the number of sinkings but only by the terror that resulted from such attacks. The gains were disproportionate to the risks involved, particularly because the strikes alienated neutral opinion. By June 1915 sinkings did average 133,000 tons monthly, auguring more extensive underwater conflict in the future .

On May 26 Germany compounded its tensions with the United States when *U-41* attacked the American steamer *Nebraskan* forty-eight miles off the southern coast of Ireland. The ship was sailing from Liverpool to New York without cargo. No lives were lost and the craft limped back to port. In mid-July Germany expressed regret and declared its readiness to make compensation but did not blame the submarine captain, claiming that the *Nebraskan* had not shown its flag and was therefore mistaken for an enemy vessel.

Jagow responded to Wilson's first *Lusitania* note on May 28, yielding no ground. He intended to investigate the *Cushing* and *Gulflight* incidents but defended the *Falaba* sinking, declaring that the captain sought to escape and had fired rockets for help. The foreign secretary offered pointed words concerning the *Lusitania*. While expressing "deep regret" over the loss of life, he accurately noted that the ship carried arms and that the British Admiralty had advised British merchantmen to fly a neutral flag and to ram German U-boats. Yet Jagow made several false claims, including statements that the vessel was armed, that it was transporting Canadian troops, that it was constructed as an auxiliary cruiser of the British navy, and that the rapid sinking resulted from an explosion of ammunition on board.[65]

If Jagow deliberately sought to antagonize Americans, he could not have been more successful. At best, the press deemed Berlin evasive, although a number of journals hoped that it had simply made an interim report. The pro-Entente *Outlook* denied that either Germany or the United States wanted war but continued: "Our fathers did not wait until they heard the war-whoop of the Indians before they began to build their stockades." The *Nation* accused the Reich of "murder on the high seas." Of course, Viereck dissented, claiming that Germany had kept its temper despite America's call for self-destruction. In a signed editorial, William Randolph Hearst said that American communiqués should be limited to such matters as attacks on U.S. ships. The United States had no right to ask Germany to refrain from using its only available maritime weapon against its enemies.[66]

Wilson felt compelled to challenge Jagow's note, even if the move meant breaking with his secretary of state. Bryan continued to stress the irresponsibility of American travel on belligerent ships. He informed Wilson on June 3: "Take the case of a riot for instance, the authorities not only endeavor to prevent shooting upon the street, but they order all citizens to remain at home in order to avoid the dangers necessarily incurred on the street." The secretary called for an investigation of the *Lusitania* incident by an international commission, a simultaneous protest against the British blockade, and adoption of his favorite solution—a "cooling-off" period to permit arbitration of differences. Wilson sympathized with Bryan's desire to prevent Americans from traveling on ships that carried munitions but believed that immediate implementation of such a ban would undercut further protest.[67]

Finding himself overruled, Bryan stepped down on June 8. "If I resign now," he told his wife, "I believe it will be possible to bring the real sentiments of this country to the surface." He had long realized that House and Counselor Lansing possessed far more influence with the president than he did. Wilson responded gracefully: "We shall continue to work for the same causes even when we don't work for them the same way." Privately the president was of two minds: he suspected something "sinister" behind the resignation but admitted it "greatly relieved" him. Bryan stoically remarked to his cabinet colleagues: "I go out into the dark. The President has the Prestige and the Power on his side." He added: "I have many friends who would die for me."[68] The two men remained on good terms.

Bryan took to the lecture circuit, calling upon the belligerents to state terms and arguing that the United States must continually offer to mediate. No German apologist, he repudiated neither his claim that America had the right to export arms nor his belief that the *Lusitania* sinking was indefensible. During the summer of 1915, he sought to nourish a coalition of labor, agricultural interests, and German and Irish Americans to foster antiwar sentiment. As with the economic issues that propelled him into fame, Bryan saw the struggle as involving a noble South and West staving off the predatory Northeast. "I have never known the New York Press to take the side of the American people on any question," he said.[69] Although unsuccessful in his efforts, he remained the nation's most influential voice for peace until the United States entered the war.

At the time of Bryan's resignation, far more voices opposed him than offered support. Roosevelt applauded the president. The Republican press aligned itself almost solidly behind Wilson; many Democratic papers concurred. Representative Robert N. Page (D-N.C.), who later left Congress in protest over American intervention, declared that the former secretary was "making an ass of himself." The congressman's brother, diplomat Walter Hines Page, spoke of "the yellow streak of a sheer fool." Kentucky editor Henry ("Marse") Watterson remarked: "Men have been shot and beheaded, even hanged, drawn and quartered, for treason less heinous." Senator Warren Gamaliel Harding (R-Ohio) called Bryan "a great and good man" but added that "no Secretary of State can be great enough to overshadow or direct the President."[70]

Bryan did receive some support in the West and the South, even if Hearst's *New York American* highly exaggerated in claiming that the secretary judged the popular temper far more accurately than those "who eat Government bread in Washington." Several leading southern Democrats supported Bryan privately but placed party unity ahead of their neutralist instincts. In the Senate, Works alone endorsed the Great Commoner. The *Fatherland* spoke for many German Americans in noting its past condemnation of Bryan, acknowledging it had portrayed him as "part of the Anglo-American conspiracy." The weekly was now relieved to know that "his heart was never in it."[71]

Judgments on Bryan have changed over time. Writing in the 1930s, journalist Walter Millis supported the secretary: "What the President did not see was that Mr. Bryan was essentially right." More recently, historians have voiced criticism. Ross Gregory believes Bryan was so obsessed with peace that he would have given away the most effective device, the threat of retaliation, to maintain it. By adhering to his proposals, "the United States would have faced economic loss, loss of national prestige, and probably the eventual prospect of a Europe dominated by Hindenburg, Ludendorff, and Wilhelm II." Ernest R. May claims that Bryan's policies would not have restrained German submarines; Americans would have experienced injuries and humiliations so great that in 1916 they would have elected a "chauvinist" as president. If the United States had retreated from its stated position, Germany would have pressed for further concessions, threatening American prosperity in the process, until Washington faced the choice of surrender or war.[72]

Just after Bryan's resignation, Wilson sent his second *Lusitania* note. Dated June 9, the communication repeated earlier demands while insisting upon specific pledges. He defended his position on the *Falaba*. Because the ship had not resisted capture, the U-boat commander violated "the principles of humanity." As for the *Lusitania,* the president denied German accusations that Britain had armed the vessel, allowed the unlawful cargo of high explosives, and made the craft a virtual auxiliary of Britain's naval forces. "Whatever be the other facts," he wrote in obvious reference to charges that the ship carried contraband, "the principal fact is that a great steamer, primarily and chiefly a conveyance for passengers, and carrying more than a thousand souls who had no part or lot in the conduct of the war, was torpedoed and sunk without even a challenge or warning, and that men, women, and children were sent to their death in circumstances unparalleled in modern warfare." He again stressed that American "shipmasters" and citizens had the right to engage in "lawful errands as passengers on merchant ships of belligerent nationality." In characteristically ringing prose, the president judged that his government was "contending for something much greater than mere rights of property or privileges of commerce. It is contending for nothing less high and sacred than the rights of humanity."[73]

In one way Wilson deviated from his first note: Germany must extend protection to "unresisting" merchantmen, rather than simply "unarmed" ones, meaning that a harried ship had a right to arm itself. Lansing at last won his battle against Bryan, in the process launching a new debate over rules of warfare that had already been proven antiquated.[74]

Wilson again received strong support. Hearst's *New York American* praised him for maintaining American rights while not forcing a quarrel upon the Germans. The *New Republic* thought the message to Germany overdue but judged it "conciliating enough to confound Mr. Bryan and firm enough to challenge German attention." Fifty-eight college presidents upheld Wilson, urging him to take the initiative in creating a league of neutral nations organized to assert common rights. Should Germany defy its wishes, it must face complete "nonintercourse."[75]

Some dissenters raised objections. To Theodore Roosevelt, the administration seemed to pursue "a course of national infamy," one of "milk and water." He called Wilson probably the worst president since James Buchanan, as he spoke of himself and his four sons possibly serving with the British in Flanders or Constantinople! Not surprisingly, George Sylvester Viereck attacked the note from the opposite perspective, declaring that it was "mild in its language, but, like the scorpion, it carries a sting in its tail." Representative James R. Mann (R-Ill.), the House minority leader, commented: "I think President Wilson has been swept off his feet by the 'Lusitania' case. It would be the silliest thing for this country to be drawn into the European war." The Chicago congressman reasoned that America could profit from the "useless war" by seizing the world's commerce from the belligerents.[76]

On June 23, Wilson made Robert Lansing secretary of state. At first, the president had found Lansing lacking in imagination, initiative, and fortitude. He had considered House but feared for the colonel's health and was reluctant to give Texas, which already had two slots, an unduly prominent role in the cabinet. He then thought of Agriculture Secretary David Houston and Thomas D. Jones, a Chicago corporation executive, but realized that both lacked foreign policy experience. House favored Lansing, though he had only once met the State Department counselor. Lansing, the colonel told Wilson, "could be used to a better advantage than a stronger man"; he "will be entirely guided by you without unnecessary argument." The chief executive agreed, thinking that Lansing would simply execute, not make, policy.[77] Besides, because of the lingering *Lusitania* crisis, time was critical.

Staunchly pro-Entente, within a month Lansing revealed his true sentiments in a private memorandum. The United States should enter the war, he wrote, if Berlin appeared close to victory. Otherwise "Germany would be master of Western Europe, of Africa, and probably of the Americas." Russia would become its ally, dominating "Scandinavia" and western and southern Asia. Japan would join the newly formed coalition in order to "control the Far East, the Pacific and possibly the West Coast of North America."[78]

Certainly events on the high seas did not wait upon diplomatic notes or new appointments. By mid-July the British had seized over two thousand

American ships, and by mid-September they had impounded American cargoes valued at $15 million. They had also confiscated two hundred thousand bales of southern cotton, causing Senator James K. Vardaman (D-Miss.) to call Britain's conduct far more reprehensible than that of Germany. Late in May, Interior Secretary Franklin K. Lane, who was Canadian-born, wrote a friend: "England is playing a rather high game, violating international law every day." On July 16, Robert Lansing warned that Britain's seizure of cotton, oil, and meat had produced such anger that it might soon be impossible to find a solution. Wilson avoided confrontation, fearing that confronting both Britain and Germany simultaneously would create a "nearly impossible" situation for America.[79]

On the last day of June, submarine *U-20* sank the escaping British vessel *Armenian* off the coast of Cornwall. Sailing from Newport News to Avonmouth, the merchantman carried close to fifteen hundred mules slated for the French army. Of some ninety-six mule tenders on board, probably twenty—most of them African Americans—were missing. Because the submarine commander first issued a warning, Wilson discerned in the incident evidence that the Germans had honored "the general principles upon which we have insisted." The pro-Entente *Outlook* suggested the United States might sever trade with Germany. The *Fatherland* countered that the Americans on board were suicidal to sail in a war zone under the British flag.[80] The public remained quite calm.

Not until July 8 did Jagow respond to Wilson's second *Lusitania* note of a month earlier. The foreign secretary evaded the whole question of sinking ships without warning as well as matters of liability and reparation. He repeated stock arguments concerning the ship's armament and British orders to ram U-boats. Commander Schwieger could not have permitted crew and passengers to board lifeboats before firing his torpedo; otherwise he would have presided over "the sure destruction of his own vessel." Similarly, if he had permitted the *Lusitania* to continue its voyage, "thousands of cases of munitions would have been sent to Germany's enemies and thereby thousands of German mothers and children robbed of breadwinners." German submarines, however, would respect legitimate American shipping and safeguard American lives on neutral vessels, provided that the ship hoisted the U.S. flag and carried no contraband. Four enemy passenger ships could pass through the German blockade. Yet the foreign secretary continued to warn that American citizens were not entitled to "protect an enemy ship through the mere fact of their presence on board."[81]

Wilson had sought German acceptance of the principle that belligerents should not attack unresisting merchantmen. Jagow was offering him a practical arrangement that assured the safety of those American travelers and ships who agreed to certain restrictions. Germany's suggested constraints did not originate with its Foreign Office, being personal proposals of Ambassador Gerard. Jagow was not signaling any general change in the U-boat campaign.

Wilson's advisers counseled firmness. On July 10 House argued that the United States could not consent to "any abridgment of those rights which civilized nations have conceded for a century or more. The soul of humanity cries out against the destruction of the lives of innocent non-combatants." A day later Lansing declared the need to check "German ambition for world domination." A victorious Reich, if allied with Japan and Russia, would constitute an "almost irresistible coalition." Furthermore, any British defeat would leave the United States isolated in the Far East. Berlin must not be allowed to "break even," much less win the war, even if "to prevent it this country is forced to take a active part." Needed were temporary settlement of the submarine issue and the strengthening of hemispheric ties by such measures as purchase of the Danish West Indies. Writing House from Berlin, Gerard reported: "The people here are firmly convinced that we can be slapped, insulted, and murdered with absolute impunity, and refer to our notes as things worse than waste paper."[82]

Wilson remained far more subdued, realizing that the controversy had cooled over the past two months. He genuinely believed that he could finally force Germany to back down over the *Lusitania*. On July 20, he wrote an old friend: "The opinion of the country seems to demand two inconsistent things, firmness and the avoidance of war, but I am hoping that perhaps they are not in necessary contradiction and that firmness may bring peace."[83]

The president's attitude was rooted in various factors: a personal sense of caution and conciliatory leanings; awareness of his nation's military weakness; a desire to serve as the world's peacemaker; and his belief, even shared by his more militant advisers, that the American public, particularly in the Midwest and the West, opposed war. Besides, he feared that the German Americans were strong enough to trigger a civil war. Other elements might include the conviction that the German people would eventually be shocked by the *Lusitania* event, that the U-boat campaign was more symbolic than real, and that Berlin would in time recognize America's latent power. Wilson spoke privately with Bernstorff about the United States challenging the

Allied blockade and a possible arms embargo. On July 14 he wrote House: "Apparently the Germans *are* modifying their methods: they must be made to feel that they must continue in their new way unless they deliberately wish to prove to us that they are unfriendly and wish war."[84]

The Congress and much of the public found little in Jagow's reply, though the *Literary Digest* discerned strong press support for some reasonable accommodation. The *Outlook* again sought to sever trade relations with Germany. Roosevelt and George Harvey, editor and publisher of the *North American Review,* desired Bernstorff's recall. The *New York American* praised the German response, asking: "Would any nation, fighting as Germany is for its existence, concede more?" The German American press endorsed Berlin's reply, the *Fatherland* calling the dispatch "an inspiring document" and noting that Germany had offered safety to American passengers and cargoes. Historians Bailey and Ryan find the German proposal worth exploring; its acceptance might well have prevented eventual war with Germany.[85]

On July 21, Wilson sent his third *Lusitania* note to Berlin. In some ways it struck the harshest tone of all. Calling the recent German answer "very unsatisfactory," the president repeated his insistence upon disavowal and reparation. American rights were based on "immutable principles"; belligerents needed to adopt any "new circumstances" to them. Continuation of the present practice must be deemed "deliberately unfriendly." Referring to freedom of the seas, he pledged: "The Government of the United States will continue to contend for that freedom, from whatever quarter violated, without compromise and at whatever cost." He rejected the German proposal concerning designated vessels. At the same time, Wilson claimed that he was ready "to make every reasonable allowance for those novel and unexpected aspects of war at sea." In fact, he continued, the past two months had shown that U-boats could wage war successfully against merchant shipping while acting in "substantial accord" with traditional cruiser rules.[86]

In a remarkable retreat, the president was no longer demanding the end of U-boat warfare. Instead, he acknowledged that under certain circumstances, the submarine was a legitimate vessel of war against merchantmen. What was deemed a "practical impossibility" in May became "manifestly possible" in July. Issues could now be limited to an indemnity and safety for Americans traveling on belligerent ships. Admittedly, the threat of war itself continued to prevail; the words "deliberately unfriendly" conveyed much.

As London applauded, Berlin proved slow to recognize Wilson's back-pedaling or the degree to which he was prepared to bargain. Wilhelm called

Wilson's stance "immeasurably impertinent."[87] Similarly, the president remained ignorant of the Kaiser's command to spare large liners, even if they belonged to an enemy.

American opinion was practically unanimous in backing the president's third note. The *New Republic* warned that a war against Germany would fail to protect American lives at sea. In addition, belligerence would cause the United States to fight over such shadowy matters as the fate of Constantinople and the Adriatic port of Trieste.[88]

Some Wilson opponents, however, were caustic. A newspaper in South Carolina quipped in the vein of John Paul Jones: "We have not begun to write." Roosevelt mused: "Did you note what its . . . number is? I fear I have lost track myself, but I am inclined to think it is No. 11,765, Series B." The *Fatherland* was mellower than usual. If the president followed his third note by an equally emphatic communication to Britain, he would be justified. The journal did find the president's missive bearing some latent threats toward Britain, stressing Wilson's insistence on freedom of the seas. The *New York American* feared armed conflict, commenting that "a note refusing to arbitrate and insisting that we are all right and another Power all wrong is practically an ultimatum." Warning that the current war threatened to cripple "the Caucasian race," Hearst's daily called for a league of neutral powers and a board of arbitration that, it claimed, would quickly terminate the conflict.[89]

Predictably, the Germans still torpedoed British merchantmen. On July 9, they fired upon the Cunard passenger liner *Orduna* just before 6:00 A.M. twenty-seven miles off Queenstown, located on Ireland's southern coast and only twenty-five miles distant from the *Lusitania* disaster. Walter Schwieger, the same captain who had attacked the *Lusitania,* commanded the U-boat. Sailing to New York from Liverpool, the *Orduna* carried 227 passengers, including 21 Americans. Schwieger mistook the vessel for a large merchantman because the ship possessed just one smokestack. Not a torpedo reached its target. News of the incident reached America nine days later. On July 24 the State Department asked the German Foreign Office for an explanation.[90] Jagow refused to reply, arguing that the incident involved an enemy ship on which no American lives had been lost. Wilson let the matter drop; he was still engaged in sensitive diplomacy over the *Lusitania.*

On July 25 *U-41* sank the American freighter *Leelanaw* sixty miles northwest of Scotland's Orkney Islands. En route from Archangel to Belfast and owned by the cotton brokerage of Harriss-Irby-Voss, it was carrying a cargo of flax, an article deemed contraband. In this case, the ship had been warned in advance; all passengers and crew were taken safely to Kirkwall. Lansing deemed the sinking a breach of a treaty with Prussia that had been made one hundred years earlier. The incident resembled the *Frye* case, but the State Department limited its protest to diplomatic representations.[91]

Not surprisingly, during the spring and summer of 1915, Germany continued to agitate for an arms embargo. In February Gerard reported Berlin's belief that the United States had supplied huge quantities of munitions to the Allies, citing a military dispatch that revealed the discovery of American ammunition behind Entente lines. That April House reported from Berlin: "Upon the streets one hesitated to speak in English, for fear of being insulted." In the same month Kaiser Wilhelm said to the American military attaché: "I will not see the ambassador of a country which furnishes arms and ammunition to the enemies of Germany." On April 4 Bernstorff sent a memorandum to Bryan and released it to the press a week later. The United States, he claimed, had created a massive new arms industry, something that per se violated "the spirit of true neutrality." He pointed to Wilson's munitions embargo during the current Mexican civil war to show the hypocrisy of American policy.[92]

Most press opinion revealed bitter hostility toward Bernstorff, labeling his note "insulting," "preposterous," and "insolent." The *Nation* accused the ambassador of imitating Citizen Edmond Genêt, a French emissary who had sought to undercut President George Washington by "going over the head of the Government to appeal to the voters. . . . An ambassador does not make offensive remarks about the Government to which he is accredited." If, remarked Senator John Sharp Williams, the United States levied an embargo while Germany controlled the seas, "the Emperor would declare war on us by telegram!"[93] Certainly Bernstorff had done irreparable damage to his own standing, not to mention lessening his influence with the American government.

Seventeen days after the ambassador submitted his note, Bryan replied. "Any change in its own laws of neutrality during the progress of a war, which would affect unequally the relations of the United States with the nations at war, would be an unjustifiable departure from the principle of strict neutrality." Although George Sylvester Viereck denigrated Bryan's reply as "the most dishonest document that was ever submitted by one great Government to another," most opinion leaders offered little criticism. To the *New Republic* the "good manners" of the secretary's note were "crushing"; it predicted that Germany would send no further official memoranda.[94]

Pro-German forces kept up their pressure. On April 5 a full-page "Appeal to the American People" appeared in a hundred foreign-language papers. It urged Americans "not to manufacture, sell or ship powder, shrapnel or shot of any kind or description to any of the warring nations of Europe, or Japan." Although these newspapers collectively claimed 8 million readers, some were too inconsequential to list in any press catalog. Of the 308 editors and publishers—Italian, Polish, Slovak, Hungarian, Jewish, French, and Dutch—not a one could be classified as German, though a German American head of a large advertising agency financed the petition.[95]

The advertisement evoked a surprising number of responses. The *New York American* defended the arms traffic on the ground that the United States must develop its own munitions industry: "We have no Krupps nor are we likely to develop any institution of like character." The *New Republic* saw German effort as pointless. Even if America refused to supply Britain with weapons, it remained doubtful that the British, who possessed such massive sea power, would ever surrender to Germany.[96]

The "Appeal" had some impact. The Socialist *New York Call* boasted that 8 million people supported the declaration. Oswald Garrison Villard's *New York Evening Post* believed that purely from a humanitarian point of view, most Americans sought to end the arms traffic.[97]

Conversely, Germany's defenders often pointed to an advertisement in the *American Machinist* of May 6, 1915. Issued by the Cleveland Automatic Machine Company, it appeared to revel in the damage its shells inflicted on human beings. "Fragments become coated with these acids in exploding and wounds caused by them mean death by terrible agony within four hours if not attended to immediately. From what we are able to learn of conditions in the trenches, it is not possible to get medical assistance to anyone in time to prevent fatal results."[98] The notice was placed on the desk of every member of Germany's Reichstag.

The *Toledo Blade* quoted the company president, who denied that his firm made such weapons and asserted that the printer had mistakenly inserted material from a different article. Another official said the firm sought to "put ginger into our advertizement" by conveying the horrible character of modern war. The pro-Entente *New York Times* found the whole situation rooted in a hoax to discredit American manufacturers.[99]

The munitions issue again came to the fore on the morning of July 3, when Erich Muenter (alias Frank Holt), a teacher of German at Harvard, attempted to kill financier J.P. Morgan Jr. in his Long Island home. Armed with three sticks of dynamite and two loaded revolvers, Muenter forced his way into the house and managed to shoot Morgan twice. He confessed that on the previous day he had placed a bomb that had damaged the reception room of the U.S. Senate. In a letter to the *Washington Times* he focused on his opposition to "this blood-money madhouse." He gave a prepared statement to a justice of the peace, in which he denied that he had intended to harm Morgan; rather he had sported a pistol and dynamite because "I intended to stay there until something was done" to end munition shipments and loans to the Allies. A grand jury had indicted Muenter six years previously for killing his first wife. He committed suicide three days after arrest, jumping twenty feet onto a concrete floor. The *Fatherland* deplored the attempted assassination but condemned as well press efforts to blame all German sympathizers for Muenter's action.[100]

Because the British blockade deprived American cotton producers and shippers of their lucrative central European market, several members of Congress sought a retaliatory arms embargo, even if it meant calling a special session. John Bull must "toe the mark," commented Representative Michael E. Burke (D-Wis.). Senator Thomas J. Walsh felt similarly, finding Britain's activity even more offensive than in 1812.[101]

Some cabinet members, angered over the British blockade, considered a munitions embargo. Early in May Interior Secretary Lane reported to House that the British "are holding up our ships; they have made new international law. . . . Each day that we [the cabinet] meet we boil over somewhat at the foolish manner in which England acts." Wilson told the colonel to warn Sir Edward Grey that Britain must stop its "endless delays and many wilful interferences"; otherwise arms embargo sentiment might become irresistible. Yet, according to House, the president informed the cabinet at one point: "Gentlemen, the Allies are standing with their backs to the wall, fighting wild beasts. I will permit nothing to be done by our country to hinder or embarrass them in the prosecution of the war unless admitted rights are grossly violated."[102]

The Central Powers would not drop the matter. On June 29 Austria-Hungary's foreign minister, Baron Stephan Burián, claimed that America's extensive arms trade jeopardized U.S. neutrality. Citing a preamble to a Hague agreement, Burián claimed that a neutral nation could legally impose such an embargo only to protect its own rights, that is, to "maintain an attitude of strict parity" between the belligerents. On August 12, Lansing responded: such a concept of neutrality "would obscure the field of international obligation, produce economic confusion, and deprive all commerce and industry of legitimate fields of enterprise." Were any nation to follow Austria's suggestion, it would have to stockpile supplies sufficient for any emergency. Each country would be turned into an armed camp, "ready to resist aggression and tempted to employ force in asserting its rights rather than appeal to reason and justice for the settlement of international disputes." House, as noted, warned Wilson that an embargo on munitions and foodstuffs would create an outcry among "our whole industrial and agricultural population."[103]

The diplomatic exchange created some debate. In the pro-Entente *Outlook*'s view, Burián would force every nation to adopt "the militarism of Germany and establish for itself its Krupp works." The *Nation* warned that any threatened country would devote its total energy to arms manufacture, forcing weaker lands to live "in fear and trembling." In contrast, Frederick Franklin Schrader, the *Fatherland*'s Washington correspondent, asserted that the secretary of state had ignored the humanitarian issue. George Sylvester Viereck's father Louis accused the United States of abandoning precedents reaching back to President Grant.[104]

Other matters pressed upon the administration. Colonel House traveled to Europe, there to investigate the possibilities of mediation. German and Austrian agents engaged in undercover operations that embarrassed their countries. The preparedness movement continually gained momentum. The Germans sank a British steamer, the *Arabic,* that carried Americans. Even had the *Lusitania* incident not taken place, such matters would still have bedeviled policymakers.

4

Toward the *Arabic* Crisis
January–August 1915

In 1921 West Point graduate Philip Dru, stationed at Fort Magruder, Texas, near the Rio Grande, became lost in the desert and suffered a sunstroke. Discharged from the army, he learned that a secret plutocratic oligarchy had gained control of the United States. Once the American people discovered the plot, civil war broke out, in which Dru successfully led an insurrectionary army. After the war, he ruled America, not as president but as "administrator." In reality a dictator, Dru fostered a host of domestic reforms that created greater equality and revolutionized the structure of the American government. Just as important, he prevented a coalition of Germany, Japan, and England from forming an anti-American alliance, for their combined military power would have enabled them to invade the United States itself. As a result of a major shift in ministry within the British government, the embryonic coalition dissolved.

Now administrator Dru could work with London to alter political alignments throughout the entire world, in the process advancing peace and freedom everywhere. Dru gave Germany freedom to control southeastern Europe and Asia Minor and to spearhead economic development in Latin America. He authorized Japan and China to divide Asia into spheres of influence, thereby checking the expansion of Russia. The Philippines became a Japanese protectorate while opening trade to all comers. The United States dominated the entire Caribbean and assumed Britain's role in Canada. Because the nations of Central America were engaging in destructive revolution, Dru defeated them at the Battle of La Tuna, fifty miles north of Mexico City, and turned them into U.S. protectorates. When he deemed his work done, Dru surrendered his powers and left his nation, sailing away with his beloved wife Gloria to a far-off Slavic land.[1]

Thus ran the plot of a novel, *Philip Dru, Administrator,* published anonymously in 1912. It was written by Colonel Edward Mandell House, who in 1917 confided to his diary: "Philip Dru expresses my thought and aspirations, and at every opportunity, I have tried to press rulers, public men and those influencing public opinion in that direction. Perhaps the most valuable work I have done in this direction has been in influencing the president."[2] There is no evidence that Wilson ever read, much less gained any insights, from this work, although he took it with him on a trip to Bermuda.

If House never entertained illusions about becoming the reincarnation of Philip Dru, he still sought to advance some of the agenda of the "administrator." Like Dru, the colonel would help to reorder the world so as to advance the causes of peace and justice. In May 1913, he journeyed to Europe, where he met with British leaders. He stressed the need for a "working understanding" with Britain, something that could lead to "some sort of coöperative understanding with the great European Powers that might help to preserve the peace of the world." In order to reduce international tensions, and in particular to weaken the intense German-British naval rivalry, he advanced a scheme that would have given Germany a sphere of influence in Asia Minor and Persia and a freer commercial hand in the Latin American republics.[3] His fictional hero could not have expressed himself better, although Wilson had no foreknowledge of House's scheme. The colonel returned home in July with his grandiose goal unfulfilled.

Sailing to Europe again late in May 1914, House met with Foreign Secretary Grey and Kaiser Wilhelm II. The emperor was impressed with the colonel's military rank, not realizing it was strictly honorary. Speaking to Wilhelm on June 1, House stressed that a naval accord between Britain, Germany, and the United States could preserve world peace. It could also check the Asiatic peoples, an argument more to the Kaiser's liking. Although the assassination of Francis Ferdinand at Sarajevo had not yet taken place, the colonel feared that "some spark might be fanned into a blaze." After conferring with Germany's naval chief, Admiral Alfred von Tirpitz, House cautioned Wilson concerning the atmosphere in Berlin: "The situation is extraordinary. It is jingoism run stark mad." In a blatantly self-serving comment, he suggested that only "some one acting for you can bring about a different understanding." Upon visiting France, the colonel maintained that its leaders no longer dreamed of revenge, much less the recovery of Alsace and Lorraine. When he returned to London, Grey told him that the current alignment of England, France, and Russia was not formalized in any written agreement; their relationships remained "purely sympathetic."[4] House departed from Europe on July 21 but did not meet with the president until the end of August. His first effort at great power politics had failed ignominiously. Furthermore, he kept Wilson ignorant of his objectives, a pattern of behavior that eventually ruined their friendship.

On August 22, 1914, soon after war broke out, the colonel wrote Wilson, hoping that neither side would conquer the other. An Allied victory would simply lead to Russian domination of the European continent; a German triumph would inflict upon Europe "the unspeakable tyranny of militarism for generations to come." In addition, the United States would be forced to "build up a military machine of vast proportions." That October, in further communication with the president, House said: "England should be held to the letter and spirit of the law if we are to maintain our attitude of strict neutrality." Germany should not be crushed, he added. Rather it must be forced to abandon its militarism, after which Europe could undertake general disarmament. It did not take long, however, for House to back the Allies; he viewed Britain in particular as the preserver of Anglo-Saxon governmental institutions. Certainly the presidential confidant was much closer to Page, Grey, and Spring Rice than to their German counterparts. He even gave the British ambassador informal advice. In November House warned the president that the Kaiser sought to exploit Latin American nations south of the equator.[5]

A month and a half later, Wilson asked House to revisit the major belligerent capitals. On the surface the timing appeared propitious. Germany had failed to take Paris, much less turn its entire army against Russia. Britain dominated the seas, denying them to the Central Powers. No real military breakthrough for either side remained in the offing.

The colonel's specific mission centered on—in Wilson's words—expediting parleys that "must be the first step in discussing and determining the conditions of peace." Ambassador Bernstorff assured the colonel that once the belligerents ceased fighting, his government would evacuate Belgium and indemnify it. Conversely, Spring Rice told him that Britain could consider peace on the basis of disarmament and German compensation to Belgium. The colonel was sensibly cautious, informing Wilson on the day after Christmas that "the European situation is not quite ready for us. . . . Keep the threads in your hands as now and [do] not press unduly."[6] Under no illusion that he could expedite a peace, House wanted to determine whether the situation was as gloomy as it appeared.

The colonel's caution was justified, for in reality neither side sought negotiations. Inside Germany the leadership was divided. Wilhelm and his civilian advisers, believing that prospects for victory were steadily waning, favored a return to the prewar status quo. Most military leaders and rightist parties, however, would settle for nothing less than annexations and indemnities. Chancellor Bethmann could only continue Germany's internal party truce, known as the *Burgfrieden,* if he avoided discussion of war aims. The issue was simply too divisive. Besides, many Germans disliked Wilson, who was perceived as leading a nation that was arming their enemies. Could there be a less appropriate person to serve as mediator?

Similarly, the Allies opposed intercession. At the time of House's visit, they were promising such neutral powers as Italy, Greece, and Rumania spoils from the dismembered Central Powers in return for joining the Entente. The colonel had already learned from American emissary Chandler P. Anderson that the Allies not only sought an indemnity for Belgium; they wanted one for France, as well as Russian acquisition of Constantinople and the Dardanelles.[7] With the German drive to Paris stalled and Britain remaining in control of the oceans, London saw no need for House's efforts.

House departed on January 30, 1915, on the Cunard liner *Lusitania,* launching his mission just as Germany was declaring the British Isles a war zone and warning neutral shipping of submarine attack. The colonel made one stop after another: London, Paris, Berlin, Nice, Biarritz, then again Paris and London. Everywhere he met the highest civilian officials. Conferring with Sir Edward Grey early in February, he discussed general disarmament, postwar international organization, and immunity for merchant shipping in peace and war, the last item the basis for what later was called freedom of the seas. Grey suggested that the United States serve as a participant in peacemaking in possible return for ending the war "as a drawn contest." The colonel replied that "it was not only the unwritten law of our country but also our fixed policy, not to become involved in European affairs." America could not entangle itself in such matters as Alsace-Lorraine, Constantinople, and a possible league of nations.[8]

Grey also told House that the Allies would not propose peace negotiations until a forthcoming spring offensive produced a "convincing military victory." House readily concurred, assuring the foreign secretary that he did not intend to push matters.[9] The foreign secretary could only feel relieved that Washington would defer any peace initiative until the Allies desired it. The colonel failed to communicate to Wilson that he had assured the British of his sympathies and had thereby deceived the president, who believed that House had sincerely pressed for negotiation. Possibly the emissary did not want to disappoint Wilson by revealing that the Allies had spurned Washington's peace bid.

House did tell Wilson that even if Germany evacuated Belgium and considered peace proposals, Russia and France would balk at negotiations. Moreover, the Union of South Africa would not give up recent conquests of German colonies on its northwest borders and Australia its possession of the Caroline and Samoan islands in the Pacific. The colonel wrote the president: "Germany may be successful. If France or Russia gives way, she will soon dominate the Continent; and it is not altogether written that one or the other will not give way. Even if the Allies hold together, there is a possibility that war may continue for another year." While House was in London, German undersecretary Arthur Zimmermann sent him a note, contradicting Bernstorff's avowal regarding Belgium. Because of the Reich's "infinite sacrifices of human lives," the German undersecretary of state for foreign affairs wrote the colonel that any indemnity was out of the question.[10]

When House arrived in Paris on March 11, he learned from Ambassador Gerard in Berlin that Germany harbored annexationist goals of its own: an indemnity from France; retention of Namur, Liège, and the Meuse valley; and territory within the Belgian Congo. When House repeated the terms to Théophile Delcassé, the French foreign minister dared Germany to "come and get it." The colonel's skepticism about Germany's desire for negotiation was reinforced when, just over a week later, he arrived in Berlin. Zimmermann told him that "if peace parleys were begun now upon any terms that would have any chance of acceptance, it would mean the overthrow of this Government and the Kaiser."[11]

In April House returned to Paris, though this time he did not even raise the question of peace, realizing there was less chance for it than ever. Germany was driving the Russians out of Poland while the French were planning a major offensive in their own northeastern region. The British and the French sought to outflank the Central Powers by initiating a major campaign in the Dardanelles.

Arriving again in London on April 28, the colonel pressed upon Grey his plan for freedom of the seas. The foreign secretary was quite aware that House's proposal involved surrender of England's most indispensable weapon, the blockade. Grey claimed that he personally concurred with House but that any such commitment depended upon the agreement of the entire cabinet and all of Britain's allies. It also required Germany's evacuation of Belgium and France. Nonetheless, House outlined a plan to institute immediate communication between London and Berlin, which would be followed by a peace conference. Grey must have thought, writes Link, that "the good Colonel had left some of his reason in Berlin to be talking so seriously about peace, which, he had been plainly told in the three belligerent capitals, was at present completely out of the question."[12] To compound the obstacles to a negotiation, in March France and Britain formally agreed to Russian annexation of the Straits and Constantinople. A month later the Treaty of London promised Italy such territory as Trentino, Trieste, the Tyrol, the Dalmatian coast and adjoining islands, and territory in east Africa—all in return for joining the Allies.

Apparently House believed that Italy's imminent entry into the war and a British success in the Dardanelles would force Germany to its knees. With both sides repelled by the mass killing, he thought that the French might compromise on Alsace-Lorraine and that Germany's civilian leaders might wrench control of foreign policy from its military. Not until May 25 did the colonel concede to Wilson that Europe might be facing a long war. The fate of the United States, he maintained, was so tied to that of the Allies that America should do nothing to weaken their good will. A week later, he confided to his diary that he foresaw an inevitable war between America and Germany.[13]

Given that the *Lusitania* controversy remained unresolved, House left for home on June 5 assuming that his nation would soon become Britain's ally. In mid-June he wrote the president that American entry into the war would have its "compensations." "The war would be more speedily ended, and we would be in a strong position to aid the other great democracies in turning the world into the right paths." That summer House backtracked somewhat, causing Wilson to write his fiancée that his lieutenant was getting "re-Americanized."[14]

In August Lansing warned Wilson that the Central Powers alone would welcome a peace bid. They occupied so much land that they could demand major Russian territories as well as part of Belgium and France. Because of this advantage, the secretary continued, the Allies could not pursue any overture, although ultimately, they believed, their enemies could not sustain continued loss of men and resources.[15] Certainly, House's journey had proved highly embarrassing to both sides. Neither alliance, however, could shun him without antagonizing the world's most powerful neutral and appearing to desire the conflict continued at any cost.

While the colonel was involved in summit diplomacy, some of the nation's most prominent women were setting their own agenda for mediation. On January 10, 1915, Jane Addams ("Saint Jane"), the internationally renowned humanitarian, addressed nearly three thousand women in the Grand Ballroom of Washington's New Willard Hotel. Here delegates representing various societies organized the Woman's Peace Party (WPP). Addams served as chairman; the leading suffragist, Carrie Chapman Catt, was chosen honorary chair. In reality a pacifist body rather than a political party, the WPP offered a most comprehensive platform. Some planks were quite visionary, among them democratic control of foreign policies, removal of war's economic causes, and a concert of nations to replace the traditional balance of power. Others appeared slightly more attainable: woman suffrage, limitation of armaments, the nationalization of munitions-making. Anna Garlin Spencer, a Unitarian minister and a sociologist at Meadville Theological Seminary, offered the rationale for a peace organization based solely upon female membership: "As women, we are especially the custodians of the life of the ages."[16]

Julia Grace Wales, a Canadian and an instructor of English at the University of Wisconsin, offered the party its most significant plank, an immediate convening of neutral nations to advance an early peace. A commission of experts, appointed by the governments of the neutral powers, would meet in continual session, acting as an agency of mediation and exploring various peace proposals, which would be continuously offered to all belligerents. As both sides genuinely sought an accord, they would eventually reach a settlement. Wales had placed her proposal before the legislature of her state; both houses approved this "Wisconsin Plan."

Not limiting herself to the United States, Addams hoped to mobilize the women of Europe. On April 28, 1,136 delegates, representing twelve different countries, gathered for four days at the largest hall in The Hague, a curious pseudo-Moorish structure located in the city's Zoological Gardens. There they formed the International Congress of Women. The United States sent the most delegates, well over forty, followed in turn by Germany, Austria-Hungary, Norway, Sweden, and Britain. Of the major belligerents, Russia and France alone did not send representatives, refusing to issue passports. Not surprisingly Addams was again chosen chair. Resolutions specified an end to secret treaties, democratic parliaments for all peoples, nationalization of armaments, political rights for women, a permanent international court, no transfer of territory without consent of the inhabitants, and compulsory arbitration along with pressure on those nations that refused it. The assembly asked neutral nations to create a conference that would offer continuous mediation without delay. There would be no waiting for an armistice, no seeking permission from the belligerents. The Hague congress established the International Committee of Women for Permanent Peace, located in Amsterdam.

The Congress chose Addams as one of its three delegates designated to visit most of the warring capitals. The trio met with Asquith, Grey, Bethmann, Jagow, Pope Benedict XV, and the prime ministers of Austria, Hungary, Italy, and France. They arrived in London just two days after the *Lusitania* was sunk and reached Italy as it was joining the Allies. Another American, economist Emily Greene Balch of Wellesley College, was part of a separate five-woman delegation assigned to Russia and the neutral powers. From May 7 through July 8, the two delegations, between them, visited fourteen countries. Balch deplored the draconian war aims of both sides but added that if "the disinterested neutrals" delayed until neither side possessed advantage, they would wait "long indeed." Conversely, continuous offers of outside mediation could put the entire negotiation on a "higher level."[17] Leaders of the belligerent leaders offered, at best, vague and tentative responses. British foreign secretary Grey expressed his personal belief that the war would be fought to the finish; his French counterpart, Théophile Delcassé, admitted that he sought to destroy Germany to the point where it would not rise again for a hundred years.

All such peace efforts ended in failure, and Addams told the press that every warring nation sought total victory. Finding mediation impractical, she stressed the need for a continuous conference of neutrals, guided by the United States and ready to act as opportunities arose. Balch blamed Wilson for balking at this suggestion, although on August 18, 1915, the president personally assured her that he would offer America's good offices when the right moment came. Wilson privately feared that Balch's solution would fail, costing the United States future influence among the belligerents. Addams, too, conferred with Wilson, visiting him six times between July and September 1915. In mid-July the president told her that the timing was inauspicious.

In conferring with Lansing, Emily Balch met with still greater frustration. The secretary informed her that the time was inopportune, for the victorious Germans alone sought peace. Furthermore, any conference of continuous mediation would prove impractical because the intermediary would simply offer to intercede and then withdraw. Were the belligerents to reject the women's terms, they might be closing the door to any intervention offered more propitiously. In addition, the secretary was scandalized at the very idea of neutral parties proposing terms, asserting that nations were by nature selfish and that America must avoid "meddling in other peoples' affairs." The would-be negotiators, wrote Lansing to Wilson, ignored "the perversity and selfishness of human nature." Wilson concurred. Balch in turn privately assailed Lansing's "absolutely amoral and cynical attitude."[18]

Why, given his views, did Wilson agree to receive the peace activists? There are several reasons. If he decided to propose mediation, he would need their support. In fact, they might make some suggestions that could prove helpful. As the women were all progressives of one type or another, their backing would be welcome on domestic issues, not to mention the forthcoming presidential election of 1916. In due time, he predicted to his fiancée, the Allies would win, not—to be sure—in a great single battle but in *"a great endurance test."*[19]

The Woman's Peace Party represented the more progressive wing of the peace movement, as it emphasized popular participation in foreign policy. So did the National Peace Federation, a body launched by the spring of 1915. It, too, stressed Wales's plan for continuous mediation. Hamilton Holt, editor and publisher of the *Independent,* a progressive weekly, served as president, Addams as vice president. Louis P. Lochner was chosen general secretary. He was serving as secretary of the Chicago Peace society and director of central west development of the American Peace Society.

Theodore Roosevelt opposed such groups strongly, calling the pacifists "copperheads" and "physical cowards." He called Addams "one of the shrieking sisterhood"; she was "poor bleeding Jane" and "Bull Mouse." Writing Chicago reformer Raymond Robins, he maintained that such peace advocates as Jane Addams, Nicholas Murray Butler, Stanford chancellor David Starr Jordan, and steel magnate Andrew Carnegie stood for "unrighteousness," for they condoned "hideous wrongdoing at the expense of the helpless and the innocent." The women responded by denouncing the ex-president as a "fire-eater," a man fifty years out of date.[20]

Another organization embodied the peace movement's more conservative side. On June 17, 1915, some three hundred people, gathering in Philadelphia's Independence Hall, established the League to Enforce Peace (LEP).

The roster embodied a veritable "who's who," drawing from the world of business, diplomacy, higher education, and the Protestant clergy. The LEP chose William Howard Taft as president and Harvard's president A. Lawrence Lowell as chairman of the resolutions committee. The major impetus came from publisher Hamilton Holt, who, with Theodore Marburg, recently minister to Belgium, sponsored a series of dinners that lay the groundwork.[21]

The LEP envisioned nothing less than a league of nations, binding signatories to (1) a tribunal for any controversy of a "justiciable" nature; (2) a council of conciliation for other questions; (3) joint economic and military force against any member that engaged in hostilities before seeking adjudication; and (4) periodic conferences to formulate international law. It focused more on eliminating wars before they erupted than on ending them after they began. According to historian William C. Widenor, it might have been better described as the League to Enforce Conciliation. Victor Berger, formerly a Socialist congressman from Milwaukee, and George Kirchwey, Columbia law professor and president of the American Peace Society, sought to eliminate the word "force" from the resolutions. Lowell, however, was adamant, stressing that coercion might be needed. Though any nation could join this league, Taft emphasized its great-power base by emphasizing that small nations would lack equal representation.[22]

The proposal inevitably drew opposition. A day after the LEP was organized, Bryan warned Americans against abandoning the tenets of George Washington and the Monroe Doctrine to become "partners with other nations in the waging of war." Besides, such intervention could well backfire, for the United States could hardly involve itself in Europe without that Continent interfering in the Western Hemisphere. Ironically, the League's founders acknowledged indebtedness to Bryan's "cooling-off" treaties, though they displeased the Great Commoner by adding the element of force. In a private letter to Lowell, former senator Elihu Root said he feared any entangling alliance and found that too much power had been given to the new tribunal. Therefore, he declined the invitation to join, much less serve on its executive committee. Senator Boies Penrose (R-Pa.) branded the league's program "fantastic and nonsensical," regarding it as no substitute for a large navy and military training.[23]

To Roosevelt, the LEP embodied "discreditable folly," for the organization sought world peace before the United States possessed the military force needed to enforce global tranquility. The former president, however, had recently advocated a "world league for the righteousness of peace," in which the United States, major European nations (including Germany and Russia), and selected Latin American states would mutually guarantee the honor, territorial integrity, and vital interests of each other. Participants would pledge their "entire military force, if necessary," against violators.[24]

As 1915 began, the administration still exhibited a peacetime mentality, even considering the actual reduction of armed forces. In January the House Military Affairs Committee rejected the request of War Secretary Garrison, who was somewhat isolated in the Wilson administration, for a 25 percent increase in army personnel, though it did provide for a small enlargement. Chairman James Hay (D-Va.) opposed adding a single soldier, saying: "Isolated as we are, safe in our vastness, protected by a great navy, and possessed of an army sufficient for any emergency that may arise, we may disregard the lamentations and predictions of the militarists."[25] Representative James R. Mann deleted a small appropriation to send military observers to Europe.

A minority of opinion leaders was less complacent. "As at present organized and equipped," commented the *New Republic,* the U.S. Army could merely serve as a "national police force."[26] To show the nation's weakness, Congressman Gardner invited the army's entire enlisted reserve to dine with him at Washington's New Willard Hotel. All sixteen appeared.

Similarly, Congress failed to press the issue when Navy Secretary Daniels sought two battleships a year. On February 5, 1915, a House amendment to cut the allocation to one battleship failed by sixteen votes. Of the 155 economy-minded representatives, 139 were Democrats, four-fifths coming from the South and the Midwest. Familiar charges of militarism and war profits surfaced. Shall the United States, asked James Manahan (R-Minn.), yield to the same avarice that brought hopeless woe upon Europe's millions? Congressman Samuel A. Witherspoon (D-Miss.) saw no logic to the claim that increased armaments would keep the United States at peace.[27]

Some countered by speaking in geopolitical terms. Congressman Peter Gerry (D-R.I.) included enforcement of the Monroe Doctrine among the navy's tasks. The United States, claimed Representative Hobson, had been on the verge of war with Japan for an entire decade; America must either "surrender the open door policy or fight." Moreover, Britain's attitude, too, appeared "nothing short of menacing." Without a strong navy," warned Assistant Secretary Franklin Roosevelt, "we should lose, in war time, Cuba, Samoa, Puerto Rico, the Panama Canal, Hawaii, and the Philippines." Even the biblical figure Noah, remarked one of Roosevelt's predecessors in the Navy Department, Herbert L. Satterlee, built an ark to meet any emergency![28]

Others debated the value of certain weapons. Representative Joseph Taggart (D-Kan.) denied that battleships protected Britain and then asked how they could shield America. Senator Claude A. Swanson (D-Va.) countered that Britain's supremacy of the sea rested on its dreadnoughts. To Senator Charles S. Thomas (D-Colo.), the submarine possessed such destructive force that it alone could maintain peace. In introducing an amendment for constructing fifty underwater craft, Senator Reed Smoot offered a commercial argument. "If the war lasts two years longer, the United States will control the commerce and finances of the world; but she will have nothing with which to defend her advanced position."[29]

Yet the preparedness cause was gaining headway. Early in March, the president signed a bill that provided for two battleships, six torpedo destroyers, eighteen submarines, and one oil ship. Daniels called the legislation the most generous naval measure that Congress had ever enacted.[30]

Opinion leaders had already begun shifting. In late January the *Literary Digest* conducted an editorial poll on military increases. America's editors, the weekly revealed, believed two to one that defenses were inadequate. By a vote of almost three to one they favored a naval buildup, and a healthy majority backed a larger standing army. Newspapers from every section endorsed this increase, though the weekly might have underplayed midwestern and southern opposition.[31]

In May 1915 the preparedness movement achieved tremendous impetus, for the *Lusitania* crisis fostered rearmament sentiment. Two weeks after *U-20* sank the liner, Wilson called for an even greater naval buildup. Financial and industrial leaders increasingly joined the boards of the defense societies, sponsored dinners, bankrolled rearmament publicity and spectacular parades, and served on such quasi-governmental bodies as the Committee on Industrial Preparedness and the Naval Consulting Board. No longer was preparedness simply the cause of a numerically insignificant, if highly articulate, upper-class minority living in the Anglophile Northeast; it drew upon the middle classes throughout the nation. The U.S. Chamber of Commerce offered support. Urban newspapers manifested all the zeal of a convert, although rural and small-town journals, which often gave overseas battlefronts limited coverage, remained unenthusiastic. Farmers, being relatively isolated from public opinion, voiced the greatest opposition. Labor, too, was suspicious, fearing that the social discipline accompanying military training would lead to strike-breaking. Editor Simeon Strunsky noted: "The big army sentiment is strong in the clubs and weak in the cheap restaurants." Military historian John Patrick Finnegan went further, writing that "The best people might back defense, but the voters did not."[32]

Certain preparedness advocates foresaw a postwar scramble for commercial dominance. Commented Rear Admiral William S. Benson, newly appointed chief of naval operations: "Already the eyes of avarice have been turned upon us. What the result will be God only knows." Leonard Wood observed that trade rivalries created nine out of every ten wars. Early in 1916 the *New York American* identified three postwar competitors: England, Japan, and Germany. It warned with typical hyperbole: "WE WILL BE SO WEAK AND CRIPPLED THAT WE CANNOT START."[33]

Rearmament enthusiasts usually put far greater stress on enemy invasion, advancing arguments that peaked in 1915. The United States, warned Captain Matthew E. Hanna, former aide to General Wood, possessed a mere day and a half's worth of ammunition with which to repel one hundred thousand troops. According to George Harvey's *North American Review,* "a great European military empire . . . could easily throw an expeditionary force of 250,000 men upon our shores." America, lacking the one-third of manpower needed to repulse it, would be no match. The Army Committee of the National Security League cited recent Allied landings at Gallipoli as evidence that "troops unquestionably can be landed here."[34]

Preparedness spokesmen often deemed New York the nation's most vulnerable target. Battleships with fifteen-inch guns, claimed Congressman Gardner, could remain out of range of the city's shore batteries while demolishing lower Manhattan. In December 1914 former war secretary Henry L. Stimson wrote in *Harper's Weekly* that an unknown enemy could seize New London, Connecticut, and move south. An infantry officer warned Hearst readers that Germany could land 1.5 million men in six weeks, occupying the area from Erie, Pennsylvania, to Washington, D.C. Retired major general Francis V. Greene, formerly governor general of the Philippines and a New York police commissioner, elaborated on this scenario in his book *The Present Military Situation in the United States* (1915). German forces would take over Queens County, then capture Manhattan. They would hold the city's leading millionaires as hostages, including John D. Rockefeller, Andrew Carnegie, and Jacob Schiff, until the nation paid a $5 billion indemnity. Julius W. Muller offered a somewhat different scenario. His book *The Invasion of America* (1916) portrayed the initial attack taking place in Rhode

Island; the seizure of Boston and New York would follow. Kansas editor William Allen White envisioned German armies landing at Galveston and moving "cross country to the Missouri Valley."[35]

One major work, J. Bernard Walker's *America Fallen!* (1915), described how on a single day, April 1, 1916, a thousand German troops captured major forts that overlooked New York harbor. Hours later they seized Boston and Washington, D.C., as well as all arsenals, arms factories, and powder works between the Atlantic Ocean and the Allegheny mountains. Soon the Battle of the Caribbean took place, the greatest naval engagement in history, in which the Kaiser's battleships pulverized the American fleet. Every U.S. dreadnought was destroyed. In his endorsement, Admiral Dewey asserted that the work revealed "a state of affairs which might well exist if our country is not prepared to maintain itself at peace with the world."[36]

Occasionally Britain and Japan were portrayed as aggressors. In a book titled *The United States and the Next War* (1915), George Lauferti described how the Royal Navy overwhelmed America's Atlantic fleet, which possessed fewer than one-fourth the number of Britain's ships, while a Japanese force engaged a U.S. Pacific squadron half its size. Similarly, Congressman Hobson foresaw a war between the United States and an Anglo-Japanese alliance. The victorious combination would seal up the Open Door in Asia. Even if, reasoned the *New York American,* Germany were victorious in the European war, its surplus population would not be contained at home; it would spill over to Brazil and Argentina. Or a triumphant Britain would intervene in the Western Hemisphere in order to protect its interests in Mexico, its Japanese ally joining in this action.[37]

The Army War College, drafting a document titled "Epitome of Military Policy," drew up its own script. Dated July 1915, the paper portrayed over 1 million Germans invading America within six months. First, three waves of soldiers would occupy the area reaching from Baltimore and Washington to Erie, Pennsylvania. Next, reinforcements would seize Pennsylvania, New York State, and New England, thus conquering over 35 million Americans as well as dominating the heart of the nation's steel and munitions industries. Indeed, the entire operation proved "commonplace," "ridiculously easy of accomplishment." Other nations posed dangers as well; a British-Japanese alliance practically placed "a powerful army on our northern frontier."[38]

Hudson Maxim's *Defenseless America* (1915) received the most public attention. A prominent inventor, Maxim developed a potent form of smokeless powder; his brother Hiram created the famous "Maxim" machine gun.

Overtly Darwinist, the book maintained that continuous war was inevitable. Whoever won the current conflict would fight the United States because neither coalition would forgive America for remaining neutral. The author wrote: "If our country should be invaded, we should not only have to furnish food, clothing, cigar, cigarettes, and wine for the armies of the enemy, but also our wives and our daughters and our sweethearts would be commandeered to supply the women and song."[39]

A screen adaptation of Maxim's book titled *The Battle Cry of Peace* showed spiked-helmeted soldiers despoiling America's East Coast, leaving Times Square in flames, the Capitol building in ruins, and mansions on Long Island destroyed. The English-born producer J. Stuart Blackton consulted with Wood, Garrison, and Theodore Roosevelt.

One of the more imaginative defense schemes came from Robert R. Mc-Cormick, president of the *Chicago Tribune,* who proposed yielding the coastal states to an invader until defenders spent several years organizing a force powerful enough to repulse it. In the meantime, the regular army and militia would stop the enemy on the nation's "natural barriers," operating from forts as far-flung as Buffalo, Atlanta, and the passes of the Sierra Nevada and the Rocky Mountains.[40]

In an effort to counter scenarios of a German attack, the *Fatherland* presented a most imaginative portrayal of a British incursion. Written by Irish-American nationalist Shaemas O'Sheel in the form of a diary under the pseudonym of one "Gustav Bauerfeldt, War Correspondent for the *Berliner Rundschau,*" the series was titled "The War of 1920." Running in Viereck's weekly from early August to mid-November 1915, the account envisioned three coordinated invasions: Mexico overran Texas, the Japanese took over the Pacific Coast, and Britain bombed New York City. One passage cataloged Allied atrocities: "the burning of homes and cities, the cruel fate of thousands of women and girls, the savage repression of the patriots of California, the hideous negro uprising and all the nameless cruelties inflicted on a white people by other whites and their Japanese, Mexican, Hindu and Senegalese mercenaries, to further the plots of the gang of English politicians for whom humanity blushes!"[41] Only when a German fleet defeated the British in "the greatest naval battle in history" did the despoilers withdraw.

Other opinion leaders rejected these predictions. Increase the number of torpedo boats, said the Bryanite House majority leader Claude Kitchin, and no nation could transport armies within 250 miles of American shores. How, asked the *Nation,* could any country land one hundred thousand troops over such barriers of water, as it pointed to the transportation difficulties the Japanese had faced in Manchuria and the United States in the Philippines? The *New Republic* denied that either San Francisco or New York could be captured; in fact, Germany could never retain London, England. Congressman Isaac R. Sherwood (D) of Toledo, Ohio, once a brevet Civil War general, saw the European powers as too bankrupt to launch any strike. "Was there ever such an utterly idiotic proposition before exploited, since civilized man was evolved from the prehistoric cave man?"[42]

In 1915 the Navy General Board determined that Germany was unable to threaten the Western Hemisphere, its population having already been decimated by war. Subject to commercial blockade, it could not engage in any struggle for world markets. Conversely, the United States remained unable to assist the Allied war effort. Even were the United States to land fifty thousand expeditionary troops on European soil, such a force would little threaten a German army already fighting some 3 million Allied soldiers.[43]

Of course, these invasion calculations were, as historian Finnegan notes, "all nonsense," "exercises in arithmetic, not war." Proponents took scant consideration of the strength of the American navy, much less the difficulties of an enemy landing armies against an equipped foe. The German navy lacked storage capacity to cross the Atlantic; it was strictly designed for fighting on the North Sea. Finnegan finds the Army War College politically ignorant, "captive of its own rigid ideas," and lacking coordination with naval planners. Offering a worst-case scenario and demanding maximum security to avert the greatest possible harm, its report laid the groundwork for hundreds of journalistic scare stories. The plan was not applicable to current diplomatic crises, being totally focused on repelling a full-scale invasion. Historian John Whiteclay Chambers II writes that the invasion fantasies "deflected discussion from the real issues: the possibility of military intervention in the European war, the probable nature of long-term U.S. foreign policy, and the most appropriate military and naval forces for both of those." Military resources were never linked with strategic goals.[44]

In March 1915 an organization named the American Legion was formed to serve as the base of a reserve force. Not to be confused with the massive veterans organization formed immediately after World War I, this Legion sought to enroll males in a volunteer army once the nation found itself at war. Supposedly, the idea emerged from a letter from an explorer, one E.D. Cook, to *Adventure* magazine, a journal devoted to exotic exploits. The Legion targeted former army and navy personnel as well as concerned civilians.

In case of emergency, such men would enter service immediately, having been trained in army, navy, militia, or ad hoc volunteer units. Preferred occupations included seamen, surgeons, engineers, mechanics, chauffeurs, cooks, police, firemen, and guides. No military training was involved. In fact the Legion's main task lay in collecting a list of names. Contributing twenty-five cents in dues, members simply pledged "to serve my country, and to serve her as she says, not as I say."[45] Within the first month, the Legion registered fifty thousand men.

Not surprisingly, the ubiquitous Theodore Roosevelt chaired the Legion's executive committee. An advisory council included former president Taft, three of Roosevelt's secretaries of war (including Root), two of Taft's secretaries of war (one being Stimson), and Taft's secretary of the navy. Leonard Wood publicly endorsed the body, at which point Secretary Garrison admonished him to avoid further involvement.[46] The admonition was not a harsh one, though it was certainly a reprimand. The War Department considered the entire effort counterproductive, deeming it either an instrument to further Roosevelt's political ambitions or a gimmick that would impede the formation of a genuine reserve. Because the department showed no interest in accumulating a card file, the American Legion lay stillborn.

How then should preparedness be achieved? For what exactly was the nation being prepared? Usually the War Department's contingency plans centered on occupying Mexico or repelling a hypothetical invasion. Of the nation's military leadership, only Major General Tasker Bliss, assistant chief of staff, worked on a hypothetical plan to send twenty-two divisions to Europe. Aside from increasing guards at several depots, the department made no provision for any military emergency.

By May private organizations had become more active than ever. Two days after the *Lusitania* sinking, the National Security League called for massive rearmament, asking for a volunteer army of a million men. Other demands included an improved National Guard, an integrated military policy, a stronger and more balanced navy, and adequate reserves for each branch of the service.[47]

That same month the Navy League sought a special session of Congress to appropriate $500 million for naval expansion, claiming that a powerful fleet would create respect for American rights. By October it demanded a council of national defense, a reserve of fifty thousand men, and sufficient ship construction over five years to prevent any enemy from crossing the seas. League officials also sought a coalition cabinet that might include either former Senator Root, a sharp critic of the president, or Joseph Choate, a strong Anglophile. The League's new president, Colonel Robert M. Thompson, predicted that after the war, the European nations would attempt to seize the world's gold supply, stored in New York. To combat this threat, the United States needed a force of a million men and a massive naval appropriation and must store incoming bullion in a vault west of the Alleghenies.[48]

On August 4, 1915, a new organization, the American Defense Society (ADS), was organized. Like the National Security League, the ADS called for a larger army and navy. Unlike the NSL, the ADS directly attacked Wilson, Garrison, and Daniels. Stanwood Menken, a corporation attorney, a nominal Democrat, and the League president, had forbidden his NSL to distribute literature critical of the president. In protest, George Smedley Thompson, the NSL publicity director, met with other Wilson foes, including Hudson Maxim, *Outlook* editor Lyman Abbott, and former naval secretaries Charles J. Bonaparte and George von L. Meyer. Their goal: to create a new and more militant association. Thompson believed that German sympathizers had infiltrated the NSL and were attempting to hinder the whole preparedness movement. (Menken's wife Gretchen was a German American). Perhaps more important, the NSL had just cut Thompson's salary in half.

Elon Hooker, president of Hooker Electrochemical and a Roosevelt Progressive, chaired the ADS. Theodore Roosevelt, who thought the NSL too nonpartisan, stood most prominent among the ADS advisory board members and later became honorary president. His second cousin Philip edited its monthly, *American Defense.* Other prominent board members included Maxim; Bonaparte; Princeton president John Grier Hibben; former diplomat David Jayne Hill; former congressman Perry Belmont (D-N.Y.), vice president of the Navy League; and Henry B. Joy, president of Packard Motor and the Navy League's vice president. Advice also came from retired rear admiral Bradley Fiske, inventor Lee De Forest, naval historian and illustrator Henry Reuterdahl, former diplomat and Morgan partner Robert Bacon, and a son of Admiral Mahan.[49]

Despite ADS's prestigious backing, its launching proved most difficult. Recruitment was slow, the prestige of the advisory board was ignored, and Roosevelt's name did not elicit the expected contributions. Its professional fund-raiser turned out to be a confidence man, who was fired amid considerable bickering. Essentially it served as the Republican branch of the National Security League, concentrating on opposing Wilson. The ADS defection did not significantly harm the NSL, which by December 1915 boasted thirty thousand members and seventy branches, with particularly strong chapters in Chicago and St. Louis. By the end of 1916, one hundred thousand Americans had joined. The NSL received the endorsement of at least twenty-two governors and fifty mayors, including New York's reformist mayor, John Purroy Mitchel.[50]

From August 10 to 16, twelve hundred upper-class volunteers began training at Plattsburg, a small town on Lake Champlain near the Canadian border. The camp was modeled on ones created by Leonard Wood at Gettysburg and Monterey in 1913, but this one drew more conspicuously from America's elite. Among those enrolled were a Morgan partner, the football coach of Harvard, the leader of the Philadelphia bar, the mayor and police commissioner of New York, and three sons and a cousin of Theodore Roosevelt. Most participants were in their thirties and forties, although a few were older. Many came from the Middle Atlantic and New England and were recruited from elite colleges and clubs of the East Coast. Half hailed from Harvard, which outdrew the number from Yale because, according to Roosevelt, "the middle classes are not naturally gallant."[51] Each participant paid one hundred dollars to go though thirty-five days of drill, marches, and various maneuvers. Leonard Wood, booted in spurs and sporting a dog-headed riding crop, supervised the training. Robert Bacon, once briefly secretary of state, acted as a sergeant, obeying the orders of his son, a first lieutenant. The Episcopal bishop of Rhode Island suddenly became a mere private. Not unexpectedly, most trainees were strongly pro-Entente. Within a month similar camps operated at San Francisco's Presidio; Fort Sheridan, Chicago; and American Lake, Washington State.

Training was not easy. In the words of historian John Garry Clifford, Plattsburg involved "a good deal more than Marie Antoinette playing milkmaid." Exercises began at 5:45 A.M., followed by calisthenics and drill. After lunch volunteers received training in one of the army's special branches—cavalry, engineering, artillery, or signal corps. The preparation ended with a nine-day hike during which one toted a pack weighing forty-two pounds. Overall the program aimed far less at producing qualified officers, something most difficult given time constraints, than at promoting a more "manly" and democratic spirit, thereby fostering a kind of social regeneration. Moreover, the Plattsburg program could act as the entering wedge for universal military training. Though never endorsing such a policy, in mid-August Wilson praised the Plattsburg concept, congratulating Wood on its success.[52]

Such preparedness measures, TR believed, could transform the nation. Military training assimilated immigrants, rationalized industries, and fostered a militant nationalism. It might stimulate overdue social reforms, uniting the causes of patriotism and progressivism. As John Patrick Finnegan writes: "The proposals which had frightened businessmen at Ossawatomie," the Kansas town where Roosevelt launched his radical progressive agenda in 1910, "now could be put forward as simple necessities for the home front."[53]

Suddenly and inadvertently, General Wood interjected politics into the program, for on August 25 he invited Roosevelt to address the volunteers. "For thirteen months," said the former president to some four thousand people, "America has played an ignoble part among the nations." He went on to attack "college sissies," men with "mean souls," and "mere money-getters and mere money-spenders." While praising loyal Americans of German descent, he deemed "the professional German-American" an "enemy to his country as well as to humanity." While speaking, he saw a wire-haired Airedale terrier roll over on his back, his paws ingratiatingly limp in the air. "That's a very nice dog," Roosevelt commented. "I like him—his present attitude is strictly one of neutrality." Wood had warned Roosevelt to be discreet and carefully edited the speech, but Roosevelt's secretary released an unexpurgated copy to the press. Just before leaving the camp, Roosevelt was even more stinging, telling reporters that Americans should stand by the president "only so long as the President stands by the nation." High-sounding words could never replace actual deeds, he went on, such activity being "proof of a mind that dwells only in the realm of shadow and of shame."[54]

The next day Garrison wired Wood, rebuking the general for allowing Roosevelt to air such controversial issues at a government training camp. When Wood remained silent, Roosevelt rushed to the general's rescue, telling the press that he took full responsibility for his remarks. TR being TR, he could not let matters go without accusing the administration of countenancing "the murder of American men, women, and children" on the high seas and of condoning continued upheaval in Mexico. On August 27, the former president again took the offensive: he accused Garrison of practicing "buffoonery" and the Wilson administration of using "peculiarly mean and unfair" methods against Wood. Also in late August, Roosevelt wrote his son Kermit, calling Wilson "this infernal skunk in the White House," either "at heart an abject coward" or one "entirely willing to sacrifice the honor and interest of the country to his own political advancement."[55]

Much of the press criticized the former president. The *Chicago Tribune,* usually a strong Roosevelt supporter, called the attack on the commander in chief a "lesson in insubordination."[56]

Antipreparedness forces struck back at their foes. To Bryan, the "same old gang" of reactionaries and plutocrats had adopted "the same old tactics" of stifling reform and reaping profits. Congressman Clyde H. Tavenner asserted that "war trafficking firms" sought self-enrichment while jeopardizing the peace of 10 million people. Some in Congress offered alternatives to rearmament. Senator La Follette, for example, sought to nationalize munition manufacturing, saying: "We can take away from private interest all incentive to increase army and navy appropriation bills."[57]

Covert operations emanating from the German embassy did little to ease tensions. Trouble first arose when the embassy forged American passports for German reservists residing in the United States. Had these men attempted to return home on their own passports, the British would have taken them off passenger ships and interned them. The German military, therefore, considered such forgeries justifiable, even if the activity violated U.S. law. American authorities were undoubtedly relieved at the departure of people who might pose a danger if the United States severed relations with Germany. Hence, they never confronted Berlin over the matter.

The Wilson administration was less aware of the curious purchase of the *New York Evening Mail* in April 1915. Bought for $1.3 million by a syndicate of German American businessmen backed by Berlin, it hid its true ownership. Edward Rumely, an Indiana manufacturer of diesel tractors, acted on the combine's behalf and became publisher. Educated in Germany, Rumely strongly supported the Central Powers and the cause of Irish freedom. Ironically, the noted muckraker S.S. McClure, who was genuinely pro-British, was appointed editor. To keep its credibility, the *Mail* found itself forced to mute its pro-German bias, so much so that even its own staff did not know who really controlled the journal.

Similar activities became known to the public only when, on the afternoon of July 23, 1915, Treasury Department agent Frank Burke seized the briefcase of Heinrich F. Albert, a commercial official of the German embassy, on an elevated train in Manhattan. Immediately aware of the theft, he chased Burke but could not nab him. Secret Service chief William J. Flynn, Treasury Secretary McAdoo, and President Wilson quickly learned of propagandistic news leaks; encouragement of strikes; an attempt to corner the market in liquid chlorine, used in making poison gas; subsidies to Viereck's *Fatherland* and to German American and Irish American organizations; and efforts to rally Texans angry at Britain's cotton restrictions.

The administration leaked the incriminating evidence to the *New York World,* which began publishing the documents on August 15. A militantly pro-Wilson paper, the *World* accused Berlin of "fomenting internal discord among the American people to the advantage of the German empire." Other newspapers voiced anger. In a private letter, Roosevelt predictably labeled the incident proof that Wilson ("a physically timid man") "intended to favor Germany as much as he safely could." He continued: "It has been only the successive brutalities of the Germans which have prevented him from throwing his weight on their side and against the Allies." The *Nation* struck a different note, finding that the documents revealed "extraordinary stupidity" but no conspiracy. Disapproving of the theft, it said: "The *World* must square with its own conscience their publication."[58]

Viereck countered that he had done nothing "incompatible with my integrity as a publicist or my loyalty as an American citizen." Claiming that his weekly was totally independent, he cited a purloined letter dated July 1, 1915, in which Albert specifically denied that Berlin exercised any influence over the *Fatherland.* Later, though, Viereck compared the incident to Germany's losses on the Marne River. Albert, the prime culprit, defended Berlin's publicity campaign and denied engaging in illegal action.[59]

Legally, none of the described activities violated American neutrality. Nonetheless, to the public, Germany appeared guilty of surreptitious efforts to weaken the United States at a time when diplomatic relations remained tense. Henceforth, even legitimate efforts to present the German case became increasingly suspect.

A similar exposé caused the Central Powers even more embarrassment. On August 30, the Holland-American liner *Rotterdam,* which had left New York seven days before, arrived at Falmouth, England. British agents arrested James F.J. Archibald, an American war correspondent employed by the German Embassy. A search of his stateroom showed that he was carrying documents to officials in Berlin and Vienna, though he denied knowledge of their contents. Among them was a handwritten letter from Dr. Konstantin Theodor Dumba, Austro-Hungarian ambassador to the United States, to his foreign minister, Count Stephan Burián. The emissary boasted that he could "very much disorganize the manufacture of munitions at Bethlehem [Pennsylvania] and in the Middle West and hold it up for months. . . . These white slaves now work at Bethlehem for twelve hours a day on seven days of the week! All the weaklings go under and get consumption." Appealing for funds to expedite his scheme, he promised "a means of escape" for such workmen through an already existing "private German employment bureau." [60]

Other documents were equally damning. Burián had instructed Dumba to warn Austro-Hungarian subjects living in America that it was an act of treason, punishable by imprisonment or death by hanging, to work in any factory that manufactured war matériel for enemies of the Hapsburg Empire. Another letter, written by Martin Diennes, a New York correspondent for a Hungarian-American newspaper in Cleveland, revealed a scheme to foster strikes in munition and steel-making factories from Chicago to Bethlehem, Pennsylvania. The foreign-language press, paid agitators, bribed union officials—all could serve the cause. Also captured was a missive of Franz von Papen, a German military attaché and future chancellor, to his wife, in which he remarked: "I always say to these idiotic Yankees that they had better hold their tongues." [61]

Within a week, news of these documents reached the American public, provoking popular anger. Possessing an absolute genius for bad judgment, Dumba admitted that he had subsidized foreign-language newspapers. More significantly, he told reporters: "There are thousands of workingmen in the big steel industries, natives of Bohemia, Moravia, Carniola, Galicia, Dalmatia, Croatia, Slavonia, and other peoples of the races from Austria-Hungary, who are uneducated and do not understand that they are engaged in a work against their own country." He added: "a peaceful walkout of these workingmen would be of the greatest advantage to my Government." At one point, he asked the American government to find alternative employment for such laborers so as to stop "no end of misery to my countrymen and prevent trouble and unrest in the labour conditions of this country." [62]

In meeting with Dumba on September 7, Lansing questioned the propriety of employing an American citizen to carry official dispatches through enemy lines. On the following day, Wilson demanded the ambassador's recall, writing Burián that Dumba sought "to cripple the legitimate industries of the people of the United States and to interrupt their legitimate trade." Upon departing the United States, Dumba remained unrepentant, informing Colonel House: "As to the unfortunate incident which is the cause of my departure I was certainly wrong, because I made the mistake of being found out." [63]

The American press supported the Wilson administration. The *Outlook* conceded that Austria possessed the right to circulate such a proclamation openly among its nonnaturalized citizens but stated that, according to international law, an ambassador could not do so. The *New Republic* saw Vienna advancing a form of extraterritoriality "which Turkey has repudiated and even China resents." Bryan, usually conciliatory toward the Central Powers, denied that the ambassador enjoyed "the confidence necessary for a proper discharge of his duties."[64]

Viereck remained one of the few holdouts, asserting that Dumba's "impropriety" was merely technical. In fact, Dumba had done no more than an American ambassador would in a parallel situation. Suppose, the German American editor mused, the United States was fighting Japan and certain ammunition plants in Austria, that were supplying the Japanese, employed American citizens; such American employees would be committing treason. And why, asked Berlin defender Frederick F. Schrader, did not Henry Van Dyke, U.S. minister to Holland, protest when the British seized Archibald, an American citizen, on a neutral vessel and deprived him of his belongings? Instead, Van Dyke, "a notorious German baiter," canceled Archibald's pass, sending him home as a prisoner for carrying a sealed message from the Austrian ambassador.[65]

Despite continued discord with the Central Powers, the *Lusitania* controversy appeared to wane. On July 29 Bethmann indicated to Gerard that Germany might submit the question of an indemnity to the Hague Tribunal.[66] In August Wilson hinted at arbitration, stressed that he would not insist on an immediate apology and reparation, and invited Germany to join him in advancing freedom of the seas. The safety of U.S. citizens traveling on belligerent ships remained the only sticking point.

At the same time, enmity grew with Britain. On July 23, finally replying to Washington's note of March 30, London yielded no ground concerning the blockade, much to the chagrin of the American press. Lansing called British behavior "indefensible and beyond belief."[67]

And on August 19, tensions with Germany drastically increased when, at 9:15 A.M., *U-24* sunk the British White Star liner *Arabic* in eleven minutes. Traveling from Liverpool to New York, the *Arabic* went down just a few miles from the spot where the *Lusitania* had been struck. Though the massive vessel ranked as the heaviest carrier of contraband in the North Atlantic, this voyage was far more innocent, the cargo consisting primarily of mail. More than four hundred passengers and crew were rescued, but forty-four people were killed, among them two Americans. *U-24*'s commander gave no warning.

The Germans argued that the *Arabic* lacked identification marks. When the U-boat approached the liner, they claimed, the *Arabic* altered course and headed directly for the submarine, thus giving the commander good grounds for fearing an attack. Four days previously a large passenger steamer, apparently belonging to the British Royal Mail Steam Packet Company, had fired on the German submarine. Bernstorff later maintained that *U-24*'s commander was ignorant of German orders, issued immediately after the *Lusitania* had been torpedoed, not to sink liners without warning and assuring protection to noncombatants.[68]

The crisis could well have been the most serious yet, as Germany was defying American warnings and continuing to violate neutral rights. The American press was furious; some newspapers demanded the recall of Ambassador Gerard. The *Nation* viewed the sinking of the *Arabic* as even less excusable than that of the *Lusitania;* in the *Arabic* case, the ship was sailing westward and carried no munitions. The ever-strident *North American Review* asserted: "No war of Israel was so righteous as that which is being waged at this moment for Freedom of the World." The *Fatherland* responded that an American note protesting the British blockade "would have stopped the torpedo that struck the *Arabic*."[69]

Wilson's two leading advisers sought to break diplomatic relations. The American public and Allied leaders, House warned the president, would interpret further notes as a sign of weakness. "I would begin preparations for defence and for war," he went on, labeling the Germans "bloody-thirsty monsters." Lansing, too, welcomed a conflict, though he did concede that it would lack popular support. He assured Wilson that war would restore the "friendship and confidence" of the Entente. When the war ended, the United States could foster a lenient peace. Wilson claimed to concur with Lansing, saying that his thought ran "very much along the same lines."[70]

For a week the president remained calm, fully aware that he might have to sever ties with Germany. When Ambassador Page urged him to demand satisfaction, Wilson wrote Edith Bolling Galt that his emissary needed to "visit his native land" so as to absorb genuinely American views. Even if the *Arabic* sinking did produce "the final parting of the ways," he would convene a conference of neutral nations, one seeking to defend freedom of the seas against both sets of belligerents. "The people of this country rely upon me to keep them out of war," he told his fiancée. Entering the conflict would be "the worst thing that could possibly happen *to the world*," for the United

States would "lose all chance of moderating the results of the war by her counsel as an outsider."[71]

To add to the president's anxiety, on August 21 Britain took advantage of the *Arabic* crisis to declare cotton contraband, though it wisely bought a quantity sufficiently large to alleviate major discontent. By the end of October, cotton prices surpassed the prewar level of over twelve cents a pound.

On August 22, Wilson leaked his position to the press: Germany could retain diplomatic relations only by disavowing the sinking and assuring the safety of passenger ships. On the following day, in writing to Edith Galt, he conceded that Bryan's strictures on Americans traveling on belligerent ships might well be "reasonable and practical." "It is not," however, "the doctrine of international law, and we must base our claims of right on the undoubted practice of nations,—for which Germany is showing such crass and brutal contempt."[72]

Within five days, Lansing, acting without Wilson's authorization, informed Bernstorff that unless Berlin refrained from further attacks on passenger ships, the United States would certainly declare war. Robert W. Tucker notes that Wilson would not have gone that far, for he did not equate breaking relations with armed conflict. "Lansing was considerably in front of Wilson," writes Tucker. "He knew this, yet he acted." Conversely, another authority, Arthur Walworth, finds the secretary of state tacitly allowing a graceful withdrawal. If tensions led to an absolute break, it would not have been the president himself who made any threat.[73]

Germany was not ready to call anyone's bluff. On August 24, Foreign Secretary Jagow privately told Ambassador Gerard that if the U-boat commander had not warned the *Arabic,* he had violated his instructions. A day later, a German Imperial Conference met at Pless Castle, a residence of the Kaiser located in the Silesian hills. Tirpitz spoke for the admirals in warning against further concession to America. General Erich von Falkenhayn, the army's supreme commander, replied that the United States remained a most formidable foe. Furthermore, an expanded war risked severing relations with such neutral nations as Denmark, the Netherlands, Switzerland, Greece, Bulgaria, and Rumania. During the past six months, he maintained, submarine warfare had proved itself ineffective against Britain. On August 25 Chancellor Bethmann issued a formal statement promising America "complete satisfaction" if Germany had wantonly sunk the ship.[74]

Seven days later, on September 1, Bethmann and Jagow authorized Bernstorff to issue what is known as the *Arabic* pledge. They instructed the ambassador to tell Lansing privately: "Liners will not be sunk by our submarines without warning and without safety of the lives of noncombatants, provided that the liners do not try to escape or offer resistance." Indeed, Bernstorff told Lansing, the new policy had been decided before the *Arabic* was sunk. Bernstorff made the note public, for which the German Foreign Office reprimanded him. Only by publicizing the new policy, the ambassador believed, could Germany convince the American people of its good intentions.[75]

The Kaiser, probably at Bethmann's insistence, ordered German U-boats away from England's west coast, rendering them virtually impotent. When Tirpitz again protested, Wilhelm responded: "America must be prevented from taking part against us as an active enemy. She could provide unlimited money for our foes. . . . What I do with my navy is my business *only*."[76]

Never was Wilson so popular. The press responded with great enthusiasm, the *Literary Digest* carrying an article titled "Germany Yields to Wilson." Bryan congratulated the president but still stressed the duty of American citizens to avoid the war zone. Even Theodore Roosevelt called the results "most gratifying," although he remained cautious as to Germany's future intentions. The *New Republic* did not concur with the self-congratulatory tone, noting that Berlin still had not taken responsibility for the *Arabic*'s sinking. Unless more satisfactory explanations were forthcoming, Wilson should recall Gerard and send Bernstorff home. The *Fatherland* wryly remarked: "Victorious on every front Germany could afford to be generous." Now, it continued, Wilson must send an ultimatum to London.[77]

Amid the euphoria, tension with Berlin remained. Germany had given the *Arabic* pledge most reluctantly. The commitment applied solely to passenger vessels; the note did not mention merchantmen. Would armed merchant or passenger ships receive protection? Germany reserved the right to revoke its order if it believed that conditions required it. Wilson wrote Mrs. Galt on September 3: "I tremble a little bit over this 'triumph.'"[78] During the coming winter, however, Germany did not sink any more liners without warning.

In reality the *Arabic* matter was far from closed. On September 7 Jagow defended the sinking, asserting that the submarine commander believed that the liner was about to ram him. Therefore, Berlin would pay no indemnity, even if the skipper's fear proved invalid. Historian Patrick Devlin muses that although the U-boat's log had not mentioned any attempted attack, it might have been politically impossible for the German Foreign Office to challenge the word of a naval officer, much less repudiate it in public.[79]

Once Americans learned of Jagow's position, they were furious. Many editors demanded a showdown. Both Wilson and Lansing thought that the German reply made a mockery of the *Arabic* pledge. The secretary recommended a final break.[80]

The sinking of the *Hesperian* increased tensions. On September 4, at 8:30 P.M., about fifty miles west of Queenstown, Ireland, a German submarine torpedoed the passenger liner *Hesperian,* a Canadian ship bound for Montreal from Liverpool. The *Hesperian* made no attempt to fire upon or ram the attacking submarine. U-boat captain Schwieger, who had previously sunk the *Lusitania,* ordered the attack because he thought that the *Hesperian,* which bore a six-inch gun astern, was an auxiliary cruiser. The ship stayed afloat for thirty-four hours, but 8 of the 650 people on board were apparently killed. The sole American traveler was unharmed.

The German Admiralty and Foreign Office argued that the *Hesperian* could well have struck a mine, for no submarines were in the vicinity. Jagow told Gerard that Germany would not respond to any requests for a report, for, unless American lives were lost, it was none of the United States' business.[81]

Officials in Washington correctly doubted Berlin's rationale, but they lacked proof. On September 7, Wilson wrote House: "Shall we ever get out of the labarynth [*sic*] made for us by all this German 'frightfulness'?" Just over two weeks later, the president informed the colonel that America might well have to participate in the war, particularly if Germany was winning the conflict.[82]

Much of the press questioned the German explanation. The mere mounting of a gun for defense, declared the *New Republic,* did not deprive a peaceful merchant ship of immunity. The *Fatherland* accused the British themselves of sinking the *Arabic* and the *Hesperian* in order to embroil the United States in conflict with Germany.[83]

On September 27, Jagow told his ambassador that the commander who sank the *Arabic* had ample reason for his fears. Nonetheless, acting out of friendship, Germany would pay an indemnity for the death of the two drowned Americans. On October 5, again acting on his own authority, Bernstorff mentioned the indemnity and told Lansing: "The Imperial Government regrets and disavows this act." Berlin had instructed the ambassador to make his apology conditional on British behavior, but he did not do so. As the ambassador had exceeded his instructions, the Foreign Office privately rebuked him. He had put his own position in jeopardy to satisfy Washington. In addition, Jagow—in a sense—"disavowed Bernstorff's disavowal," but with such ambivalence that Washington did not recognize the shift. Certainly Germany wanted no further confrontation over the matter.[84]

American editors hailed the ambassador's note to Lansing. The *Literary Digest* titled its lead story "America's Diplomatic Victory," as it reported the many commendations of Wilson's handling of the crisis. The *Nation*'s editorial heralded "A Great Controversy Ended." House wrote an unimpressed Page that Wilson had gained "the greatest diplomatic triumph of this generation." Furthermore, Washington would not use the *Hesperian* incident to jeopardize the *Arabic* settlement. In his first *Lusitania* note, Wilson had emphasized the safety of "unarmed merchantmen," a matter on which the Germans had given way. Both Wilson and Lansing realized that the British were not merely arming merchantmen but using them offensively and perhaps illegally. The American press manifested little support for any confrontation over ships that were armed.[85]

Several historians have praised Wilson's handling of the *Arabic* crisis. Link lauds his endless patience and subtle use of diplomatic pressure. To Devlin the president was neither too threatening nor too passive: "Wilson played his hand just right." A bit more critical, Tucker finds this particular success mostly due to Lansing's intransigence, which, the historian claims, frightened Berlin. Tucker adds that Wilson remained locked in the rigid neutrality policy he had declared months earlier.[86]

Efforts at negotiated settlement, debates over preparedness, German subversion, incidents on the high seas—these matters intensified throughout 1915 and well into the following year.

5

Frustrating Times
August 1915–March 1916

On August 19, 1915, seventy miles off Queenstown, Ireland, at about three in the afternoon, the German submarine *U-27* halted the British mule steamer *Nicosian*. Acting in accordance with the rules of international law, the U-boat was waiting for the *Nicosian*'s crew to evacuate, when a vessel that appeared to be a tramp steamer, flying the American flag, approached. Once the oncoming vessel reached within one hundred yards of the submarine, it hoisted the English flag, opened fire, and immediately sank it. In reality the supposed rescue craft was a British "Mystery Ship" or "Q-boat," a decoy ship named *Baralong*. Eleven German sailors were shot as they floundered in the ocean and sought refuge on the *Nicosian*. The *Nicosian*'s crew murdered the U-boat captain in the water while his hands were raised in surrender. Within ten days, several of the forty-five American "muleteers" on board the *Nicosian* revealed what had transpired.[1]

"Isn't this one of the most unspeakable performances?" asked Wilson upon hearing the news. "It's horrible." Lansing ruled Britain's behavior "shocking," though he did not lodge a protest, claiming that the affidavits of the ten or so American muleteers conflicted in some details. Such use of the American flag, the State Department maintained, had occurred during previous wars; the United States had engaged in this practice.[2]

London quickly defended the *Baralong*'s action. The ship, it said, was merely a defensively armed steamer, although it possessed twelve-pound guns and was commissioned in the British Navy. Foreign Secretary Grey curtly remarked: "The British Government does not think it necessary to make reply to the suggestion that the British navy has been guilty of inhumanity." Britain did propose that an impartial tribunal of American naval officers

investigate the affair. Such a probe, however, must include three other incidents as well, one being the *Arabic,* another involving a German destroyer
alleged to have fired on the crew of a British submarine off the Danish coast.
The German government rejected the proposal.[3] To Berlin, "playing by the
rules" had proven futile.

Certain Allied seizures appeared particularly outrageous. On October
31 a prize crew from a British warship brought the steamer *Hocking,* headed
from New York to Norfolk, into Halifax, Nova Scotia. Just about that time
a British cruiser forcefully searched the *Zealandia.* Bound from Pensacola to
Tampico, it was seized just off Progreso, a port in Yucatán. In autumn the
British detained another ship, the *Genesee,* at St. Lucia; it was carrying coal
from Norfolk to Montevideo. One boat, the *Kankakee,* ended up at Port
Stanley in the Falkland Islands. Similarly, in December the French confiscated the *Saginaw* at Marseilles. British men-of-war chased the *Vineland,* an
American cargo ship of Danish registry, as it sailed from New York to Norfolk; the craft escaped its pursuers. In mid-December the Marquis of Crewe,
Lord President of the Council, blatantly told the British House of Lords that
his government sought to starve Germany: "There is no difference from the
point of view of humanity in besieging a city and besieging a country."[4]

In October Hearst's *New York American,* admittedly a neutralist newspaper, expressed great anger, declaring that London had no right "to confiscate
our beef cargoes, to make our cotton contraband, to seize our ships bound
to neutral ports, to restrict our trade, suppress our commerce and limit our
free rights upon the seas—all of which things she has done without warrant
of international law." Americans suspected Britain of deliberately enticing
Americans to travel on its ships so as to create a crisis with Germany. One
advertisement in a New York newspaper ran: "Help Wanted—Male. Men
feeding horses to France receive pay and return transportation; American
and British only. Greenwich Agency."[5]

Wilson now decided that he could not press American claims against
Germany and Britain simultaneously. Though Wilson and Lansing in private had expressed support for the Allies, they increasingly thought it necessary to challenge British behavior. On October 21, Lansing, acting under
administration pressure, sent Grey such a sweeping indictment that he
risked breaking off further relations. Admittedly, the note made no retaliatory threats and maintained that it acknowledged the "legitimate" prerogatives of British sea power. Nevertheless, the missive accused London of
seriously violating international law and indeed took on the entire British

maritime system, clearly implying that the resumption of cordial relations dependent upon its modification. Britain stood accused of violating promises concerning America's commercial rights. It searched ships in port when they should have been examined at sea and detained neutral cargoes even if it lacked proof concerning an enemy destination. The secretary considered the blockade legally invalid because it could not be enforced. Besides, it discriminated against the United States while leaving certain German ports on the Baltic Sea open to Danish, Norwegian, and Swedish trade. In short, London's activity was "ineffective, illegal, and indefensible."[6]

Historian John Milton Cooper Jr. labels the note "a typical Lansing production, fifty-five pages that alternated between copious legal citations and truculently worded accusations that the British were using the blockade as a cloak for advancing their own economic interests." Arthur S. Link is more positive: the communication embodied a powerful protest, one that involved "a fair warning from one friend to another to expect no benevolent neutrality, no special help or favors." With this message, "the construction of the edifice of American neutrality was finally completed."[7]

Within three weeks American editors learned of Lansing's protest. They strongly backed the administration, while voicing skepticism that the protest would produce any results. Even the pro-British *Outlook* called Lansing's message "sound, well reasoned, just, and courteous," but the weekly could not help asking why Germany had not received a similar note of protest when it invaded Belgium. Bryan considered the dispatch sound, though he vaguely added that the United States might need to "resort to force" after the war ended. Ambassador Page was much in the minority in calling the message "an uncourteous monster of 35 heads and 3 appendices." Lansing himself confidentially told Frederick Dixon, editor of the *Christian Science Monitor,* that the note served as "a political safety valve, [and] not much was expected of it, as it would certainly not be pressed."[8] Aware of the secretary's tactics, London would not budge.

In the summer of 1915, the Allies needed additional credit to pay for continuing war contracts. In July Britain experienced a flight from the pound; its efforts to rush gold across the Atlantic and sell American securities offered no lasting solution. A month later, in a letter to Wilson, Treasury Secretary McAdoo implied that Britain, "our best customer," was underwriting America's agricultural boom and, by its munition purchases, the nation's industry as well. "Our prosperity is dependent on our continued and enlarged foreign trade," which in turn relied on America's financing of this affluence; the alternative would be "disastrous." Early in September Lansing warned that if Europe lacked the ability to pay for American goods, the nation would face a most serious financial situation: "restriction of outputs, industrial depression, idle capital and idle labor, numerous failures, financial demoralization, and general unrest and suffering among the laboring classes."[9] By September American exporters were terrified to see the purchasing power of their best customer disappear.

On September 10, an Anglo-French financial mission, headed by Lord Chief Justice Reading, arrived in New York in search of a $1 billion loan. The sum would be used to purchase such American supplies as munitions, breadstuffs, meat, cotton, wool, and leather. The commission was not prepared to pledge collateral, claiming that the general credit of both nations was sufficient. A bit apprehensive, it noted that Wall Street, sensitive to public opinion, was reluctant to market bonds of belligerent nations. "Sympathy makes the door easy to open," reported Reading to the British Treasury, "but once inside finance looks to hard facts."[10] Nevertheless, on October 15, a nationwide banking syndicate headed by J.P. Morgan and Company underwrote an unsecured Anglo-French loan of $500 million. Bonds would mature in five years and bear 5 percent interest. Proceeds would be applied solely to pay British and French trade balances in the United States. The Allies grumbled over the interest rate but speedily acquiesced, realizing that the loan buttressed their credit amid a financial crisis and linked American material interests with their own.

Some investors were motivated by pro-Ally sentiments, which had been strengthened after the recent sinking of the *Lusitania* and the *Arabic*. Others deemed the loan essential to sustain the rising volume of exports. To many, the Allies possessed a strong financial reputation and were bound to win the war. These individuals had press opinion on their side, for after a year of hostilities, a *Literary Digest* poll conducted in August revealed that most editors predicted that in the long run the Entente would emerge victorious, though they did judge the immediate conflict a virtual stalemate.[11]

Opponents of the loan offered predictable criticism. Foes found the loan inhuman, prolonging the war. It violated Wilson's call to be neutral "in spirit." It was a poor credit risk, or at the very least of doubtful merit. It would simply benefit bankers and, borrowing the phrase of jurist Louis D. Brandeis, the "Money Trust." It would enrich munition firms at the expense of more useful industries. It would deprive the nation of capital needed at home. It would channel funds to war-torn Europe at a time when investments would be more productive in such underdeveloped regions as Latin America. The *New York Times* responded by accusing loan opponents of sacrificing American prosperity because of "sentimental attachment" to foreign lands.[12]

German Americans sought to abort the loan by creating a run on major banks, but their credibility was questioned because they promoted imperial bonds themselves. By the end of 1915, U.S. investors bought $10 million worth of such securities. Despite accusations within America that Morgan was serving as Britain's lackey, London in turn believed that the Wall Street giant was both greedy and arrogant.

As far as immediate results went, the bonds found few buyers. Significant purchases were made only in the East, the center of industry and shipping. Underwriters were forced to assume 60 percent of the amount. In time, though, the loan marked America's rise as the world's leading creditor.

Anger against Britain did not imply support for the Central Powers. In Brussels on October 12, a German firing squad executed a middle-aged British nurse, Edith Cavell, who was accused of helping British and French prisoners of war escape to neutral Holland. Cavell freely admitted that she had used her clinic to shelter Allied soldiers lost behind enemy lines and thereby expedited their flight. She obviously abused her immunity as a Red Cross worker, thus betraying a trust, though she never conducted these troops to safety. Amid outcry from the neutral press, Berlin added to its own denunciation, falsely stating that she smuggled dynamite with which to blow up bridges.

The American press denounced the execution. The *Nation,* for example, wrote of "this pure and good woman" who fell victim to Germany's "brutal callousness." German Americans followed Berlin's lead in accusing Cavell of spying. Frederick F. Schrader's *Handbook for German Americans* claimed that she headed "a widespread organization" that helped hundreds of prisoners to escape. Viereck and Schrader argued that Germany had simply followed Allied precedent, citing the execution of one Julia Van Wauterghem in mid-August 1915 at Louvain and two other German women that March. Herman Ridder regretted that the German commanders had not taken her case to the Kaiser, who probably would have pardoned her.[13]

Turkey's behavior caused the Central Powers even greater embarrassment. The Ottoman Empire, embittered because of heavy losses on the Caucasus Front, accused the Armenian population of assisting the Russian invaders. Beginning in mid-April 1915 and continuing for several months, the Turks executed hundreds of thousands of Armenian civilians. The Committee on Armenian Atrocities was organized, headed by Professor Samuel Train Dutton of Columbia University Teachers College. Members included such prominent figures as New York rabbi Stephen S. Wise; William W. Rockhill, former ambassador to Turkey and Russia; Oscar S. Straus, once secretary of commerce and labor and ambassador to Turkey; business leader Cleveland H. Dodge; and John R. Mott, general secretary of the Young Men's Christian Association. After examining testimony from Armenians, Turks, Bulgarians, Greeks, and other nationalities, the committee concluded that a half million Armenians either had been murdered or had faced certain death in the desert. In its report dated October 3, the committee accused the Turks of engaging in outright extermination; nothing in the past thousand years equaled these persecutions.[14]

To the *New Republic,* the Armenian plight revealed the degree to which the war makers "let loose anarchy in all the ends of the earth." Hearst's *New York American* accused the Turks of conducting "wholesale massacre" of the region's Christians. The *Fatherland* deemed such charges "fictitious," referring to Armenian "conspirators" who betrayed Turkey to the Russians. The United States, the weekly asserted, was acting hypocritically because it had not protested czarist persecution of the Jews.[15]

Far greater tension arose on November 7 when the German *U-38,* flying the Austrian flag, sank the Italian ship *Ancona* near Sardinia. Sailing from Naples to New York, the liner carried 412 passengers, mostly in steerage, and 160 crew members. Of 27 lives lost, 9 were Americans. Survivors accused the submarine commander of firing numerous volleys as passengers attempted to flee.

A week later the Austrian Admiralty asserted that the *Ancona* had ignored a warning shot and sought to escape. The submarine commander claimed to have seen a potentially hostile vessel approaching and therefore felt forced to torpedo the ship. Even though *U-38* gave the passengers forty-five minutes to leave, some refused to do so, and the crew cared merely for its own survival.[16] Vienna did not acknowledge that the U-boat was a German ship, not an Austrian one, and only later did the United States become aware of its true identity.

Though the American press debated whether the nationality of the offending submarine was Austrian or German, it believed that the attack was a savage one, hauntingly reminiscent of the *Lusitania.* The *Outlook* asked whether the Wilson administration would call Austria to account or simply resume its "long correspondence." The *Fatherland* blamed the deaths on the

Ancona's skipper, who supposedly ignored orders to stop, and the American government, which had not warned Americans against traveling on belligerent vessels.[17]

Lansing and House pressed the matter. Acting on the assumption that the submarine was German, not Austrian, Lansing warned Bernstorff on November 17 that American opinion was sufficiently irate to seek a declaration of war. House desired to sever relations with Austria immediately, though he believed that the Central Powers would "now do almost anything to keep from an open rupture."[18]

Wilson sought to maintain peaceful relations, but on December 6 he permitted Lansing—unthinkingly, according to Link—to send a virtual ultimatum to Vienna. Demanding an indemnity, prompt disavowal, and punishment of the U-boat captain, the secretary practically accused the Austrians of murder. Within a week, House wrote Page: "We are nearer a break with the Central Powers than at any time before." On the fifteenth, Austria-Hungary's foreign minister Stephan Burián asked Lansing to prove his allegations. The secretary repeated his accusations and demands, labeling the Austrian reply "almost an insult to one's intelligence." On December 21, Lansing told Baron Erich Zwiedinek, counselor of the Austro-Hungarian Embassy: "Either the commander is guilty, or your government is guilty." A week later Lansing informed Wilson that the United States might have to sever relations with Austria, an event that would probably trigger war.[19]

On December 29, as the president tried to calm Lansing, Burián discovered a solution. Although defending the motives of the submarine commander, he promised Washington that Austria would honor the safety of passengers and crew on merchantmen. Furthermore, he pledged an indemnity and the punishment of the U-boat captain. On New Year's Day 1916, American newspapers jubilantly published the notes, praising the settlement.[20]

Nonetheless, relations with the Central Powers remained strained. On December 30, 1915, the *Persia*, an armed British liner belonging to the Peninsular and Oriental Company, was torpedoed off Crete; it sank within five minutes. Of passengers and crew lost, two were Americans, one of whom was en route to Aden as consul. Within a day the American consul at Alexandria reported that the ship carried a 4.7-inch gun. Disputes also centered on whether the ship had really been torpedoed or had suffered an internal explosion.

On January 4, Wilson, who had married Edith Bolling Galt on December 18, cut short his honeymoon at Hot Springs, Virginia, and returned to the capital. Deeming the *Persia* situation grave, he promised that the United States "will act just as soon as information is obtained." He told his secretary Joseph Tumulty that he knew the nation sought activity, "but I will not be rushed into war, no matter if every damned congressman and senator stands up on his hind legs and proclaims me a coward." Lacking sufficient knowledge, the president allowed the crisis to lapse. On January 7, Lansing, after conferring with Bernstorff, released a conciliatory statement from the German government. U-boats in the Mediterranean would sink nonresisting merchant vessels only after crew and passengers had been accorded safety.[21]

Meanwhile, the *Lusitania* matter remained unresolved. On October 2, Bernstorff met with Lansing. He gave no ground on Germany's right to sink the liner but regretted the loss of American lives and offered to submit the issue of liability to the Hague. Exactly a month later, Lansing told the ambassador that Berlin's position was unacceptable and that American public opinion demanded a quick resolution. On November 17, he warned Bernstorff that the crisis should be solved before Congress went into session; otherwise, given the "present resentment of public opinion," that body might declare war. Four days later Wilson informed Lansing: "The matter of the *Lusitania* is just as important and just as acute now as it was the day the news of her sinking arrived."[22]

The president may have been seeking a confrontation. How otherwise, ask historians Thomas A. Bailey and Paul B. Ryan, could one so sensitive to public opinion "have put down on paper the incredible miscalculation that the public had not cooled down substantially in six months"? Perhaps Lansing sought to strengthen the president's hand in the upcoming presidential elections of 1916. Possibly the secretary truly desired a break with Germany. At any rate, he had initiated what Link calls "the Second 'Lusitania' Crisis." Bailey and Ryan suggest that Wilson and Lansing actually feared that the Hague might rule that a U-boat had every right to sink ships carrying munitions, running a blockade, and possessing instructions to ram. According to the two scholars, American leaders considered justice "clearly all on the side of the United States, so why risk arbitration by foreign neutrals who might concede that the Germans had a case?"[23]

On December 20, Lansing informed Bernsdorff that national sentiment was becoming daily "more bitter. . . . This state of affairs cannot continue much longer without the gravest consequences." The pro-Allied secretary was sounding increasingly belligerent just as the Central Powers had made major gains in the Balkans. At a meeting of the German War Ministry, army chief Falkenhayn noted that Bulgaria was now allied to the Reich, Serbia lay helpless, and the road to Constantinople appeared secure. The United States, still unarmed, posed no threat should the Admiralty launch a major submarine campaign.[24]

In January 1916 Lansing became more subdued, confiding to his diary that he hoped to defer further confrontation until Americans perceived the German danger. At the same time, if Germany's "oligarchy triumphs over the liberal governments of Great Britain and France, it will then turn upon us as its next obstacle to imperial rule over the world." On the twenty-ninth, the secretary, identified simply by the press as a "high officer," told reporters: "The situation is now graver than it has been for some time—and the country has a right to know."[25]

House, writing from Europe in February, noted increasing German agitation for indiscriminate U-boat warfare and predicted an eventual showdown. Given such an outcome, the United States would be in a far more advantageous position if it avoided a controversy nine months old and that centered increasingly on the wording of an apology.[26] During a preparedness tour of the Midwest, the president found little support for confrontation with Berlin but widespread backing for challenging the British.

Germany still would not concede that the *Lusitania*'s sinking was illegal. Otherwise it was glad to accommodate the United States. On February 4 Jagow expressed "profound regret" for the suffering of American citizens, offering to make reparation. Even Lansing conceded that the foreign secretary's note came "near meeting all our demands." Within days the administration informed journalists that the crisis was over.[27] Because, however, new disputes were already arising concerning the arming of Allied merchant ships, the *Lusitania* matter remained unresolved. Never again, though, was it a matter of contention.

Tensions with Berlin centered instead on various cases of sabotage. On February 2, 1915, a German national, Werner Horn, unsuccessfully attempted to blow up a major bridge of the Canadian Pacific Railroad spanning the St. Croix River between Canada and the United States; the explosion took place near Vanceboro, Maine. Alarmed by increasing U.S. munition exports to the Allies, in April the German war ministry sent a young naval reserve officer, Commander Franz von Rintelen, to the United States. Armed with apparently unlimited funds and using numerous aliases, Rintelen set up headquarters in New York. Among his activities were attempting to destroy Canada's Welland Canal, thus severing the Great Lakes from the St.

Lawrence River; manufacturing time bombs to destroy ships at sea and munitions installations in New York harbor; forming Labor's National Peace Council, a pseudo–trade union that sought to promote wildcat strikes among longshoremen and munitions manufacturers; and spending $12 million to restore the anti-American Victoriano Huerta as dictator of Mexico. That August British security officers arrested Rintelen, then sailing to Europe on a Dutch ship, and held him as a prisoner of war. In April 1917, he was extradited to the United States, where he spent nearly four years in prison.

Because Rintelen worked closely with military attaché Franz von Papen and naval attaché Karl Boy-Ed, the German Embassy was strongly implicated in his activities. In such cities as Chicago, St. Paul, Seattle, and Detroit, Papen, who had recruited Horn, sought to organize groups of fifty to one hundred German reservists to serve as shock troops against Canada, a nation targeted in part because Japanese soldiers were passing through it on their way to European battlefields. In mid-February 1915, Bernstorff revealed his complicity; he reported back to the Foreign Office: "All preparations made for armed action with purpose of destruction of railway in case of Japanese troops." Such activity included disabling the locks of the Panama Canal if the Japanese took a southern route. Several years later the ambassador conceded that Rintelen had gravely compromised German representatives in America, affording "our enemies an excellent opportunity of inflaming public opinion."[28] In December Lansing forced the recall of Papen and Boy-Ed, accusing both attachés of improper activities. Wilson's advisers recommended similar treatment for Bernstorff, but the president deemed him indispensable to the possibility of mediation.

Germany engaged in other covert activities. A number of American steamers were destroyed at sea, at least some of the sinking undoubtedly caused by German-planted explosives. Berlin provided $3 million for detective work, $3 million for propaganda, and $2.5 million for supplying German warships. It allocated $5 million to buy the Bridgeport Projectile Company; the firm was to fill orders for Germany and, by skillful placing of orders with such firms as Aetna Powder, absorb business that might otherwise be channeled to the Allies. In July 1915 a federal court in San Francisco indicted some ninety-eight persons, including consuls, for planning to foment revolution in India. Late in October several Germans were arrested near Grantwood, New Jersey, for plotting to dynamite such installations as the New York Central and New Haven railroads; the Allis-Chalmers Company, a major manufacturer of steam engines; and the Brown-Sharpe munitions plant in Providence. The accused confessed that they were employed by the German secret service and that they reported directly to Papen and Boy-Ed. Several years later Papen remarked: "It was not exactly a quieting factor when the [American] public realized how we had been leading them by the nose."[29]

The press highlighted these activities, so much so that the *Fatherland* complained that any squelched rumor was immediately replaced by another. In November the *New York Journal of Commerce* reported about forty mysterious fires and detonations in munition plants or on ships carrying arms to the Allies, leaving a score of people dead and property losses of more than $5 million. In one week alone, there was a fire in the Thomas P. Skelly Bolt Company of Philadelphia; $1.5 million worth of damage in the Bethlehem Steel Company's ordnance plant; a fifty-five-thousand-dollar blaze in the Baldwin Locomotive Works, which built engines for the Russian government; the destruction of two buildings of the Midvale Steel and Ordnance Company, which had manufactured some 3 million Lee-Enfield rifles for the British; a $1 million fire in the Roebling steel rope plant at Trenton, which prepared wire cables for the Allies; and a blaze in the Synthetic Color Company of Stamford, Connecticut, which developed aniline dyes, a product that had recently been a German monopoly. In February 1916 a federal grand jury indicted the German consul general in San Francisco for conspiring to blow up ships and ammunition plants. He was sentenced to two years in prison. Historians Walter Millis and H.C. Peterson, writing the wake of postwar disillusionment, suggested that occupational accidents triggered some explosions. Admittedly, mishaps were a natural risk in some booming industries, but enough Germans confessed to enough crimes to confirm suspicions.[30]

By the summer of 1915, a rash of sensationalist books accused German sympathizers of participating in outright subversion. Titles included *The German-American Plot* and *German Conspiracies in America*. Howard Pitcher Okie's *America and the German Peril* described trained German American soldiers capturing the nation's coastal defenses, then turning guns on U.S. vessels as enemy troops disembarked in New York harbor.[31]

The Wilson administration was apprehensive, particularly after discovering the materials in Dr. Albert's briefcase. Early in August the president thought that the United States was "honeycombed with German intrigue and infested with German spies." House warned Wilson that Teutonic sympathizers might be engaged in armed uprising, to which the president queried where such an outbreak might take place. The colonel responded: "Attempts will likely be made to blow up waterworks, electric lights and gas plants, subways and bridges in cities like New York. . . . I do not look for any organized rebellion or outbreak, but merely some degree of frightfulness in order to intimidate the country." Yet, when McAdoo called for public denunciation of Bernstorff and his entourage of "secret agents & commercial agents," Wilson balked, warning the Treasury secretary against oversimplifying matters. Neither Lansing nor Attorney General Thomas W. Gregory wanted to pursue the issue further.[32]

German activities in Latin America also were subject to official scrutiny. Back in 1913 the State Department had acquired information concerning Berlin's effort to control Haiti's customs administration. Other rumors concerned contacts with various Mexican factions, placement of cruisers in the Caribbean, and construction of bases in the Dominican Republic and the Galápagos Islands. Possible German designs on the Danish West Indies, later named the Virgin Islands, led to American possession in late March 1917. Lansing feared that the Reich might occupy Denmark, then secure legal title to its Caribbean holding.[33]

German Americans sought to dispel suspicions concerning clandestine activities. The *Fatherland* published Germany's official denial of sabotage. The journal noted that owners of Bethlehem Steel and Du Pont powder denied any foul play in connection with recent explosions. Accusing "the entire Federal machinery" of creating an atmosphere hostile to Germans, the weekly deplored the deportations of such figures as Dumba, Papen, and Boy-Ed. "Are we secretly pledged to England?" it asked. The weekly accused pro-Allied elements of tormenting German Americans, claiming that they had assassinated a Lutheran minister in Gary, Indiana. Certain labor leaders were also vilified, as was scientist Charles P. Steinmetz, a German-born Socialist. The *Irish World* went further: the Wilson administration "persecuted" those Germans who placed explosives on trains but tolerated British passenger ships that carried munitions.[34]

Continuing international tension generated new attempts to settle the conflict. Proponents of a neutral conference took heart from the continuing military stalemate, growing war-weariness, a sense of moral responsibility for the human suffering, and conditional endorsements of the proposal from Sweden and the Netherlands.

On November 12, 1915, Stanford chancellor David Starr Jordan, a director of the American Peace Society, and Louis Lochner, now secretary of the National Peace Federation, met with Wilson. They presented petitions and resolutions calling for a conference of neutral governments. Six state governors and congressmen from fifteen states were among the signers. Jordan advocated Jane Addams's plan of continuous mediation, declaring that the neutral nations of Europe stood ready to promote this plan. The president countered that the Allies might find uninvited mediation blatantly partisan, that some neutral governments lacked the support of their own people, and that other nations could outvote the United States; hence, such a meeting might do more harm than good. Wilson did express a general belief in conciliation but would not commit himself further, asserting that he alone would determine the right moment to act. After the meeting ended, Lochner privately claimed that Wilson "has no plan outside of a fight to the finish." If a European neutral, he added, were to invite the United States, public pressure could press the president to accept the offer. Just over a week later Colonel House received Addams, social reformer Lillian Wald, and Hungarian peace activist Rosika Schwimmer, telling them that Wilson would not officially appoint such a peace commission but did not object to informal activity.[35]

Supposedly the greatest chance for mediation lay in a plan of Henry Ford to send a delegation to Europe that would, in his words, "get the boys out of the trenches and back to their homes by Christmas." The eccentric automobile manufacturer acted on the basis of impulse and hunch and was known for his short attention span. He envisioned an international machinery whereby peace-lovers in belligerent nations could maintain contact with each other. In late November he fantasized a worldwide general strike, when on Christmas day, "war-torn men will climb from their trenches, throw down their arms and start home."[36]

From the time the war had broken out, Ford branded the conflict absolute folly, a "wasteful sacrifice of human life and the world's resources." "The word "murderer," he told a *New York Times* interviewer, "should be embroidered across the breast of every soldier." He maintained that the hostilities emerged from the greed of moneylenders and munitions makers, one group of nations desiring what the opposing group possessed. Let people occupy themselves productively and profitably, and international conflict would cease. Peace again would allow Europe to spend its money on tractors, not guns.[37]

Ford soon turned his peace sentiments into a personal crusade. "New York wants war," he said in June 1915, "but the United States doesn't. The peoples west of New York are too sensible for war." Speaking in Denver in midfall, he predicted that the conflict could end within two months if "the money bags of the world's richest men" were conscripted. Persuaded by such pacifist leaders as Lochner and Addams to send a peace mission to Europe, Ford commissioned the *Oscar II* of the Scandinavian-American Line to transport delegates. Supposedly when pacifist Rosika Schwimmer remarked that it would be pleasant for the deputation to have its own ship, Ford snapped, "We'll get one!"[38]

Meeting with Wilson in November, Ford invited the president, Treasury Secretary McAdoo, and two Wilson daughters to travel with him. He asked the chief executive to nominate expedition members. After the baffled president refused the manufacturer's overtures, arguing that he needed to retain his freedom of action, Ford told Lochner the president was "a small man."[39] He encouraged prominent Americans, including all state governors, to join him and sought a student delegate from each university. Members of Congress, he believed, should remain in Washington to fight preparedness. Unfortunately for Ford, not a single business leader accepted his invitation. Neither did any major figures from the world of science, education, or government. Addams wanted to participate, but a kidney infection hospitalized her. Bryan offered supporting words, although curiously comparing the voyage to Noah's Ark. He saw the party off, promising to join it later; he never booked passage. Some prominent reformers signed on, among them Unitarian minister Jenkin Lloyd Jones, editor S.S. McClure, and Denver juvenile court judge Ben Lindsey.

A cynical press ridiculed the project. The most common epithets were "farcical," "fantastical," "mischievous," and "quixotic." More imaginative phrasing included "Ford's Folly," the "innocents abroad," and "that wonderful yachting party." The *New Republic* titled an editorial "A Little Child Shall Lead Them." The *London Spectator* suggested an inscription for the sides of *Oscar II*: "SOF," which could mean either "Ship of Ford" or "Ship of Fools." Newspapers in Germany were not much kinder, one labeling the voyage a "manifestation of American eccentricity."[40] Ford cared little; he welcomed the publicity, even if it was often hostile.

On December 4, the *Oscar II* left Hoboken, New Jersey, arriving two weeks later at Christiania (now Oslo), Norway. On board were 163 adults and 3 children, among them 55 pacifists, 44 journalists, 25 students, and 42 staff and family members. Though Ford himself made the journey, much of the planning fell to Schwimmer and Lochner. The delegates continued to

Stockholm, Copenhagen, and finally The Hague, where they established the Neutral Conference for Continuous Mediation. Despite its grandiloquent name and lofty goal, the conference proved markedly ineffective.

Its failure was hardly surprising. Ford, as expedition historian Barbara S. Kraft notes, manifested almost a schizophrenic personality, being "both modest and vain, sensitive and crass, kind and cruel, persevering and impulsive, naive and cunning." Suffering from a cold, he left abruptly for the United States while the party was still in Christiania, promising to return if he could expedite a peace. Upon his return home, he claimed no longer to blame bankers, militarists, and munition-makers but "the people," who had "neglected to select the proper heads for their Governments—the men who would prevent such chaotic conditions." He no longer kept in regular contact with his peace expedition.[41]

Ford's personal surrogates did not take the mission seriously, seeing it as wasting both the time and the money of his automobile company. Schwimmer acted dictatorially, at times manifesting a paranoid personality. She irritated many by her insistence that she supervise every cable, letter, and speaker. She always carried a black bag, which she boasted was full of secret documents, although the contents involved nothing more than confidential statements of European leaders vaguely supporting neutral mediation. Both American and European delegates were chosen in a haphazard manner, leading to many inappropriate selections. The press emphasized the circuslike nature of the voyage, ignoring a sober appeal drafted by the conferees and signed on April 12, 1916. The manifesto endorsed postwar disarmament, freedom of the seas, a new international organization, self-determination for Europe's nationalities, parliamentary control of foreign policy, and the lifting of many trade barriers. By far its greatest handicap, however, lay in the attitude of the belligerents, none of whom proved willing to sacrifice the possibility of ultimate victory, particularly to a group of unauthorized participants.

Yet, argues Kraft, all was not lost. In the short run, the conference allowed hundreds of thousands of neutral citizens to press for mediation, in the process transmitting ad hoc peace proposals across boundaries and campaigning for open diplomacy and a league of nations. Taking the long view, for the first time in history "a gathering of neutral citizens, acting in the name of the people, asked warring nations to stop fighting and settle their disputes, not on the basis of military conquest, but according to the principles of justice and humanity."[42]

By this time, few Americans stressed mediation. Submarine warfare, overseas commerce, and the controversy over military preparedness all took precedence. Wilson experienced severe qualms concerning immediate peace-making. The U-boat controversy with Germany needed to be settled first. The Central Powers dominated the Continent to such a degree that the Allies would deem American intervention as an unneutral act. The president feared that the participation of other neutral powers in Europe and Latin America would hinder effective action. More important, he would not commit himself to any peace plan that sudden military moves might make obsolete. Wilson, writes historian David S. Patterson, would have been unwise to commit himself to premature and amorphous schemes, thereby jeopardizing a major political reverse if the belligerents condemned his intervention.[43]

House's own plans for mediation involved personal diplomacy and the risk of war. Late in August 1915, Sir Edward Grey wrote to the colonel, hinting that the Allies would welcome American mediation provided terms included disarmament on land and sea and U.S. membership in an international organization. In mid-September Grey elaborated on just what he meant by a world body: "a League of Nations binding themselves to side against any Power which broke a Treaty; which broke certain rules of warfare on sea or land. . . . ; or which refused, in case of dispute, to adopt some other method of settlement than that of war." He intimated that Britain might negotiate on the basis of a Russian outlet to the sea, Belgium's restoration, the evacuation of France, and French annexation of Alsace- Lorraine.[44] The foreign secretary was far from candid, for as noted, England and France had promised Russia the Turkish straits and the city of Constantinople and Italy territory in southern Austria, the Dalmatian coast, and eastern Africa.

The colonel never envisioned such imperialistic aspirations but remained ever hopeful of a possible settlement. On September 22, during the unresolved *Arabic* crisis, House made a bold suggestion to Wilson. If the United States were to demand peace, threatening to use its military power against the side that refused to accept the proposal, the warning might frighten the belligerents into negotiations. "Much to my surprise," House confided to his diary, Wilson "said he had never been sure that we ought not to take part in the conflict and if it seemed that Germany and her militaristic ideas were to win, the obligation upon us was greater than ever." On October 8, House met with the president, warning Wilson that if Germany won the war, "our turn would come next." As the United States was isolated and unprepared, "we should do something decisive now—something that would either end the war in a way to abolish militarism or that would bring us in with the Allies to help them do it." If the Central Powers refused, "diplomatic relations would first be broken off, and later the whole force of the Government—and perhaps the force of every neutral—might be brought against them." Wilson did not speak, acting startled but appearing to agree.[45]

Believing that he possessed a presidential mandate, House wrote Grey on October 17, outlining his scheme and stressing the need for haste. Were the Allies to experience military setbacks, American intervention would become increasingly difficult, if not impossible. Wilson approved the message, though insisting upon adding the word "probably" before any assurance of joining the Allies. The president commented: "I do not want to make it inevitable quite that we should take part to force terms on Germany, because the exact circumstances of such a crisis are impossible to determine."[46]

At this point, Grey sought to dampen House's hopes, writing him on November 11 that France, Russia, and Britain had decided on a winter campaign. France, he continued, viewed itself as secure in the west. In the east, Russia believed that the worst was over. Only in the Balkans and "the Mohammedan world" might trouble appear.[47]

When the undaunted colonel visited the president ten days before Christmas, House denied that he sought American entry into the war. Nonetheless, he wanted to let "the Allies know we are definitely on their side and that is not our intention to permit Germany to win if the strength of this country can stand [it]."[48]

Despite the *Arabic* pledge of September 1, Wilson realized the need for further diplomacy to resolve outstanding grievances with Germany. On December 24, he authorized House to visit London and Paris. In his written instructions, the president stressed that Britain must modify its blockade, adding that American shippers and merchants needed support. In fact, the colonel was "primarily bound" to put "further, immediate, and imperative pressure on England and her allies." The president told his emissary to limit discussion of the future peace to general guarantees, that is, military disarmament and a league of nations that would both protect nations against aggression and maintain "absolute freedom of the seas." The colonel should avoid the matter of indemnities and territorial questions, which Wilson perceived as purely "local settlements." The president stressed exercising "our utmost moral force," by which he meant diplomatic pressure, although such influence risked triggering a break in diplomatic relations with Germany and could lead to war.[49]

House recorded in his diary on Christmas Day that Wilson "clearly places the whole responsibility back on my shoulders where I would gladly have it, for if I am to act, I wish to act with a free hand." He wrote the president a day later: "I think we agree entirely." On December 17, the president had informed his comrade, "You need no instructions. You know what is in my mind and how to interpret it."[50]

Link writes that House could not have misunderstood Wilson's instructions. Nevertheless, the colonel soon flagrantly misrepresented and misinformed the president, doing so because he perceived the stakes so high and the objectives so noble. Historian Robert W. Tucker notes that Wilson had just expressed greater concern over the British blockade than over any grand scheme of Colonel House.[51]

One must stress that the two leaders perceived the broader aspects of the mission in sharply different terms. House believed that German submarine activity would drive the United States into war by 1916. He therefore emphasized the need to support the Allies and, if necessary, to engage in armed intervention. If such be the case, it was better to have American belligerency focus more on a just and permanent peace than on American rights and honor. Looking at the immediate situation, the colonel perceived a severely wounded Russia that had lost Poland, Lithuania, and Courland. He viewed the chances of Allied success in western Europe as poor because during that autumn a major French offensive between Rheims and the Argonne forest had failed. Hence he considered his proposal most propitious. Conversely, Wilson desired a genuine effort to engage in American mediation, leading to general disarmament and a postwar international league.

House arrived at Falmouth, England, on January 5 and immediately headed for London. On the eleventh he met with Ambassador Page and leading British officials, including Munitions Minister David Lloyd George, Chancellor of the Exchequer Reginald McKenna, Secretary of State for India Austen Chamberlain, and Lord Chief Justice Rufus Daniel Isaacs, first marquis of Reading. The presidential agent assured the gathering: "The United States would like Great Britain to do those things which would enable the United States to help Great Britain win the war." During lunch the following day with Page, Foreign Secretary Grey, and Lord Robert Cecil, parliamentary undersecretary of state for foreign affairs, House communicated

Wilson's desire that Britain lift its shipping restrictions. Any such move, Grey and Cecil retorted, would result in the public's removing them from office, adding that the French were even more inflexible on the matter. Cecil, soon to become minister of blockade, stressed that he did not believe in "half way measures"; restrictions must "be rigid, or not at all."[52]

The colonel neither pressed the issue nor reported to Wilson his indication of American support for the British war effort. House did write the president on January 16, warning that pushing Britain too hard on commercial restrictions could lead to Grey's resignation. "I am sure that our policy should be to have no serious break with the Allies over the blockade, and to keep upon such terms with Germany that our diplomatic relations may be maintained."[53]

During his meetings with British leaders, the colonel communicated his personal vision of a reasonable peace: a settlement that returned Alsace-Lorraine to France, gave Constantinople to Russia, freed Belgium and Serbia, and created a league of nations. Finding the British overconfident, he warned them several times of a possible Russian surrender, an event that would lead to France's capitulation. Even if Germany returned Alsace-Lorraine to France and restored much of Belgium, it could dominate the Hapsburg Empire and maintain a free hand in Egypt, India, Asia Minor, and parts of Africa. Under such conditions, British control of the seas could not last three months, merely because other nations would protest against its commercial domination. On January 14 Lloyd George told House that Wilson's diplomatic intervention alone would prevent continuation of the war. However, not until around September 1, after "the big battles" of the summer had been fought, should the president undertake mediation.[54]

Undeterred, House continued on to Berlin, where from January 26 to 29 he met with Germany's civilian leaders. Conferring with Chancellor Bethmann, whom he found "most unreasonable," he learned that any settlement must include indemnities from Britain and France as well as German control of Belgium and Poland. Bethmann told him that the army, which did not want peace, now directed matters. Gerard quoted the Kaiser, who remarked bizarrely: "I and my cousins, George [of Britain] and Nicholas [of Russia], will make peace when the time comes."[55]

On January 30 House wrote Wilson, then on a preparedness tour of the Midwest. Germany's naval leaders, he reported, believed that unrestricted submarine warfare could effectively blockade Britain. In fact, they were so confident over the matter that they would willingly risk war with the United

States. The civilian government supported the Admiralty and would not admit the illegality of submarine warfare: "They will yield anything but this. If you insist on that point, I believe war will follow." Four days later, the colonel urged Wilson not to break with Germany over the *Lusitania*, saying that a delay in negotiations might foster House's "original plan in regard to intervention. And if this cannot be done because of German's undersea warfare, then we will be forced in, in a way that will give us the advantage."[56]

By early February, House had arrived in Paris, meeting with Foreign Minister Jules Cambon on the second. The colonel denied that the Allies could achieve victory on any front, repeating his warning that Germany might make a separate peace with Russia. "I am trying," he wrote the president, "to impress upon both England and France the precariousness of the situation and the gamble that a continuance of the war involves." By now discouraged about advancing any imminent peace, Wilson's envoy predicted: "Hell will break loose in Europe this spring and summer as never before. I am sure as I ever am of anything that by the end of the summer you can intervene."[57]

Meeting again with Cambon and Prime Minister Aristide Briand on February 7, House outlined certain peace terms, including the return of Alsace-Lorraine to France, compensation for Russia in Armenia, and German control of the Asian part of Turkey, known as Anatolia (all reflecting the vision of Philip Dru). Turkey itself "must disappear." He pointed to Germany, Russia, and Japan as the world's only aggressive powers; the trio sought "domination and conquest." After the war France, England, and the United States should be "closely united and allied." More important, according to Cambon's narrative, House told both men that "if the Allies should have a little success, this spring or summer, the United States will intervene in favor of peace, but if they have a setback, the United States will intervene militarily and take part in the war against Germany." The two Frenchmen responded quite candidly: public opinion, much less the military situation, would not permit a peace initiative. Immediate mediation remained out the question.[58]

That very day House wrote Wilson concerning "the most important conference I have had in Europe." "We had a complete and satisfying understanding," he said. Two days later, the colonel reported to the president: "It was finally understood that in the event that the Allies had some notable victories during the spring and summer, you would intervene; and in the event that the tide of war went against them or remained stationary, you would intervene." The former intervention would be on behalf of negotiation; the latter would involve direct military participation in the war. He went on: "A great opportunity is yours, my friend, the greatest, perhaps, that has ever come to any man."[59]

House's French diplomacy revealed singular ineptitude. Link wonders how he could have been so naive, for Briand and Cambon stressed that a negotiated peace was currently impossible. Victory was France's sole agenda, a fight to the finish. Furthermore, House intended to use the word "intervention" to connote diplomatic action, whereas the French cabinet thought it signified military support. Cambon told Lord Bertie, British ambassador to France, that the colonel had informed him "the war will be long, that the Allies will win in the end, and that in a year's time America will be with us." House not only misrepresented Wilson's intentions; he distorted his own.[60]

On his way back to Britain, House visited King Albert of Belgium, standing fast in La Panne, an unoccupied corner of his country. Here the colonel's diplomacy took an even more curious turn, for he asked the monarch if Germany could purchase the Belgian Congo. The ruler replied that he could not sell the Congo Free State, the creation of his uncle, Leopold II.[61]

By February 9, House had returned to London, telling his hosts that Berlin was not suffering economically; it possessed sufficient manpower on the western front to sustain an assault. Grey brought up the possibility of lifting the British blockade, indicating a reversal of his position a month earlier. This time House spoke against the proposal, claiming that Germany was continuing its inhumane warfare; he had apparently forgotten Wilson's instructions.[62]

On February 14, House engaged in his most significant meeting. Those attending included Prime Minister Herbert Asquith and First Lord of the Admiralty Arthur Balfour, as well as Grey, Reading, and Lloyd George. Lloyd George insisted upon a preliminary understanding with Wilson about minimum Allied peace terms. House responded that the president probably favored the restoration of Belgium and Serbian independence, the ceding of Alsace and Lorraine to France, compensation for Germany in "other places outside Europe," the "liberation" of those Italian communities under "the Austrian yoke," and a Russian outlet to the sea. The colonel wrote in his diary: "We all cheerfully divided up Turkey, both in Asia and Europe." Asquith turned to the matter of Wilson's mediation, asking the envoy what action the president would take if "Germany proposed something totally unfair."

The colonel replied: "In these circumstances, I thought the President would throw the weight of the United States on the side of the Allies."[63]

Within three days, the colonel and the foreign secretary drafted what historians have since called the House-Grey memorandum. Grey wrote: "Colonel House told me that President Wilson was ready, on hearing from France and England that the moment was opportune, to propose that a Conference should be summoned to put an end to the war. Should the Allies accept this proposal, and should Germany refuse it, the United States would probably enter the war against Germany." If, however, the Allies delayed acceptance of Wilson's offer and later faced military defeat, "the United States would probably disinterest themselves in Europe and look to their own protection in their own way."[64]

By signing the agreement, Grey was clearly humoring House, although he might well have personally favored mediation. He realized full well the tenuous nature of this understanding. The Americans had really made no commitment whatsoever. Could the British afford to put their fate in the hands of any foreign leader, no matter how friendly? Ambassador Page, who considered the scheme sheer "moonshine," was far more realistic concerning British sentiment; he wrote in a memorandum that "such an indirect scheme is doomed to failure—is wrong, in fact." "Nobody here would dare talk about peace," he personally told House, "and . . . if they did dare, nobody would dare accept the President's 'intervention.' They no longer have confidence in the President." He also commented to House: "If the British public learns that this is going on, you will be lucky if you are not thrown into the Thames."[65] Upon learning of the House-Grey memorandum, the French leaders dismissed the agreement, finding it unworthy of discussion with their British allies.

Because the British had cracked House's code, they were fully aware of the colonel's duplicity toward both them and the president. Asquith deemed House's plan "pure humbug," "a mere manoeuvre of American politics." Balfour denied that the United States would enter the struggle: "Wilson wants votes and the country does not want war." The proposal was "not worth five minutes thought."[66]

Link is trenchant concerning the entire matter. He maintains that Wilson undoubtedly believed that once an armistice was signed and a peace conference launched, the peoples of Europe would not allow their governments to resume hostilities. The House-Grey accord contained "no promises of American military intervention by a certain date, no reassuring words about seeing the Allies through to the end." America would simply promise to throw its "weight," whatever that might mean, to either side if it followed Wilson's lead. The United States did concede the possibility of returning Alsace-Lorraine to France, slight compensation for Germany, and minor territorial changes, but the agreement suspiciously suggested a return to Europe's 1914 boundaries. Despite the silence of British and French officials, House blithely assumed that they sought American mediation, in the process deceiving not only the president but himself. The colonel, writes Link, was involved in "one of the most startling instances of self-delusion in history." Moreover, as Wilson biographer Ray Stannard Baker notes, House assured the Allies of American support without inquiring as to their real objectives.[67]

John Milton Cooper Jr. portrays the accord as revealing House's "characteristic deviousness." The approach backfired, contributing to Wilson's growing antagonism toward the British and the waning of the colonel's influence. "The great realist did not always come off as a shrewd operator."[68]

For the United States itself, the scheme possessed some danger. Suppose Berlin refused to participate in an American-led peace conference? Or suppose Germany, once attending, rejected terms "not unfavorable to the Allies"? The Reich would have violated no international law, whereas the United States, in the words of Patrick Devlin, would be entering the war "simply on the ground that she thought the fighting ought to stop," in the process single-handedly discharging the duties of any embryonic international league.[69]

In addition, could America make good on such an implicit promise? Most scholars are doubtful. How, asks House biographer Godfrey Hodgson, could one depend on the good faith of a president who added the word "probably" to a major pledge? By so acting, he in effect compromised his commitment to carry out a bargain that might mean "life or death to the Allies." Kendrick A. Clements emphasizes that Wilson himself realized he could not enter the war without congressional approval. In stressing the need for the Allies to act quickly, House was warning the British that the Republicans might emerge victorious in 1916 or that conceivably Wilson might die. Offering a different view, Joyce Grigsby Williams suspects that Grey was not really distressed because the document supplied evidence that America tacitly supported the Entente.[70]

The colonel departed for the United States on February 25, firmly believing that Wilson could soon end the war. The president, meeting with House on March 6, could not have been more appreciative: "I cannot adequately express to you my admiration and gratitude for what you have done." Two days later Wilson expressed his agreement with the House-Grey memorandum, though he insisted that House stress the world "probably" in communicating the chief executive's approval to Grey. Yet clearly House had ignored the president's instructions, encouraging the British blockade and implying that America would intervene on the Allied side. Historian Robert W. Tucker suspects that Wilson might well have been aware of House's intriguing but admired his emissary's sincerity. The president might not have wanted to jeopardize their friendship and feared severe diplomatic consequences were he to disown the colonel. At any rate, House remained most optimistic. Bolstered by the resignation of Admiral Tirpitz, America's arch naval foe, on March 12 and by conversations with Bernstorff, he wrote in his diary that day: "If we can get the Allies to give the word, I believe Germany will acquiesce."[71] House did not realize that his memorandum was already dead.

House had another obsession—preparedness. He confided to his diary on July 10, 1915: "If we had gone actively to work with all our resources to build up a war machine commensurate with our standing among the nations, we would be in a position to-day to enforce peace. If war comes with Germany because of this submarine controversy it will be because we are totally unprepared and Germany feels that we are impotent." The colonel bemoaned Wilson's "one-track mind," his inability to realize the "gravity" of the situation. He wrote the president on July 14: "I feel that we are taking a terrible gamble ourselves in permitting our safety to rest almost wholly upon the success of the Allies, and I wonder whether the time has not come for us to put our country in a position of security." After citing House's comments, historian John Garry Clifford concurs, suggesting that Germany would never have risked renewing unrestricted submarine warfare in 1917 against a well-armed United States.[72]

Within the administration, House, Garrison, and Franklin Roosevelt maintained informal liaison with the preparedness advocates. On July 21, the day Wilson sent his third *Lusitania* note, he publicly asked Garrison and Daniels to draft comprehensive security proposals. The crisis triggered by the Cunard liner had obviously forced the president to change his stance radically, shifting from distancing from the war to engaging in outright deterrence. On October 6 he told the Naval Consulting Board that the United States needed to be "prepared, not for war, but for defense," a theme he soon repeated to others. Six days later the General Board of the navy, headed by

Admiral George Dewey, submitted a program sweeping enough to achieve naval equality with Britain by 1925. Construction would include ten battleships, six battle cruisers, ten scout cruisers, fifty destroyers, one hundred submarines, and eighty smaller vessels. The time span, five years; the cost, $500 million. This proposal met the most ambitious goals of the Navy League. The president, believing the navy more valuable than the army, approved the proposal.[73]

On October 28 Garrison submitted his recommendations for the army, which were published on November 6. The product of the War Department, they were praised by Chief of Staff Hugh L. Scott as the culmination of forty years of military planning. Although the secretary of war sought to increase the regular army to 140,000 troops, the crux of his program lay in a new "Continental Army" of 400,000. Recruits for this Continental Army would serve on active duty two summer months a year for three years, then spend another three years in a ready reserve. Officers would be drawn from the National Guard, retired members of the regular army, and graduates of military colleges.[74]

The conception was deeply flawed. Despite the costs—$183 million the first year alone and $1 billion over five years—the Continental Army would lack necessary equipment and quite possibly sufficient recruits. The plan bypassed the National Guard, a creation of the states and responsible to them alone. The Guard would receive a minor funding increase but was basically ignored. Politically the plan's fate was most precarious, for the militia drew considerable political support in the South and East. Writes historian John Patrick Finnegan: "What the United States needed was a strong armed force in hand while the European War raged; what it got was competing long-range blueprints."[75]

Although the *New Republic* welcomed preparedness as a "Trojan horse" for domestic reform, pacifist-leaning Americans remained suspicious. Any large standing army emitted overtones of European militarism. On October 29, 1915, the Woman's Peace Party, led by Jane Addams, petitioned Wilson, telling the president that the preparedness movement would compel poorer nations to enter an arms race, thus creating "rivalry, suspicion and taxation in every country." Rabbi Stephen Wise wrote Wilson that new military appropriations, "at other times and in other hands than yours," might well serve "the interests of aggression." The chief executive, remarked Oswald Garrison Villard, was "sowing the seeds of militarism," "raising up a military and naval caste." He privately called Wilson a "bloodless and calculating man."[76]

On November 4, 1915, Wilson spoke to New York's Manhattan Club. He denied that the United States was "threatened from any quarter" but stressed the need for "security and self-defense on the part of every nation confronted with the great enterprise of human liberty and independence." Although he endorsed Garrison's Continental Army plan, he was sufficiently mindful of the promilitia sentiment in Congress to promise that the National Guard would train this new force. In an obvious reference to German subversion, he attacked those who "spoke alien sympathies," "who loved other countries better than they loved America." It was, the president maintained, "high time that the nation should call a reckoning."[77]

The address, as historian William Henry Harbaugh notes, possessed "all the appearances of a political compromise." Wilson neither identified potential aggressors nor discussed international alignments. Indeed, he denied that the nation was threatened from any quarter. The *New Republic* deemed the president far too vague. "A speech more resolutely confined to platitudes, to large and dull abstractions, has rarely been offered to an anxious nation." "Unless a government knows what it is going to defend," the journal continued a week later, "it cannot be said to have a program of national defense.[78]

In undertaking a radical switch on preparedness, Wilson made his most important domestic decision of 1915. In part, political considerations were at work. Admittedly, his Democratic party contained many neutralists. They were extremely vocal, controlled major committees in the Congress, and supplied essential support for domestic reform. Nonetheless, if the public perceived the president as too soft on defense matters, his party would be weakened, particularly if Roosevelt became the opposition candidate. Furthermore, President Wilson was genuinely apprehensive, fearing German influence in Latin America. He was particularly worried about the influence of the Hamburg Colombian Banana Company, a firm that held extensive tracts of land.[79]

Nevertheless, the president enjoyed a surprising consensus, even before he delivered his Manhattan Club speech. The *Outlook,* often critical of Wilson, predicted that a stronger military force would prevent future attack. According to one press survey, the most influential newspapers, including those in inland sections, backed preparedness, as did business groups, educators, and a number of governors. The White House mail was most complimentary. A poll conducted by the admittedly biased National Security League found strong congressional support.[80]

Wilson received the backing of major congressional leaders, among them such powerful figures as Senate majority leader John W. Kern (D-Ind.), Bryan's running mate in 1908; Lemuel P. Padgett (D-Tenn.), chairman of the House naval affairs committee; and James Hay, chairman of the House Military Affairs Committee. Holdouts included House majority leader Claude Kitchin, who blamed all preparedness agitation on "jingoes and manufacturers of war equipment" and who stacked the military and naval affairs committees of the lower chamber with its foes. The American navy, Kitchin argued, was already twice as large as Japan's and exceeded that of Germany.[81] During the summer the North Carolina Democrat organized a "peace coalition" of thirty Democrats from the rural South and West. Recognizing allies among certain labor and Progressive Party constituencies in the North and among some midwestern Republicans, the bloc hoped to obstruct increases in defense spending. Though Bryan had left office, such activity showed that he still retained avid disciples in Congress.

Many German Americans endorsed increases in military strength, though others feared that such efforts suggested an impending war against their ancestral home. The *Fatherland* was selective in endorsing preparedness, favoring military training in colleges and secondary schools and the type of "people's army" existing in Switzerland and Germany. It sought a navy "strong enough to check the mightiest armada that England can send out against us." At the same time, German Americans would join no war "to slaughter their own kind at the behest of the cruelest plutocracy the world has ever seen."[82]

In December 1915 publisher George Haven Putnam organized the American Rights Committee (ARC), serving as its chairman. Other prominent members included Lawrence F. Abbott, president of the *Outlook* company; international lawyer Frederic R. Coudert; Columbia sociologist Franklin H. Giddings; and New York attorney Charles P. Howland. Unlike the defense societies, the ARC was openly interventionist, warning that a Teutonic triumph would imperil human liberties and proposing the immediate severing of diplomatic relations with Germany. Its influence centered in the Northeast. Not until the eve of war in April 1917 did any substantial portion of Americans adopt its position.[83]

Wilson's shift alienated the great majority of progressives. Almost every farm spokesman opposed the chief executive, as did the American Federation of Labor, the United Mine Workers, the *American Socialist,* and much of the clergy. To Bryan, the president departed from American traditions, menaced the nation's peace and safety, and challenged "the spirit of Christianity itself." Republican leaders, however, remained Bryan's primary culprit; the Great Commoner accused them of seeking a large army to suppress labor unrest and a large navy to conduct trade wars. Such reformers believed that the United States must lead by example, not cave in to Wall Street bankers, munitions-makers, and market-hungry industrialists. To Villard, even the manufacturers of more mundane products, for example, typewriters and sewing machines, supported this new "militarism."[84] Wilson's new critics entertained simple alternatives: let the nation retain its modest military establishment, promote compulsory arbitration, and repudiate war as an instrument of national policy. This was the proper way to "prepare" in such times.

In November various progressives and pacifists organized the Anti-Militarism Committee. Among its leaders were such prominent reformers as Rabbi Wise, *Masses* editor Max Eastman, *Survey* editor Paul U. Kellogg, Unitarian clergyman John Haynes Holmes, settlement leader Lillian Wald, prison reformer George W. Kirchwey, Florence Kelley of the National Consumers' League, Socialist party leader Allan Louis Benson, and Crystal Eastman Benedict, who was vice chairman of the Woman's Peace Party and committee secretary. It sought to fight the "cult of preparedness" and associated war budgets. Concrete proposals by the group included closer hemispheric cooperation, a panel of experts to study tensions with the Orient, and the payment of military expenses by income and inheritance taxes, "not by taxes which place the burden on the poor."[85]

On December 7, 1915, Wilson made preparedness the dominant theme of his annual message. Avoiding all discussion of the European war, he outlined a program that emphasized concerns about Mexico and continental defense. He stressed the War Department plans and the navy's five-year program; Americans must be able "to fight effectively upon a sudden summons," "know how modern fighting is done," and "be fitted to play the great role in the world, and particularly in this hemisphere, for which they are qualified by principle and by chastened ambition to play." Addressing himself to German American subversion, he warned against those "who had poured the poison of disloyalty into the very arteries of our national life."[86]

Several historians suggest that Wilson missed a major opportunity to educate the public. Link notes that the address was too long and disjointed to elicit much enthusiasm. William Henry Harbaugh argues that the president offered no intimation that the United States might soon be fighting in defense of neutral rights, that an Allied defeat would betray the national interest, or that a great navy was needed to check Japan. Harbaugh concedes that given the nebulous diplomatic situation and the antiwar feeling of the Congress, Wilson undoubtedly had little choice.[87]

Many newspapers were enthusiastic, although Bryan criticized the message as "revolutionary," while the pacifists on Ford's ship called it "reactionary." In Roosevelt's opinion the president met "blood and iron" with "milk and water." The German American press concentrated on the loyalty issue, claiming that the chief executive had pilloried their kinsmen. Socialist congressman Meyer London, who represented New York City's lower East Side, accused Wilson of pronouncing a "monstrous doctrine" of ethnic distrust.[88]

If Democratic congressional support remained questionable, most Republicans sought a program at least as comprehensive as Wilson's. The House and Senate minority leaders, James R. Mann of Illinois and Jacob H. Gallinger of New Hampshire, promised Republican support for a nonpartisan defense program. Mann suggested an army of a half million men and a navy powerful enough to confront Britain, the nation he believed most likely to fight the United States. Nonetheless, certain progressives within the Grand Old Party balked at preparedness. Robert La Follette espied a "glorious group of millionaires" lying behind the rearmament movement; he listed a number of Morgan partners in its ranks. More important, Wilson still lacked essential support from Majority Leader Kitchin, who maintained that four-fifths of the House Democratic members opposed the president's program. The North Carolina congressman presented his own defense agenda, which focused on submarines, mines, and coastal defenses.[89] Such rearmament could ostensibly meet demands for increased defense while making it impossible to carry out offensive operations. Preoccupied by his forthcoming marriage, the president provided no leadership.

Once he returned from his honeymoon, Wilson commenced a ten-day campaign on behalf of his military agenda. Because he knew support in the South was relatively secure, he focused on the East and the Midwest. Launching his campaign in New York City on January 27, he denied that any threat of invasion existed but warned against "indirect, roundabout, flank movements" that would menace America's hemispheric dominance. Two days later, he spoke in Pittsburgh, stressing America's "right to the equal and just treatment of her citizens wherever they go." "When the world is on fire," he asked, "how much time do you want to take to be ready?" Addressing Cleveland's residents, he confessed that he might find it impossible to maintain the nation's honor and still remain out of war.[90]

As his tour continued, Wilson escalated his rhetoric. In Kansas City he confessed that war might "creep in towards both coasts," threatening some of the nation's "great cities." Certainly he "could not tell twenty-four hours at a time whether there is going to be trouble or not." At Topeka the president emphasized the need to protect the rights of Americans traveling on "legitimate errands" of commerce and relief. He deemed the right to ship major exports overseas as crucial, specifying wheat as a prime example. St. Louis audiences heard him warn that one reckless submarine commander, acting on his own, "might set the world on fire." In a statement that aroused much controversy, he asserted that the United States should possess "incomparably the greatest navy in the world."[91]

On this trip Wilson spoke directly to a million people. Business and professional groups offered strong support, as did urban areas. But while the trip was a personal triumph, it failed politically. Rural regions, which dominated the Congress, ranged from indifferent to hostile. Bryan's *Commoner* responded: "The President says that the world is on fire, and then he suggests that we try to extinguish it by pouring on gasoline." The National Security League endorsed Garrison's plan but added universal training. George Sylvester Viereck feared that certain passages in Wilson's speeches foreshadowed a grave crisis with Germany. Wrote journalist Ray Stannard Baker: "The trouble with Wilson's policy of preparedness is that it does not tell us *what* [it is] *for*. No vision of internationalism. No constructive policy."[92]

Throughout this time, Garrison's plan for a Continental Army remained in jeopardy. For nearly a year the relevant House and Senate committees had worked on a plan to "federalize" the militia, a proposal that Garrison discarded. Why, the legislators asked, abandon the National Guard, an existing force, for an untried scheme? On January 6, 1916, when the secretary testified before the House Military Affairs Committee, he encountered much hostility. If his plan were turned down, he warned, the nation would need some form of compulsory training. Chairman Hay suggested "federalization" of the National Guard, which would require a dual oath to both state and nation, and increasing this militia to 425,000 men. He wrote Wilson on February 5 that in wartime the militia could be drafted into national service.[93] The product of advice from former adjutant general Fred C. Ainsworth, Hay's plan allocated federal funds to pay Guard units and supply them. In turn they would have to meet certain standards in equipment and training and, if required, serve under the president's direction. The option was far less expensive than Garrison's and was supposedly bereft of militarism.[94] Hopefully, thought Hay, his compromise could forestall more radical measures. The secretary of war responded that federalization was unconstitutional.

Critics found Garrison's training period too short, the six-year enlistment too long, and the implication that the state militias must surrender their identity too authoritarian. Lieutenant General Nelson A. Miles, who subdued Puerto Rico in 1898, opposed both conscription and a Continental Army; he sought to expand the National Guard, saying, "You cannot Germanize American citizens." No enemy, he maintained, could land a sizable number of invaders on American shores because the nation's coastal defenses equaled any in the world.[95]

Other critics believed Garrison's proposal too weak. Army chief of staff Hugh L. Scott and his predecessor Leonard Wood deemed Garrison's proposal most inadequate, both endorsing universal training instead. Wood warned a Senate committee that a force of only 150,000 troops could successfully invade the United States; the American coastline was totally exposed. Roosevelt insisted upon compulsory military preparation: "I would have the son of the multi-millionaire and the son of the immigrant who came in steerage, sleep under the same dog-tent and eat the same grub. It would help mightily to a mutual comprehension of life." The former president advanced a counterscheme that called for forty-eight battleships, federal control of the National Guard, a regular army of 250,000, sufficient officers to command an army of 1.5 million, and the construction of munitions plants west of the Alleghenies.[96]

Garrison faced pressure from the National Guard lobby, antimilitaristic Democrats, and Republicans who labeled his proposals inadequate. He drew just twenty-four congressional supporters. Within a week after the secretary testified, Hay told Wilson that his Continental Army plan lay dead on arrival. At this point the president undercut Garrison, whom he considered arrogant. The chief executive informed the Virginia congressman that he remained entirely flexible concerning the structure of any refurbished army. In fact, he would even accept Hay's federalization proposal, provided it proved constitutional.

Beseeching Wilson to intervene personally, Garrison portrayed any federalized militia as a shadow force, Hay's plan a "betrayal of the trust of the people." The president responded by calling the House committee "well informed"; he remained flexible as to the ways in which the new army would be created, provided that the legislation resulted in "a national reserve under unmistakable national control." To "shut the door" on Hay's solution would be "a very serious mistake." Garrison also criticized an abortive proposal by Senator James P. Clarke (D-Ark.) that would grant the Philippines independence within five years. The islands, the secretary insisted, were unprepared for self-rule and lay easy prey to Japanese domination. Finally, on February 10, Garrison resigned his office. Wilson released his correspondence with Garrison to reporters, undoubtedly a factor in Garrison's later claim that the president was a "man of high ideals but no principles." Wilson named General Scott acting secretary.[97]

Press reaction varied. Democratic newspapers blamed Garrison; Republican journals attacked Wilson's "partisan politics." The *New Republic* reproached the president, claiming that he had neither argued his case forcefully nor delivered any follow-through: "He is not up to the job." Villard noted that Garrison had resigned with universal respect, but the liberal publisher called the preparedness program itself "the biggest humbug perpetrated upon the American people since the Free Silver agitation." How could additional troops enhance the nation's security when proper organization and training facilities did not exist?[98] The defense organizations backed Roosevelt, demanding the type of comprehensive program that Wilson would never accept in peacetime.

At first, Wilson considered Agriculture Secretary David F. Houston and Interior Secretary Franklin K. Lane for the War Department post but soon judged them more valuable in their present slots. He finally settled on Newton Diehl Baker, a reformist mayor of Cleveland who had previously so impressed Wilson that he was twice asked to head the Interior Department. Baker entertained pacifist sentiments, having been a member of the American League to Limit Armaments and an endorser of a film titled *Lay Down Your Arms.* War, he believed, was an anachronism, professional soldiers relics from a barbaric past. With this appointment the president sought to conciliate foes of preparedness and temper demands of the army. Although Baker to this point had opposed preparedness, he showed himself a personable and able administrator who possessed the flexibility that Garrison sorely lacked. He endorsed the Military Training Camps Association, criticized the Hay plan as inadequate, and approved a flying corps for the army. Americans, he said, were a "fighting race," "more inclined to love the eagle than the dove."[99]

Once Garrison resigned, Wilson overcame any constitutional qualms concerning Hay's plan to federalize the militia. Despite opposition from the

War Department, which raised both legal and practical arguments, such major administration figures as Treasury Secretary McAdoo, Postmaster General Albert S. Burleson, and Attorney General Thomas W. Gregory supported the move.

The hearings of the House naval affairs committee, held in January and February 1916, lacked the controversy generated in its army counterpart, but they revealed sharp differences within the service leadership. Naval Secretary Daniels, Assistant Secretary Franklin Roosevelt, and rear admirals Victor Blue and William S. Benson claimed that the American fleet was battle-ready. Arguing to the contrary, Rear Admiral Austin M. Knight, president of the Naval War College, found the navy operating at only 50 percent efficiency; Rear Admiral Bradley A. Fiske ranked effectiveness at 75 percent. Rear admirals Charles J. Badger, a member of the General Board, and Cameron M. Winslow, commander in chief of the Pacific Fleet, both maintained that the Pacific coast lacked genuine naval defenses. Winslow was particularly vocal, claiming that his fleet possessed no first-class battleship and that one good enemy battleship could defeat America's present force. Vice Admiral Frank F. Fletcher testified: "We need battle-cruisers, sixteen-inch guns, and cruising submarines." Other testimony revealed shortages of ammunition, "hydroaeroplanes," and enlisted men.[100]

Within months the United States found itself involved in far greater debates. The nation experienced outright sabotage efforts, a major diplomatic proposal to strip belligerent merchant ships of their arms, a full-scale congressional rebellion over the right of American passengers to travel on belligerent ships, and the sinking of a British passenger ship in the English Channel, a matter that brought the United States to the brink of war.

6

Tensions with Germany and Britain

January–September 1916

BEFORE WILSON JOINED THE preparedness crusade, he faced a major challenge: Britain's arming of merchant ships. The practice, accepted in international law, had begun over a century earlier. A merchantman would have a small gun on deck to ward off pirates or "privateers," that is, private vessels that governments commission in wartime to attack enemy ships.

The German navy had long contended that submarines could not safely surface and warn armed merchantmen before sinking them. In mid-November 1915 a U-boat captured a copy of secret British instructions; these orders confirmed long-held suspicions that armed commercial vessels were obligated to pursue submarines, then destroy them. German press coverage of the diplomatic correspondence between Berlin and London over the *Baralong* incident of August 1915, in which Britain denied any wrongdoing, further inflamed national sentiment.

During the first months of the war, the State Department classified merchantmen, even if armed, as by definition involved in peaceful tasks and thereby immune from attack. Until the summer of 1915, when the British Admiralty began arming ships that voyaged to the United States, the issue remained abstract. On September 12, Lansing informed Wilson that the British steamer *Waimana,* which carried a 4.7-inch gun, had entered Newport News, Virginia, to take on a load of coal. Such armament, the secretary argued, was no longer "clearly defensive"; it "may now be employed for offensive operations against so small and unarmored a craft as a submarine." As even ocean liners engaged in the practice of search-and-destroy, it was difficult "to demand that a submarine shall give warning and so expose itself to the heavy guns carried by some of the British passenger vessels." Henceforth, the United States should treat such craft as warships.[1]

The president appeared sympathetic to Lansing's argument, remarking to House: "It is hardly fair to ask Submarine commanders to give warning by summons if, when they approach as near as they must for that purpose they are to be fired upon." In a note to Wilson on January 2, 1916, after the suspected torpedoing of the armed British liner *Persia,* the secretary urged the administration to revise its rules quickly, positing that Germany had a good case. Ambassador Gerard concurred, finding it absurd that "a submarine must come to the surface, give warning, offer to put passengers and crew in safety, and constitute itself a target for merchant ships."[2]

In a memo dated January 7, Lansing advanced a diplomatic initiative that could have changed the entire nature of the war. Allied merchantmen should either disarm or risk being treated by the enemy as warships and hence subject to immediate sinking. In return, the Central Powers would observe normal rules of cruiser warfare, that is, they would agree to rescue all people on board and launch torpedoes only after giving warning.[3]

Lansing assumed both sides would back his proposal. German U-boats would no longer face enemy fire. Allied craft would be spared underwater attack. American citizens and ships could safely cross the Atlantic. Such a policy might foster peace with Germany as well as pleasing a Congress that hoped the entire submarine issue would disappear.

At first Wilson welcomed Lansing's scheme. Britain, he claimed, was "going beyond the spirit" of maritime practice by using guns for offensive purposes. On February 16, the president wrote House, then in London negotiating the House-Grey memorandum. Disarming merchant ships, claimed the president, would leave the Germans without excuse "to throw off all restraints in under-sea warfare. . . . We are amazed the English do not see this opportunity to gain a great advantage without losing anything."[4]

On January 18, Lansing, with Wilson's backing, submitted his modus vivendi to the Allies. The United States, he threatened, was seriously considering treating armed merchantmen as auxiliary cruisers, hence no longer recognizing their immunity from attack.[5]

London was appalled, fearing that the proposal would have legalized the wholesale sinking of merchant ships. British vessels would be deprived of a defense that the United States itself had formerly held legitimate. In a memorandum to the cabinet, Grey accused the United States of attempting to readjust "the balance of sea power in favour of our enemies."[6]

When, on January 29, the secretary's proposal reached the American public, it was extensively debated. Pro-German elements backed Lansing while pro-Allied ones opposed him. To *Fatherland* contributor Frederick Franklin Schrader, Lansing was advancing "precisely the points for which Germany has been contending with only a slight variation of terms." Hearst's *New York American* concurred, declaring that any armed ship was really "a war vessel." The *Nation* praised the secretary for understanding the viewpoints of both belligerents. The *Outlook* countered that America was telling peaceful merchantmen: "America has not protected you, and now America declines to allow you to protect yourselves." To the *New Republic,* the justice of the proposal could hardly be questioned, but the liberal weekly confessed that it could not bring itself to embarrass the Allies. Within a month it admitted that "every attempt to be fair to one of the belligerents involves unfairness to its enemies."[7]

Historians have reacted negatively toward Lansing's proposal. Patrick Devlin gives several reasons for finding the modus vivendi totally unrealistic. While the scheme would admittedly save civilian lives, it would leave British cargoes at Germany's mercy. "Would not the Germans continue to torpedo just as before, accusing the British of arming their ships?" Furthermore, periscopes were far from ideal for discerning whether a suspect ship was truly armed. Ross Gregory adds an additional objection: the arrangement left London with the decided impression that America remained at best confused. Assuredly, "it was contradictory to House's babbling in London and Paris about American eagerness to intervene in the war."[8]

Arthur S. Link is even more trenchant, calling Lansing's plan "one of the most maladroit blunders in American diplomatic history," a scheme revealing "the immaturity and inherent confusion of the President's policies." The proposal would jeopardize House's mission. More significantly, it could systematically destroy Britain's merchant marine.[9] In the skirmishes between submarines and armed merchantmen, U-boats usually escaped or protected themselves. The *Baralong* incident remained the exception.

On January 26, Lansing confidentially told the Austrian chargé about his scheme. Baron Erich Zwiedinek responded that the Central Powers were considering all-out war against armed ships. The secretary of state replied that "the sooner it was done the better." Lansing's reaction reached German chancellor Bethmann, who assumed that the United States welcomed maritime war against British armed merchantmen.[10]

Lansing had misled the Central Powers, later offering the curious explanation that he believed Germany's announcement would help expedite the pending *Lusitania* negotiations. In his memoirs he noted that one condition of settlement with Germany could involve an American demand that it withdraw any new U-boat orders. More likely, argues historian Ernest R. May, the secretary hoped any such declaration would force the Allies to disarm their merchantmen.[11]

Early in January 1916, Admiral Tirpitz predicted German defeat if his U-boats remained leashed; conversely, submarine warfare would force the British to sue for peace within two months. Admiralty chief Henning von Holtzendorff gave his enemy six months. A month later Tirpitz denied that an America at war could offer Britain much help.[12] By mid-February Erich von Falkenhayn, chief of the general staff, endorsed widespread submarine use. The battle of Verdun, launched on February 21, made Berlin more strident, particularly given the surprising French resistance. So, too, did the British defeat of the Turks at Erzurum, which increased peace sentiment among the Ottomans.

On February 10, Germany presented the State Department with exhibits designed to show that Britain had armed its merchantmen with the intent of attacking enemy submarines; in some cases, gun crews had been placed on board. Therefore, neutral governments should warn their citizens against traveling or transporting goods on such vessels. On the same day the Imperial Government issued its order: as of February 29, "Enemy merchantmen carrying guns should be regarded as warships and destroyed by all means." In short, in Berlin's eyes, there was no such thing as a defensively armed merchantman. Initially Bethmann and the Kaiser objected, fearing American entry into the war and questioning whether the U-boats could severely injure Britain. On February 22 Wilhelm told his chancellor: "Were I captain of a U-boat I would never torpedo a ship if I knew that women and children were on board."[13] Lansing inadvertently helped create the very situation he wanted to prevent.

Wilson and Lansing backtracked. After conferring on February 15, the president and his secretary of state agreed that they had committed a major error. In speaking to reporters, Lansing announced that the United States would not seek to change the rules in time of war. While hoping for an agreement and affirming that merchantmen should not carry guns, he stressed that merchant vessels had the legal right to arm defensively. He did not directly challenge the legality of Germany's announcement; rather he maintained that Americans reserved the right to travel on merchantmen armed solely for defense, something he had not asserted previously. If American lives were lost on such craft, the U.S. reaction would depend on whether the ship's armament was truly defensive. The secretary also announced that because of Berlin's "recent manifesto" of February 10, the United States must refuse Germany's *Lusitania* apology issued six days earlier.[14] Nevertheless, that matter remained buried.

The British waited until March 23 before officially rejecting the modus vivendi, although Grey gave informal assurances that all armament was solely defensive. On April 26 Lansing made public America's position. Merchantmen could arm for defense. If, however, these ships remained under orders to hunt down and destroy submarines, the United States would regard them as auxiliary cruisers.[15] The entire matter became somewhat moot, at least as far as entering U.S. ports was concerned, for the British avoided sending their ships to America until autumn and very few craft were dispatched afterward.

Motives for the administration's reversal are clear. House warned the administration that Lansing's proposal put his peace mission in jeopardy. Were the secretary's scheme implemented, the Allies, at best already suspicious, would have totally rejected Wilson as mediator. Not accidentally, the House-Grey memorandum was drafted just as Wilson abandoned his armed-ship plan. As it was, Britain remained fearful that the United States preferred to end tensions with Germany over the matter rather than risk war by backing the Allies.

Wilson's reversal did not come without its price. Some congressional leaders, ignorant of Wilson's wider diplomatic strategy, suspected that the president sought to become a belligerent. According to Claude Kitchin, "the President is anxious for war with Germany—his sympathies are so strong with the allies." On February 17, two days after Lansing repudiated his own proposal, Democratic representative Jeff: McLemore introduced a resolution requesting that the president warn American citizens against traveling on armed merchant ships.[16] McLemore was a former cowboy, gold prospector, and newspaperman who for some curious reason placed a colon between his first and last names.

On the next day, Senator Thomas Sterling (R-S.D.) countered with a resolution maintaining that the United States should resist Germany's new decree. He blamed Germany's U-boat directive on Lansing's modus vivendi, asserting that the secretary had encouraged Berlin's announcement. Lodge supported Sterling. The fresh policy indicated "a step toward war," with the United States aiding the Germans by the obvious threat of closing American ports to armed British merchantmen.[17]

On February 21, Wilson met with three leading congressional figures: Senate majority leader John W. Kern; William J. Stone, chairman of the Senate Foreign Relations Committee; and Hal Flood, chairman of the House Foreign Affairs Committee. The consultation focused on a bill, similar to McLemore's resolution, introduced on January 5 by Senator Thomas P. Gore (D-Okla.), a former Populist and a staunch agrarian. Submitted at Bryan's request and supported by House majority leader Kitchin, Gore's bill went beyond the mere warning embodied in McLemore's proposal; it prohibited the State Department from issuing passports to Americans traveling on belligerent ships. Even American and neutral craft could not carry U.S. passengers if such vessels transported contraband. In his supporting remarks, Gore proclaimed: "No single citizen should be allowed to run the risk of drenching this nation in blood merely in order that he may travel upon a belligerent rather than a neutral vessel."[18]

The three legislators feared that a German submarine, acting without warning, might sink an armed ship carrying Americans. During the meeting, Wilson showed himself unwilling to reveal the substance of the House mission, much less the memorandum that the colonel drafted with Grey. He voiced his personal endorsement of Lansing's modus vivendi but affirmed the Allies' right to arm their merchantmen. He also believed that such ships could legitimately enter American ports. In addition, Americans retained the right to travel on merchantmen sporting defensive arms. The United States would go so far as to sever diplomatic relations with Germany if it torpedoed such vessels without warning. Stone, among Wilson's strongest backers in the Senate, denied that the public would enter the war in order to vindicate the transit rights of a minuscule number of Americans. "You have no right to ask me to follow such a course," he told Wilson. "It may mean war for my country."[19]

On the day after Wilson conferred with the three congressional leaders, Foreign Secretary Gottlieb von Jagow announced that Germany would sink belligerent armed merchant ships, even if they carried passengers. Congress manifested unprecedented panic. Surely, many members reasoned, if Berlin proclaimed that armed merchantmen took on the character of a ship of war, the administration should not defend any obsolete right of its citizens to travel on them. Led by Bryan Democrats, critics engaged in open revolt.

Flood reported back to the Democratic members of his committee that Wilson stood firm in opposing McLemore's resolution. All present responded that the president had forty-eight hours to reverse himself; otherwise the House would adopt the measure. A partial canvass conducted on February 23 indicated that such a resolution would pass by three or four to one; the "ship of state," Gore warned, was "driving headlong upon the breakers."[20]

Wilson faced the gravest political challenge to date. Adopting McLemore's proposal would ruin the chief executive's standing with the Allied governments and possibly destroy potential influence over Germany's leaders, because no one would know whether it was the president or the Congress who made American policy. Wilson particularly feared that Capitol Hill would ruin possible mediation efforts.

On February 24 a crucial exchange took place between Wilson and Stone. In an open letter to the president, the Missouri senator argued that those Americans "recklessly risking their lives on armed belligerent ships" were committing "a sort of moral treason against the Republic." At the suggestion of his secretary, Joseph Tumulty, Wilson replied the same day. He publicly pledged to do everything possible to keep the nation out of war but denied that he could abridge any right of Americans without sacrificing the nation's honor and self-respect. "Once accept a single abatement of right and many other humiliations would certainly follow, and the whole fine fabric of international law might crumble under our hands piece by piece. What we are contending for in this matter is of the very essence of the things that have made America a sovereign nation."[21] In short, the nation would be justified in entering the conflict if the lives of its citizens were lost on Allied merchantmen, even if such ships were armed.

In this message Wilson pursued several aims. By manifesting firmness, he tried to convince Allied leaders that he could be trusted with an early peace bid. Moreover, such resoluteness might force the Germans to give up their new policy. In addition, the president sought to rally the American public behind his leadership, especially if the United States found itself forced to confront Germany on the high seas. Wilson also desired to preempt congressional initiative before any crucial votes took place, so that he would not appear to be yielding under pressure. Reasons existed for this last concern. Former Senator Root, for example, had recently accused him of being "brave in words and irresolute in action."[22]

By and large, the American press supported the president, the monthly *Current Opinion* noting a "phenomenal outburst" of newspaper backing.

Wilson's "clear phrasing of the issue of American rights," remarked the *Nation*, "will make it impossible to assail him successfully in Congress." The *New Republic* claimed that the president had brushed aside Congress in the same manner as Imperial Germany's rulers had ignored its Socialists. In the American instance, however, the legislative branch had forced Wilson's hand. Moreover, the president was acting "in a good cause."[23]

Scholars differ concerning the wisdom of the letter to Stone. Robert W. Tucker calls it "the most extreme expression of the domino theory made in the twentieth century by an American president." Once uttered, the words formed "a procrustean bed" from which the president could not easily escape. Edward H. Buehrig declares that it manifested an "extraordinary legalism" that violated Wilson's own doubts about the workability of traditional rules. To Thomas A. Bailey and Paul B. Ryan, the chief executive's communication was "extraordinary." The president kept claiming that his fellow citizens not only possessed the right to embark on armed munitions-carriers; their presence actually conferred the status of immunity on these ships. The chief executive did not perceive that his "fine fabric of international law" had already crumbled. Arthur S. Link faults Wilson for resorting to hyperbole, engaging in historical inaccuracy (he had already consented to many abridgments of American rights), and failing to manifest the flexibility concerning armed ships that marked his true position. John A. Thompson, however, finds that the message was most effective; it ultimately defeated congressional opposition and weakened Germany's truculent Admiralty.[24]

Wilson still faced Congress as a whole. At 9:00 A.M. on February 25, in what is called the "Sunrise Conference," Majority Leader Kitchin, Representative Flood, and House Speaker Champ Clark (D-Mo.) conferred with the president in the White House. When Clark reported that the House stood two-to-one in favor of McLemore's resolution, Wilson reiterated his opposition. If an armed Allied ship was torpedoed and American lives lost, he would break relations with the Central Powers, even risking war in the process. In fact, American belligerency might end the war much sooner than predicted. When accused of desiring war with Germany, the president snapped: "In God's name, could any one have done more than I have to show a desire for peace?"[25]

On the same day, with McLemore's resolution pending in the House, Gore introduced a resolution, this one expressing "the sense of the Congress" that Americans avoid traveling on armed ships belonging to belligerent powers and that any such passengers be refused passports. A Senate poll indicated that this resolution would be defeated 70 to 25. The blind Oklahoman was not optimistic concerning passage, content to see in the mere discussion of his resolution an unofficial warning against dangerous travel.[26] Congressional backing for the dissenting legislators was proving itself unexpectedly flimsy.

One day later, Lansing told reporters that American travel rights remained valid for those voyaging on defensively armed merchant ships, though not on those fitted for offensive warfare. Besides, the United States would gladly discuss with Germany the specific meaning of defensive armament. At least temporarily, congressional agitation came to a halt. McLemore said that he would not press immediately for a House vote; Gore's Senate resolution drew just twenty supporters.[27]

Wilson confidently demanded that the House Rules Committee vote on McLemore's resolution. On February 29, he wrote its acting chairman, E.W. Pou (D-N.C.): "The report that there are divided counsels in Congress in regard to the foreign policy of the Government is being made industrious use of in foreign capitals. I believe that report to be false, but so long as it is anywhere credited it cannot fail to do the greatest harm and expose the country to the most serious risks."[28]

The *New York World* strengthened Wilson's hand by publishing documents implying that the National German-American Alliance had spearheaded the Gore-McLemore resolutions. The Alliance denied complicity. George Sylvester Viereck later gave the claim some credence. In his memoirs he asserted that Shaemas O'Sheel, a young Irish-American poet and politician close to the *Fatherland,* had suggested the resolution to McLemore and drafted it himself.[29] Certainly the preamble was couched in pro-German language that McLemore himself soon sought to delete.

Initially Germany appeared obstinate, refusing to rescind its renewed warfare against armed merchantmen and correctly claiming that it was not violating the *Arabic* pledge. Nevertheless, on February 28, the Foreign Office assured Lansing that new orders had been issued to German naval commanders: no armed liner would be sunk "unless such armament is proved."[30]

During the debate in the Senate, Lodge insisted that the president should not be crippled in diplomatic negotiations. Suppose, speculated William E. Borah, a German submarine caused the death of one hundred Americans; would Gore's resolution prevent the United States from demanding just reparation? Support for Wilson came from John Sharp Williams, who asked: "Shall I exclaim 'America First' or shall I sing 'Deutschland über Alles?'" Gore pointed to the Sunrise Conference as proof that Wilson sought war, though the Oklahoma senator had not been present. Gore falsely claimed that the president denied that American entry into war was in itself "an evil." Stone and Flood instantly repudiated Gore's account, while Wilson branded the accusation "too grotesquely false to deserve credence for a moment."[31]

Though few in Congress sought a showdown with the president, Treasury Secretary McAdoo and Postmaster General Albert S. Burleson were taking no chances. They threatened to withdraw patronage from Democratic backers of McLemore's resolution, especially pressuring members of the House Foreign Affairs Committee. Lansing submitted a memorandum to Flood arguing that the McLemore resolution would usurp executive powers, deprive Americans of legitimate rights, jeopardize current negations with the belligerents, and condone Germany's "wanton slaughter on noncombatants."[32]

The first confrontation arose in the Senate. On March 3, Gore radically altered his resolution, an action obviously designed to embarrass the president. It no longer denied passports to Americans traveling on armed belligerent vessels. By striking out the single word "not," it specified that the loss of American lives on armed merchantmen "without notice or warning" would constitute grounds for war. The gambit created virtual chaos on the floor. Lodge led eastern Republicans in helping to table the resolution by a vote of 68 to 14. Even Gore concurred.[33] Wilson ended up with a vote that set aside a resolution, hostile in intent, that, ironically, embodied his policies.

Not many senators desired to go on record over such a controversial matter. Besides, the parliamentary situation was so confusing that James P. Clarke complained that few senators really knew what they were voting on. Reed Smoot wished to be excused on those very grounds. Twelve of the fourteen opposing the tabling motion were Republicans, usually of progressive leanings. Foremost among them were La Follette, Norris, Cummins, and Works. One party progressive, Wesley Jones of Washington, denied that the Senate had ruled on the fundamental issue: "We have only done like the ostrich, and in the face of danger have covered our heads in the sand." The confrontational Borah protested administration efforts "to cut off discussion." Although some administration foes hailed from midwestern states with large German American populations, none voiced support for the Central Powers. Historian John Milton Cooper Jr. sees genuine isolationist sympathies at work.[34]

Certain commentators pointed out that the Senate tally indicated no victors. In examining his colleagues' votes, Senator Norris deduced that "the real majority" lay "on the other side," that is, against the president. Journalist Willis Abbot of the *New York American* denied that Wilson had won; the president was denied the thorough discussion he had requested. His own views were relegated to a shelved resolution. Similarly, David Lawrence of the *New York Evening Post* concluded that larger issues had been ignored; a considerable number of senators favored the warning concerning belligerent ships. The *New Republic* accused the Senate of acting in a "cowardly spirit" by skirting its duty of overtly backing the president. The *New York Times* referred to the fourteen "Germans" in the Senate.[35]

March 7 marked the House's turn. It voted 276 to 142 to adopt a resolution, made by the Foreign Affairs Committee, to table the McLemore resolution, thereby, like the Senate, refusing to commit itself concerning the matter of traveling on armed merchantmen. The debate lasted seven hours, consuming 4.5 million words. Both parties split on the issue: 182 Democrats, 93 Republicans, and 1 Progressive supported the tabling motion; 33 Democrats, 102 Republicans, 5 Progressives, 1 independent, and 1 Socialist opposed it, therein defying the president. Despite anti-German statements by such leaders as Root and Roosevelt, Republican backers of McLemore's proposal included Minority Leader James R. Mann, former House Speaker Joseph G. Cannon (Ill.), and other Old Guard stalwarts. Mann hoped that "our citizens will never be put to the test of having to fight because some fool has involved us by entering upon a joy ride."[36]

The sectional alignment foreshadowed debates over neutrality legislation during the 1930s. Upholding Wilson were the Solid South and much of the Middle Atlantic region. Strong dissent came from the Midwest, including entire delegations from Iowa, Nebraska, Minnesota, and Wisconsin. Of the 33 Democrats who bucked the administration, 25 resided west of the Alleghenies. Bryan called the tally irrelevant, for "the real object has been accomplished by discussion. The people of the United States are not willing to go to war to vindicate the right of Americans to take these risks; neither is Congress." Historian William Henry Harbaugh writes: "Probably a majority of congressmen voted contrary to their convictions."[37]

Party loyalty strongly bolstered Wilson's ranks, as did fears of patronage loss. Some disliked McLemore's wording, believing it was too pro-German. Many supporters did not want to embarrass the president overseas. In the words of Congressman Cyrus Cline (D-Ind.), the question centered on "whether we shall stand by the president in this crisis or not."[38] Undoubtedly, many Democrats felt most grateful for the New Freedom reforms that the administration had spearheaded, bills that included the Underwood Tariff, the Federal Reserve Act, and the Clayton Antitrust Act.

These congressional votes gave the president the flexibility he sought. Among his fellow Democrats, only two lone senators and fewer than one-quarter of his party's congressmen had backed the Gore-McLemore resolutions. Wilson had shown himself the unquestioned leader of his party and in full control of his nation's foreign policy. Both *Current Opinion* and the *Literary Digest* reported overwhelming editorial support for the chief executive. At the same time, Bernstorff was undoubtedly correct in believing that the president had won a Pyrrhic victory, for Wilson promised that he would do everything possible to avoid war. The majority of both houses, the ambassador maintained, wanted Americans to keep off armed ships.[39]

Germany was fully aware of the American debates. When its press published Wilson's letter to Stone, the Wilhelmstrasse feared war with the United States. On February 29 Bethmann, citing massive statistical data, denied that Germany's existing submarine fleet was sufficient to blockade the British Isles. Conversely, unrestricted U-boat warfare would bring the United States into the conflict, a move that would encourage France and Russia, discourage Berlin's allies, and cause many Germans to doubt the possibility of eventual victory. More concrete risks included the dispatch of several thousand U.S. volunteers to the western front and greatly increased American credit and supplies to the Allies. In addition, Rumania, Denmark, and the Netherlands might join the Entente.[40]

On March 4, at a German Imperial Conference, the Kaiser asserted that Germany would begin unrestricted submarine warfare around April 1, to which Bethmann warned that an American response would guarantee the Reich's defeat in an exhaustive war. The chancellor denied that he could assume responsibility for such a catastrophe. On the following day, after meeting alone with Wilhelm, Bethmann reported that the Kaiser would reserve any action concerning a comprehensive U-boat campaign. As this imperial judgment involved a severe reprimand of naval secretary Tirpitz, the admiral resigned on March 12. Not only were the decisions a major victory for Bethmann, who now held renewed hope of avoiding war with the United States. They were a triumph for Wilson, whose recent confrontation with Congress had been the principal factor in spurring the chancellor to challenge his emperor.[41]

Yet, on March 13, Admiral Holtzendorff issued new orders: Germany would sink armed enemy merchant ships encountered in the war zone without warning. Conversely it would spare similar ships if they were disarmed or if they were ocean liners. By these dictates Germany was resuming the U-boat policy it had maintained until October 1915, except that now passenger ships were promised protection. The decision by no means alleviated tensions with the United States, as submarine captains often found it impossible to distinguish whether ships were armed or unarmed, neutral or enemy, merchant or passenger. In his memoirs, Bernstorff wrote that mistakes were inevitable.[42]

Such errors arose quickly. In mid-March, for example, a submarine struck the Dutch passenger steamer *Tubantia* off the Netherlands coast; the sinking violated the *Arabic* pledge of September 1915, by which U-boats were obligated to spare passenger liners. Far more important, at 2:41 P.M. on March 24, 1916, *U-29* fired a torpedo without warning into the passenger ship *Sussex* in the English Channel. Flying the French flag and owned by the London, Brighton & South Coast Railroad Company, the vessel was following its usual route from Folkestone to Dieppe. Aboard were 325 voyagers, of whom 22 were Americans. Because its boilers did not explode, the ship did not sink; rather it was towed to Boulogne. The blast, though, killed or injured about 80 people, including 4 wounded Americans. The captain of *U-29*, Herbert Pustkuchen, mistook the *Sussex* for a minelayer.

Lansing sought an immediate break in diplomatic relations, writing Wilson three days after the sinking: "We can no longer temporize in the matter of submarine warfare when Americans are being killed, wounded, or endangered by the illegal and inhuman conduct of the Germans." On March 28 the president's cabinet supported an ultimatum.[43]

Two days later, House met with the president. The colonel suggested that Wilson send Bernstorff home and make a "dispassionate statement" of the Allied case. He volunteered to go the Netherlands, where in midsummer he would confer with the Allies and convey to Berlin American terms for ending the war. Wilson feared that breaking diplomatic relations would prolong the conflict indefinitely, there being "no one to lead the way out."[44]

On April 3 the colonel wrote Wilson, telling him that immediate belligerency would strengthen the president both at home and with the Allies. "Your influence at the peace congress would be enormously enhanced instead of lessened, for we would be the only nation at the conference desiring nothing except the ultimate good of mankind. We could still be the force to stop the war when the proper time came." Within three days, the president tersely cabled Grey: "It now seems probable that the country must break with Germany." He asked whether Britain would act upon the House-Grey memorandum.[45]

The Wilson administration, however, drew little domestic support for any confrontational policy. Congress lacked any martial spirit. Interior Secretary Lane thought that 80 percent of the American people favored peace at any price. Navy Secretary Daniels warned of recrimination in the 1916 election. On April 8, House shifted his position, cautioning Grey that both he and Wilson thought that American belligerency would indefinitely lengthen the war. The colonel confessed skepticism concerning sufficient popular backing for entering the conflict. On the same day Sir Edward replied that he was not ready to apply the House-Grey memorandum. Referring to sentiment in France, Grey said: "Feeling there was that war must yet continue to have any chance of securing satisfactory terms from Germany." Yet that very day House met with Bernstorff, telling the ambassador that Wilson would have to break relations with Germany unless it stopped sinking passenger ships without warning.[46]

Although Wilson hoped that Britain would act upon the House-Grey accord, he would not let Lansing and House push him further. He kept his own counsel, meeting with few people and even leaving Washington for a weekend cruise on the presidential yacht *Mayflower.*

At first, Gottlieb von Jagow denied culpability, writing a public communication to Ambassador Gerard on April 10. The German foreign secretary admitted that at the same place and time that the *Sussex* had been hit, *U-29* had struck what Commander Herbert Pustkuchen had identified as a "mine-layer of the recently built English *Arabic* class." Comparing photos of the *Sussex* with the commander's sketches of what he had torpedoed, Jagow concluded that *U-29* had not hit the *Sussex* but rather "a war vessel." As if to argue that Germans were not barbarians, he cited the German sinking of three other British merchantmen in which, in each case, crews had been evacuated. Admiral Holtzendorff contended that an English submarine, using a German torpedo, had sunk the *Sussex,* a claim Admiral Georg Alexander von Müller, chief of the naval cabinet, deemed "very picaresque."[47]

The American press reacted to Jagow's epistle most negatively, insisting that Germany had engaged in deception. Remarked the *New York Evening Post:* "We have had something too much of all this, ever since the day of the

monstrous crime of May 7, 1915; the time has come for making an end of it."
Bernstorff later labeled Jagow's note "probably the most unfortunate document that ever passed from Berlin to Washington," especially because the
discovery of torpedo shrapnel in the *Sussex*'s hull "placed the matter beyond
all doubt."[48]

German Americans acted defensively, deluging Washington with cables
and petitions calling for peace. The *Fatherland* denied that Germany had
torpedoed the *Sussex*. Irish American partisan Jeremiah O'Leary claimed
that as the ship was struck on the bow, it had hit a mine. Publicist Schrader
accused Wilson of seeking to divert American attention from Mexico, where
a "punitive expedition," led by General John J. Pershing, was encountering
resistance.[49]

On April 18, Wilson sent an ultimatum. He denounced Germany's U-
boat campaign, be the target belligerent or neutral, freighters or passenger
liners. Because of the nature of the submarine and its method of attack,
he deemed its current use "utterly incompatible with the principles of humanity, the long-established and incontrovertible rights of neutrals, and the
sacred immunities of noncombatants. . . . Unless the Imperial Government
should now immediately declare its purpose to abandon its present methods of submarine warfare against passenger and freight-carrying vessels, the
Government of the United States can have no choice but sever diplomatic
relations with the German empire."[50] The president was threatening war.

Three days earlier, Jagow had cabled Bernstorff: "We have modified submarine war to maintain friendly advantages with America [sacrificing] important military advantages and in contradicting [contradiction] to excited
public opinion here. We therefore trust that American Government will appreciate this and not put forward new demands which might [bring] us into
impossible situation." Bernstorff immediately told Lansing, but the secretary
did not inform Wilson of the news.[51]

It might not have mattered. The president sought a showdown. Admittedly he shared the public's deep aversion to war and retained his hope of
mediating the European conflict. Yet he believed that to remain silent would
humiliate him personally, make U-boat warfare more ruthless, increase Allied mistrust, and intensify domestic chauvinism so strongly that he might
lose control of events.

Addressing Congress on April 19, Wilson spoke for sixteen minutes, repeating his demands on Germany and invoking the rights of Americans,
neutral nations, and humanity at large. He deliberately left unclear whether

Germany could attack armed merchantmen, fearing that such a concrete stipulation would jeopardize current negotiations and undermine popular consensus. In addition, he and Lansing doubted whether Berlin should be held to such a rigid stipulation. Therefore, Germany was left "an out." It could accept Wilson's note without totally giving up submarine warfare.[52]

Many Senators praised Wilson's speech. To Senator Atlee Pomerene (D-Ohio), who expressed the majority sentiment, the choice lay between approving the president's message or continuing to witness neutral vessels torpedoed and innocent citizens killed. Lodge asserted that Wilson could not have done less. In the House, opposition was more marked. A survey from the admittedly neutralist *New York American* revealed a mere 20 congressmen favoring a break in diplomatic relations, 112 opposed, and 187 uncommitted. The newspaper could not reach 100 representatives.[53]

Some dissenters in Congress offered biting comments. William S. Kenyon (R-Iowa) said that if the United States entered the conflict, those who insisted on traveling on armed belligerent ships should be the first to enlist. Representative Mann deemed Wilson's address "a campaign dodge," maintaining that the president hated the Germans and sought to force a conflict. Senator James K. Vardaman accused the chief executive of involving America in "the bloody conflict" so as to protect British and French commerce.[54]

Caught up in a wave of jingoism, the American press—particularly in large cities—offered strong endorsement, as did journals in Paris and London. The *Nation* reported that an overwhelming majority of the president's fellow citizens supported him. The *Outlook* stressed that Wilson should have spoken out a year ago, at the time of the *Gulflight* incident; nonetheless, Americans should prepare for war with "loyalty, unity, and high resolve." The United States, wrote the *New Republic,* must not fight to restore the antiquated doctrine of neutrality but rather to drive the Central Powers from occupied lands. America should become a guarantor of Belgian neutrality and maintain the inviolability of postwar buffer states. All nations must pledge "to use their resources against the Power which refuses to submit its quarrel to international inquiry."[55]

Not surprisingly, German American organizations beseeched Congress to prevent war. So, too, did many American newspapers. The *New York American* judged Wilson's note a "peremptory ultimatum" in the tone of those issued by emperors Francis Joseph and Wilhelm in July 1914. Writing in the wake of Pancho Villa's raid on Columbus, New Mexico, which took place on March 9, it noted that the Mexicans had killed infinitely more Americans than the Germans had. Bryan called hostilities with Berlin a "crime against civilization," asserting that the controversy should either be submitted to an international tribunal for investigation or postponed until the war ended. To Henry Ford the note embodied "political bunk." Attacking Wilson from the opposite perspective, Roosevelt accused Wilson of repeating his "strict accountability" note of the previous year while irresponsibly allowing his nation to remain disarmed.[56]

Throughout the world, nowhere more than in Berlin, people predicted war. But because the Reich had just experienced a bloody repulse at Verdun and was awaiting Britain's Somme offensive, it would not risk taking on a new adversary, at least not while it lacked sufficient submarines to wage an effective struggle. In April 1916 Germany possessed just 43 working U-boats; 9 more were under construction.

On April 22 Bernstorff, alarmed at the possibility of impending war, asked House what terms would satisfy Wilson. Within a week Lansing cabled Berlin, declaring that Germany must abandon "illegal" methods of submarine combat, though he implied that adherence to normal rules of cruiser warfare was acceptable. Chancellor Bethmann wanted to end the new submarine policy, fearing that any break with the United States would strengthen Britain, leading to Germany's defeat. Chief of Staff Falkenhayn challenged him, warning the emperor that current U-boat warfare must continue; otherwise the general would have to terminate his continuing assault on Verdun. Admiral Holtzendorff came to Bethmann's rescue, warning that continued unlimited submarine assaults would bring the United States into the conflict: "From the military point of view—at least from the naval point of view—this risk could be accepted if need be, but from the economic point of view our situation would be considerably worsened. This rich and inaccessible country [the United States] can carry on a war for ten years; it will bring to our staggering enemies considerable moral and material aid and will strengthen them and prolong their resistance—*and in particular England*."[57]

The Kaiser reluctantly supported his chancellor. A week before, Wilhelm had attacked Wilson's invocation of the term "humanity," caustically remarking that America's "sending millions of shells & cartridges to England and her Allies to kill and maim 1000s of German soldiers is not '*inhuman*' but quite proper because *lucrative*." Lunching with the emperor, Ambassador Gerard retorted: "If two men entered my grounds and one stepped on my flowerbeds and the other killed my sister, I should probably first pursue the murderer of my sister."[58]

On May 4, Germany changed course. In a note from Jagow to Gerard that soon became known as the *Sussex* pledge, the foreign secretary pledged that hereafter submarines would observe rules of cruiser warfare, including provision for the passengers and crew of unresisting merchant vessels. Jagow did add a warning. If the United States would not compel the British to observe international law, Germany would be facing "a new situation in which it must reserve itself complete liberty of decision." The note remained silent regarding the controversial issue of armed merchantmen because Wilson had not raised the matter. Berlin could not have announced total repudiation of submarine warfare and retained its domestic support. Four days later, in addressing the specific matter of the *Sussex*, Jagow accepted evidence supplied by the American State Department and admitted that *U-29* had sunk the ship. The commander, whom Jagow claimed had honestly miscalculated, had been punished; in addition, Germany expressed "sincere regret" and promised to indemnify American citizens.[59]

Within the Wilson administration, opinions were divided. Lansing found Germany's concession a "gold brick" swindle, claiming that the message was insolent and required further examination: "The more I study the reply the less I like it." House was delighted that Germany had made such major concessions.[60]

Berlin, however, had won few American converts. In surveying editorial comment, the *New York Times* tallied forty-five newspapers disapproving Jagow's note, eighteen approving, and twelve uncommitted. As expected, the South and the Midwest voiced relief that war could be avoided. Viereck argued that Germany had met America's demands, its reply to Wilson's ultimatum being "dignified, just, unassailable." The president should dispatch an ultimatum to Britain within thirty-six hours.[61]

In one of the shortest diplomatic notes on record, the president simply accepted the German avowal, expecting "scrupulous execution" of its commitment. In reference to Berlin's insistence that he pressure the British, Wilson replied that he could not accept conditions concerning "the attitude or action of any other government." As Bailey and Ryan note, "There was no meeting of minds."[62]

Wilson's response met with strong domestic approval. A congressional poll taken by the *New York American* revealed much support. The House supported the president 83 to 10, the Senate 18 to 3. Another congressional poll, taken by the more belligerent *New York Tribune*, revealed that only a minuscule number deemed that Germany had supplied grounds for war.

The *Outlook* dissented from the consensus, observing that Berlin had merely suspended its policy, not abandoned it.[63]

Historians debate Wilson's role in the entire *Sussex* matter. Writing in the 1930s, Walter Millis saw Wilson building "an iron trap for himself and his countrymen," for he had so positioned matters that further flexibility was impossible. Once Germany decided that U-boat warfare was more beneficial than American neutrality, the president would be helpless. Writing over seventy years later, Robert W. Tucker finds little merit in Wilson's stance; threatening war over American travel rights violated "almost any rational calculus of national interest." Better to have compromised with the Germans while pressuring Britain to moderate its blockade. Ernest R. May differs, asserting that the *Sussex* sinking had left the chief executive "no alternatives except to confess impotence or to deliver a virtual ultimatum." Link praises Wilson for taking a calculated risk, continuing that the president's demarche probably prevented war in 1916. During that summer, he continues, Germany showed itself able to avoid new incidents while revealing that it could still engage in highly successful submarine warfare. To Wilson biographer August Heckscher, the chief executive had made a brilliant diplomatic stroke, winning "a solid victory for the United States and all neutral nations."[64]

Submarine warfare was not the only source of contention with Germany. In April 1916 Department of Justice officials arrested eight men in New Jersey, accusing them of placing explosives in the cargoes of ships sailing from American ports. Authorities charged the suspects with making these incendiary bombs on board the North German Lloyd line's *Friedrich der Grosse,* which had sought refuge at Hoboken at the outbreak of war. Furthermore, a federal grand jury in New York indicted several prominent Germans for conspiring to blow up Ontario's Welland Canal. Among the accused were military attaché Franz von Papen, who had already left the United States.

On July 30, at 2:00 A.M., an earsplitting explosion took place on a promontory jutting out from New Jersey into New York harbor. Located across from Bedloe's Island, where the Statue of Liberty is located, the site was somewhat inaccurately called Black Tom Island. Here lay a huge freight yard where gunpowder and munitions were deposited. These goods, manufactured in the Northeast and the Midwest, awaited shipment to Britain and France. Loss of life was negligible, although the shock reached Philadelphia and Maryland. Thousands of skyscraper windows were shattered, shrapnel ripped into the giant Statue of Liberty, gaping holes were blasted in walls on nearby Ellis Island. German nationals were immediately interrogated, though it took more than two decades before the Mixed Claim Commission established that Berlin was responsible. The *Fatherland* simply remarked that the incident "seems like the judgment of God on the hideous traffic in murder."[65]

Despite such incidents, tensions with Germany were waning, while they were increasing with Britain. On April 24, 1916, the Easter Rebellion broke out in Dublin, triggered by a German promise to ship munitions and arm anti-British insurgents. Rebels captured the post office, raised the nationalist flag, and proclaimed a republic. Unfortunately for the rebels, the Germans had to scuttle their supply ship. The British rushed sufficient troops in to crush the insurrection, then executed fifteen rebel leaders. Among them was Sir Roger Casement, who had been knighted by the Crown for his exposés of brutality in the Congo and who had just arrived in a German U-boat, ironically to quell any premature uprising. Making no secret of his sentiments, Casement, while visiting friends in America in August 1914, had told the *Brooklyn Eagle* that he hoped Germany would win the war. Shelly Skeffington, editor of the *Irish Citizen,* was also shot during the rebellion. He had taken no part in the rising; his murderer was later judged insane. Three thousand other Irishmen, usually seized at random, were interned in England.

When news came to America that the rebellion was ruthlessly squelched, Irish Americans protested vehemently. At the time of the revolt, they had been divided over the merits of the uprising. The more militant had been quite open concerning their anti-British feelings, the Clan-na-Gael working closely with Bernstorff and military attaché Papen to secure German arms and officers for an Irish uprising.

In early March 1916, an "Irish Race Convention" met in New York. John W. Goff, a Tammany judge who was born in the Emerald Isle, addressed the gathering, saying: "I want to see the power of England broken on land and sea. It is treason to our race to hope for or help in an English victory." The convention formed a new organization, the Friends of Irish Freedom. Upon hearing the news of the abortive Easter uprising, various Irish American societies in New York gathered to denounce England, passing a resolution "to see Ireland recognized as a belligerent and as an ally of the central powers."[66]

Just a week before the rebellion began, Wilson learned that New York Supreme Court Justice Daniel Cohalan, an ardent Irish American nationalist, was in secret contact with the German embassy. In a cable to Ambassador Bernstorff, Cohalan suggested that Germany attack England from the air and divert the Royal Navy the moment the Irish began their rebellion.

If possible, Germany should land troops and arms. Such activity would enable Ireland to close its ports to England while permitting the Reich to use them as submarine bases. Furthermore, Papen had been in direct contact with Casement. Bernstorff, who was close to the Clan-na-Gael, was fully informed about plans for the coming rebellion.[67]

Some Casement supporters accused the American government of having betrayed their hero to Britain. There might have been some truth to the charge, for on April 18, 1916, six days before the uprising, federal officials raided the office of Wolf von Igel, Papen's successor as military attaché and director of German intelligence operations in the United States. Confiscated papers included telegrams describing arms shipments and preparations for the uprising.[68]

The repression jolted the American public, with even Anglophiles condemning the executions. Britain had inadvertently bolstered neutralist sentiments. The Senate, with an eye on the Irish American vote in the forthcoming elections, adopted a resolution requesting that Wilson seek clemency for Casement, but it reached London after the nationalist had been executed. The *Fatherland* published a cartoon showing a half-naked Ireland nailed to a cross. The caption: "John Bull: Savior of Small Nations." The *New York American* compared Casement to Washington, Jefferson, and Franklin. The more moderate *New Republic* aptly remarked that the Dublin executions had created more American isolationism than any event since the war began. Even such a pronounced Anglophile as author William Dean Howells denounced the shooting of Irish insurrectionists as resembling German *Schrecklichkeit,* meaning terror. The British had reason to worry.[69]

Americans considered British activities in Greece far less important, but occasionally they expressed criticism. In October 1915 the Allies occupied Salonica, in time taking over Greek bases, demanding the demobilization of the Greek army, and seeking the resignation of King Constantine, whose wife was the sister of Kaiser Wilhelm. The *New York American* accused Britain of having "seized his [the Greek king's] seaports, occupied his lands, forcibly blockaded his merchant ships, destroyed his railroads and bridges, attempted to incite revolution against his rightful authority and hold Greece captured against the will of her sovereign and her people." Noting England's excuse of military necessity and promises to pay for damage after the war ended, the Hearst daily found its reasoning exactly the same as Germany's concerning Belgium.[70]

From the spring of 1915, London continually tightened its blockade, moving to bring all neutral trade under control. In October Britain initiated a practice called "bunkering"; it would withhold "bunker" coal from American ships unless assured that their destination was friendly.[71] Britain claimed it needed the coal for its own war effort. Furthermore, it was difficult to haul coal to distant ports for the indiscriminate use of neutrals. In most cases, however, the British did not withhold this resource and the United States never suffered much inconvenience.

Not until April 24, 1916, in a thirteen-thousand-word memorandum, did Britain respond to Lansing's indictment of the previous October. The blockade, it insisted, met the fundamental criteria of legality, for few ships were able to slip through. The "doctrine of continuous voyage" justified the ongoing crackdown. As American trade with Germany's neutral neighbors had increased many times over, it was obvious that the Reich was serving as the ultimate destination. Why otherwise, for example, had American exports of lard to Sweden increased tenfold in 1915? By September Britain had slightly relented, issuing "letters of assurance" that would permit large American exporters to trade with Germany's adjacent neighbors.[72]

Of greater concern to America were Allied seizures of American mail. In December 1915, the British honored a most significant French request: it would remove first-class mail and parcels containing contraband from neutral ships journeying between America and Europe's neutral ports. By the end of the month, they seized hundreds of bags from ships bound for the Scandinavian countries.

Finally, on May 24, 1916, having made several futile protests, Lansing—strongly backed by Wilson—sent French ambassador Jules Jusserand a stern note. The United States, warned the secretary, "can no longer tolerate the wrongs which citizens of the United States have suffered and continue to suffer through these methods." Exactly one month later, Britain made a partial reply, reporting merely that its Foreign Office found incidents of censorship few in number. In mid-October Jusserand forwarded a British and French memorandum justifying the mail searches; they had stifled "hostile acts" and "dangerous plots" against the Allies.[73]

In an article titled "British Hands in Our Mail-Bags," the *Literary Digest* reported strong press support for the administration's protest. The *New Republic* downplayed the quarrel, arguing that "we are suffering inconvenience and commercial loss that can be repaired." Moreover, given American sympathy for France and England, "legal 'rights' seem less important than the greater issues at stake." The far more neutralist *New York American* supported a resolution of Congressman Peter F. Tague, a Democrat from Boston, who called upon the American navy to convoy the mails between the United States and neutral ports. The daily editorialized: "THEN LET THE BRITISH ATTEMPT TO SEIZE THAT MAIL IF THEY CARE TO DO SO."[74]

In September the American embassy in London reported that Britain had opened consular mail dealing with commercial matters. Even the pro-Entente Lansing later recalled incidents in which the London Board of Trade read business communications with the intent of passing on secrets to British firms.[75]

The Allies presented more serious evidence of economic threat. On June 14–17 Entente nations held an economic conference in Paris. They accused the Central Powers of inaugurating a Central European Zollverein, that is, a protectionist customs union. To match this challenge, they sought restrictive trade regulations against their enemies, some provisions of which would remain after the war ended. They vaguely spoke of "a common economic policy" that would foster agricultural and industrial independence and greater shipping, telegraphic, and postal coordination.[76]

Americans were quick to show alarm. In a memo to Wilson, Lansing found the Paris agreement proposing "to continue the war industrially after actual warfare ceases," something that would "cause the Central Powers to hesitate in taking steps toward a restoration of peace." "Perhaps," warned Senator Stone, it would be only natural for the victorious Allies "to turn a cold, icy face to America and all the rest of the world." Such a policy, he threatened, would "be short-sighted, resulting in retaliatory measures." Colonel George Harvey of the *North American Review*, who was usually pro-British, accused the Allies of seeking to isolate the United States. The National Foreign Trade Council feared a return to mercantilism at the expense of U.S. trade. The *New Republic* stressed the necessity of German markets for American copper, cotton, tobacco, and foodstuffs; in addition, Latin America depended on importing German manufactures and exporting such items as coffee, hides, and tobacco. The Allies could offer a defeated Reich no compensation for the loss of this trade.[77]

Fatherland contributors used particularly explosive rhetoric. Political scientist John W. Burgess sought to retaliate by blacklisting all of Britain. To financial writer Charles A. Collman, "England tried to knife us in the back." After the conflict, wrote engineer Frank Koester, "the American manufacturer will be in the position of a fat dog among a pack of wolves."[78]

In August Prime Minister Herbert Asquith denied that Allied economic policy was aimed at the United States; his nation only contemplated measures of self-defense. Sir John Simon, recently home secretary, warned his countrymen that the proposed measures would backfire, shifting the center of world trade from London to New York.[79]

Despite such tensions, all during the spring of 1916, House beseeched Grey to consult his partners and request American mediation. On March 24, Britain's foreign secretary maintained that the fighting at Verdun was still in doubt and that the Allies needed greater success before entering into negotiations. House wrote Grey on April 7: "We are not so sure of the support of the American people on the submarine issue, while we are confident that they would respond to the higher and nobler issue of stopping the war." Early in May, House stressed that Britain must act quickly on Wilson's bid: "If it is not done now the opportunity may be forever lost." Conversely, he noted, full-scale U.S. belligerency would be destructive for England, because Germany and Austria would be completely crushed, while Italy and France would divide the spoils. Grey informed House in mid-May that if Wilson called for a peace conference without offering definite terms, the Allies would construe his bid as favoring Berlin, which still possessed the military advantage. When, in the fourth week in May, Grey, Asquith, and Balfour met together, they expressed fear of American mediation. Addressing the House of Commons, Grey stressed a fight to the finish. At this time an army council, led by the general chief of staff, Sir William Robertson, threatened to resign if the Asquith ministry raised "the peace question."[80]

To Grey, despite Germany's setback at Verdun, the Reich operated from a position of strength, its influence stretching from the North Sea to the Adriatic and from the Marne River to the Vistula. What bargaining power, the British asked, did the Allies possess? Would not any peace involve recognition of Germany's conquests? Even if one reverted to Europe's 1914 boundaries, Berlin would have been strengthened vis-à-vis Paris and Petrograd.

Bethmann added to Britain's anxieties. Speaking to the Reichstag on April 5, the chancellor claimed that Germany would never concur in a settlement based on the destruction of its military might. In addition, it would not surrender Belgium or Poland without security guarantees. Nor would Germany return peoples "freed from Russian bondage." Nonetheless, later that month and in May, he hinted that Germany might welcome an American peace initiative.[81]

By mid-May Wilson was becoming increasingly frustrated with the British. On the sixteenth he wrote House to claim that British maritime policy and mail seizures were "altogether indefensible." The United States, he continued, must either make "a decided move for peace" or insist upon its international rights with "the same firmness and plain speaking" against Britain as it had against Germany. House responded immediately, accusing the Allies of ingratitude. He asked the president to "press for a peace conference with all the power at your command—for, whether they like it or not, I believe you can bring it about."[82]

On May 27 Wilson made his "decided move" in the form of a speech that relied heavily on a House draft. Addressing an audience of two thousand members of the League to Enforce Peace at Washington's New Willard Hotel, he shared the podium with Senator Lodge, who described the LEP program as the best promise of world peace. The president averred that the current conflict had arisen from "secret counsels" and bitter rivalries but continued that "with its causes and objects we are not concerned." The scope of the conflict reached "every quarter of the globe," affecting "our own rights as a nation, the liberties, the privileges, and the property of our people. . . . Henceforth alliance must not be set up against alliance. . . . Every people has a right to choose the sovereignty under which they shall live." The territorial integrity of small states deserved as much respect as that of great and powerful nations.

Advancing a theme stressed by Grey in his exchanges with House, the president called upon his nation "to become a partner in any feasible association of nations" that would advance these aims. In an effort to allay German concerns, the president stressed that this league would maintain the freedom of the seas, or, to use his language, "the inviolate security of the highway of the seas for the common and unhindered use of all the nations of the world." It would "prevent any war begun either contrary to treaty covenants or without warning and full submission of the causes to the opinion of the world—a virtual guarantee of territorial integrity and political independence." He vaguely referred to the creation of "some common force" to "safeguard right," speaking of coercion in "the service of a common order, a common justice, and a common peace."[83] The LEP had not made such a radical proposal.

The Allies should have been pleased with parts of the president's address. He stressed the need to protect small states, an aim that the Entente had repeatedly emphasized. They were far from gratified, however, with Wilson's claim that the war had been caused by a system of international alliances and intrigue, not German aggression, and that the United States was indifferent to the conflict's "causes and objects." Therefore, in France and Britain, support was limited to those of a decidedly liberal bent. Sir Eric Drummond, Grey's private secretary, expressed much British opinion in saying: "The Good Samaritan did not pass by on the other side, and then propose to the authorities at Jericho a bill for the better security of the highroads."[84]

In Germany Wilson received little backing; only the Social Democrats backed the president. Gustav Stresemann, leader of the National Liberal Party, received strong approval in the Reichstag when he rejected Wilson's bid as a mediator. Reich editors deemed the LEP speech politically motivated, given with an eye to the forthcoming presidential election; they also viewed the American president as a most unsuitable intermediary. In addition, they argued, if one focused on the rights of small oppressed peoples, one must condemn British rule of Ireland, India, Egypt, and the Boers. Besides, in late May Falkenhayn was sufficiently optimistic to predict Germany's victory within a year, even without having to wage unrestricted U-boat warfare. France, the commanding general predicted, might leave the Entente, making a separate peace. Frederic C. Penfield, American ambassador to Austria-Hungary, warned that the Hapsburg monarchy feared granting self-government to such subject peoples as Bohemians, Slavs, and Croats.[85]

At home Wilson garnered strong press support. The *Nation* commented: "We believe it to be true that the great majority of Americans are ready to have this country cast in its lot with the nations of the world seeking a way to maintain peace." The *New Republic* spoke in superlative tones: the most significant statement of the war; the most important foreign policy proclamation since the Monroe Doctrine; possibly "a decisive point in the history of the modern world." The president offered Britain aid against an aggressor, France a guarantee of defense, and Germany security in return for abandoning aggression. Senator Warren Harding, who was far more conservative than the progressive weekly, remarked: "I will always welcome such an alliance as proposed by President Wilson. Peace is an aim commendable enough to justify almost any kind of arrangement with other Powers." Senator Charles Curtis (R-Kan.), later Herbert Hoover's vice president, denied that Wilson's proposal was "entangling in the sense meant by [George] Washington."[86]

Several critics opposed the president's brand of internationalism. Senator Gore said, "Our policy of isolation is our greatest security." Do Americans, asked Congressman Gardner, really want an organization that might wield jurisdiction over the Monroe Doctrine or America's policy of Oriental exclusion? Roosevelt attacked the entire notion of mediation, fearing "a premature and disastrous end to the war" while the Central Powers dominated so much of Europe. Like Pope Benedict XV, who sought a negotiated peace, Wilson was governed by "cold-blooded opportunism."[87]

Even Lansing expressed reservations, foreshadowing his opposition in 1919 to the League of Nations. Writing Wilson just two days before the speech, he endorsed regional arrangements and economic pressure while balking at any suggestion that foreigners might control America's armed forces. He asked: "Who may demand international intervention? What body will decide whether the demand will be complied with? How will the international forces be constituted? Who will take charge of the military and naval operations? Who will pay the expenses of the war (for war it will be)? . . . I do not believe that it is wise to limit our independence of action, a sovereign right, to the will of other powers beyond this hemisphere."[88]

The *Outlook* harbored mixed sentiments, welcoming Wilson's endorsement of an international organization but stressing that every patriot must study the causes of the conflict. Writers for the *Fatherland* offered divergent opinions. Schrader denied that the address could be construed as a sincere peace bid. To Viereck, however, the discourse was "a great speech." As "the new Woodrow Wilson" was no longer a British dupe, Germany was prepared to meet him upon "the plane of his idealism."[89]

Wilson sought to meet criticism in his Memorial Day speech of May 30, when he denied that he would consent to the type of "entangling alliance" condemned by George Washington. He favored "a disentangling alliance—an alliance that would disentangle the peoples of the world from those combinations in which they seek their own separate and private interests and unite the peoples of the world to preserve the peace of the world upon a basis of common right and justice."[90]

As summer approached, House continually expressed his disappointment with London. In early June the colonel warned Grey of overconfidence. While the British blockade was "gnawing" at Germany, he maintained, the Reich still had infinite food supplies. In his diary, he denied that either Britain or France sought a just peace or even that England had entered the war to save Belgium. On June 23, he confided to his journal: "I believe the French and English are prolonging the war unnecessarily. It is stupid to refuse our proffered intervention on the terms I proposed in Paris and London." Grey wrote House on the twenty-eighth, stressing that the British army must bolster French forces before any American mediation took place.[91]

In three days Britain launched the Somme offensive, a campaign that in its first day cost it twenty thousand lives. After fighting through mid-November, it advanced only seven miles, making no significant gains. The campaign marked the greatest military tragedy in British military history. House and Wilson realized the futility of their bid. Britain and France had made all too clear their desire to continue the conflict. Efforts to bring Rumania into the war reinforced Allied confidence, for the move would supposedly force Austria-Hungary to fight on a new front.

Though never desiring a German victory, the president and his closest adviser took a more neutral posture. Wilson believed that a European stalemate would best serve American interests. The public, noted the president, appeared more focused on Bethmann's hints concerning possible U.S. negotiation than on any similar British sentiment. "Germany's complete change of attitude, both here and abroad," House remarked early in July, "has done much towards lessening the war spirit in America."[92]

By the middle of 1916, Wilson and House realized that the Allies did not desire a negotiated peace. The Entente in turn perceived the House-Grey memorandum as far from airtight. One Foreign Office official had written Asquith in mid-March, "I fear if House could deliver the goods the goods are not good enough. It is not enough that we should secure a partial victory—it is not enough that Germany should be punished by her own self-inflicted material damage. We must win a complete victory and that I think House cannot secure us."[93]

House and Grey did not envision Germany's total defeat; its army, navy, industrial complex, and fighting machine could remain intact after the war. Even if the Reich's army remained intact, London remained confident that its fleet and dominions could ensure the continuation of the British Empire as a great power. In addition, many Englishmen thought that a strong Germany could help contain an expansionist Russia. Yet even for Britain, the House-Grey agreement was a risky undertaking. France remained the agreement's most adamant opponent, envisioning the military destruction of Germany as essential to French survival.

For Britain the price of Wilson's mediation was always too high, the risks too great. Looking across the Channel in the summer of 1916, it faced a Germany that occupied Belgium, northern France, and much of eastern Europe. To compound London's anxiety, Wilson repeatedly announced his indifference concerning territorial matters, indicating that the belligerents must resolve such issues themselves. Better to place one's efforts on the

Somme offensive, irrespective of the toll it was taking. Besides, Ambassador Page continually told the British, the president faced defeat in the forthcoming November elections. Who could guarantee that a successor would not ignore, and perhaps repudiate, any House-Grey memorandum?

To Link, the Allies bore a heavy responsibility for prolonging the war. Wilson's mediation carried some chance of Germany's acceptance. Berlin's civilian leadership denied that the Kaiser's armies or U-boats could crack the existing stalemate; at the same time it feared the intense Anglo-French offensives on its western front. Hence Bethmann pressed Wilson to implement his peace moves quickly. Because Grey lacked courage and resolution, argues Link, he played a particularly strong role in prolonging the conflict. Though the foreign secretary endorsed the House-Grey memo, he did not object when powerful hard-liners within the cabinet vetoed his proposal and did not apply pressure on the intransigent French.[94]

British leaders, in turn, faced popular pressure to continue the conflict. Laborers lost patience with the American president, while "Tommies" in the trenches referred to dud shells as "Wilsons." On September 28 David Lloyd George, now secretary of state for war, publicly challenged what he called "a defeatist spirit working from foreign quarters to bring about an inconclusive peace." Warning Wilson not to "butt in," the fiery Welshman told the United Press's Roy Howard, "The fight must be to the finish—to a knockout!" Grey had long felt similarly, though he believed Lloyd George's public warning was unnecessary and probably harmful. Similarly, French premier Aristide Briand endorsed total victory.[95]

Still greater friction ensued on July 18, 1916, when Britain released a "blacklist" of some 85 American and 350 Latin American firms suspected of trading with the Central Powers. British subjects could have no dealings with alleged offenders, not even being allowed to correspond with them. London banned British steamships from carrying cargoes owned by proscribed firms. Offending ships could be refused coal at British ports. Companies were given to understand they might be blacklisted at any time and without notice. The British practice went back to November 1914, but at first American firms were not included. France followed suit, adopting the entire British list early in August. After the list was publicized, bankers of neutral powers refused to grant loans to offending firms while neutral merchants hesitated to contract for their goods.

The Great War marked the first time blacklisting was used on a massive scale. It was employed not only by such Allied powers as Britain, France,

Italy, and Australia, but by Germany and Austria-Hungary and, once it entered the war, the United States. But the wording of Britain's announcement appeared particularly insulting, thereby maximizing American anger. State Department Counselor Frank L. Polk wrote House concerning the enumeration: "It is nothing new and if the British Government could only keep quiet it could have been handled comparatively easily."[96] Released at a time when tensions were already high, it appeared to show deliberate hostility.

Newspapers condemned the move, with even the pro-British *New York Tribune* finding it "foolish and futile." Ambassador Page, an ardent Anglophile, thought the practice unwise, a bad tactical error. Allied stupidity, House wrote Wilson, was "beyond belief." The *New Republic,* fearing "a war after the war," remarked: "To the American mind this looks like mere commercial aggression not for the objects of the war, but in the interests of British merchants."[97]

Several congressmen were quite candid in expressing their anger. William S. Bennet (R-N.Y.) feared that a "trade bludgeon" would seal off all of South America; he demanded that American warships meet the challenge. "Through the operation of the British black list the commercial flag of Great Britain floats from the Rio Grande to the North Pole," he warned. James A. Gallivan (D-Mass.) introduced a resolution to sever relations with Britain.[98]

Certain senators manifested equal ire. Wesley L. Jones accused Britain of "making war on American citizens." James K. Vardaman demanded a retaliatory arms embargo: "I hardly think the American people will submit much longer to this rather contemptuous disregard of their rights." The *Star* of Marion, Ohio, published by Senator Harding, averred that a ban on all exports might end the war.[99]

On July 23, Wilson denounced Britain's "intolerable course" to House. Considering a ban on loans and export restrictions, the president said: "I am, I must admit, about at the end of my patience with Great Britain and the Allies. This black list business is the last straw. . . . It is becoming clear to me that there lies latent in this policy the wish to prevent our merchants getting a foothold in markets which Great Britain has hitherto controlled and all but dominated."[100]

Writing Britain's Foreign Office on the twenty-sixth, Wilson asserted that the blacklist would cause "harsh and even disastrous" effects upon his nation's commerce. Americans possessed the right to trade with whomever they pleased. Even were the proscription legal, it violated "that true justice, sincere amity, and impartial fairness which should characterize the dealings of friendly governments with one another." "Serious consequences" would result if Britain continued its ban.[101]

Blockade Minister Robert Cecil responded in Parliament, maintaining: "All we have done is to declare that British shipping, British goods, and British credit should not be used for the support and enrichment of those who are actively assisting our enemies." Offenders were accused of sending money to Germany, engaging in pro-German propaganda, subscribing to German war loans, and abusing cable facilities by using codes. Historian Patrick Devlin finds Cecil unnecessarily confrontational, for an unpublicized list had been working satisfactorily: "A British subject in wartime would not dream of disregarding governmental advice not to trade with someone who was suspected of aiding the enemy."[102] Britain and France never alleviated American grievances.

Despite the furor, the list added little to the effectiveness of the British blockade, for the business conducted by the designated companies had always been sparse. The overwhelming majority of firms blacklisted were located in New York City and were owned by individuals born in Germany or Austria.[103] Though public outrage soon cooled, the Wilson administration would not let go of the issue, obviously aware of the impending presidential election, in which German Americans might play a decisive role.

Once it became clear that Britain would not withdraw the blacklist, the United States moved swiftly. Despite unanimous Republican opposition, the Democrats pushed through measures creating a government-owned and -operated merchant fleet. Though not directly aimed at Britain, it obviously gave the United States far greater control over its own commerce. Treasury Secretary McAdoo, who believed that merchantmen were essential to naval strength, wrote the legislation in late January 1916. The bill created the five-member Shipping Board, which possessed the authority to spend up to $50 million to buy, construct, or charter merchant ships suitable for use as naval auxiliaries. It contained a retributive amendment authorizing the president to deny clearance to vessels that refused to carry the freight of blacklisted American citizens. Although opposed by shipping companies and the Merchant Marine Association, both of whom branded the bill socialistic, on May 20 it passed the House by a vote of 209 to 191. On August 18, the Senate approved the measure, the president signing it on September 7. Unlike McAdoo's proposal of the previous year, it did not authorize the government to purchase vessels belonging to belligerent powers; in fact, it specifically forbade this activity. Wilson's dream, stymied the previous year, was now fulfilled. For the first time since the Civil War, the United States possessed its own merchant marine.[104]

On September 8 Wilson signed an even more radical measure. In passing the Revenue Act, Congress included an amendment, introduced by Senator Charles S. Thomas, that empowered the president to deny discriminatory nations access to American ports. The United States could use its armed forces as enforcement. Senator James D. Phelan had offered a more threatening proposal, but this one met with defeat. Accusing the British of interfering with American commercial mails to China, the California Democrat sought to deny use of U.S. mails, telegraph, cables, and wireless to nations that interfered with American communication. His bill passed the Senate, but Wilson opposed the move and the conference committee dropped it.[105]

Such legislation could cripple the Allied war effort, for Wilson now controlled the means of retaliation. As the *New Republic* noted, he could meet "discrimination with discrimination, embargo with embargo." In fact, he possessed the authority to wield a death blow to the Allies. Because of such pressure as well as protests from its own merchants, by October Britain had begun relaxing the blacklist.[106]

Lansing feared that the United States could end up siding with Germany. "Nothing in our controversies with Great Britain must be brought to a head," he confided to his diary, adding that Wilson focused more on "violations of American rights by both sides" than on "the vital issues" at stake. "German imperialistic ambitions threaten free institutions everywhere." On September 23, the secretary undercut Wilson by personally assuring Ambassador Spring Rice that the president had simply acted to assuage public opinion during an election campaign; the chief executive would only use retaliatory legislation as a last resort.[107]

Throughout 1916 other British actions angered Americans. Britain banned the export of hospital supplies to the Central Powers. It prevented a group of German Americans, led by former Harvard professor Edmund von Mach, from shipping canned milk to German children. On February 18, officers from the British cruiser *Laurentic* boarded the American passenger ship *China* close to the entrance of the Yangtse River, forcibly removed thirty-eight subjects of the Central Powers, and detained them as prisoners.

When, in August, Walter Hines Page returned to America, Wilson refused to discuss concrete policies with him, finding the ardent pro-British ambassador useless in conveying his nation's anger to London. The president considered removing Page by making him secretary of agriculture but could find no spot for incumbent David F. Houston. As for the wider issues at stake, Wilson spoke vaguely to Page of "England's having the earth and Germany's wanting it," the war itself being "a quarrel to settle economic rivalries." He found "the German system" directly opposed to "everything American," but his continual harping on Britain's offenses gave Page little comfort. Conversely, Page privately referred to Wilson's "lamentable failure" to lead the nation; Lansing was simply a "manikin."[108]

Tensions with Britain could not mitigate one overreaching fact: America's trade with the Allies had become highly lucrative. Back in December 1915, Spring Rice had written Grey: "Before the war began the United States was threatened with a great crisis. Owing to the war this crisis has been averted."[109] During the years of neutrality, exports to Britain, France, Russia, and Italy totaled $7 billion. Of this sum, $2 billion came from munitions, the other $5 billion from foodstuffs, cotton, raw materials, metals, and manufactured goods. Particular beneficiaries included Bethlehem Steel, United States Steel, meat-packers, mining companies, oil firms, and Worth Brothers, an armor plate concern.

As summer 1916 turned to fall, the United States confronted major debates, centering on how best to defend the nation and just who would be its president during the next four years.

7

Preparedness Debates and the Presidential Election

March–November 1916

"WHO IS ATTACKING the institutions of this country?" asked Congressman James Hay in mid-March 1916. "What nation on earth is attacking them? My friends, there is not a country on earth today that has any idea of making war on the United States." So spoke the chairman of the House Military Affairs Committee and author of one of the most provocative bills of the Wilson presidency. Representative Frank L. Greene (R-Vt.) responded that after the war a prosperous United States would find itself subjected to the jealous rivalry of "any or all the powers of the Old World." Hay in turn rejoined that the European nations would not cross the Atlantic, much less seek indemnity for their losses. Socialist Meyer London concurred; never in the history of modern warfare had a far distant power attacked a great industrial nation.[1]

On March 6, within a month after War Secretary Garrison resigned, Hay's committee unanimously reported its Army Reorganization Bill, which modestly increased the strength of the regular army from about 100,000 to 140,000 men. In time of war this force could reach 275,000. The bill federalized the National Guard of 129,000, placing it directly under the control of the War Department. The legislation also authorized the department to raise a volunteer force of 250,000 men. Ironically, by so doing, it was adopting a version of Garrison's Continental Army, although a strongly modified one. At the end of six years, over 1.4 million men could be on call. Wilson backed the proposal, supported by Attorney General Thomas W. Gregory, who argued that the federal government possessed the authority to assume direct control of the Guard. Although the president believed the bill gave the militia a more prominent role than he desired, the National Guard Association supported the plan.

Even such weak legislation met with some opposition. Some members of the House Military Affairs Committee denied the constitutionality of militia federalization. James H. ("Cyclone") Davis (D-Tex.), a former Populist leader, accused Wilson of conspiring with northern business to draw America into war; the ultimate issue lay in "democracy" versus "plutocracy." Meyer London offered a Marxist critique, claiming that the European conflict centered on a quest for markets and commercial supremacy: "Wars are nowadays shopkeepers' quarrels."[2]

Certain editorialists found the Hay bill inadequate, the *New York Tribune* commenting that it would create a "paper army" unable to meet any attack. The *Literary Digest,* polling five hundred editors, revealed that the average estimate of desired troop strength for the regular army was 285,078; the reserve force should tally 1.2 million. Augustus Gardner said that to regard Hay's legislation as adequate for the nation's defense was "as sensible as to regard the peanut tendered by some child's hand at the circus as an adequate satisfaction of an elephant's demand for food." Historian John Patrick Finnegan calls Hay's proposal "a minimum response to a new national mood. In 1912, it would have been welcomed. In 1916, however, events seemed already conspiring to overtake and render inadequate any preparedness legislation whatsoever."[3]

The raid of Mexican chieftain Pancho Villa against Columbus, New Mexico, on March 9 revealed America's vulnerability. Machine guns failed to load promptly, needed reserves were lacking, and the cavalry unit on duty was caught short. Six days later, Wilson ordered General John J. Pershing to launch his "punitive expedition" with four thousand regulars. Assistant Chief of Staff Tasker Bliss told his superior, Hugh L. Scott, that the army lacked the strength to "reasonably guarantee American territory from hostile invasion and American citizens and property from injury." Gerard, writing House from Berlin, warned of eventual German attack on the American continent, "probably by way of an infringement of the Monroe Doctrine in Brazil or Mexico."[4]

The German-born Julius Kahn of California, a former actor and a ranking Republican member of the House Military Affairs Committee, introduced an amendment that would immediately increase regular army strength to 220,000. Douglas MacArthur, an army major attached to the

General Staff, advised Kahn on the matter. Just as birds, animals, and insects devour one another, said the congressman, "in all history in like manner men have preyed upon their fellow men." Hay scoffed at Kahn's scheme, arguing that in a real emergency a million men would be needed. Other opponents asserted that the amendment committed the United States to spending $8 million in peacetime.[5]

Manifesting a sectional division, the House defeated Kahn's proposal by a mere twenty-two votes. Eastern Republicans and Democrats favored it; southerners and midwesterners of both parties were opposed. Successful additions included the Reserve Officers Training Corps and an amendment, introduced by Carl Hayden (D-Ariz.), which was buried in an obscure paragraph and which permitted conscription if enlistment dragged. Though Wilson stressed that the clause applied only in wartime, the "Hayden joker" remained law until May 1917. On March 23, after brief debate, the House passed the Hay bill by 403 to 2. Representative London and a lone preparedness advocate, the former prize fighter Fred A. ("Pop Gun") Britten (R-Ill.), voted nay.[6]

Such preparedness foes as Majority Leader Kitchin welcomed the Hay bill: "We have scored a victory." Similarly, more militaristic advocates felt defeated. The *Outlook* estimated that the total number of men to be added to the army equaled estimated German casualties for a mere eight days. Furthermore, the Hay bill gave power and prestige to "forty-eight little armies" that, by their very nature, could never be welded into an effective national force.[7]

Hay's Senate counterpart was far more strident. George E. Chamberlain, chairman of his chamber's Military Affairs Committee, considered Wilson far too moderate on the matter. The Oregon Democrat favored universal military training and the creation of a powerful council of national defense that would coordinate security matters. Fearful that the Monroe Doctrine would prove vulnerable once the Great War ended, he continually warned against the British, who held up many American merchant ships and who, acting with the Japanese, might menace the Northwest.[8]

Reported on March 4 to the full Senate, Chamberlain's Army Reorganization bill was more acceptable to preparedness advocates than the House legislation. It slated peacetime army strength at 178,000, a sum far exceeding the House's specification, though in wartime the enrollment could reach as high as 250,000. The bill increased infantry, cavalry, and artillery regiments so as to meet War Department recommendations. It incorporated the Plattsburg system while it curtailed the role of the militia. Thanks to Enoch

Crowder, judge advocate general, some 261,000 volunteer reservists would receive thirty days of training each year. Chamberlain's bill also included a provision for vocational training, short-term enlistment, reserve instruction in high schools and colleges, federalization of the National Guard, and an increase of Guard strength to 280,000.

Although this bill was more popular than any competing plans, the powerful National Guard Association strongly resisted it. Senator Porter McCumber (R-N.D.) warned that military expansion could make the United States more militant in asserting the right to travel on belligerent vessels. Moreover, America's true protection lay in the two major oceans and the exhaustion of Europe's powers, not in any "nonproducing official aristocracy" created by huge armies and navies. Senator Vardaman feared that African Americans would flock to the training camps and thereby threaten the white South. Opposition was finally overcome by intensive efforts of the Military Training Camps Association, led by the young New York attorney Grenville Clark. An entire week was spent in debate before the Senate adopted an amendment that provided for a $15 million nitrate plant at Muscle Shoals, Alabama. Because a government-owned facility would take the profit out of munition manufacture while producing cheap fertilizer for farmers, it drew some rural support for the legislation. Senator Lawrence Y. Sherman (R-Ill.) remarked: "I think amendments have been offered now for everything except a rural-credit bill, possibly a parcel-post bill and a hard road system, and I look for them to come on apace in due time."[9]

Certain proposals failed. Senator Works, for example, offered a scheme that would create a "Constructive Army"; half its time would be spent on military undertakings and the rest on such public projects as roads, reclamation, irrigation, forestry, and river and harbor improvement. Although Wilson himself endorsed such an idea on January 27, it gained little support.[10]

Knowing that pressure from the militia lobby almost destroyed Garrison's volunteer scheme, Chamberlain told his fellow senators: "If the National Guard comes here with a determination to prevent all other legislation for national defense, I say it ought to be wiped out of existence." Major General John F. O'Ryan, commander of the New York State National Guard, countered that the new volunteer army would duplicate functions of the militia. As Finnegan notes, the two sides "regarded one another with the natural and implacable hostility of two scorpions in a bottle."[11]

The *Sussex* crisis, however, led the Senate, acting by voice vote, to pass the Chamberlain bill on April 18, just when Lansing dispatched the American ultimatum to Berlin. Upon hearing that Wilson would address the Congress, Frank Brandegee had introduced an amendment calling for a peacetime army of 250,000 men, the size recommended by Theodore Roosevelt. The Connecticut Republican pleaded ignorance as to "where the danger is coming from" but stressed the need to meet it from any quarter. This amendment passed 43-37, although southern Democrats and midwesterners of both parties opposed it. The *Sussex* emergency probably saved the volunteer scheme, although here the margin was closer, 34-32. Commenting on the deliberations in a letter to Hay, Wilson approved the development of artillery and engineer units but viewed the Brandegee amendment as creating too large a force. Early in May a survey of editors revealed a 4:1 ratio in favor of Brandegee's proposal.[12]

On May 5, the day after Germany issued the *Sussex* pledge, a conference committee decided on the final bill. Congressmen Hay, Kahn, and S. Hubert Dent Jr. (D-Ala.), ranking member of the Military Affairs Committee, could not reach an accord with Senate counterparts Chamberlain, Francis E. Warren (R-Wyo.), Robert F. Broussard (D-La.), Henry A. Du Pont (R-Del.), and J.C.W. Beckham (D-Ky.). Three days later the House rejected Senate provisions for the volunteer army by 251 to 109 and Brandegee's regular army of 250,000 by 221 to 142. Thanks to progressive and farmer support, the House accepted the government nitrate plant.[13]

Preparedness-minded newspapers were furious, accusing the legislators of irresponsible and elusive behavior. Roosevelt continued his plea for a quarter of a million men, "so constantly trained and manouevered" as to be ready at "the highest degree of fighting efficiency at any point of our border or coast line." The nation, he said, must adopt the type of universal service existing in Switzerland or Australia. Taft sought universal military training. The *Fatherland* claimed to favor preparedness but "not as a weapon in the hands of those who are at present exploiting the issue." Making direct reference to TR, it asked: "Would you place a loaded revolver into the hands of a baby?"[14]

Because the *Sussex* crisis became resolved early in May, Wilson saw no need to push Congress into large-scale preparedness. Perhaps he feared a split in Democratic ranks or possibly he thought that further measures would commit America to unwise actions in both Europe and Mexico. The president did exercise sufficient pressure so that, when the conference committee met again on May 13, it drafted a bill acceptable to both houses. The legislation federalized the National Guard, which would take a dual oath to both state and national governments. It doubled the size of the regular army, increased the force to 17,000 officers and 400,000 men within five years, and promised nearly a half million troops by 1921. The committee abandoned the volunteer reserve force while retaining a nitrate plant, the wartime draft, the Reserve Officers Training Corps, and camps modeled on the Plattsburg pattern.

On May 17 the Senate adopted the revised Army Reorganization Act, now called the Hay-Chamberlain bill, without a roll call. Three days later the House passed the legislation 351-25. Those opposed included 18 Republicans, 5 Democrats, 1 Progressive, and the 1 lone Socialist. Mann attacked Wilson, declaring that the president did not fight for legislation that would have met the dangers the chief executive had described in his recent speaking tour. Gardner voiced particular anger, referring to "a fake preparedness bill that every pacifist in the House can support and will please every pacifist throughout the country." Hay countered that the measure met peacetime needs, while Scott Ferris (D-Okla.) expressed gratification that the bill satisfied neither Augustus Gardner nor Meyer London, neither Henry Ford nor Theodore Roosevelt.[15] Wilson signed the bill on June 3. In mid-June Congress created the Council of National Defense to coordinate the relevant government departments.

Despite the congressional consensus, the Hay-Chamberlain bill engendered fierce opposition. The National Security League remained unconvinced. Furious that the bill preserved the National Guard, Roosevelt deemed it a "foolish and unpatriotic . . . bit of flintlock legislation." To the *Outlook* the increase in regular forces remained "totally inadequate except as part of a first line of defense." General Scott called it a "gold brick."[16]

Leonard Wood noted that the legislation lacked the support of the General Staff, much less that of the army itself; it would have been better to have passed no bill at all. The scheme, he wrote House, was "dangerous to a degree exceeding anything ever attempted in legislation in this country." In January 1916 Wood had argued that America's accumulation of most of the world's gold supply would invite attack. The nation's navy, he asserted, could not hold out more than sixty days. Needed were two hundred thousand regulars and a 2-million-man reserve.[17]

Some voices were slightly more moderate. The *New Republic* praised the conference bill for creating a larger and better equipped army but claimed that the new military force remained insufficient. Wilson, the progressive weekly continued, still conceived of the army as an instrument of domestic politics. Others favored the legislation. "From the purely military point of view," said Oswald Garrison Villard, "it ought to satisfy every militarist who has not suddenly gone daft." It doubled regiments, established a regular reserve, and kept a million men connected to the army while retaining their civilian status.[18]

Historians say little positive about the Hay-Chamberlain act. Finnegan finds the legislation "a huge windfall for the militia lobby" while "remarkably unrelated to the foreign policies of the country." William Henry Harbaugh views the act as the handiwork of resentful agrarian and progressive isolationists, who repudiated any suggestion that the United States should prepare to participate in the European War.[19]

On June 18, as the Mexican situation continued to deteriorate, Wilson called out the newly federalized National Guard, then over one hundred thousand men, to serve on the border. (Militia units from Texas, Arizona, and New Mexico were already mobilized.) This move would free about thirty thousand regulars to serve within Mexico in case of full-scale war.

By the end of July, the Guard was almost depleted. At most its units trained just one a week a year. Many troops lacked weapons and in some cases uniforms. Much equipment was unsuitable, camp sites often miserable. Eighteen percent of Guardsmen reporting for duty failed the medical examination. In eleven states over one-third either failed to appear or did not meet the physical requirements. To former secretary of war Henry L. Stimson, China could scarcely have acted more ineptly.

The Hay-Chamberlain bill had failed its first test. By the end of 1916, tension with Mexico had greatly eased, but the National Guard appeared to disintegrate. Chief of Staff Scott, together with much of the public, believed that federalization of the militia, far from turning it into an efficient fighting force, had proved disastrous.[20]

All this time, preparedness advocates sought to mobilize the public. Many cities sponsored parades. On May 13, 132,000 marched in New York, among them Thomas A. Edison and Hudson Maxim. A bomb was thrown during the procession in San Francisco; the accused perpetrator, Tom Mooney, became a cause célèbre. On June 14 President Wilson, sporting the colors, led a column of 60,000 down Washington's Pennsylvania Avenue. When the march ended, he delivered a Flag Day address at the base of the Washington Monument. "There is," he remarked, "disloyalty active in the United States, and it must be absolutely crushed." Such treachery, he added, came "from a minority, a very small minority, but a very active and subtle minority."[21]

Antipreparedness forces were far from inactive. Wilson, speaking at St. Louis in February 1916, had challenged them to take their case to the people directly. Calling Wilson's bluff, opponents held a major rally on April 6 in New York's Carnegie Hall with perhaps four thousand people in attendance. Social reformer Lillian Wald mocked fears of German invasion while Unitarian minister John Haynes Holmes labeled "security at any price" thinking damnable.[22] Soon the Anti-Preparedness Committee, chaired by Wald and boasting a host of reformers, sponsored rallies in Chicago, Kansas City, Pittsburgh, Cincinnati, St. Louis, Des Moines, Minneapolis, and Detroit— roughly the same territory covered by Wilson. Speakers included Rabbi Stephen Wise, millionaire reformer Amos Pinchot, and Congregationalist minister A.A. Berle. The gatherings possibly totaled forty thousand people in all. Usually speakers did not attack the president directly; they were most enthusiastic about his domestic reforms.

In April 1916 the Anti-Preparedness Committee became the American Union Against Militarism (AUAM). Wald and social reformer Crystal Eastman Benedict ran the organization. A national clearinghouse of information and activity, it established local committees in twenty-two cities and twenty-one states and spanned an area from Boston to San Francisco. It soon received over fifty thousand dollars; it boasted 6,000 dues-paying members, 5,000 volunteers, and 60,000 "friends." Such numbers are questionable, since only a fraction of the membership ever contributed financially and the AUAM was usually in debt. If America entered the war, the body maintained, constitutional liberty, democratic institutions, and popular control of government would no longer be possible. Far from being isolationist, it sought a lasting peace settlement that would evolve into a democratic world federation.[23]

On May 8 some prominent AUAM members met with Wilson. Amos Pinchot spoke against proposed legislation in New York State, soon adopted, that would provide for compulsory training camps for boys between ages sixteen and nineteen. *Masses* editor Max Eastman compared the unanimous vote of the United Mine Workers against the preparedness program with the "military excitement which seems to have possessed our upper and leisure classes." The president replied by contrasting "reasonable preparation" to "militarism," arguing that "it is not inconsistent with American traditions that everybody should know how to shoot and take care of himself." He defended a proposed naval increase and stressed the need for troops to patrol the Mexican border. "In the last analysis," Wilson warned, "the peace of society is backed by force."[24]

Bryan, who might still have retained political ambitions, echoed the AU-AM's sentiments. In his house organ, the *Commoner,* he wrote of a "munitions-militarist conspiracy" led by professional soldiers and such firms as Du Pont and Bethlehem Steel. "The big corporate employers of labor are aiding and abetting the conspiracy because they want a large army—not made up of state militia but of regulars—to keep their workmen under subjection." At the end of 1916, the annual convention of the American Federation of Labor ignored its own president, Samuel Gompers, by deciding to oppose "militarism."[25]

Such foes offered several arguments. Rearmament, some claimed, would inevitably draw the nation into the conflict. To publisher Oswald Garrison Villard, preparedness would "complete the vicious military cycle of the world," depriving it of "the one great beacon-light of a nation unarmed and unafraid." The large-scale spending would bleed American taxpayers, squander the nation's treasury, and—particularly anathema to Democrats—possibly lead to a tariff increase. Such huge outlays involved a massive transfer of wealth, aiding Wall Street, the trusts, and armament manufacturers. In criticizing recent defense proposals, the *Saturday Evening Post* observed: "The taxes . . . will be real. The soldiers and armaments will be mostly paper." Such sacrifice, critics asserted, was sheer folly; after the war the European powers would be too exhausted ever to threaten the United States.[26]

Despite such opposition, agitation grew to support naval expansion. A peculiar coalition was formed; it was composed of traditional nationalists who possessed a militarist bent, southern and western farmers who sought to coerce Britain into lifting its blockade, and jingoists who sought either war with Germany or confrontation with Japan.

In May House stressed to Wilson that a strong fleet would "give us the influence desired in the settlement of European affairs, make easier our South American policy, and eliminate the Japanese question." The presidential confidant was well aware that the United States had recently experienced tension with the island empire. In 1913 California passed a law prohibiting Japanese aliens from owning land in the state. Japan's recognition of Mexican dictator Huerta the next year helped matters little. In January 1915 Japan made its famous Twenty-one Demands, which, had Britain and the United States not intervened, would have made China a de facto Japanese protectorate. Wilson became even more intent on developing American sea power. When House told him in September 1916 that the United States had become Britain's chief commercial rival, the president replied: "Let us build a navy bigger than hers and do what we please!"[27]

Agitation for a stronger navy also developed. George von L. Meyer, Taft's secretary of the navy, declared that the American fleet lacked balance and that its ships remained undermanned. The *Outlook* quoted Secretary Daniels, Assistant Secretary Franklin D. Roosevelt, and Admiral Bradley Fiske on the need for dreadnoughts. Of the fastest battleships currently being built, argued the *New York Tribune,* England possessed twenty, Germany fourteen, Japan four, and the United States none. Maritime artist Henry Reuterdahl told members of New York's National Security League that Secretary Daniels should resign; he was simply the "Father of the Pork Barrel."[28]

Many navalists discerned a genuine foreign threat. After the war, predicted the *New York American,* the United States would face "two enormously powerful empires who have beaten all Europe"; both rulers and people were "highly incensed against us for the sympathy given to their enemies and the unqualified and unjustified hostility displayed toward them." The lesson: "We must have a navy that can meet their navies on their way over here and sink them." When the European war ended, warned journalist John Callan O'Laughlin, Europe would be equipped with superb fleets and millions of veterans who would enviously eye American markets. "Will not the debt-ridden belligerents, when they have returned to peace as between themselves, look with envy upon our riches gained from their needs?"[29]

Some naval proponents again expressed fear of foreign invasion. America must seek, said the General Board of the navy, "to meet the enemy at a distance and defeat him before he reaches the neighborhood of the coasts." Rear Admiral William S. Sims, who had recently commanded the Atlantic Torpedo Flotilla, warned that a hostile fleet armed with one hundred submarines could shell New York. Colonel Edwin F. Glenn noted 116 unprotected landing places along the Atlantic Coast between Portland, Maine, and the capes of Virginia. Long Island's coast, admonished Admiral Dewey, remained particularly vulnerable.[30]

Other opinion makers spoofed talk of attack. In a paid advertisement, Henry Ford pointed to the British setback in the Dardanelles as revealing the limitations of the "greatest battle fleet in the world's history, backed up by a magnificent army." He noted that England, which controlled the seas, required thirty-three days to move thirty thousand unequipped troops from Quebec to Southampton. Could four hundred thousand enemy troops really land on American shores almost overnight? Congressman Oscar Callaway (D-Tex.) asked, "How is Germany going to come across 4,000 miles of ocean, crippled, a bankrupt, horrified by the war through which she has just passed, crepe on every door for lost son, husband or brother, with an enemy at her back, and sweep from the seas, a navy . . . pass our forts . . . and levy tribute on New York, Boston and Philadelphia!"[31]

On May 18 the House naval affairs committee presented legislation that postponed the construction of two dreadnoughts, thereby rejecting a five-year program that the General Board had sought in October. In this sense, the proposed bill met the wishes of such small-navy Democrats as Walter L. Hensley (Mo.), who offered a rider calling for American participation in a postwar disarmament and arbitration conference. Yet the recommended tonnage remained impressive, totaling five battle cruisers, four cruisers, ten destroyers, and twenty submarines.[32]

When committee chairman Lemuel P. Padgett introduced the bill to the House six days later, Republicans sought to raise the number of submarines from twenty to fifty (forty-seven of them slated for coastal defense) and increase the appropriation from $2 million to $3 million. They filed a minority report demanding a "big navy" program—the construction of two dreadnoughts and six battle cruisers for the current year—and the establishment of a council of national defense. The Republican bill lost by only six votes. After this final minority stand, on June 2 the House passed the bill itself 358 to 4.[33]

Just before the final tally, news of the battle of Jutland off the Danish coast reached the United States. Americans learned that the Germans had downed some of Britain's thinly armed battle cruisers but that battleships on both sides had escaped a similar fate. Writes Finnegan, "The small-navy program of the Democrats was sunk along with part of the British fleet."[34]

On June 30 the Senate naval affairs committee, reflecting a bipartisan consensus, introduced a bill strikingly similar to the House legislation. Drafted by ranking committee member Claude Swanson and Henry Cabot Lodge, it added four dreadnoughts, envisioning a total of 157 vessels in comparison to the House's 72. It set a three-year goal, not the five years proposed by the administration.

Debate commenced in the Senate chamber on July 13. Swanson stressed the protection of American commerce, finding it crucial to the nation's prosperity. While specifically denying that Britain embodied a concrete threat, the Virginia Democrat noted that its "unjust restrictions" necessitated "a navy large enough to demand and enforce our rights." Tracing the predatory imperialist record of the European powers before the current war began, he predicted that such ambitions would not cease with the coming of peace.[35]

In backing the naval bill, Senator Borah, too, stressed commercial aims. The war, he maintained, was caused by economic rivalry between the Allied and Central powers. The United States needed the military means to "protect our own" as it sought "an outlet for our trade, a market for our goods, and thereby a living wage for our workingmen, insuring efficiency and prosperity at home." Evidence of the nation's peril included the drowning of two hundred American citizens, an obvious reference to U-boat warfare; a thousand "assassinated and murdered on land," a pointed allusion to Mexico; and the closing of the Open Door in the Orient, a clear inference to Japanese penetration of China.[36]

George Norris was quick to challenge such claims. Far from being a threat after the war, he argued, Germany would be bankrupt, the majority of its soldiers dead, and the balance crippled. The much-touted British navy had proved itself unable to seize the poorly fortified Dardanelles, and Japan could not transport troops across four thousand miles of water. The Nebraska senator introduced an amendment to postpone battleship construction; in addition, he proposed the establishment of an international court empowered to enforce its decisions with its own navy. Just eleven senators, however, stood behind him.[37]

In opposing massive naval development, Robert La Follette asserted that it would take just eleven thousand men to make American coasts impregnable; he cited military actions at such places as Egypt's Alexandria and Russia's Port Arthur to show the effectiveness of shore fortifications. The American navy was already superior to Germany's, while an exhausted Britain would be left with a much smaller fleet after the war. To support his arguments, he drew upon a host of military experts, among them rear admirals Frank F. Fletcher and Austin M. Knight, Lieutenant General Nelson A. Miles, and Brigadier General Erasmus M. Weaver, former chief of coast artillery.[38]

On July 21 the Senate voted for the navy bill, passing it 71 to 8 and appropriating $315 million. The legislation included funds for an armor plate factory and a rider that attached Hensley's peace declaration. Albert Cummins, while claiming to favor a naval buildup, sought to limit battleships to two and cruisers to four but garnered just fourteen votes.[39]

When the conference committee met, Wilson pleaded with House representatives for the stronger Senate bill. Though the president never set down his reasons, he was aware of possible tensions with Germany, Britain, and Japan. Moreover, in his speech to the League to Enforce Peace, he had recently asked his nation to participate in a postwar international organization that might need an enforcement mechanism.[40]

The House met the president's wishes on August 15, passing the Senate measure 283 to 51. Opposed were 35 Democrats (primarily "little navy" congressmen from the rural South), 15 Republicans, and the lone Socialist. Ninety-nine members did not vote.[41] This tally revealed that the Democrats feared naval expansion much less than they did a large army.

Fourteen days later Wilson signed a bill that, as Harbaugh notes, affirmed unequivocally the vision of the naval publicist Alfred Thayer Mahan. Certainly it contained by far the largest naval budget in the nation's history. To dissenter Claude Kitchin, the legislation made the United States "the most militaristic nation on earth." Pacifist Oswald Garrison Villard noted that America had just reached an accommodation with Germany, a country weakened by the heavy naval losses experienced off Jutland. "Where is this sort of madness to end?" he asked.[42]

To finance the new military expenditures, on July 10 the House and on September 6 the Senate passed a revenue bill that raised the income tax on upper brackets and added inheritance and munitions taxes. Never before in peacetime had the United States levied such heavy burdens on the wealthy. Resistance from eastern Republicans inadvertently supplied ideological support for such progressives as La Follette. The Wisconsin senator accused the preparedness movement of being the creation of munitions makers and Wall Street finance. Now they were refusing to pay their fair share. Wilson signed the legislation on September 8.

In several ways the entire preparedness debate was quite revealing. Few, if any, proponents stressed the need to supplement the British navy or preserve Europe's balance of power. Though Germany was still deemed America's most dangerous potential enemy, the implication remained implicit: America's role in world politics rested entirely on its own sovereignty and strength.

Some scholars question the basis of the entire crusade. Arthur S. Link notes that most Americans endorsed preparedness because it strengthened American defenses against "some vague and ill-defined future threat." If they favored the Allies, they did so without fervor. Just a small minority believed that the United States must prepare to fight a major war in Europe. Robert Endicott Osgood finds that the entire movement "actually amounted to miseducation"; it focused on "arming a metaphysical fortress to resist a hypothetical assault." John Patrick Finnegan faults Wilson for failing to co-ordinate diplomacy with armed might, that is, linking power to policy. He suspects that the president feared that an emergency military force might create the very crisis it was designed to prevent. Finnegan sees Congress as more focused on the notion of a Continental Army, something rooted in the thinking of the 1880s, than on the exigencies of the Great War. All the same, a more rational program, he continued, would probably have made little dif-ference, for nothing that was politically possible in 1916 could have kept the nation out of war in 1917.[43]

By the summer of 1916, public attention had become less centered on rearmament and more on the coming national elections. For the past half year Republican leaders had blasted Wilson's foreign policy. In mid-Feb-ruary 1916, former New York senator Elihu Root, temporary chairman of the New York State Republican convention, told an audience gathered at Carnegie Hall that Wilson's diplomacy was "brave in words and irresolute in action," "blindly stumbling along the road that, if continued, will lead to in-evitable war." Attacking the administration for failing to protest Germany's violation of Belgian neutrality, the former secretary of state denied that one could be "neutral between right and wrong, neutral between justice and in-justice, neutral between humanity and cruelty, neutral between liberty and oppression."[44]

In a *Literary Digest* poll of 751 Republican editors, senators, and rep-resentatives published in mid-December 1915, Root appeared as his par-ty's front runner, drawing 249 votes. (Second place went to Charles Evans Hughes, associate justice of the Supreme Court and previously a reform gov-ernor of New York; the jurist garnered 152 backers.) To publisher George Harvey, Root was "the foremost statesman now living in this country or in the world." The *New Republic,* more cautious, deemed him "a patient, shrewd, experienced man," who "supplies to the aggressive element in public opinion an encouragement and a leadership for which it has been waiting."[45]

Root received the backing of Wall Street and the "regulars" of his state's party machinery but suffered major handicaps. By the time of his inaugu-ration he would be over seventy-two years old. His domestic conservatism alienated progressive Republicans, while his strident pro-British attitudes estranged German Americans. Kansas editor William Allen White warned that Root could not carry one state west of the Mississippi River. The relatively moderate Taft considered him too close to the socially prominent "400 circles of New York City." In a signed editorial, William Randolph Hearst called the retired senator "the attorney of privilege."[46]

Roosevelt, too, hoped for the Republican nomination. No longer denouncing the "malefactors of great wealth," he simply sought benevolent state supervision of large industries. In response he received support from such conservative journals as the *New York Tribune,* the *Bankers Magazine,* and the *North American Review.*

No prominent Republican matched TR for sheer vitriol. Speaking in mid-May 1916 in Detroit while on a midwestern tour, he assailed the nation's policy of "culpable weakness and timidity," asserting that the loss of life on torpedoed ships exceeded the total deaths suffered by both Union and Confederate navies during the Civil War. He denounced the "politico-racial hyphen" as a "breeder of moral treason," an obvious reference to German American agitation. While in heavily Teutonic St. Louis, he posited: "It is our purpose this fall to elect an American president and not a viceroy of the German emperor."[47]

Far from seeing himself as taunting Berlin, Roosevelt maintained that his policies would keep the nation out of the conflict. Writing the prominent Progressive banker George Perkins in that April, he said that after the *Lusitania* was sunk, the United States should have interned the Reich's ships lodged in American ports, a move that "would have prevented all the trouble we have had last year with Germany." He did add: "If it were necessary to go to war to put a stop to repeated killings of American men, women and children I would go to war."[48]

Roosevelt retained control of the Progressive Party, which he hoped to use as a device to secure the Republican nomination for himself or a candidate sympathetic to his views. In May the Progressive executive committee asked both parties to nominate the same candidate. TR sought to make sure the platforms of the two parties were quite similar. By June the Progressives were no longer a conventional political party; they were a band of dedicated Roosevelt followers, sharing the desire to make their idol the nominee.

In March Roosevelt publicly denied that he would campaign for the White House but coyly continued: "It would be a mistake to nominate me unless the country has in its mood something of the heroic—unless it feels not only devotion to ideals, but the purpose measurably to realize those ideals in action." On May 11, he wrote the Roosevelt Non-Partisan League, formally entering the race for the Republican nomination. Roosevelt biographer John Milton Cooper Jr. questions whether TR genuinely thought he had a chance at the Republican nomination, which, given the crushing Progressive losses in the 1914 congressional race, was the sole candidacy worth having. Rather, Cooper goes on, he sought primarily to control the Grand Old Party.[49]

The ex-president was aware of certain handicaps. In June 1915 Roosevelt informed Progressive Party leader Raymond Robins that it would "be utterly hopeless" to run for president; bigoted anti-Protestant Catholics, "professional" German and Irish Americans, "professional" pacifists, and "the ultra-Protestants" would oppose him. A year later he wrote Brigadier General Pershing: "I do not for one moment believe I shall be nominated. Just at present the American people are passing through a yellow streak, and their leaders have sedulously done everything in their power to broaden the yellow streak."[50] By the time he returned to his home in Oyster Bay, Long Island, after a spring tour of the Midwest, his criticism of German Americans had ruined his slim hope for the GOP nomination.

In early February 1916, Lodge informed the former president that many Republicans were as "engaged in keeping neutral as Wilson, and as silent about international duties." He noted that a majority of the Republican congressmen, particularly those from the Progressive-leaning Midwest, backed the McLemore resolution, which warned Americans to stay off armed merchant ships. Taft expressed his party's consensus in noting public indifference to such Roosevelt causes as American rights, universal military service, and "Americanism."[51] Regulars correctly held Roosevelt responsible for splitting the Republicans in 1912, an action that put Wilson in the White House.

Even the Bull Moosers of 1912 did not unite behind Roosevelt's foreign policy. Such prominent party figures as Amos Pinchot, Jane Addams, and former Indiana senator Albert J. Beveridge opposed intervention in the European war, and they often spoke for fellow party members. As the Kansas editor William Allen White wrote in his autobiography, "many Progressives heard Roosevelt's war drums with distaste and uneasiness."[52]

Ordinarily the "armed progressive," General Leonard Wood, would have had a excellent shot at the nomination. Although a short boom on his behalf surfaced early in May, his closeness to Roosevelt handicapped him. He did not want to harm the ex-president's chances, though TR privately envisioned the general as a possible compromise candidate.[53] Wood's ostentatious promotion of preparedness, however, led to the popular impression that he was a political general.

Within Republican ranks were various "dark horses." Included were Ohio's former Senator Theodore Burton, a staunch regular known for budget-cutting; Senator Albert B. Cummins of Iowa, both a "lower case" progressive and a strong opponent of military increases; Senator John W. Weeks of Massachusetts, a major backer of defense appropriations; Senator Lawrence Y. Sherman of Illinois, an irascible conservative; former senator Philander Knox of Pennsylvania, who had fostered "dollar diplomacy" as Taft's secretary of state; and governors Charles S. Whitman of New York and T. Coleman Du Pont of Delaware. Two candidates harbored pronounced foreign policy views: Wisconsin's La Follette, who supported Wilson's domestic legislation but opposed his conversion to preparedness, and Idaho's Borah, an erratic progressive who leaned toward the foreign and domestic policies of Lodge and Root.

Few of these individuals possessed lasting strength. Cummins garnered many delegates from Iowa, Minnesota, South Dakota, Colorado, and Montana, but a poor showing in the Oregon primary ruined his chances. La Follette, Sherman, and Du Pont appealed exclusively to their home states.

On April 5 Henry Ford won Michigan's Republican presidential primary, then Nebraska's on the eighteenth. In Michigan the auto magnate received a five-thousand-vote margin over Senator William Alden Smith, who received the support of his state's party press and machine. Although one of the most vocal peace partisans in the nation, Ford tried to keep his name off the ballots. Yet he could still be most useful to midwestern Republicans, who wanted to warn their party against nominating an interventionist candidate.

German Americans offered a list of preferred candidates. *Fatherland* writer Frederick Franklin Schrader praised Sherman, "a strict American"; Borah, who opposed castigating "hyphenates"; and Cummins, who supposedly would contest British maritime policy. Viereck added the names of Hughes, Knox, Massachusetts governor Samuel McCall, Charles Nagel (Taft's secretary of commerce and labor), and senators George Norris of Nebraska and William S. Kenyon of Iowa. "It is inconceivable," the editor wrote, "that any Republican can reach the White House without the German Americans and the Swedes of the Northwest."[54]

Wilson's foes took comfort in certain state and local elections. Texas Democrats, for example, renominated Jeff McLemore by increased majorities. (In the one-party South, nomination was tantamount to election.) Former diplomat Robert Bacon, who had driven an ambulance behind French lines, met defeat in New York's Republican primary. "I am an avowed un-neutral," he said, as he deemed the electoral result a "German victory."[55]

On June 7, the Republican and Progressive parties simultaneously opened their conventions in Chicago. Hughes was the GOP front-runner, though he still lacked a clear majority. He drew twice as many delegates as Root, his closest competitor, and up to four times as many as Roosevelt. Until then he had remained silent on major political issues, a wise attitude given the divisions in party ranks.

Because the Wilson administration had recently enacted a host of re-forms—including the Child Labor Act, workman's compensation, and a rural credits bill—Roosevelt's Progressive Party viewed its only possible appeal as lying in its foreign policy. Its platform included universal military service, an increase in the regular army to 250,000 officers and men (the Brandegee amendment), an increase of at least $300 million for the armed forces, and the second-largest navy in the world. (TR maintained that the United States should not challenge British supremacy at sea.) In some ways, the platform was evasive, ignoring such matters as "hyphenates," Mexico, and the means of financing military appropriations, matters heavily bearing on foreign policy. Also absent were concrete calls for domestic reform; instead it referred to mobilizing national resources and transcending factional interests. Possibly fear of offending German Americans and remaining antiwar elements within its ranks made the party more cautious. The *New Republic* judged the platform "a reflection of Mr. Roosevelt's recent speeches, which were profoundly influenced by the necessity of saying nothing which would prove a bar to his nomination by the Republican party."[56]

The Republican platform endorsed "a strict and honest neutrality" in the European war: "We must perform all our duties and insist upon all our rights as neutrals without fear and without favor." By means of "shifty expedients," the Wilson administration had "destroyed our influence abroad and humiliated us in our own eyes." The party endorsed "a sufficient and effective Regular Army," "a provision for ample reserves," and a navy sufficiently powerful to prevent an enemy from invading either coast. Other foreign policy planks included a world court and reaffirmation of the Monroe Doctrine. Lodge and Borah sought preparedness provisions similar to those of the Progressive platform, but the platform committee overruled the two senators. La Follette's plank for a munitions embargo similarly met defeat 45-1.[57] In addition, the GOP remained silent over confrontation with Germany and the possibility of a postwar league of nations. The program never indicated how a Republican administration would differ from Wilson's rule.

Within three days after the Republican convention assembled, Roosevelt realized that he could not win its nomination. He wrote his Progressive backers from home at Oyster Bay, Long Island, suggesting that they rally around Lodge, whose preparedness views he praised.[58] As the Massachusetts senator had been at best the mildest of reformers, TR's effort was hopeless. The former president's admirers felt insulted.

On June 10, the Republicans nominated Hughes, undoubtedly the figure most able to reconcile party regulars and Progressive dissenters. In his acceptance letter, the standard-bearer sought "the firm and unflinching maintenance of all the rights of American citizens on land and sea." He endorsed "adequate" preparedness, an "honorable peace," and the maintenance of "our rights under international law; insisting steadfastly upon all our rights as neutrals, and fully performing our international obligations."[59] These statements reflected the fact that the nation's neutralist sentiment had destroyed Roosevelt's chances.

If Hughes's language remained infuriatingly vague, it still might reconcile his party's pro-German, pro-Allied, and neutralist camps. Harbaugh finds the letter shortsighted concerning postwar economic problems, chauvinistic in its focus on protecting American lives and property, and foolish in defining military and economic preparedness exclusively in terms of defense. What the candidate's words "implied for the future no man could foretell; but that they were ominously nationalistic any man could perceive."[60]

The Progressive Party stubbornly nominated TR, though believing strongly that he had betrayed them. Wrote journalist Walter Lippmann: "The spirit of that nomination was to strike back at Theodore Roosevelt. It was a nomination made in order to make trouble for him." The former president conditionally declined the offer, then placed the entire matter in the hands of the Progressive National Committee, which, at his prompting, wasted no time in endorsing Hughes. In his letter to the national committee, Roosevelt accurately noted that the party's national organization lacked the means to be truly effective. Furthermore, he asserted, a third-party ticket would aid Wilson and injure Hughes, who "is beyond all comparison better fitted to be President."[61]

Foreign policy divided the Democrats far less. By early May they were no longer fearful that Bryan might bolt the party. House speaker Champ

Clark, Wilson's convention rival in 1912, was rumored to have sought the presidential nomination, but he repudiated any presidential boom on his behalf. Once controversies over preparedness and the *Sussex* were resolved, Democrats united behind Wilson, realizing that he held the keys to victory.

The president took a strong personal hand in drafting the party platform, which combined domestic reform with promises to foster a neutralist foreign policy, an army "fully adequate to the requirements of order," and a navy "fully equal to the international tasks which this Nation hopes and expects to take a part in performing." Taking an obvious slap at German American agitation, the program condemned "the activities and designs of every group or organization, political or otherwise, that has for its object the advancement of the interest of a foreign power." It supported an international organization in language that the League to Enforce Peace might have written. Although it sought "protection of the nation's rights," it never defined them, thereby begging the whole question of war and peace.[62]

On June 14, three days after the Democratic convention opened in St. Louis, New York's former governor, Martin H. Glynn, inadvertently set the tone for the party campaign. In his keynote address, he touched upon one international crisis after another throughout American history, beginning with the *Chesapeake-Leopard* affair of 1807 and proceeding down to the *Alabama* claim controversy of 1869–71. After each incident he whipped up the crowd by bellowing, "We didn't go to war, we didn't go to war!" On the following day, the convention's permanent chairman, Kentucky senator Ollie M. James, boasted that Wilson, "without firing a single gun or shedding a drop of blood, . . . wrung from the most militant spirit that ever brooded over a battlefield an acknowledgment of American rights and an agreement to American demands." Then Bryan electrified the convention. While admitting that he differed from the president, he joined his countrymen "in thanking God we have a President who does not want the nation to fight."[63]

Desiring to make "Americanism" the theme of the convention, Wilson was most wary concerning the campaign's emerging slogan "He kept us out of war," telling Daniels: "I can't keep the country out of war. They talk of me as though I were a god. Any little German lieutenant can push us into war at any time by some calculated outrage." Historian John A. Thompson notes: "The American people had been encouraged in their desire to believe that the exercise of power in the world would be cost-free."[64]

On the eve of the campaign, Wilson showed himself increasingly eager to avoid participating in the conflict. On August 30, he met with representatives of the American Neutral Conference Committee, a group that included Hamilton Holt, David Starr Jordan, and Mary Woolley, president of Mount Holyoke College. When the delegation proposed mediation by the neutral nations, the president replied that he was waiting for the right moment to make his peace bid. "Nobody knows what the war is about," he told them. The struggle merely involved an effort "to see who is strong enough to prevent the other from fighting better."[65]

On September 2, Wilson accepted his party's nomination at Shadow Lawn, his new summer home on the Jersey shore. In his speech, he maintained that the United States bore the responsibility for preventing the spread of hostilities. America must save its strength "for the anxious and difficult days of restoration and healing which must follow when peace will have to build its house anew." Yet "no nation can any longer remain neutral as against any wilful disturbance of the peace of the world." He vaguely requested the countries of the world to "unite in joint guarantees" against those who would break the peace. At the same time, he condemned the new British maritime measures, asserting that "direct violations of a nation's sovereignty" would encounter "direct challenge and resistance." Holding little brief for "hyphenates," he asserted: "I neither seek the favor nor fear the displeasure of that small alien element amongst us which puts loyalty to any foreign power before loyalty to the United States."[66]

Much of the press praised the address. The *New York Evening Post* claimed that Wilson had "never penned a more brilliant document." Minority voices included the *Outlook,* which found Wilson apathetic concerning the unresolved *Lusitania* affair, and Viereck, who declared that Wilson remained pro-Entente.[67]

Realizing that the peace theme was the most popular one in the campaign, Democrats soon exploited it. Speaking on September 30 at Long Branch, New Jersey, Wilson warned that a Republican victory offered the "certain prospect" that the United States would be drawn "into the embroilments of the European war." His midwestern campaign director, Montana Senator Thomas J. Walsh, told party orators to highlight the issue, which Bryan certainly did during travels to some nineteen states of the Midwest and the Great Plains.[68]

At the same time, Wilson made sure that he was not seen as a tool of the Central Powers. Late in September the Irish American spokesman Jeremiah O'Leary cabled Wilson: "Your foreign policies, your failure to secure compliance with all American rights, your leniency with the British Empire, your approval of war loans, the ammunition traffic are issues in this campaign." The president immediately snapped back, "Your telegram received. I would feel deeply mortified to have you or anybody like you vote for me. Since you have access to many disloyal Americans and I have not, I will ask you to convey this message to them."[69]

When the press published Wilson's rejoinder, the president met with such a warm response that House later called it the campaign's turning point. Even Republican journals praised the chief executive. Hearst's *New York American* dissented. If any American who placed the welfare of his nation above that of England was disloyal, "then the majority of us Americans are disloyal." *Fatherland* contributor Charles A. Collman reacted similarly, writing that Wilson's "single-track mind again led him to refer to his political opponents as traitors to the country." Ironically, a week after the controversy erupted, O'Leary confessed that he was undecided as to whom he favored, noting that Wilson had protested British trade practices while Hughes remained silent.[70]

Several times during the campaign, Wilson claimed ignorance concerning the war's origins. Speaking in Omaha early in October, he drew his greatest applause when he maintained that no one understood the causes of the current conflict; they were grounded in "obscure European roots which we do not know how to trace." Speaking toward the end of October to the Women's City Club of Cincinnati, he asked: "Have you heard what started the present war? If you have, I wish you would publish it, because nobody else has, so far as I can gather. Nothing in particular started it, but everything in general. There has been growing up in Europe a mutual suspicion, an interchange of conjectures about what this Government and that Government was going to do, an interlacing of alliances and understandings, a complex web of intrigue and spying, that presently was sure to entangle the whole of the family of mankind on that side of the water in its meshes." The president also stressed the need for an international organization. "What disturbs the life of the whole world," he stated in Omaha, "is the concern of the whole world." The United States, he continued, was duty-bound "to lend the full force of this nation, moral and physical, to a league of nations which shall see to it that nobody disturbs the peace of the world without submitting his case first to the opinion of mankind." Wilson's antiwar rhetoric won the support of Henry Ford as well as that of many peace progressives, including Stephen Wise, Amos Pinchot, Lillian Wald, and Jane Addams. Villard was the only AUAM leader who refused to back the president.[71]

In their effort to maximize popular support, the Democrats made overtures to German Americans. They linked Hughes's views, in reality more
moderate than Roosevelt's, to those of the ex-president. Were Hughes elected
president, some warned, he would appoint the truculent Roosevelt secretary
of war. (Certain German American alarmists envisioned TR as secretary of
state.) Senator Stone met with such German American leaders as Viereck
and Victor Ridder, who had recently replaced his late father as publisher of
the *New Yorker Staats-Zeitung*. Wilson sharply downplayed his attacks on
hyphenates, obviously aware that emphasizing the peace issue could draw
Teutonic support. Bernstorff preferred Wilson, being fearful of Roosevelt's
pro-Allied stance. The president, the ambassador believed, possessed the determination and the power needed to create a settlement.[72]

The Hughes campaign sought to capitalize on hyphenate discontent but
feared antagonizing its pro-Allied wing. In his acceptance speech, delivered
on July 31 before an audience of three thousand at New York's Carnegie
Hall, the Republican candidate endorsed an international court and a postwar world organization. "There is no national isolation in the world of the
Twentieth Century. . . . The peace of the world is our interest." Turning
to tensions with Germany, he alleged that genuine enforcement of "strict
accountability" would have prevented the *Lusitania* sinking. "The essential
assurance of security," he added, lay in increasing the regular army and creating a federal reserve force.[73]

The address met with some criticism. Hughes attacked the administration with "great energy," the *Nation* remarked, but never indicated what
specific policies he would pursue. A mere opposition to Wilson, the *New Republic* observed, united "the Roosevelt following, the Republican machine,
the active pro-ally sympathizers, the pro-Germans, and Mr. Hughes's own
passion for efficiency." The candidate's stress on maintaining all legal rights
proved hollow, for "not all 'rights' are of equal value, nor can all of them
be maintained at the same time." As Hughes put the issue before a crowd
gathered in Madison Square Garden just before Election Day: "It is idle for
any one to say that a criticism of the policies of the present administration
implies either a desire for war or a tendency to war."[74]

At times Hughes indicated that he would not tolerate German behavior.
In mid-October, in confronting a heckler at Louisville, the former justice
proclaimed that he would have broken relations over the *Lusitania* sinking.
Later that month, he was badgered again at Columbus, Ohio. When asked

President Woodrow Wilson

President Wilson and his wife Edith en route to his second inaugural, March 5, 1917

Colonel Edward Manville House

Wilson and Cabinet members, 1916

Secretary of State William Jennings Bryan

Secretary of State Robert Lansing

Secretary of the Navy Josephus Daniels

Secretary of War Lindley M. Garrison

Secretary of War Newton D. Baker

British Foreign Secretary
Sir Edward Grey

General Paul von Hindenburg, Wilhelm II, and General Erich Ludendorff

German Chancellor
Theobald von Bethmann-Hollweg

Walter Hines Page,
American Ambassador to Britain

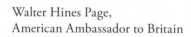

James W. Gerard, American Ambassador to Germany

Johann von Bernsdorff, German Ambassador to the United States

Sir Cecil Arthur Spring Rice, British Ambassador to the United States

Captain Franz von Papen

Lusitania coming into port

Senator Henry Cabot Lodge

James Hay, Chairman of the House Military Affairs Committee

William J. Stone, Chairman of the Senate Foreign Relations Committee

Senator Thomas Gore

Representative
Jeff: McLemore

Claude Kitchin, House Majority Leader

Senator George W. Norris

Senator Robert M. La Follette

Theodore Roosevelt

Theodore Roosevelt and General Leonard Wood

Elihu Root

Charles Evans Hughes

William Howard Taft

Jane Addams

William Jennings Bryan and Henry Ford discussing the final plans for the peace ship
expedition

Outlook editor Lyman Abbott

Fatherland editor
George Sylvester Viereck

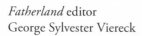

about levying embargoes and guaranteeing passenger prerogatives, he responded: "I, Sir, am in favor of the maintenance of every right, including the right of travel and the right of shipment."[75]

Such remarks did not preclude overtures to German Americans and citizens of more neutralist sentiments. In his keynote address to the GOP convention, Senator Warren Harding called foreign-born citizens a valued part of "our American citizenship." Hughes met with leaders of the American Independence Conference, an ad hoc pro-German body partially financed by Berlin and spearheaded by Jeremiah O'Leary. His running mate, Charles W. Fairbanks, once TR's vice president, sought to curry favor by saying that America's greatest danger lay not in the man who loved two countries but the one who loved none. The National German-American Alliance unofficially cooperated with the Republican Party. More overt support came from much of the German-leaning press, including Ridder's *New Yorker Staats-Zeitung*. To some such supporters, Hughes was "the Bismarck of America" or "the new Lincoln." The more militant *Fatherland* made no endorsement, Viereck labeling the Socialist Allan Benson "a violent pro-Ally" and asserting that neither Wilson nor Hughes manifested genuine neutrality.[76]

In mid-September Hughes told a Milwaukee audience that he would "protect and enforce American rights on land and sea without fear and unflinchingly with respect to American rights, American property, and American commerce." As tension over such matters currently rested far more with Britain than with Germany, the candidate met with a particularly warm reception among the city's large German American population. On October 9, speaking in Philadelphia, he pledged that his administration would tolerate neither a blacklist nor interference with its mails. His speeches alarmed the *New Republic,* which claimed that his polices aided the Central Powers. Hughes backtracked at the end of his campaign, informing a New York audience that he repudiated the support of anyone "who would not instantly champion the rights and interests of our country against any country on earth, who wants impunity for foreign aggression, or who would have the power of this nation held captive to any foreign influence or served by alien motivations." More concretely, he opposed embargoes on war supplies and legislation that warned Americans to stay off belligerent merchant ships.[77]

Roosevelt remained active. Privately he labeled the Republican convention a "sordid set of creatures." He deemed Hughes a "bearded iceberg," at times "the bearded lady," whose silence on major issues made him "a good deal of a skunk." Nevertheless, believing Hughes's progressivism to be "far ahead of all the other leading Republicans," TR persuaded himself that the candidate possessed the temperament to "rise to a very big height" in crisis. Within three weeks of Hughes's nomination, he met with the candidate for three hours, after which he gave his endorsement, immediately letting the press know he and the standard bearer were "in absolute accord."[78]

Speaking in Lewiston, Maine, on August 31, Roosevelt attacked Germany vehemently, maintaining that a Hughes administration would have prevented a host of Teutonic measures: invading Belgium, murdering Edith Cavell, torpedoing merchant vessels, bombarding churches and hospitals, massacring women and children, and attempting to exterminate Armenian and Syrian Christians. The former president condemned the "moral treason" of "professional German-Americans," adding that he would denounce English, French, or Irish Americans who acted similarly. Wilson's neutrality, he added, was worse than that of Pontius Pilate. Hughes publicly congratulated Roosevelt on the address, declaring that he, too, considered any attempt to organize citizens on ethnic lines "a foul and evil thing."[79]

Speaking at Battle Creek, Michigan, on September 30, Roosevelt accused Wilson of inviting "the murder of our men, women and children by Mexican bandits on land and by German submarines at sea." Had TR been chief executive at the time of the *Lusitania* sinking, he would have seized every German ship docked in the United States, telling Berlin: "Now we will discuss not what you will give but what we will give back." In late October he told a Denver audience that, if necessary, he would have gone to war over the matter. The slogan "He kept us out of war" Roosevelt branded "the phrase of a coward." As the campaign was ending, the former president spoke at New York's Cooper Union, acidly playing on the name of Wilson's summer home on the Jersey shore:

There should be shadows now at Shadow Lawn; the shadows of the men, women and children who have risen from the ooze of the ocean bottom and from graves in foreign lands; the shadows of the helpless whom Mr. Wilson did not dare protect lest he might have to face danger; the shadows of babies gasping pitifully as they sank under the waves; the shadows of women outraged and slain by bandits. . . . Those are the shadows of Shadow Lawn; the shadows of deeds that were never done; the shadows of lofty words that were followed by no action; the shadows of the tortured dead.[80]

By such language Roosevelt gave credence to Democratic accusations that the Republican Party sought war. Bryan's *Commoner* noted: "Mr. Roosevelt is still waging war on Mexico and Germany, but his shells are falling in the camp of one Charles Evans Hughes." The *Fatherland* warned: "It is time for Mr. Hughes to cry halt to this treacherous ally." As Harbaugh notes, the former president divided his party and abetted Hughes's defeat in the West while contributing little to American understanding of Europe's turmoil.[81]

The candidate became somewhat apprehensive, requesting Roosevelt in mid-August to avoid the term "hyphenated American." Not until late October did Hughes's managers try to curb TR, suggesting he tone down themes of Americanism and preparedness.[82]

Pro-Hughes representatives asked the defense societies to avoid participating in the campaign. Many interventionists remained silent; Root gave just one speech. On August 1, thirty-seven progressive journalists wrote an open letter to the former justice asking a series of questions: Would he have filed an immediate protest against Germany's invasion of Belgium? Would he have enforced this remonstrance with naval force? Did he favor universal military training?[83] Hughes never responded.

Wilson realized that his opponent was running a weak campaign, writing financier Bernard Baruch in mid-August that it was never wise to "murder a man who is committing suicide." By early October he confessed to having "a sort of sympathy" for Hughes: "He is in a hopelessly false position. He dare not have opinions: he would be sure to offend some important section of his following."[84]

In the last days of the campaign, Lodge accused Wilson of insincerity in drafting the first *Lusitania* note. Surreptitiously, according to the senator, the president sought to moderate its demands and offered to submit the entire matter to arbitration. Although Lodge identified his informant as Henry Breckinridge, steel manufacturer and assistant secretary of war during Garrison's service, his supposed source denied the accusation; so did Wilson and his cabinet. In reality the president's disclaimer was highly evasive, seizing on a technical inaccuracy, for, as shown, Wilson had sought to "tip-off" the press concerning a possible negotiation. In the words of historian Arthur Walworth: "There was just enough truth in Lodge's accusation to draw blood." Nevertheless, the senator felt himself forced to accept Wilson's disavowal.[85]

The election was one of the closest in American history. Because California remained in doubt, polling results were not known until the evening of November 9, two days after the election. A shift of fewer than four thousand votes would have carried the state for Hughes. Wilson captured the electoral college 254 to 237. The popular vote tallied 9,129,606 to 8,538,221, the chief executive gaining nearly 3 million votes over his tally in 1912. The president remained strong in the West and the "Solid South," although Hughes captured much of the East and the Old Northwest. In the Senate, the Democratic majority fell from 16 to 10. In the House, each party possessed 214 members, though the 2 Progressives, 1 Socialist, and 1 Prohibitionist assured Democratic control.

The Socialist vote dropped from close to 1 million in 1912 to less than six hundred thousand in 1916, with the strong likelihood that Wilson benefited from defections far more than Hughes did. In the intervening, years the party had sustained a vigorous press, encompassing dozens of newspapers and journals that undoubtedly reached several hundred thousand people. Its geographical strength, however, was usually limited to urban areas populated by immigrants from central and eastern Europe. In February 1916 it sought a peace based upon gradual disarmament, international arbitration, evacuation of occupied territory, liberation of oppressed nations, freedom of the seas, political rights for Jews, and self-determination for Alsace-Lorraine and Poland.[86]

The Socialists selected Allan Louis Benson of Yonkers, a New York City suburb, as their presidential candidate. A newspaper editor in Detroit and Washington, D.C., Benson was unquestionably a strident voice against entering the conflict. He wrote *Inviting War to America* (1916), in which he suggested that the preparedness movement might be "the greatest attempt of its kind in all history to stampede a nation into committing an act of monumental folly."[87] He based his campaign on the war issue, saying he hoped to save America from Europe's fate. As long as capitalism remained dominant, he argued, the nation's industries depended upon foreign markets, something that would inevitably bring the United States in conflict with others. George R. Kirkpatrick shared the ticket. His prewar book *War—What For?* (1910) long offered the strongest party statement on the topic.

The Socialist platform endorsed a war referendum, abandonment of the Monroe Doctrine, mediation by neutral nations, and repeal of preparedness legislation. During the campaign, Benson repudiated the support of German American groups, saying he merely sought individual converts to socialism. The *Fatherland* in turn abjured him, although it endorsed such Socialists as Representative Meyer London and the New York City congressional candidate Morris Hillquit. Certain leading Socialists endorsed Wilson, including Congressman London and *Masses* editor Max Eastman. The president's stress on peace and progressivism cut deeply into party ranks, as did internal party struggles and Benson's lackluster campaign.[88]

Political figures read the results differently. Roosevelt referred to Hughes's "over-caution, his legalism, his sluggish coldness of nature, and his sheer inability to grapple with great issues," all of which made him "a complete failure." Had the candidate made "a straight-out fight," he would have won, ending up a better president than Wilson. Writing William Allen White, TR argued that the West abandoned Hughes because of his "pussy-footing and lack of vision" as well his "machine and reactionary support." Taft ascribed Wilson's victory to "the emotional votes of the women, to the extreme speeches of Roosevelt, and to the besotted comfort of the western farmers."[89]

Varied journals offered their own analysis. The *New York American* found that such recent domestic reforms as a child labor law outweighed Wilson's negative foreign policy. Accusing Hughes of being pronouncedly pro-British and anti-German, Hearst's daily asserted that the majority of Americans highly approved of the president's "firm attitude toward German aggression" while opposing "his feeble submission to English and Mexican aggressions." Wilson won his majorities, said the *New Republic,* "because of the net results of his administration—peace at the moment, prosperity, a general sense of goodwill to the rest of the world and of some fellowship for the humble within the nation." Hughes "seemed strangely content to play the rôle allotted to him by the Democrats, and the Republicans went before the western electorate as a tory war party."[90]

In his analysis of the wider public, Link believes that the president's victory resulted from peace, prosperity, and progressive legislation. The economy was booming: farm income stayed high, labor received good wages; manufacturers were drawing the best prices yet for their goods. The peace issue helped Wilson considerably in the Midwest and the West, although one could well argue, as does John Milton Cooper Jr., that the election did not serve as a national referendum on the matter.[91] As the threat of war receded, Americans believed they could again focus on domestic issues.

In the race for congressional seats, preparedness played little role. Certain outspoken antipreparedness figures were defeated, among them such Democrats as Clyde H. Tavenner of Illinois, Warren Worth Bailey of Pennsylvania, and Oscar Callaway and "Cyclone" Davis of Texas. Others, however, were returned, the outspoken Claude Kitchin, for example, winning the North Carolina Democratic primary.

Rank-and-file German Americans often split their vote, although they slightly tilted toward Hughes. The Democratic stress on peace, combined with Roosevelt's baiting of "hyphenates," smashed possible ethnic unity. Despite the endorsements given to Hughes by their press, rank-and-file Irish Americans remained in Wilson's camp.

After his reelection, Wilson could act as he had long wished, that is, make an effort to mediate between the belligerents and thereby end the Great War. The resignation of Herbert Asquith as prime minister complicated matters, because on December 6 David Lloyd George, a far more assertive figure, replaced him. Arthur Balfour filled Grey's position at the Foreign Office. Similarly, early in December 1916, Gottlieb von Jagow resigned as Germany's foreign secretary, being succeeded by the belligerent Arthur Zimmermann. The president would be advancing his peace bid at a most inopportune time.

8

To End a Conflict
October 1916–January 1917

AFTER TWO YEARS OF fighting on the various fronts, the belligerents were merely continuing their mutual slaughter. By September 1916, France and Germany had experienced 1 million casualties at Verdun; by November Britain had lost 400,000 men in the Somme offensive. If, that summer, Russian offensives cost the Central Powers 600,000 men, the czarist regime lost 1 million of its own. In battles on the Isonzo River that lasted most of the year, Italy repulsed the Austrians but sustained losses of 150,000 by early summer.

Though the Germans occupied most of Belgium and parts of northern France, the Central Powers felt far from assured of victory. In August Wilhelm II so feared Austrian defeat that he experienced a nervous breakdown. By the time Austrian emperor Francis Joseph died in November, he had lost hope of military triumph, simply expressing the wish that his empire could "last out the winter." His grandnephew Charles I, who inherited the throne, resented his nation's dependence on Germany and opposed increased submarine warfare. Within a year he surreptitiously sought peace with the Allies. Already Baron Stephan Burián, Austro-Hungarian foreign minister, desired negotiation.

On the home front, Germany suffered food shortages, leading to strikes and food riots. As early as June 1915, bread had been rationed; in May 1916 the government parceled out meat. Potatoes, sugar, and fats remained scarce. The fall harvest proved dismal. Neutral nations supplied meat, butter, and cheese, but these items went to troops or munitions workers, not the civilian population. Many Germans ate turnips, normally used as cattle fodder. By November authorities conceded that much undernourishment existed.

Frustrated by failure to achieve a breakthrough on the western front and facing a crisis in domestic morale, Germany increasingly placed its hopes on U-boat warfare. By sinking massive tonnage of merchant shipping and deterring neutrals from carrying goods to British ports, it sought to threaten Britain's very existence. Whereas on April 1, 1916, the Reich possessed just thirty-six submarines, by July 1 the number rose to fifty-four and by December 20 to eighty-five. Despite the limitations specified in the *Sussex* pledge, U-boat warfare proved most successful. Between October 1916 and January 1917, German vessels sank an average of 350,000 tons a month.

On August 31, meeting at Pless Castle, the Admiralty endorsed unrestricted submarine warfare, arguing that the measure would defeat Britain by the end of the year. Otherwise, said Admiral Holtzendorff, "time is working against us." Foreign Secretary Jagow retorted: "Germany will in such case be looked upon as a mad dog against whom the hand of every man will be raised." On August 27 Rumania had joined the Allies, its sole motive being territorial gain. Germany's leadership agreed to postpone any maritime decision until the Balkan nation was defeated. Late in September Admiral Georg A. von Müller, naval adviser to the emperor, warned that such U-boat combat would simply lead to "prolongation of the war and our ultimate exhaustion." On October 6, Holtzendorff ordered a new campaign against merchant shipping, although he stressed that submarines must observe the rules of cruiser warfare scrupulously.[1]

A minor crisis arose on October 7, when a new long-range submarine, *U-53,* arrived at Newport, Rhode Island, having left Heligoland, an island off Germany's northwest coast, close to three weeks earlier. The submarine remained in port just six hours, for Commander Hans Rose possessed orders to attack Allied warships hugging the American coast. The next day Rose sailed fifty miles off Nantucket, where he sank several British steamers and two others, one Norwegian and one Dutch. Included was the Red Cross liner *Stephano,* a Canadian ship en route from Halifax to New York and carrying American passengers returning from summer vacations. A U.S. destroyer flotilla, lying nearby, helped pick up crews and passengers. All lives were saved. On the next day, Rose sank three more ships and then headed home.

Americans betrayed genuine apprehension, manifest in a stock market panic that liquidated $500 million in fifteen minutes. Marine insurance rates jumped 500 percent as the press expressed anxiety. In public, Wilson remained calm, merely asserting that he would hold Germany to its pledges. Privately, he told Ambassador Bernstorff that he could not control public outrage. American naval authorities investigated, then reported that Berlin had not violated neutrality rules. The British were furious, accusing the United States of tolerating a violation of its own neutrality.[2]

Reactions followed predictable lines. Wilson's critics found that such incidents proved American vulnerability to European attack. Roosevelt accused Wilson of acting in a "Pontius Pilate–like manner," telling the press: "War has been creeping nearer and nearer, until it stares at us from just beyond our three-mile limit, and we face it without policy, plan, purpose, or preparation." The more moderate *Nation* affirmed that Germany might be acting legally but found its behavior at best foolish. By entrusting maritime encounters to "a naval officer under a terrific strain," Germany was "playing with dynamite." Viereck maintained that nothing would please Americans more than the sinking of "every Allied cruiser nosing about in our waters."[3]

German authorities immediately asserted that they still honored the *Sussex* pledge. More important, they ceased sinkings off the U.S. coast, sending no more submarines to American waters until the United States entered the war. On October 11, Grey hinted to Page that the United States shared partial responsibility for *U-53*'s raid, because the United States insisted that British cruisers avoid the U.S. coast and opposed visits by defensively armed merchantmen.[4]

Although submarine commanders attempted to follow instructions, American lives continued to be lost. On October 28, *U-55* sank the armed British steamer *Marina* without warning off the Irish coast, killing six American crew members. The commander mistook the merchant vessel for an auxiliary naval ship. Within eight days, a German U-boat torpedoed the British liner *Arabia,* also armed, in the eastern Mediterranean; again it gave no notice. Of the fifty-seven lives lost, none was American. By early December Admiral Georg von Müller conceded: "We have broken our promises to America." Even though the Germans were violating the *Sussex* pledge, something that Lansing pointed out to embassy counselor Joseph C. Grew, the administration made no protest.[5]

On November 2, in talking with House and Vance McCormick, chairman of the Democratic National Campaign Committee, Wilson expressed his reluctance to press the Germans on the matter of attacking armed Allied ships. "I do not believe," he contended, "the American people would wish to go to war no matter how many lives were lost at sea." He maintained that the *Sussex* pledge merely applied to passenger ships, not merchantmen, a false claim that alarmed Lansing. Writing House on November 24, Wilson asked him to inform Grey that American sentiment was "as hot against Great Britain as it was at first against Germany and likely to grow hotter still against an indefinite continuation of the war." He wanted the foreign secretary to know that the militant Anglophile Page no longer spoke for the United States.[6]

House and Lansing remained far more belligerent than the president. Early in December the colonel first broached the revival of the House-Grey memorandum, then undercut Wilson by informing an English friend that America's pro-British attitude had not changed over the past year and a half. For several months Lansing faulted Wilson for not realizing that "German imperialistic ambitions" threatened "free institutions everywhere"; the issue, he insisted, lay strictly between autocracy and democracy. "When we do go into the war," the secretary confided to his diary, "and we might as well make up our minds that we are going in, we *must* go in on the side of the Allies, for we are a democracy." On December 8, Lansing wanted to sever relations with Germany over the *Marina* and the *Arabia:* "We ought not to let matters drift along with Germany continuing at intervals to sink vessels on which Americans have taken passage," he wrote Wilson. "The longer we delay the more frequent I believe will be the outrages and the less regard Germany will give to our declaration in the SUSSEX case."[7] The president would not even reply. During the next few weeks, thanks to a German Imperial Order dated December 2, no Allied passenger ships were sunk, although many merchantmen went to the bottom. Hence State Department communications to Berlin were limited to requests for information; they did not include protests.

To American observers, conflict over German U-boats was simply a matter of time. In mid-October, Joseph Grew warned House from Berlin that the United States must be fully prepared for eventual resumption of indiscriminate submarine warfare, an admonition repeated early in November in a report that riots in Kiel revealed an alarming food situation.[8]

German naval commanders continually underestimated American strength. In October Admiralty officials assured Hindenburg that U-boats could prevent U.S. armed forces from ever setting foot on European soil. Ludendorff reportedly remarked: "I do not give a damn about America." Bethmann remained opposed to their use, warning that a blockade of England was impossible, particularly if such neutral nations as the United States, Denmark, Spain, and the Netherlands entered the conflict. In speaking to the main committee of the Reichstag, Karl Helfferich—deputy chancellor and secretary of both treasury and interior—warned that massive numbers of American troops could arrive in Europe. "If the cards of the unrestricted U-boat war are played and are not trumps, . . . then we are lost for centuries."[9]

On December 22 Holtzendorff warned that Germany faced a major dilemma: either it must engage in total war, which would include sinking *all* shipping, neutral as well as belligerent, or experience certain destruction. Neutral shipping supplied about one-third of Britain's tonnage needs. Because of limited cargo space and poor harvests in North America and Canada, Britain depended upon supplies from Argentina, India, and particularly Australia. It also received fats from Denmark and Holland, metal from Spain, and wood from the Scandinavian countries, the last item contributing to iron, steel, and munition production. If submarines could frighten many neutral vessels away, Britain would lose almost 40 percent of its shipping, which the admiral considered as "a final and irreplaceable loss." The U-boats, he predicted, could sink six hundred thousand tons a month, thereby reducing England, the mainstay of the Entente, to starvation within half a year.

Though such all-out warfare would certainly bring the United States into the conflict, Holtzendorff saw little reason to worry. In entering the war, America would lose "the sources of that commercial prosperity which has given it the towering political prominence which it now occupies." Besides, he continued, the United States stood "face to face with the Japanese peril," a reference to recent tensions over immigration and Nippon's aggressive moves in China. Therefore, America "can neither inflict material damage upon us, nor can it be of material benefit to our enemies. . . . I guarantee that for its part the U-boat war will lead to victory." Quartermaster General Erich Ludendorff, Germany's "silent dictator," echoed the admiral's sentiments. Either commence the sinking of all merchantmen by January 31, he warned, or he could no longer retain responsibility for directing Germany's military effort.[10]

Although Wilson could not make any conciliation bid until after the 1916 election, he knew that he must act soon. "Unless peace could be quickly attained," his aide Joseph Tumulty noted in October, in paraphrasing the president's views, "the European struggle would soon enter upon a phase more terrible than any in the preceding two years, with consequences highly dangerous to the interests of the country."[11]

Bernstorff welcomed American efforts, cabling Berlin on September 8: "If Wilson is re-elected, I think there is good prospect of his mediation before the end of the year. From this point of view the attainment of peace through unrestricted submarine war seems hopeless, since the United States would inevitably be drawn into the war—no matter what the result of the election—and consequently the war would be prolonged." Throughout the fall the ambassador begged Berlin to delay a U-boat decision until Wilson made a negotiation effort.[12]

Although Germany perceived its current situation as weak, historian Karl E. Birnbaum argues that it possessed a good bargaining position. Admittedly, it lost colonies in Africa and the south Pacific, but it suffered few territorial privations. It occupied large tracts of enemy territory both to its east and west, valuable pawns in any bargaining. Its military power remained unbroken.[13]

On September 2 Bethmann instructed his ambassador to stress the need for America to make such overtures promptly, if possible before the presidential election: "Otherwise all-out submarine warfare would have to be seriously considered." The chancellor's note passed the scrutiny of Ludendorff and Chief of Staff Paul von Hindenburg. In signing on to Bethmann's draft, Wilhelm scribbled at the end: "The mediation must seek to achieve an armistice of limited duration—short as possible—in the course of which a preliminary peace would be arranged. Without a conference—that is to say, without the neutrals—only between the belligerents alone."[14]

Three weeks later, the German Foreign Office gave Bernstorff an ominous warning. On October 18 it stated that Wilson must offer his good offices soon or Berlin would "be forced to regain the freedom of action" reserved in the *Sussex* note; "thus the President's steps may be jeopardized." Bernstorff passed the news on to House, who wrote Wilson, calling the German dispatch a threat to resume full-scale U-boat hostilities if the president did not intervene immediately. Although Wilson believed he must wait until the election was over, the German note encouraged him to move quickly. Slightly over a month later, Foreign Secretary Zimmermann cabled Bernstorff, emphasizing that the president must make his peace overture by New Year's Day. On November 20, the ambassador told House, without being authorized to make any such claim, that Germany was willing to evacuate France and Belgium, a move that would force negotiation.[15] Nevertheless, by late November, Britain and France were intensifying their maritime warfare, arming as many merchantmen as possible and giving them orders to shoot every German submarine on sight.

Wilson felt pressed. He told House on November 14 that unless the war could be terminated, "we must inevitably drift into war with Germany upon the submarine issue." Claiming that Berlin had already broken the *Sussex* pledge, he feared that the United States might have to sever diplomatic relations if he did not "make a move for peace." The colonel balked, arguing that a negotiation bid would appear to reward Germany's flaunting international obligations. House also feared that America would become entangled in a host of thorny issues, among them Poland, Serbia, the Balkans, Constantinople, and Alsace-Lorraine.[16]

On the next day, House presented the president with a frightening scenario: Wilson would make a peace proposal; Germany would accept it; the Allies would turn down this offer; Berlin would begin unrestricted U-boat warfare; the president would attempt to break relations with the Reich; and the American people would sympathize with Berlin. Conversely, if Germany remained restrained, the United States would inevitably drift into a sympathetic alliance with it, possibly causing England and France to declare war on America. According to the colonel, Wilson "went so far as to say that if the Allies wanted war with us we would not shrink from it." German historian Reinhard R. Doerries partially concurs with House's analysis, claiming that Britain would probably have rejected Wilson's peace bid, after which Berlin could retract the *Sussex* pledge and wage all-out submarine warfare with moral impunity.[17]

The president further contended that neither power could seriously harm the United States, to which House rejoined that "Great Britain might conceivably destroy our fleet and land troops from Japan in sufficient numbers to hold certain parts of the United States." The Japanese, responded Wilson, would have to stop at the Gulf of Mexico. By the fall of 1916, notes Arthur S. Link, the chief executive was "as neutral in thought as it was possible for any American to have been."[18]

If Wilson desired to force the Allies to the peace table, the opportunity had come, and he knew it. On October 3, a British interdepartmental conference noted the nation's utter dependence upon American munitions, steel, foodstuffs, oil, wheat, cotton, and lubricants. Were the United States to engage in economic reprisals, Britain's war effort would practically stop. Of the 5 million pounds sterling needed to prosecute the war, reported government economist John Maynard Keynes later that week, 2 million must come from North America. "In a few months time," claimed the treasury official, "the American public will be in a position to dictate to this country on matters that affect us more nearly than them." Reginald McKenna, chancellor of the exchequer, concurred with Keynes, telling the cabinet in late October: "By next June or earlier, the President of the American Republic will be in a position, if he wishes, to dictate his own terms to us." At the end of December, McKenna told an American journalist that Wilson could "force the Allies to their knees any time in a moment."[19]

France, too, experienced deprivation. It lost 40 percent of its coal-producing capacity when, in August 1914, the Germans seized the Lille region, an area that also supplied steel, iron, and textiles. As such items could be obtained solely through exports from Britain and the United Stares, France accrued a massive debt.

British delegates to a meeting of the Joint Anglo-French Financial Committee reinforced the depressing analysis. On October 16, they warned that British-owned American securities were exhausted and collateral was needed. "Our financial requirements," the committee noted, "have got far beyond any total which can be met by the great capitalist interests." Britain must seek American investments "not only on the Atlantic seaboard, but in the Middle and Far Western States, where the European War is a distant and unrealized adventure."[20]

Wall Street recognized the Allied predicament. Meeting with the Anglo-French Financial Committee in London a week earlier, from October 3 to 10, J.P. Morgan Jr. and H.P. Davison, a partner in Morgan's firm, were told that France had drained its gold and dollar resources. When the Joint Committee asked the American visitors whether their banks could supply $1.5 billion by March 1, J.P. could not answer that "awful question." The two Morgan partners proposed to allow temporary bank overdrafts and short-term credits. A large, unsecured public loan was deemed too risky.[21]

On November 18, when Davison presented his plan to the Federal Reserve Board, he encountered strong opposition. Banker Paul M. Warburg wrote fellow board member Benjamin Strong, governor of New York's powerful Federal Reserve Bank, warning against undue dependence upon any single debtor. He noted Washington's guess that the war would end in a draw; continuing the conflict by extending further loans would create "needless and fruitless sacrifice of life and treasure." President Wilson and the board shared Warburg's apprehension, the Federal Reserve advising bankers on the twenty-seventh that it violated the national interest to "invest in foreign Treasury bills of this character." In cautioning against war loans, the board stressed that banks must keep large cash reserves. Aware of its dominant position, it said, "The United States has now attained a position of wealth and of international financial power, which, in the natural course of events, it could not have reached for a generation. We must be careful not to impair this position of strength and independence."[22]

British Ambassador Spring Rice reported home: "The object of course is to force us to accept the President's mediation by cutting off supplies." The Federal Reserve Board's governor, W.P.G. Harding, went so far as to write Strong that America's newly gained financial power gave it the power either to shorten or prolong the war.[23]

The Federal Reserve's admonition put London on the brink of panic. Both Allied bonds and American war stocks fell sharply. All British finance, including, of course, its American purchasing, lay in turmoil. Values on the securities market plummeted by $1 billion. According to Virginia's governor, Henry C. Stuart, Davison believed that the world's entire financial equilibrium lay at risk.[24] At first J.P. Morgan Jr. defiantly promised that his firm would market short-term British and French notes, but the British withdrew their treasury bills from sale.

With Britain on the verge of collapse Wilson remained master of the situation, able to press Britain for concessions concerning the blockade and the blacklist. After the Federal Reserve issued its statement, little could prevent the financial collapse of the Allies. Wilson was fully aware of his power, saying at the close of the presidential campaign: "We can determine to a large extent who is to be financed and who is not to be financed."[25]

The United States was not merely the sole means of Britain's financial salvation; it served as well as an indispensable armory. In mid-October an internal memorandum of the British Ministry of Munitions noted that the United Kingdom, while self-sufficient in small arms, depended upon America for explosives and metals needed to manufacture such ammunition as howitzers and shells. By November 1916 the British had spent 40 percent of their war expenditure on supplies from North America.

Britain's Board of Trade added food to its list of needed items. Because of a worldwide drought, grain production in Canada, Argentina, and the United States was markedly lower than in 1915. Were the United States to embargo wheat, Britain would experience hardship, though not comparable to Germany's "turnip winter."

Despite such handicaps, the Allies still sustained hopes of victory. Admittedly, Germany held France's richest territory and most of Belgium. It dominated central and southeastern Europe, having just checked a major Russian offensive. However, the Entente strengthened its Turkish flank, maintained a tight naval blockade of the Continent, and outnumbered German forces on the western front by close to 1.5 million. By moderating its efforts, conserving resources, and relaxing some restrictions of American trade, Britain could maintain its war effort for several more months, at which time the Allies could gain significant victories and Wilson could modify his policies.

Although involved in a desperate struggle, the British continued to apply economic pressure. On October 10 the British finally responded to Wilson's protest of July 26 against the blacklist. Britain defended the practice, calling it the "exercise of the sovereign right of an independent state over its own citizens and nothing more." London denied that the list was directed against neutral trade in general, much less American commerce. It was part of a general campaign to weaken the enemy. Foreign Secretary Grey, however, confided to Ambassador Page that his government had blundered in the matter; he predicted modification of the list.[26]

Similarly, not until October 12 did Britain and France answer Lansing's protest, issued four and a half months earlier, concerning mail censorship. In a long message, they accused Germany of using neutral mails to advance its war effort. "A few lines of a letter conveyed to the enemy may be as useful or even more useful to his warlike operations than a cargo of arms and ammunition. . . . Hostile acts have failed which had been planned through the mails." They agreed to take responsibility for "abuses, grave errors, or derelictions" concerning mail inspection but never resolved the issue.[27]

American editors deplored the British response. The *Literary Digest* reported that government and press opinion claimed that London had ignored Lansing's efforts to restore America's full neutral rights. Free use of the mails, argued the *New Republic,* was essential to the transaction of international business. The *Outlook* advanced a minority view, calling the note "conciliatory and reasonable."[28]

By mid-December the *New Republic* listed Britain's transgressions: the Japanese alliance, made in 1902, which enabled Japan to seize Shantung peninsula and several central Pacific islands; "the Irish episode"; an "indefinite extension" of its sea power; and "a good deal of discourtesy in the British press." In addition, the annexationist war aims of Italy, Rumania, and Russia made the conflict look continually less like "a clean-cut fight between right and wrong, between democracy and absolutism, between public faith and international lawlessness." On November 17, House told Frank L. Polk, counselor of the State Department, that he still would risk war with Germany but described the Allies as "irritating beyond all endurance."[29]

There remained another side to the picture. Even if American economic pressure could help terminate the conflict, it might well jeopardize the United States' own domestic economy. Toward the end of October, the Department of Commerce warned that a counterstroke against the United Kingdom would backfire. Important U.S. businesses, it noted, depended upon such imports as rubber, wool, jute, tin, and graphite—all coming from the British Empire. Were Britain to terminate existing agreements concerning such items, it could paralyze many home industries. An arms embargo would deprive the United States of a quarter billion dollars worth of business each year; one on wheat would depress the domestic price, thereby injuring American farmers. To deny the Allies ship clearance would simply harm the nation's own export trade.[30]

Such sentiments might be most perceptive. In 1916 American trade with the Entente exceeded $3 billion a year. During that year per capita income rose markedly, much of it stemming from Allied commerce. With American prosperity a reality, the United States had far more to gain materially by acquiescing to the British blockade than by challenging it. Although a prohibition on loans could have wrecked the British war effort, it would have jeopardized America's prospects. Historian Ross Gregory writes: "American economic weapons were probably too large to use," something the British understood. Furthermore, he argues, Wilson could not have coerced both sets of belligerents economically without himself going to war.[31]

Two weeks after the presidential election, Wilson deemed the time propitious for his peace bid. Deploring "this vast, gruesome contest of systematized destruction," the president noted: "Never before in the world's history have two great armies been so equally matched; never before have the losses and the slaughter been so great with as little gain in military advantage." Neither the triumph of "German militarism" nor of "British navalism" was desirable. In a memo dictated to his stenographer in the fall of 1916, he cited the example of the Franco-Prussian War to argue that victory by either side would inevitably lead to another war of revenge.[32]

Tensions with Berlin remained troublesome. By the end of 1916, the Germans had deported almost fifty-five thousand Belgians to work in their factories, and forty-seven thousand were forced to labor in occupied France. American outrage could only be compared to U.S. reaction to Germany's original invasion of Belgium in 1914. Late in November Lansing protested this action, noting that the practice took place at a time when the American public was "more nearly approaching a balance of judgments as to the issues of the war than ever before." On December 11 Germany in turn rejected Lansing's reproach, blaming the Allied blockade for creating massive unemployment in Belgium and promising to ameliorate any adverse conditions. Elihu Root, addressing three thousand protesters in New York's Carnegie Hall in mid-December, demanded that Wilson threaten Bernstorff with recall. The *Fatherland* sought to reply by claiming the Belgians were "notoriously the most illiterate" as well as being "the most immoral people in Europe." Incredibly lazy, they were becoming "a nation of tramps."[33] Although on March 2, 1917, Wilhelm II announced an end to deportations, the Germans retained Belgians who possessed the desired skills.

On December 8 Hindenburg, Ludendorff, and Wilhelm II allowed Bethmann to launch a peace campaign. Germany had recently captured the Rumanian capital of Bucharest, a conquest that might temporarily give Berlin some diplomatic maneuvering power. These leaders added a warning: if this move was rebuffed, unrestricted submarine warfare would begin in January.

Four days later the chancellor told the Reichstag that his nation did not seek to annihilate its enemies; it was ready to negotiate. Were Germany's bid rejected, the Central Powers would continue fighting until they achieved victory. Assuming a tone of confidence, Bethmann pointed to the conquest of Rumania and the repulse of Allied forces on the Somme and Italy's Carso River. In a supplementary statement, the Austrian government emphasized the uselessness of further Allied fighting. That very day Bethmann privately cabled Wilson, requesting him to use the "good offices" of the United States to expedite a parley.[34]

Bethmann's address ignored the unabashed imperialism of Germany's war aims. Conspicuously absent from his speech were such matters as the establishment of a puppet kingdom of Poland and German annexation of Courland and Lithuania. In the west, Berlin's demands involved war indemnities, strategic boundary adjustments in Alsace-Lorraine, "guarantees" in Belgium or the annexation of Liège and "corresponding areas," and annexation of Luxembourg and the French territories of Briey and Longwy, both of which possessed major iron deposits. Overseas, Germany sought to regain most of its colonies, exceptions being Kiaochow, the Carolines, and the Marianas—all in the Pacific. It also desired extensive parts of the Belgian Congo.[35] Germany could not achieve these aims unless the Central Powers possessed the power to dictate such terms.

Historians debate Bethmann's motives. German scholar Fritz Fischer claims that the chancellor sought to mollify such neutrals as the United States while paving the way for all-out submarine warfare. To Ernest R. May, the German leader held little hope for his nation's long-term prospects, particularly given the pessimism of his Austrian and Turkish allies and the suicidal nature of U-boat warfare. David S. Patterson believes that Bethmann hoped that Washington would so welcome a peace initiative that it would not break diplomatic relations if Berlin intensified submarine warfare. Besides, Allied rejection, which appeared likely, would convince the Reich's military and civilian population that their cause was just, thereby bolstering sagging morale.[36]

Within the United States, pacifists and pro-German voices welcomed Bethmann's speech. Predictably, Viereck praised "the momentous pacific bid of the Imperial German Chancellor," claiming that Germany's terms would be moderate. Hearst's *New York American* asked the United States to back Berlin's peace effort, warning that continued warfare could destroy the balance of power and lead either to Russian or German domination of Europe. The *New Republic* argued that the Allies had nothing to lose by negotiation because hope for victory remained futile. Senator Stone told the St. Louis chapter of the League to Enforce Peace that the time was ripe for the United States to intervene diplomatically. Bryan sent a personal message to Lloyd George, calling upon him to negotiate; the prime minister's "decision may mean life or death to millions."[37]

Without exception the Allies rejected the German bid. The Russian Duma unanimously spurned the proposal. So did Czar Nicholas II. The Duma sought "a decisive victory over the military power of the enemy." French premier Aristide Briand branded Bethmann's proposal "a gross trap." On December 24, France's Senate unanimously declared that peace could not be discussed as long as one enemy soldier occupied its native soil. Italy's foreign minister, Baron Sidney Sonnino, stressed the solidarity of the Entente.[38]

On the nineteenth David Lloyd George, Britain's new prime minister, publicly asserted that the Entente stood by its demand, initially made by his predecessor Herbert Asquith, for "complete restitution, full reparation, effectual guarantees." Claiming that "we shall put our trust in our unbroken Army rather than in broken faith," he warned that the British would not "put our heads into a noose with the rope end in the hands of Germany." Privately he was far less confident, remarking, "We are going to lose this war." He did tell the House of Commons that he would not totally slam the door on negotiations, thereby tacitly challenging the Germans to state their terms.[39]

American defenders of the Allies echoed the opposition of London and Paris. The *Nation* accused Bethmann of speaking as "a conqueror addressing the conquered." Senator Warren Harding struck a note of caution, observing that "the fellow who tries to bring about peace between two combatants often gets a swat in the jaw himself."[40]

Bethmann had placed Wilson in a serious predicament. The address, Lansing aptly noted in his memoirs, put Wilson "in the embarrassing position of apparently collaborating with the Germans in their endeavor to bring about a negotiated peace while the Imperial armies were occupying conquered territory." Not only was the president upstaged; he was deprived of the neutral stance he needed to secure a fair hearing from the Allies. In mid-November Bernstorff had warned the Foreign Office to remain silent concerning peace moves until Wilson was able to act.[41]

At the very time the Allies were refusing the German overture, Wilson sent a note to all belligerents. Dated December 18 and published three days later, the message requested the warring powers to offer concrete peace terms. In an effort to nullify any secret accords and maximize the chance of agreement, he asserted: "The objects which the statesmen of the belligerents on both sides have in mind in this war are virtually the same, as stated in general terms to their own people and to the world." Each belligerent sought security for its own people, wanted to protect "the rights and privileges of weak peoples and small states," and was ready to consider the formation of "a league of nations to insure peace and justice throughout the world." When the war ended, the American people would cooperate in attaining such goals. Somewhat cautious, the president denied that he was suggesting mediation; instead, he was "merely proposing that soundings be taken in order that we may learn, the neutral nations with the belligerent, how near the haven of peace we may be for which all mankind longs with an intensive and increasing longing."[42]

An early draft of the note posited an early peace conference and warned that future American policy would depend on the response of the warring states, but House and Lansing persuaded Wilson to delete such statements. The colonel found the message itself poorly timed because the Allies were in no mood to welcome any peace note. He also thought that the implication that both sides shared common aims would make the Allies "frantic with rage," adding: "I find the President has nearly destroyed all the work I have done in Europe."[43] In reality the president did not equate the war aims of the two alliances; rather he asserted that the objects of both alliances *as stated* were alike. However, the final version was stronger in the sense that the president skillfully made it difficult for the belligerents to espouse any but the most lofty of war aims. In addition, he put the belligerents on warning: he was not simply seeking to end the war quickly; their replies might force the United States to reconsider its entire neutrality policy.

Historians differ over Wilson's message. Arthur Walworth calls the paper "a landmark in the diplomacy of the century." Patrick Devlin offers more nuance, writing that any suggestion that belligerents might pause to discuss "what the war was all about" ignored the character of modern warfare. Each warring party shared one primary object, humbling the enemy. The president offered "the voice of reason but the tone was the tone of mental and moral superiority." Kendrick A. Clements dissents, holding that Wilson would have been wiser to stress the futility of the ongoing stalemate rather than to antagonize Britain and France by claiming both sides were fighting for similar aims.[44]

At home Wilson's message received much support. The *New York American* titled its endorsement: "In the Name of the American People, Mr. President, We Salute and Thank You." Bryan praised the president's "invaluable service." Senator Stone called the proposal "a very timely offer," finding in it "the beginning of the end." George Sylvester Viereck spoke for many German Americans in welcoming the note, writing: "Mr. Wilson has vindicated those who voted for him, and disarmed those who voted against him." Bernstorff remarked: "I am positive there will be a peace conference."[45]

The American Neutral Conference Committee, chaired by publisher Hamilton Holt, backed the move. Acting similarly to Jane Addams's International Committee of Women for Permanent Peace (of which the Woman's Peace Party was a member), the organization sought a conference of neutral nations that would offer joint mediation to the belligerents. Other planks included self-determination of peoples, repudiation of all military conquests, and the establishment of a world organization to settle international disputes. Emily Greene Balch, the committee's vice chairman, claimed that Germany endorsed international organization. She attacked the Allies for coveting such areas as Constantinople, the Turkish Straits, Persia, the Dalmatian coast, and Syria.[46]

Staunch pro-Allied elements attacked the president. Senator John W. Weeks branded Wilson's move "ill-timed and unwise." Roosevelt deemed the note "profoundly immoral" and "wickedly false," attacking in particular Wilson's implication that both sides shared similar goals. Lodge wrote Viscount Bryce, warning that trust in Wilson "would be a fatal mistake." To the pro-British *New York Tribune,* "American influence for real peace, for just peace, is abolished." The *Outlook* expressed concern that the president was offering a veiled warning that the United States might enter the conflict without giving any intimation as to America's true interest. At a private dinner of the Vigilantes, an organization of propreparedness writers, General Wood remarked: "Gentlemen, we have no leadership in Washington."[47]

George Wharton Pepper, a prominent Philadelphia lawyer and an Episcopal layman, warned fellow Christians about Wilson's attempt to promote a "premature" peace. On December 30, he organized a group of prominent clergy and laity, among them several leading educators, to release a statement addressed to "Christians of America." The manifesto read: "The just God, who withheld not His own Son from the cross, would not look with favor upon a people who put their fear of pain and loss, their concern for comfort and ease above the holy claims of righteousness and justice, and freedom and mercy and truth."[48]

Overseas reaction varied. Such neutral nations as Switzerland, Spain, and the Scandinavian countries endorsed the president's bid. Many German editors perceived Wilson as backing their nation, although naval, Pan-German, and conservative spokesmen accused him of seeking to rescue the Allies. On December 23 Hindenburg wrote Bethmann, denouncing the president for trying to delay the U-boat campaign. "Wilson's efforts can accomplish nothing," he added. The more moderate chancellor believed that the White House was too emotionally committed to the British cause, the American economy too dependent upon Allied commerce for America to mediate impartially. Furthermore, until now he had retained some semblance of internal unity by avoiding any discussion of war aims. The Kaiser was even more emphatic, accusing the British of starting the war and Wilson of continuing it. Assailing America's failure to institute a munition embargo and ban on loans, he remarked: "I won't go to any conference! Certainly not under his chairmanship!"[49]

Most Allied leaders proved equally hostile, believing that Wilson sought a peace conference because Germany supposedly possessed a military advantage. England's King George V reportedly wept upon hearing the news. Philip Kerr, secretary to Lloyd George, saw America as almost as much a threat to Europe's freedom as Germany. Paul Cambon, French ambassador to London, commented: "This professor, with his dogmatism and inspired airs, is acting like a knave." James Bryce wrote Wilson: "A peace concluded on any terms the German Government would now accept would be a hollow truce. . . . That is why we must fight on at whatever cost." Much of the British and French press denounced the president, in part because he appeared to place all war aims on the same moral plane. Wilson did muster some overseas support. British Liberals and French Socialists endorsed his move, the *Manchester Guardian* declaring that each nation harbored "a great volume of opinion" that sought to end the carnage.[50]

Lansing did everything possible to sabotage Wilson's effort or, to say the least, to assure that it led to entering the war on the Allied side. Not merely, he believed, did the conflict embody a global ideological struggle; America's own security lay at stake. Therefore, his countrymen must not think that peace was imminent and the world must not believe that the president supported Bethmann's recent overture. He genuinely thought that, as he wrote Wilson on December 10, the nation was "certainly drifting nearer and nearer" to war: "We cannot continue much longer by peaceful means to secure these rights."[51]

The secretary held a press conference on December 21, the day Wilson's appeal reached the press. He asserted that both sides were increasingly violating American rights and warned:

> We are drawing nearer to the verge of war ourselves, and therefore we are entitled to know exactly what each belligerent seeks, in order that we may regulate our conduct in the future. . . . The sending of this note will indicate the possibility of our being forced into the war. That possibility ought to serve as a restraining and sobering force, safeguarding American rights. It may also serve to force an earlier conclusion of the war. Neither the President nor myself regard his note as a peace note; it is merely an effort to get the belligerents to define the end for which they are fighting.[52]

The implication was clear: America's top-ranking diplomat implied that the note issued by his president was not intended to promote peace; rather it was to prepare for the nation's entry into the conflict. Lansing was hinting that his nation would meet increased U-boat warfare by entering the war on the side of the Allies.

Many Americans feared that hostilities with Germany were impending.

Panic seized Wall Street as such stocks as General Electric and Bethlehem Steel plummeted. An unscrupulous financial writer, along with a Republican congressman from Indiana, warned of an imminent presidential peace note, thereby causing the stock market briefly to tumble. After all, a ceasefire would affect American industry, whose prosperity stemmed largely from war orders. Conversely, the uncertainty created by possible American entrance into the war would depress the market. Headlines continually used the phrase "verge of war."

Seldom in American history had a cabinet official so undercut a president. Lansing ensured Allied rigidity, as if it needed such bolstering, and undermined Wilson's domestic support. "In no other country in the world," trumpeted the *North American Review,* "could a Foreign Minister use such language without being instantly called to account." The chief executive considered firing his disloyal subordinate but ended satisfied with his secretary's public "clarification," which declared that the United States was not contemplating any change in its neutrality policy. In a corrective, Lansing posited that he simply sought to suggest "the very direct and necessary interest" the United States held in the belligerents' peace terms; he regretted that "any other construction" had been put on his remarks.[53] This tacit retraction soothed the financial community.

Historians speculate as to why Wilson did not relieve Lansing. Patrick Devlin perceives a flaw in the president's character. John Milton Cooper Jr. finds sheer embarrassment at work, along with anxieties concerning the delicate nature of pending negotiations and the president's inordinate toleration of disagreement. The secretary was henceforth excluded from major decisions.[54]

By no means repentant, Lansing met with the French ambassador Jules Jusserand on December 20 and with British ambassador Cecil Spring Rice a day later. He told both diplomats that Wilson had spurned Bethmann's peace offer and desired to aid the Allies. The secretary personally endorsed the return of Alsace-Lorraine to France; indemnities for France, Belgium, and Serbia; an international commission to resolve Balkan matters; and a democratized Germany. No league of nations, he went on, was likely to guarantee the forthcoming peace. When Jusserand replied that such terms might make the Germans more strident, the secretary claimed that Berlin was prepared to negotiate. In his conversation with Spring Rice, the secretary dangled additional terms: an autonomous Poland under Russian sovereignty, Italian acquisition of the Trentino, and the expulsion of Turkey from Europe.

Lansing did not inform Wilson about these conversations. Obviously such terms could be exacted through military victory alone; their very publication would prolong hostilities. By suggesting them to the Entente, writes Link, Lansing sought to reinforce Germany's hard-liners, who were pressing for all-out submarine warfare, a move that in turn would force the United States into the conflict. "We come to what seems to be the only possible conclusion—that the Secretary of State was maneuvering to promote American intervention on the Allied side."[55]

House, too, undermined Wilson. Meeting on December 22 with a British contact, Sir Horace Plunkett, the colonel maintained that the president sought to restrain Germany's submarine policy, as he found the threat "appallingly serious for Britain." The chief executive had not changed his views, House continued; rather he was buying time, fearing that "England would not be able to hold out long enough for American assistance to become effective."[56] Despite House's machinations, Britain's leaders correctly understood—and opposed—Wilson's desire for a peace without victory.

Two days earlier, however, House had warned Wilson that "we might have trouble with England in the event she is victorious." Its navy possibly equaled the navies of the rest of the world combined; its army matched that of any other nation. Most of its population, he added, was "as war mad as Germany"; he had recently learned how unpopular the president was there.[57]

On December 26, Germany politely but firmly rejected Wilson's mediation. In a formal note, the new foreign secretary, Arthur Zimmermann, thanked the president for his "noble initiative" but declared that "the great work for the prevention of future wars can first be taken up only after the ending of the present conflict of exhaustion. The Imperial Government is ready, when this point has been reached, to cooperate with the United States in this sublime task." On the same day, Zimmermann informed Ambassador Bernstorff that a peace conference should be held in some "neutral spot" in Europe in order to free it from "American indiscreetness and intermeddling." He found that any "interposition" by Wilson, even in the form of establishing a "clearing house," would be detrimental to German interests. Within a month the foreign secretary elaborated, writing the ambassador: "American mediation for *genuine* peace negotiations is undesirable to us if for no other reason than public opinion." Bernstorff later asserted, quite correctly, that the German note was deliberately designed to eliminate the slightest possibility of Wilson's mediation. "We did not want any intermeddling by Wilson in territorial questions," he told a parliamentary inquiry in 1919.[58]

The American press condemned the German note. "The German Foreign Office," said the *New York World,* "had abruptly closed the door," leaving no basis for further discussion.[59] Ironically, had Germany responded positively to Wilson's message, the United States might have aligned itself against the Allies, the very circumstance Lansing and House feared.

Despite the discouraging wording of Zimmermann's reply, on January 3 Wilson told House that peace was in sight. During the conversation, House suggested that Wilson outline his terms in an address to Congress, the main principle being "the rights of nations to determine under what government they should continue to live." The two men concurred on freedom for Poland, restoration of Belgium and Serbia, and the right of Russia to a warmwater port. European Turkey "should cease to exist." They remained unsure about Alsace and Lorraine.[60]

Speaking to the colonel on the next day, the president remarked: "There will be no war. This country does not intend to become involved in this war. We are the only one of the great White nations that is free from war to-day, and it would be a crime against civilization for us to go in." House noted in his diary that the president had told Lansing that he did not think the American people would go to war because a few fellow-citizens had been killed on belligerent ships.[61]

Two days before the year ended, the Allied governments officially rejected the Reich's offer. They called Berlin's December 12 bid sheer propaganda, "devoid of substance and of precision"; it was "a maneuver of war," not "an offer of peace." Not only did it try to throw the onus for continuing the war on the Allies; it sought to impose a German settlement on Europe while Berlin held a transitory military advantage. The Entente would consider no peace move that lacked definite conditions, the restoration of Belgium among them.[62]

On December 21 Senator Gilbert Hitchcock introduced a resolution approving Wilson's note. The White House itself opposed the measure of the Nebraska senator, looking neither for a confrontation nor an endorsement. On January 3, 1917, when the measure came up for Senate debate, Lodge denied that the "national interest" of the United States was linked to the peace terms of any belligerent. He attacked Wilson's proposal of an international league, claiming it "makes us part of the political system of another hemisphere." To submit controversies to arbitration might threaten the Monroe Doctrine and the right to regulate immigration. Two days later, offering his support for Hitchcock, J. Hamilton Lewis commented: "War cannot continue without America being involved in a conflict." William E. Borah countered by accusing Wilson of adopting the program of the League to Enforce Peace; the president's proposal violated the Monroe Doctrine by committing American armed forces to protect the national integrity of every small European nation. Furthermore, such a world organization might, for example, force the United States to fight alongside Argentina against Brazil, with Japan against Russia.[63]

To gain Senate support, Hitchcock accepted a weaker revision of his resolution. Offered by Wesley L. Jones, it merely endorsed the president's request that belligerents state their peace terms. The body then approved the resolution 48 to 17 with 31 abstentions. All but ten in favor were Democrats; all but one of those opposed were Republicans. With two exceptions, the Republican support came from midwestern and western progressives, who did not share the more strident nationalism of their party colleagues, most of whom belonged to the Old Guard. James E. Martine of New Jersey was the lone Democratic opponent.[64]

The vote revealed that reactions to Wilson's foreign policy had become increasingly partisan. Democrats enthusiastically supported his agenda, Bryan standing practically alone in opposing membership in a world organization. On the Republican side, such hitherto globally minded figures as Lodge were manifesting opposition to collective security. Roosevelt became adamant on the issue. In a speech delivered in 1906 upon being awarded the Nobel Prize, Roosevelt had endorsed the concept of "an international police power." Now he preached against "violently meddling in every European quarrel," thereby inviting reciprocal action by the "Old World nations." The Monroe Doctrine would be subject to "an arbitral tribunal upon which Chinese and Turkish judges might deliver the casting vote." The United States might be devoting its "whole military and economic strength to a long-drawn and bloody war for a cause in which our people have no concern and in some place where we could hardly exert even a tiny fraction of our strength."[65]

The alliance of Borah with Lodge and Roosevelt suggests the embryonic development of a coalition that would bear fruit in postwar opposition to Wilson's League of Nations. The Idaho senator believed that an internationalist program would ensnare United States in the sordid world of power politics, causing America to lose its ideals. TR and his Bay State ally were far more amenable to binding alliances with such nations as Britain in order to enhance American power, their objection to the president's proposal lying in its supposed threats to the nation's sovereignty.

By now Germany saw itself facing stark choices: supporting Wilson's peace campaign, which meant forsaking hopes for military victory; continuing its policy of limited U-boat warfare, which remained sufficiently devastating to give Berlin hopes of obtaining a stalemate; or risking American intervention by launching unlimited submarine warfare, a move that, it hoped, would make Germany dominant in Europe, possibly in the world. Obstinate trench warfare promised no hope of victory. On January 10 counselor Grew reported from Berlin that Germany's masses suffered from undernourishment. Hence public morale remained low. "Well informed" Germans spoke of ceding parts of Alsace and Lorraine to France as well as certain unnamed colonies to Britain.[66] To both the German military and much of the populace, the U-boat alone could promise an Allied defeat both speedy and crushing.

Within days after Congress endorsed Wilson's plea for peace terms, Germany made its decision. On January 4 Holtzendorff predicted to Bethmann that U-boats could "finish off" America as well as England. Five days later, at a meeting held at Pless Castle that lasted just over an hour, military leaders demanded the unrestricted use of U-boats. Hindenburg warned that the Allies would launch a spring offensive that would surpass the murderous Somme assault. Therefore, Germany must immediately block their access to fresh manpower and supplies. Holtzendorff predicted that England would be defeated within six months, certainly before a single American soldier had set foot in Europe.[67]

Initially, some civilian leaders voiced opposition. If, noted Treasury Secretary Karl Helfferich, the United States entered the war, the Allies would get more, not fewer, provisions. Moreover, they could initiate antisubmarine measures. Until the last minute, Bethmann expressed disagreement, although, because of the defection of the Catholic Center Party, his control of the Reichstag was now in doubt. At last approving, he remarked: "If success beckons, we must follow."[68] In closing the meeting, Wilhelm declared that he fully expected American participation in the conflict but believed it would make no difference.

The terse imperial order of January 9 was most explicit: "I command that unlimited submarine warfare begin on February 1 with all possible vigor. You will please take all necessary measures immediately but in such a way that our intention does not become apparent to the enemy and to neutrals in advance. Basic operational plans are to be laid before me." Three days later the Admiralty issued slightly more detailed orders, beginning with the words:

"From February 1, 1917, onward every enemy merchantman met within the restricted zone is to be attacked without warning." To avoid any misunderstanding, the decree stated: "For the intimidation of neutral shipping, an effect as strong as possible at the beginning will be of great significance."[69]

Bernstorff had warned Zimmermann on January 10 that unlimited submarine warfare would not only kill Wilson's peace efforts; it would lead to war with the United States. The foreign secretary forwarded the ambassador's cable to Wilhelm, who replied that he placed "absolutely no reliance" on the president's initiative. Nine days later Bethmann cabled Bernstorff that Germany had set a deadline of February 1.[70]

On January 31 the chancellor told the Reichstag's budget committee: "If submarine warfare accomplished the expected results, America will not have time to attack before victory is certain." The naval secretary, Eduard von Capelle, added that "from a military point of view America is as nothing." Referring to U.S. troops, he asked: "How are they to cross the ocean?"[71]

Why did Germany make what Link calls "one of the greatest blunders in history," engaging in the very action that would make its own defeat inevitable? Berlin believed that if it desired victory, it had no choice.

Conversely, the German military deemed U-boats essential to ultimate triumph. The Admiralty now saw itself able to blockade the British Isles, ordering about twenty-five submarines to both western waters and the Mediterranean by February 1. The poor wheat harvest in North and South America could aid Berlin's war effort. U.S. food and raw materials, currently shipped to the Allies, would be diverted to an American army still in training. Historian Walter Millis argues that Germany actually underestimated the number of Allied ships that its submarines could sink while ironically overestimating the immediate military aid the United States might offer the Allies. After all, a year and a half elapsed from the time of the Pless conference to the engagement of American doughboys in major combat.[72]

Admittedly, at first Germany inflicted much damage on British shipping, the U-boats sinking close to 500,000 tons in February 1917 and 669,000 by June. In April one out of every four ships leaving port failed to return. Admiral Sir John Jellicoe, first British sea lord, warned: "It is impossible for us to go on with the war if losses like this continue."[73] By August, however, the amount of Allied tonnage sunk fell and Reich submarine losses began to rise.

Germany failed to make crucial estimates. On February 1 it possessed 107 U-boats, of which a mere 30 were suitable for ocean warfare. Submarines were often too slow to be effective against fast destroyers. Construction hardly kept up with losses. Codes were frequently lost or broken. Wireless seldom worked. Air leaks from torpedoes warned intended victims. Furthermore, the Germans calculated only British activity, whereas they should have taken stock of total world shipping. They overlooked in particular America's shipbuilding potential. By estimating only Britain's wheat production, they ignored the fact that other grains could compensate and that uncultivated grassland could be plowed up. Despite the relatively poor harvest of 1916, grain reserves in the United States, Australia, South America, and Canada were able to feed the Allies throughout the following year. Skillful rationing aided Britain considerably. Most important of all, the Royal Navy instituted convoys.

Ironically, Germany was introducing submarines to sever the Allied lifeline when the sorry shape of British and French finances was poised to accomplish the same result. The breakdown of the Anglo-American exchange system would have practically terminated American war exports. Not one German leader perceived the desperate Allied predicament, though an assessment of public records could have indicated the true situation. Had Berlin sought supporting documents and statistics, rudimentary espionage efforts in London or New York could have secured them. To plunge into unrestricted submarine warfare at this point, as John Milton Cooper Jr. notes, was "snatching defeat from the jaws of victory."[74]

Besides, by late summer 1916, Russia was collapsing, its major offensive led by General Alexsei Brusilov turning into a massive rout. Of course, Berlin could not predict how weak the Allies would be the following year, when they would experience defeats in Italy, mutiny in the French army, and, most significant, Russia's devastating downfall.

Despite Germany's decision, it still advanced peace terms. On January 15, 1917, Bernstorff gave House some idea of the conditions drafted by Zimmermann. His nation, said the ambassador, favored general international arbitration, a postwar league of nations, and a direct "cooling-off" treaty with the United States. Bernstorff disavowed any intention of annexing Belgium and subtly hinted at an independent Poland and Lithuania, a common border for Austria-Hungary and Bulgaria in Dobrudja (an area on the Bulgarian-Rumanian border), and unification of Serbia and Montenegro under the Montenegrin dynasty. "This is the most important communication we have had since the war began," House wrote Wilson that day, and "gives a real basis for negotiations and for peace." On January 18, in another letter to the chief executive, the colonel alleged that liberals totally controlled

Germany, a nation that was "badly pinched" and as inclined to take a stand "as advanced" as any democracy. "If Bernstorff has stated his Government's proposals correctly, peace is in sight," House said, adding: "You would be justified in forcing the Allies to consider it." Wilson responded that House greatly encouraged him.[75]

Twelve days earlier, Bethmann had authorized Bernstorff to communicate other terms confidentially. These were far more harsh: annexation of Liège, the Briey region, and strategic districts around Metz (in return for which France might possibly obtain compensation in upper Alsace); political, economic, and military protective arrangements in Belgium, to be worked out in direct negotiations with its King Albert; establishment of a Kingdom of Poland (to which would be added Lithuania and Courland) under German domination; and colonial restitution in Africa. Austria-Hungary would be permitted "territorial expansion" in Serbia, Montenegro, and Rumania, as would Bulgaria in Serbia and Dobrudja. Russia would be granted free passage through the Straits.[76]

On January 18, Bernstorff wrote House, repeating Germany's assurance that it welcomed Wilson's leadership of a conference aimed at reconstructing the international order. This time, however, the ambassador added that a preliminary meeting must come first; it would be limited to the belligerents alone and would possess the authority to execute a peace settlement. Two days later the ambassador wrote again, warning the colonel that Britain's "starvation policy" had so infuriated German public opinion that Berlin might be forced "to act accordingly in a very short time. I am afraid the situation in Berlin is getting out of our hands." Patrick Devlin compares Bernstorff's note to "the letter of a salesman who is unable to fulfill the orders he has taken because of trouble in the factory."[77]

Upon hearing this news, House wrote Wilson that the Germans were "slippery customers," who might resume "unbridled submarine warfare." The British, he went on, might be stubborn and stupid, but at least they were reliable. He deemed it essential to "tie up Germany in a conference."[78]

During this time the Allies advanced their own agenda. On January 12 the press reported their formal answer to Wilson's request for peace aims. Terms included the restoration of Belgium, Serbia, and Montenegro, together with indemnities for each; German evacuation of France, Russia, and Rumania, all with "just reparation"; liberation of Italians, Rumanians, Slavs, and "Tcheco Slovaques" under alien domination; enfranchisement of populations subject to "the bloody tyranny of the Turks"; and the expulsion of Turkey from Europe. German militarism was to be destroyed, huge indemnities exacted.[79]

Not surprisingly, the Allied aims somewhat resembled Lansing's mid-December suggestions to Jusserand and Spring Rice and House's winter conversations with Allied officials. Only military victory could fulfill such aims. They could well have been proposed in the expectation that they would trigger Germany's massive U-boat campaign, which in turn would lead to American belligerency. At any rate, Wilson believed the British terms far too ambitious, certainly impossible to fulfill. More important, he feared that the Allied agenda would stifle his peace efforts.[80]

Reactions to the note varied. The *Nation* argued that the Entente showed marked deference to Wilson, seeking to fulfill his terms and giving up thought of dismembering Germany. Finding "plenty of bargaining material," it continued: "So long as the word peace is still uttered by the belligerents, hope is not extinguished." The *New Republic* called the Allied response "a brilliantly ambiguous, a triumphantly equivocal document." The statement left the way open for some German presence in Alsace-Lorraine and possible autonomy for subject nationalities in the Ottoman Empire or a federalized Austria-Hungary. Hearst's *New York American* branded the missive "a bitter and truculent reply." The Central Powers could not yield Turkish territory to Russia. Nor could Austria surrender Trieste, Herzegovina, and Bosnia. Germany would fight "to the bitter end" before giving up "a foot of Alsace-Lorraine." To Viereck, the reply of the Allies read "as though it had been dictated by Colonel Roosevelt or Senator Lodge." The response was "written in the spirit of a gambler who, though not holding even a pair of deuces, hopes to intimidate his opponent."[81]

On January 22, believing time was crucial, Wilson addressed the Senate. Speaking in a low voice that grew increasingly stronger, he asserted that all belligerents had agreed to a postwar "concert of power" that would prevent further catastrophe. Although disavowing an American voice in determining concrete peace terms, he saw it "inconceivable" that his countrymen would not play a role in "that great enterprise," one in which Americans would "add their authority and their power" to that of other nations so as to "guarantee peace and justice throughout the world." "It will be absolutely necessary," he continued, to create an international force so powerful that "no nation, no probable combination of nations could face or withstand it. If the peace to be made is to endure, it must be a peace made secure by the organized force of mankind."

Henceforth, Wilson continued: "There must be not a balance of power, but a community of power; not organized rivalries, but an organized common peace." Needed was a "peace without victory," "a peace between equals." "Victory would mean peace forced upon the loser, a victor's terms imposed upon the vanquished. It would be accepted in humiliation, under duress, at an intolerable sacrifice, and would leave a sting, a resentment, a bitter memory upon which terms of peace would rest, not permanently, but only as upon quicksand."

Wilson first stressed such abstract aims as "equality of rights" for every nation and the principle, taken from the Declaration of Independence, that "governments derive their just powers from the consent of the governed." Suddenly becoming more specific, he maintained that "statesmen everywhere" endorsed such goals as "a united, independent, autonomous Poland"; access to the sea for "every great people"; and "freedom of the seas," by which he meant "the free, constant, unthreatened intercourse of nations." All peoples living under hostile governments must be guaranteed "inviolable security of life, of worship, and of industrial and social development." After advocating arms limitation, he asked "the nations" to "adopt the doctrine of President Monroe as the doctrine of the world," by which he meant that "no nation should seek to extend its polity over any other nation or people, but that every people should be left free to determine its own polity, its own way of development, unhindered, unthreatened, unafraid, the little along with the great and the powerful."[82] Never had an American leader sought to intervene so directly in European affairs.

The president directed the speech at "the silent mass of mankind everywhere," as he said in his text, bypassing their rulers. In writing editor John Palmer Gavit, Wilson stressed he was not addressing the American Senate or foreign powers. Rather he was speaking to "the *people* of the countries now at war." If, he continued, he could create sufficient pressure on the warring nations, their regimes would be forced to seek peace. In asking for support from the Carnegie Endowment for International Peace, he wrote: "I feel that the task of the moment is the rousing of a great body of opinion to very definite thought and purpose."[83] Yet Wilson did not neglect the belligerent governments, as seen by his offer to underwrite European security. Nor was he oblivious to domestic sentiment, stressing that his policy was deeply rooted in such historic American tenets as the Monroe Doctrine.

Historians differ on the wisdom of this message. Charles Callan Tansill, a scholar often critical of Wilson, argued that "for the first time since the outbreak of the World War, he was really neutral in his attitude towards the belligerents." Walter Millis, another revisionist of the 1930s, judged the speech "an ingenious and powerful effort of constructive statesmanship."

Writing decades later, Arthur Walworth refers to this "great manifesto of Anglo-Saxon liberalism." If both sets of belligerents, declares John Milton Cooper Jr., had been as chastened as they professed, the president might have been able to broker a grand settlement guaranteed by an international league. Wilson's proposal, notes Ross A. Kennedy, would permit Germany to retain its army, claim its right to an overseas empire, probably dominate the Balkans, and gain entry into a collective security system that offered more safety than any arms race.[84]

To Ross Gregory, however, the president relied solely upon his powers of persuasion rather than brandishing "the weapons in his arsenal, partly because he did not know how large they were." Link stresses that Wilson affirmed the necessity of a negotiated peace but in the next breath depicted a settlement that involved coercing a defeated Germany. Devlin is particularly critical. The speech appeared one-sided, failing to rebuke the Allies for the tone of moral superiority in their response of December 30. It used language that could be interpreted as threatening the Central Powers: "consent of the governed" (breaking up the Hapsburg Empire); an independent Poland (possibly depriving Germany of some Polish territory); direct outlets to the seas (ceding the port city of Danzig to Poland). "All this confirmed the Wilhelmstrasse's view that Wilson would have proved to be a most unsuitable mediator."[85]

In Europe the address received a mixed reception. Pope Benedict XV regarded the speech "the most courageous document which has appeared since the beginning of the war"; it revived "the principles of Christian civilization." Liberals and labor leaders offered strong support. The eighty-nine Socialists in the French Chamber of Deputies unanimously characterized the speech as "the charter of the civilized universe." The czar's foreign office commended Wilson's "broad humanitarian principles."[86]

Political leaders on all sides, still seeking military victory, remained either skeptical or hostile. Paris editor Georges Clemenceau, who became premier in November 1917, dismissed Wilson's remarks as utopian. Andrew Bonar Law, chancellor of the exchequer and leader of the House of Commons, said that the peace Wilson sought could be achieved only by continual fighting. Helfferich, who opposed Wilson's terms, later summarized the German reaction as: "Thank God for having kept us safe from this peace mediator!"[87]

At home Wilson met with strong support. Most journals praised the speech, the *Nation* writing that the president had uttered "a word heard round the world." *New Republic* editors were ecstatic, noting that Wilson had used the exact phrasing, "peace without victory," with which it had titled an editorial. Seven hundred prominent clergymen endorsed a world organization designed to prevent war. Never," said the American Union Against Militarism, "we believe, in the history of the world has any message of a single individual found its way into so many minds and hearts."[88]

In the Senate, Democrats and progressive Republicans expressed themselves in extravagant language. La Follette led the chamber in applause, saying: "We have just passed through a very important hour in the life of the world." Benjamin Tillman (D-S.C.) called it "the most startling and the noblest utterance that has fallen from human lips since the Declaration of Independence." Key Pittman put it on a par with "the enunciation of Monroe."[89]

Even Wilson's bid for an international organization received some warm endorsement. Senator Charles S. Thomas found Wilson's proposal "in entire accord" with the American tradition. Taft, who was president of the League to Enforce Peace, said that his entire constituency could "rejoice sincerely" in the president's statements. Congressman Frederick Gillett (R-Mass.), who became the House Speaker in 1919, declared himself "in thorough accord" with the president's position. To *New Republic* editor Herbert Croly, a peace league offered "a legal and institutional expression" for those appalled by the horrors of war.[90]

Several endorsements came from longtime critics of the president. Viereck predicted that Wilson's words would "transform the fabric of human thought." Irish partisan Jeremiah O'Leary cabled Wilson: "The document is the greatest American paper since Lincoln's Emancipation Proclamation." The *New York American* claimed that "the President's address will powerfully stimulate the masses of Europe and turn their thoughts toward peace." Bryan saluted Wilson's "wonderfully eloquent appeal," although he opposed putting American armed forces under European command.[91]

Wilson met strong criticism as well, particularly among Senate Republicans. Some thought the chief executive had acted far too presumptuously. Francis Warren, formerly father-in-law to the widower John J. Pershing, remarked: "The President thinks he is president of the world." Reed Smoot denied that the United States had any right to insist that England relinquish its right to the seas, direct Turkey as to who shall pass through the Dardanelles, or inform Germany that it must surrender Poland. Progressive Republican Albert Cummins introduced a resolution calling for congressional consultation before the president made further commitments to any world organization.[92]

Major objections centered on the president's call for peace without victory. The *New York Herald* declared that Wilson favored a settlement bearing the hallmark, "Made in Berlin." Roosevelt called the Tories of 1776 and the Copperheads of 1864 the true spiritual forebears of the president. The American Rights Committee argued that the defeat of Prussian militarism was essential to lasting tranquility. A compromise agreement, warned Elihu Root, involved "the absolute destruction and abandonment of the principle upon which this war was begun." Former senator Chauncey Depew (R-N.Y.) asserted that he very much sought "peace *with* victory," while former solicitor general James M. Beck accused Wilson of serving as the "unconscious catspaw of that nation which brought this stupendous horror on the world." Conversely, the *Irish World* accused the president of seeking to preserve the British Empire.[93]

Certainly, Senate critics argued, Wilson was most naive. Jacob Gallinger deemed the president's vision "utterly impossible of accomplishment." Lawrence Sherman said that the address would "make Don Quixote wish he had not died so soon." "Man is a fighting animal," remarked Thomas; racial hatred, commercial strife, and increased armament would continue to engender wars. Historian Charles Austin Beard, noting Wilson's remarks concerning "consent of the governed," perceived that the speech embodied "a broad, general principle, that arouses nothing but confusion when you begin to apply it in detail." How, he asked, did Wilson's concept apply to Ireland, Alsace-Lorraine, Bohemia, Croatia, and other Balkan nationalities, not to mention the peoples of American-dominated Haiti and Santo Domingo?[94]

Another objection dealt with American participation in a world association, a proposition that drew criticism across the political spectrum. Here the conservative Republican senator James Watson of Indiana concurred with Socialist leader Allan Benson. Remarked Congressman Gardner, using Rooseveltian rhetoric: "I want no conglomerate flag of all nations, with a yellow streak down the middle." Such a league, commented Senator Miles Poindexter (R-Wash.), would render the United States helpless. Senator Cummins feared that the country would involve itself in continual wars. Senator James A. Reed (D-Mo.) worried that a league would field an international army large enough to conquer the United States, particularly if Europe's monarchies chose its leadership.[95]

On January 25 Borah introduced a resolution that reaffirmed the Monroe Doctrine and the noninterventionist policies of Washington and Jefferson. "Once in the maelstrom of European politics," he warned, "it will be impossible to get out." If the United States did not agree in advance to accept league decisions concerning immigration, citizenship, or territorial propinquity, the very international force it helped create would attack the American nation.[96]

When Lodge delivered a major policy speech on February 1, he fully backed Borah, taking issue with all of Wilson's principal ideas. The Massachusetts senator asked how the United States could successfully negotiate a peace. Given the "awful sacrifices" made by the belligerents, no nation would be content "with everything left just as it was." Besides, there was nothing wrong with an imposed settlement; witness the forty years of tranquility following the Battle of Waterloo. Lasting accord "rests on justice and righteousness," which in turn might necessitate "victories in the field." He wondered whether popular government could arise in such areas as Korea, "Hindustan" (northern India), Armenia, Alsace-Lorraine, Trentino, the duchies of Denmark, and Austria's Slavic provinces.

Lodge scorned other Wilsonian propositions. "Freedom of the seas" might involve violation of long-honored rights to blockade enemy ports or seize contraband shipped by neutrals. Such access could involve America in "very difficult questions," for example, securing a right of way for Russia to Constantinople and for Germany to the Persian Gulf, not to mention privileges for such landlocked states as Bolivia, Paraguay, and Afghanistan. Monroe's manifesto, he maintained, was based on the assumption that the world was divided into two spheres "entirely separate in their political interests"; to universalize this policy meant abandoning it. "If we are to have a Monroe Doctrine everywhere we may be perfectly certain that it will not exist anywhere." Commenting on Wilson's league proposal, Lodge feared that international councils, in which the United States possessed only one vote, might be able to commit some five hundred thousand American troops to fight anywhere they chose.[97] Despite Lodge's effort to launch a major debate over Wilson's entire agenda, the Senate tabled Borah's resolution on January 30.

Much Republican dissent was principled, but partisanship played a role. The GOP wished to differentiate itself from Wilson's administration, a circumstance that led it in an isolationist direction. Similarly, the Democrats were unlikely to differ from their first president to win consecutive terms since Andrew Jackson.

There were definite issues at stake, however. As William Henry Harbaugh notes, many eastern Republicans favored intervention in Europe for nationalistic reasons, not altruistic ones. Any suggestion of peace without victory would challenge their conception of the national interest. Hence the bitterness of their assault on the president's January 22 address. The interjection of Wilson's league of nations simply strengthened their arguments. Their conception of international organization, such as it was, differed entirely from the president's, as it was based far more on balance-of-power politics.[98]

On March 7, in conversation with the French ambassador, Wilson expanded slightly on his postwar vision. Any international league, he told Jules Jusserand, must evolve slowly. One begins by submitting controversies to a conference of nations not directly involved in a clash. The president denied any desire to break up the Austro-Hungarian Empire. He deemed broad autonomy sufficient for subject peoples.[99]

Sir William Wiseman, a representative of British intelligence stationed in the United States, told House on January 26 that he "seemed now to think" his nation would entertain peace negotiations if Germany returned a favorable reply to Wilson's call for moderate terms.[100] As Whitehall's intelligence knew that Germany would launch unrestricted U-boat warfare within days, Wiseman's overture might have been an expedient way of gaining favor. Given the developing crisis and the rigidity of both parties, little chance existed of holding any such conference. Besides, Wiseman's message was at best impressionistic; he had really committed himself to nothing.

In the meantime, Wilson needed to ascertain what Berlin really wanted. The president wrote House on January 24, two days after addressing the Senate: "If Germany really wants peace she can get it, and get it soon, *if she will but confide in me and let me have a chance.*" He asked the colonel to tell Bernstorff that "this is the time to accomplish something, if they really and truly want peace; that the indications that have come to us are of a sort to lead us to believe that with something reasonable to suggest, as from them, I can bring things about. . . . Do they in fact want me to help? I am entitled to know because I genuinely want to help and have now put myself in a position to help without favour to either side."[101]

Within two days, Bernstorff warned House that all-out submarine warfare would begin with the start of the spring offensives. A day later he cabled Berlin, begging his government to delay any sweeping U-boat activities until Wilson could initiate negotiations. Predicting that the move would make war unavoidable, he wrote: "We can get a better peace by means of confer-ences than if the United States should join our enemies." Speaking on behalf of the Foreign Office, Undersecretary Wilhelm August von Stumm replied in one sentence: "Regret postponement impracticable."[102]

On January 28 Lansing drafted a memorandum, "Certainty of War with Germany." He wrote: "We must nevertheless wait patiently until the Germans do something which will arouse general indignation and make all Americans alive to the peril of German success in this war." He hoped that the Germans would blunder soon, because "the Allies in the West are having a hard time and Russia is not succeeding in spite of her man power."[103]

Lansing's wishes were soon fulfilled. Germany's public announcement of unrestricted submarine warfare marked the beginning of the end of peace with the United States.

9

The Break with Germany
January–March 1917

On January 31, Ambassador Bernstorff presented Lansing with Germany's response to Wilson's recent "peace without victory" plea. The ambassador endorsed Wilson's call for an economic open door, freedom of the seas, and equal rights for all nations. He backed the president's plea for self-government of subject peoples, though he pointedly referred to British domination of Ireland and India. He denied that Germany sought to annex Belgium; Germany simply wanted to assure itself that enemies could not use the neighboring state as a base for instigating hostile intrigues. He accused the Allies of engaging in a "lust for conquest," seeking to dismember Germany, Austria-Hungary, Turkey, and Bulgaria. Britain in particular insisted on continuing its "war of starvation" against women and children, the sick and the aged.

But the ambassador conveyed a far more important message as well: his nation was about to launch an unrestricted submarine campaign, thereby declaring total maritime war against all neutrals. After February 1, the communiqué noted, German U-boats would sink without warning belligerent and neutral ships found in a designated zone comprising waters around Great Britain, France, and Italy, and in the eastern Mediterranean. The Admiralty made one minor exception: it would permit one American steamer a week to sail between New York and Falmouth provided it carried no contraband, was painted with red and white stripes, and sported a special red and white checkered flag. Initially Germany would grant a period of grace, during which its submarines would not harm neutral ships that either were en route to the war zone or had already arrived.[1]

Much of the American press reacted with rage. The *Brooklyn Eagle* mourned, "The freedom of the seas will now be enjoyed by icebergs and fish." "A Malay pirate could not have made the announcement more bru-tally," remarked the *New York Evening Post*. The *Nation* accused Germany of madness. The *Outlook* called Germany's note "a declaration of war against the whole world." Senator Sherman noted that even Attila the Hun spared civilians. The *New Republic* sought immediate diplomatic, economic, and military conferences between the Allies and neutral powers. The United States, it continued, should help the Entente police the oceans, send Ameri-can volunteers to Europe, and train a large army on U.S. soil. Roosevelt asked the War Department for permission to raise an infantry division.[2]

Several voices dissented. Hearst's *New York American* remarked: "No sensible American expected that a high-spirited and powerful people, such as the Germans are, would continue to submit to seeing their women and chil-dren starved by sea warfare without eventually striking back at their enemies by sea." It nevertheless endorsed Wilson's peacemaking efforts: "Whither he leads, there we will follow him." Forming a league of neutral nations, a favorite Hearst scheme, could end the world war in ninety days; the body should simply refuse to trade with any belligerent that continued aggressive behavior or declined to negotiate.[3]

The *American*'s Berlin correspondent, William Bayard Hale, who had directed the German Information Service, denied that Germany would either jeopardize the lives of traveling Americans or engage in indiscrimi-nate submarine warfare. Viereck accused Britain, not Germany, of engaging in the real "reign of terror," for it converted merchantmen into auxiliary cruisers and mined the entire North Sea. Other German American journals pointed to the British "hunger blockade" and the Allies' rejection of recent peace offers. Senator Wesley L. Jones advised every "real American" to "say nothing and stay at home."[4]

Those with pacifist leanings expressed particular concern. Speaking to five thousand people in New York's Madison Square Garden, Bryan told supporters of the American Neutral Conference Committee that the United States should seek arbitration, resorting to war solely in case of invasion. The American Union Against Militarism opposed any breach with Germany. An emergency committee of the Socialist Party sought to embargo shipments bound for any belligerent nation. Such prominent reformers as philanthro-pist George Foster Peabody and settlement worker Lillian Wald petitioned Wilson, asking him to offer personal mediation.[5]

Had Germany limited its U-boat attacks to armed ships or merchantmen belonging to the belligerent powers, argues Arthur S. Link, Wilson would have acquiesced in Germany's decision, thereby accepting a modification of the *Sussex* pledge. Under certain circumstances, U-boat commanders could have even sunk American craft. By declaring war on peaceful neutral shipping, however, Berlin engaged in a "campaign of terror." The United States was forced "to choose between some form of counteraction and a major surrender of national rights," with the accompanying "diminution of national prestige" and "deterioration of the national fiber."[6]

Upon receiving the news of Germany's decision, Lansing pressed Wilson to break diplomatic relations immediately, asserting that continuing discussions would fatally jeopardize the nation's prestige. The president, according to Lansing, countered by voicing fear that "white civilization" and "its domination over the world rested largely on our ability to keep this country intact, as we would have to build up the nations ravaged by the war."[7]

On the morning of February 1, Wilson told House that Germany was "a madman that should be curbed," though he called it "a crime" to enter the conflict. In the afternoon, when Wilson, House, and Lansing all conferred, the secretary argued that Prussian militarism threatened the world's democratic institutions, at which point the president warned of unspecified dangers that would follow the destruction of the German state.[8]

At two thirty that afternoon Wilson met with his cabinet. According to Interior Secretary Franklin K. Lane: "The President said he didn't wish to see either side win,—for both were equally indifferent to the rights of neutrals—though Germany had been brutal in taking life, and England only in taking property. He would like to see the neutrals unite." According to another cabinet member, Agriculture Secretary David F. Houston, Wilson maintained that if "in order to keep the white race or any part of it strong to meet the yellow race—Japan, for instance, in alliance with Russia, dominating China—it was wise to do nothing, he would do nothing, and would submit to anything and any imputation of weakness or cowardice." Houston did not fear such powers, finding them "relatively weak intellectually, industrially, and morally." He desired to arm merchant vessels and, "if necessary," aiding the Allies with America's armed forces. Treasury Secretary McAdoo spoke vaguely of "prompt action" but other cabinet members—among them Baker and Daniels—supported Wilson's caution.[9]

When, later in the afternoon, Wilson consulted with sixteen Democratic senators, William J. Stone and J. Hamilton Lewis denied that Germany would sink American craft without warning. The others, however, favored severing diplomatic relations. It was this meeting, Link claims, that served as the catalyst in convincing Wilson to break with the Reich.[10]

At two in the afternoon on February 3, Wilson addressed a joint session of Congress. He announced that Germany's decision forced him to sever diplomatic relations with the German Empire. He could not believe that the Reich's submarines would sink an *American* ship, much less take *American* lives. "Only overt acts on their part can make me believe it even now." If Berlin undertook a "heedless contravention of the just and reasonable understandings of international law and the obvious dictates of humanity," he would ask Congress for authority to protect "our seamen and our people in the prosecution of their peaceful and legitimate errands on the high seas." Because Germany had violated the *Sussex* pledge, there lay "no alternative consistent with its dignity and honour."[11]

A careful examination of the address indicates that Wilson tacitly accepted a far more comprehensive U-boat campaign than he had in the past. He allowed Germany to attack belligerent merchantmen on which Americans served as crew. The president limited his demands to the safety of American shipping and presumably American lives on belligerent passenger ships.

Many Republicans stood behind the chief executive. Representative Gardner stressed that he "wouldn't change a word of the President's address." Senator Harding remarked that for the first time he could conscientiously applaud a Wilson speech. Taft discovered "an exhibition of patriotism" unmatched since the Civil War. Democrats were almost unanimously supportive, Senator Tillman remarking that Bernstorff should "pack his duds and go home to his barbarians." Both Kitchin and the Republican Mann did not see how the president could have acted differently. James K. Vardaman struck a dissenting note, denying that the president's course was "wise, prudent or justified by the facts."[12]

Most American newspapers backed the president. So did the religious press. Even former critics endorsed the speech. The pro-Entente *North American Review* called upon the United States to start raising an army of a million men in preparation for entering the war. "Now, thank Heaven," it said, "we have ceased to be neutral." The *Outlook* supported Wilson, though it lacked the president's confidence that Germany would not prey upon neutral shipping.[13] Because a period of uncertainty had ended, the stock market rose.

Much of the German American press defended the president while hoping for peace. The *New Yorker Staats-Zeitung* declared that Wilson spoke for the entire country, adding: "There can be only one loyalty—to the United States of America." The *Fatherland,* which had just changed its name to the *New World,* doubted whether Wilson could have softened his recent "forceful expression." The United States could still avoid war if it embargoed food and arms and warned its citizens to keep off belligerent ships. The German-owned *New York Evening Mail* reminded readers that "there are worse things than war." The National German-American Alliance endorsed the break with Berlin, promising to supply special regiments if America entered the conflict, but sought a national referendum before any war was declared. Several Teutonic journals accused Wilson of being one-sided, the *Cincinnati Volksblatt* charging the president with failing to punish Britain's far greater offenses.[14]

Socialists still opposed any confrontation. The party's executive committee denied that German submarine warfare threatened either America's integrity or its dignity; U-boat warfare simply struck at "those parasitic classes that have been making huge profits by manufacturing instruments of death or by taking away our food and selling it at exorbitant prices to the fighting armies of Europe." American citizens and ships should enter the war zone only at their own risk.[15]

A host of pacifist groups pushed the slogan "No War Without a Referendum." Cooperating organizations included the AUAM, the Church Peace Union, the Woman's Peace Party, the American Peace Society, and the American Neutral Conference Committee, the latter soon renamed the Emergency Peace Federation (EPF) and headed by Louis Lochner. (The organizations neither explained how such polling could be conducted quickly and impartially nor how one could finance a canvass of an entire electorate. To lend any official stamp to such a measure, congressional action would be needed.)

The EPF suggested a German-American joint high commission similar to one created during the recent Mexican crisis. Hearst concurred, saying that those who would have to fight should decide the matter. Bryan insisted upon keeping American ships out of the war zone, even if the nation had temporarily waived its rights, and postponing ultimate settlements until the conflict ended. Jane Addams asked Wilson to meet with other neutral nations in order to create "a league of nations standing for international rights."[16]

A small group of reformers—among them attorney Amos Pinchot, *Masses* editor Max Eastman, and *New Republic* staffer Randolph Bourne—recommended "every expedient of diplomacy and economic pressure" to foster a peace conference. They named themselves the Committee for Democratic Control. Chaired by Pinchot, the committee urged the nation's leadership to emulate George Washington and John Adams, both of whom had kept the United States out of war with France in the 1790s.[17]

Four days after Wilson's speech, the Senate voted 78 to 5 to adopt a resolution backing the president. (On February 8 Harry Lane [D-Ore.] said he would have voted against the resolution had he been present.) Stone introduced the statement, maintaining that the chief executive "had expressed a desire to avoid conflict" and had promised to submit matters for further action to Congress. Lodge, usually a sharp critic of Wilson, helped push through the measure, saying: "The President did what was demanded by the honor, the safety, and the future security of the United States." In endorsing the resolution, Borah stressed the need for independent action, declaring: "I want no alliances. I want no leagues." Stone's biographer, Ruth Warner Towne, notes that "the militant element thought of the break with Germany as a long step toward war, while the pacifists viewed it as a substitute for belligerency. Thus each side could support a resolution simply endorsing the rupture."[18]

Dissenters included La Follette, Works, Vardaman, Lane, William F. Kirby (D-Ark.), and Asle J. Gronna (R-N.D.). Three were Bryan Democrats, three progressive Republicans. La Follette and Gronna represented states with large German American constituencies. Vardaman warned against being "drawn into this vortex of blood and plunder to satisfy the greed and cupidity of those who would coin the blood of the murdered soldier and the tears of the brokenhearted woman into dollars." Works deemed the loss of a "a few thousand dollars to a very few people" as nothing compared with "the sacrifice of thousands of lives by going to war to protect this trade on the high seas." La Follette accused preparedness advocates of deliberately distracting the public from such pressing concerns as skyrocketing food prices. "Taking advantage of a people stunned by a world catastrophe and flaunting a government laboring under the strain of international affairs, the financial barons and food kings opened wide the flood gates of exploitation."[19]

On the following day, Representative Oscar Callaway, an agrarian radical close to Bryan, introduced a resolution in the House calling for a popular referendum on entering the conflict. Representatives Warren Worth Bailey and Isaac Sherwood and labor spokesman Frank Buchanan (D-Ill.) took similar steps. Sherwood accused "the J.P. Morgan interests," as well as steel, shipbuilding, and powder groups, of purchasing control of twenty-five of the nation's greatest newspapers so as to frighten the nation. In the Senate, Stone made similar charges, saying that "a cabal of great newspapers" deliberately circulated false news to increase war sentiment. Publisher William Randolph Hearst personally denied such charges, though his *New York American* asserted that Britain had spent over $76 million to propagandize neutral nations.[20]

Several war opponents proposed extreme measures. James Maurer, a Socialist member of the Pennsylvania legislature and president of its state federation of labor, endorsed a national general strike to handicap defense preparations. Publisher Oswald Garrison Villard said he would not even fight to resist an invasion.[21]

The Wilson administration faced pressures from interventionists as well. On February 17 the American Rights Committee sought entry into the conflict. Lodge privately wrote Theodore Roosevelt that Wilson sought "to avoid war at any cost," for "he flinches in the presence of danger, physical and moral." TR replied that the president was "yellow all through," a man who would "accept any insult or danger from a fighting man." La Follette he deemed "considerably inferior, in morality and capacity, to Robespierre."[22] Just a small minority, though, held this attitude. Even in mid-February there was no popular desire for war.

On February 3, the day that Wilson severed relations with Germany, his administration, as was its legal right, seized certain German vessels. Among them were two auxiliary cruisers, the *Kronprinz Wilhelm* and the *Prinz Eitel Friedrich,* in Philadelphia; the liner *Appam* in Newport News; the liner *Kronprinzessin Cecilie* in Boston; and four ships in Cristobal harbor, Panama. In New Orleans naval guards were placed on two German and three Austrian steamers. Two days later, Wilson announced that other German property continued to enjoy the full protection of American law.

Immediately Germany began to sink American and British merchantmen and passenger vessels. On February 3 *U-53,* the very submarine that had been so active off Nantucket the past October, torpedoed the U.S. steamer *Housatonic.* Named after the prominent river in Connecticut and until 1915 a German freighter, it was operated by a one-ship firm. It was attacked twenty-five miles off Britain's Land's End while carrying grain from Galveston to London. The German submarine gave advance warning, Captain Rose saying in perfect English: "You are carrying foodstuffs to an enemy of my country, and though I am sorry, it is my duty to sink you." He rescued all crew members, dropping them off at the Cornish coast. Both the

State Department and the American press reacted cautiously, believing that Germany had not yet committed an "overt act" of war.

On the following day, a U-boat struck the British merchantman *Turino* without warning eighty miles southwest of Fastnet, Ireland. It was bound from New York to Liverpool. The lone American sailor on board was saved, although several others were not. On February 5 Ambassador Page reported the death of an American crew member when lifeboats of the *Eavestone,* an escaping British merchantman en route from Galveston to Liverpool, were shelled one hundred miles from the British coast. Two days later, the armed British passenger liner *California,* sailing to Glasgow from New York, was torpedoed off Fastnet. The one American aboard remained alive, although forty-one people went to the bottom.

On February 12 the German *U-35* sank the American schooner *Lyman M. Law* off the coast of Sardinia. Owned by a Bangor shipping firm, the *Law* was carrying box shooks (thin strips of lumber used to construct lemon crates) from Stockton Springs, Maine, to Palermo, Italy. Germany considered such cargo contraband. The submarine had warned the ship and given the ten-man crew provisions. After twenty-five hours the lifeboat arrived safely at the port of Cagliari. Thus far, in dealing with American ships, Germany was obeying traditional cruiser rules.

Wilson did not protest these incidents, indicating his desperate desire to avoid intervention. His failure to act when torpedoes sank belligerent merchantmen proved that he was prepared to abandon stipulations specified in the *Sussex* pledge. His failure to complain about the *California* revealed that he would ignore Germany's violation of its *Arabic* commitment concerning passenger ships. Wilson privately noted that the British armed several of the besieged craft, possibly for offensive purposes; others, by seeking to escape, almost invited attack. "Such argument was so strained and concerned with technical detail," writes historian Ross Gregory, "that it suggests the president was seeking to rationalize his inaction. While he made no public effort to describe what events would provoke him to war, some perceptive observers concluded that he would act on nothing less than a deliberate assault on an American ship."[23]

Between February 1 and 21, the Central Powers had sunk 128 ships bearing 252,621 tons. Of these, 40 belonged to neutral nations and 80 to the British. Other belligerents owned 8. Ships of the American Line suffered damages of $1 million per week. In March the toll increased to 564,497 tons per month, in April to 860,334.

At first the Wilson administration did not allow warships to escort merchantmen through the war zone. Foreign trade became virtually paralyzed because owners refused to venture onto the seas. As vessels lay in port, rail lines and storage facilities became clogged, damaging the sales of American products. Standard Oil radioed its steamers to return home. The International Merchant Marine Company postponed sailings indefinitely. For three weeks after the German announcement, only five American freighters went to sea. Spring Rice reported to Foreign Secretary Arthur Balfour "a stoppage of trade, a congestion in the ports, widespread discomfort and even misery on the coast and inland, even bread riots and a coal famine." The *New Republic* claimed that American merchant shipping was being terrorized: "The war against neutrals is as drastic as the war against the belligerents." Stressing the need to punish Germany, the journal hoped the United States would enter the conflict before the British Navy could achieve victory. "The Americans are just bluffing," Ludendorff told a young officer. "They have no intention of declaring war against us."[24]

Responding to the U-boat sinkings, historian Carlton J.H. Hayes of Columbia University proposed a means for waging at best limited war. In an article published in the February 10 issue of the *Survey*, the scholar asked the neutral maritime nations to form an armed league to protect their legitimate commerce. In 1780 Russia, Denmark, Sweden, Austria, and Portugal had combined to safeguard their neutral rights against England, France, and Spain. The powers convoyed merchant ships and submitted united protests until one set of belligerents conceded the disputed principles and the other moderated its practices. At the outset, Hayes's new league would concentrate on opposing unlawful submarine attacks; subsequently it might ameliorate abuses of blockade, visit and search, and contraband lists. Naval convoys would provide enforcement, as in 1780.[25]

The AUAM, the Woman's Peace Party, and the Committee for Democratic Control backed the proposal. Pacifist publisher Oswald Garrison Villard declared that Hayes's plan could keep America out of war while preserving its moral prestige. Congressman Irvine L. Lenroot (R-Wis.) endorsed Hayes's reasoning, declaring that Congress would support the use of force to maintain "our liberties upon the sea" but oppose efforts to "send our men to the trenches of Europe."[26]

On the surface the scheme seemed attractive. American ships would possess guns to resist U-boat attack. The United States could uphold traditional principles against an illegal and immoral method of warfare. At the same time, it would escape military involvement on the Continent and ensnarement in power rivalries.

The Navy Department soon reported difficulties. Resistance to a U-boat attack invited a torpedo. So did treating German submarines as hostile ships. American captains might err in sinking such craft, giving Berlin an excuse to wage war against the United States. Few nations would seek membership in Hayes's league; Wilson had snubbed the neutral Scandinavian powers far too often to gain their cooperation. Sweden quickly recalled that the United States would not join the Scandinavian countries to assert collective rights. The proposal caught Wilson's attention, but it did not gain his support. Patrick Devlin writes: "Armed neutrality is no better adapted to keeping the peace than unarmed belligerency would be to winning a war."[27]

On February 13 the question of protecting American merchantmen arose in the cabinet. Houston and McAdoo wanted to place naval guns and crews on such ships. Wilson responded that such action was precipitous, risking outright war. The move would force the hand of Congress, whose authority he still deemed necessary. The navy had told him additional convoys would simply increase the target. He worried about fifty-five American seamen who crewed for three armed British merchantmen after a German surface raider sank the vessels. The men were transported to Germany aboard the prize ship *Yarrowdale* and were held hostage against possible U.S. seizure of German ships and internment of their crews. On March 12, after one of the Americans contracted typhus, the Germans released the sailors.

The president remained cautious. On February 19 Wilson told the philosopher Henri Bergson, who sent reports on American policy to France's foreign ministry, that his countrymen remained divided over such matters. Many in the American West, he maintained, favored peace at any price. He accused England of fighting solely for commercial supremacy, an aspiration for which he lacked sympathy. Conversely, he thought that the German people were tired of Prussian militarism and possibly the Imperial regime. When the cabinet met a day later, the president remained silent about the arming of merchant ships, although immediately after the meeting he asked Lansing to prepare a memorandum justifying such a move. The following day, the secretary supplied data justifying the right of merchantmen to arm for defense.[28]

When the cabinet gathered again on February 23, Agriculture Secretary Houston warned that a German victory would make it "mistress of the world," adding: "We would be next on her list." Wilson accused the more belligerent members, including Houston, Lane, and McAdoo, of seeking to adopt the "dueler's code." The United States, he continued, would not run the risk of war. Responding to the president's inquiry, Daniels assured him that the navy possessed sufficient guns and gunners to protect American merchant ships. The cabinet endorsed the move. Yet Wilson sounded so conciliatory toward Germany that after the meeting Houston considered resignation.[29]

On February 16 Britain had issued a retaliatory order. Ships entering or leaving the port of a neutral power close to enemy territory must first call at an Allied port. Otherwise they would be deemed as "carrying goods with an enemy destination or of enemy origin." Devlin finds this stance a "novel provision in international law, which said in effect that anyone who failed to call at a police station should be presumed guilty." Even French ambassador Jusserand strongly protested the British action, declaring that it violated the 1856 Declaration of Paris, an international agreement that had granted immunity to neutral vessels carrying noncontraband property. The move, he believed, could inflame American sentiment, although the United States made no objection. In addition, the United States granted clearance to Allied merchantmen without questioning the weight of their armament or its use.[30]

As far as preparedness was concerned, Wilson sought to avoid alarm. In late January the Maryland League for National Defense urged the president to adopt universal military training, pointing to the "actual present danger" of embroilment in the European war. Wilson replied that the group had not proven its case: "These things are of utmost intricacy and are not to be settled ex cathedra." On February 16 he told his cabinet that he opposed "any great preparedness." When the war ended, he declared, the belligerents would lack men and money and would therefore pose no threat. He ordered Newton Baker to do nothing that suggested incipient mobilization. Concretely, the secretary of war should not order any unusual troop movements. At the same time, the president opposed peace demonstrations, writing a Federal Reserve governor that they falsely conveyed the impression of "divided counsels among us."[31]

In mid-February S. Hubert Dent, the new chairman of the House Military Affairs Committee, reported that this body had unanimously decided that "this was not an opportune time for any radical changes in the military policy of this country." The House's army appropriation bill of 1917 provided for a regular force of just 135,000 men, causing Pennsylvania congressman

Thomas S. Crago (R) to call it "a great peace measure."[32] Bryan Democrats still controlled the lower chamber.

Nevertheless, in certain quarters, panic prevailed. When the Defense Advisory Council met, the War College Division feared that a foreign invasion, obviously German, might compel American troops to evacuate ports on the North Atlantic and retreat to the Appalachians. A few prominent naval officials went public. "In case an attacking force is sent against us," warned Admiral Bradley Fiske, "we shall have only three weeks to get ready to fight." Rear Admiral Robert E. Peary, Arctic explorer, cautioned that foreign aircraft might descend upon the United States within thirty days, destroying such cities as Washington in a single night.[33] Construction began on gun emplacements at Rockaway Beach off New York City.

Wilson's policy did not satisfy more militant Americans. Late in January the National Security League held the Congress for Constructive Patriotism in Washington. Prodded by Roosevelt and Root, the organization endorsed universal military training. John D. Rockefeller Jr. told his Sunday school class at New York's Fifth Avenue Baptist Church that "compulsory military service is the one thing that will do away with class spirit in this democratic country, and for that reason alone I feel it would be justified."[34] Senator Chamberlain introduced a bill that required six months of training for all males between the ages nineteen and twenty-six, but the measure never reached a vote.

Flaws existed in such proposals. John Patrick Finnegan finds such sweeping measures impractical; they were inefficient and costly. For mechanized warfare, the country needed trained specialists, not a massive number of recruits. Late in January Major General Tasker H. Bliss, soon to become acting chief of staff, demanded: "We should not waste time, energy or money in the training of people who are not to be immediately called into active service in the field." Toward the end of March, Baker wrote Wilson, referring to a "selective draft," not a universal one.[35] The drive for all-encompassing preparation did have some effect, because it conditioned the public to accept conscription once the nation entered the war.

On February 13 the House passed the largest naval bill in American history, which provided for forty-two ships and an appropriation of $368 million; the vote was 353 to 23. Among the bill's opponents were Democratic congressmen Oscar Callaway of Texas and George Huddleston and William B. Oliver, both of Alabama. The three representatives sought just one battleship, not three, while wanting to increase the number of submarines and destroyers. Minority leader Mann added an amendment endorsing international arbitration, a measure that passed by voice vote. On March 3, after a conference committee met, the appropriation was reduced to $335 million. The revised bill provided for three battleships, one battle cruiser, fifteen destroyers, and twenty submarines.[36] Because of a filibuster in March, the Senate passed neither an army nor a navy bill until the United States entered the war.

For a brief time Wilson hoped that Austria-Hungary might broker an agreement. On February 5 Count Ottaker Czernin, the new foreign minister, cabled Lansing to accuse the Allies of seeking to dismember the Hapsburg Empire. Nonetheless, he claimed that the empire was ready to negotiate on the basis of peace without victory. Were the president to press his agenda on the Entente, "not only the terror of submarine war, but war in general would come to a sudden end." The message marked the first positive response to the president's appeal for a negotiated peace. The American ambassador, Frederic C. Penfield, personally supplemented the note, adding: "Economic life of Austria-Hungary seems paralyzed. . . . People [of] all classes praying for peace."[37] At that moment Prince Sixtus of Bourbon, a Belgian officer and brother-in-law of Emperor Charles, was secretly negotiating with Allied leaders.

Acting on Wilson's direct orders, Lansing immediately cabled Ambassador Page, claiming that he sought to keep "channels" open to the Central Powers. If Britain's leaders could assure Austria that they did not seek its dismemberment, they might advance a settlement. A concert of nations could guarantee the Hapsburg Empire continued access to the Adriatic coast "without depriving the several Balkan states of their political autonomy and territorial integrity."[38]

Lloyd George, using Page as his intermediary, informed Wilson that he was aware of Austria's initiative and that Vienna "had never wanted war." The Hapsburg state, he observed, was "an increasing military and economic burden to Germany," who commanded the Austro-Hungarian armies. While Britain harbored no objection to Austria's retaining Hungary and Bohemia, "the principle of nationality" must apply to such allies as "the Roumanians, the Slavs, the Serbians, and the Italians" as well as to Bosnia and Herzegovina. He hoped that the United States would enter the war, not so much because of its military or economic aid but for its potential influence during the ensuing peace. Wilson must personally attend the postwar conference because his nation alone desired "nothing but justice and an ordered freedom and guarantees of these for the future."[39]

Bernstorff, who did not leave Washington until February 14, sought to reopen American-German negotiations. Using the Swiss minister to Washington as his conduit, he cabled his foreign office that the "huge majority" of Americans merely wanted peace, still a possibility if U-boats refrained from sinking ships that did not carry contraband. He hoped that, during the following month, the principals could negotiate the submarine issue, then convene a "conference of powers." He alluded to a congressional resolution of Congressman Walter L. Hensley, which suggested just such a meeting.[40]

Germany's leaders proved singularly uncooperative concerning Czernin's and Bernstorff's overtures. In a note to Vienna, Foreign Secretary Zimmermann accused Wilson of serving as "an adherent of the Entente at all costs"; the president would "exert all his influence against us." He similarly rebuffed Bernstorff, claiming that not even the resumption of diplomatic relations would cause his government to reconsider its submarine policy. "Under no circumstances" would Germany restrict U-boat warfare. When Zimmermann's stance became public, Lansing maintained that Berlin's policies precluded any parley. Although Colonel House and Ambassador Gerard considered Zimmermann a most approachable diplomat, his predecessor Jagow correctly labeled him a "fanatical U-boat warrior" who would "swim with the stream and with those who shouted loudest."[41]

Tensions drastically increased on February 25 when Wilson learned that Germany sought to entice Mexico into war against the United States. On January 19 Zimmermann had sent Heinrich von Eckhardt, his nation's minister to Mexico, a communiqué marked "absolutely confidential." The foreign secretary instructed Eckhardt to inform Mexico's "First Chief," Venustiano Carranza, that on February 1 Germany would begin unrestrained U-boat warfare. Should the United States enter the war against the Reich, he proposed a military alliance: "Joint conduct of the war. Joint conclusion of peace. Ample financial support and an agreement on our part that Mexico shall gain back by conquest the territory lost by her at a prior period in Texas, New Mexico, and Arizona." The foreign secretary added that Germany would attempt to persuade Japan, hitherto one of the Allies, to become an associate of the Central Powers.[42]

Britain intercepted the German wireless but did not inform the United States until it obtained an additional copy from Mexico, for it needed to disguise its ability to read Berlin's wires. Zimmermann's scheme originated with a Latin American expert in the German Foreign Office. In early November 1916, Carranza had offered submarine bases to the Germans. Although Germany declined the offer, the expert pushed the matter, finally winning over the foreign secretary.

Berlin's proposal was absolutely ludicrous. Germany faced financial crisis and could hardly afford "ample financial support" to Mexico. A power lacking shipping facilities and under blockade was obviously unable to supply such a distant nation. The Kaiser's forces were too deeply engaged in Europe to aid a Mexican invasion of the United States. Without such assistance, Mexico could not regain the American Southwest.

Knowledge of the plot caused Wilson, as yet not converted to war, to lose all faith in the German government. Berlin had encouraged a Mexican attack while still formally at peace with the United States. If Zimmermann's gambit was absurd, it led the president to believe that Germany ruthlessly sought to dominate the world. On February 28, upon meeting with leaders of the Emergency Peace Federation, Wilson snapped at Professor William Isaac Hull of Swarthmore College, who pressed the cause of conciliation: "Dr. Hull, if you knew what I know at this present moment, . . . you would not ask me to attempt further peaceful dealings with the Germans." House informed Wilson that he was not surprised to hear of the Reich's proposal: "I have been satisfied for some time that they have laid plans to stir up all the trouble they could, in order to occupy our attention in case of hostilities."[43]

Germany had long been involved in Mexico. When, in February 1911, Victoriano Huerta seized power, deposing the democratically elected Francisco Madero, Berlin supplied the new despot with arms. In April 1915, the ousted Huerta landed in New York and met with such German agents as Rintelen, Papen, and Boy-Ed. According to Reinhard R. Doerries, this activity could not have taken place without Bernstorff's knowledge.[44] The pro-German tone of the Mexican press, Carranza's bid to prohibit arms and foodstuffs to European belligerents, and negotiations with Germany over loans, a wireless station, and a U-boat base—none of these matters endeared Mexico to its northern neighbor.

On February 26, the day after Wilson learned of Zimmermann's communication, he addressed a joint session of Congress. After noting that the *Housatonic* and the *Lyman M. Law* were warned before they were torpedoed, he conceded: "The overt act which I have ventured to hope the Germans would in fact avoid has not occurred." Nonetheless, U.S. commerce was suffering because so many ships were "timidly keeping to their home ports."

Each day, the resulting congestion grew increasingly serious. Americans simply desired to pursue "peace and goodwill" as they affirmed rights long recognized by the world's civilized nations. He requested authority to "supply our merchant ships with defensive arms, should that become necessary, and with the means of using them, and to employ any other instrumentalities or methods that may be necessary and adequate to protect our ships and our people in their legitimate and peaceful pursuits on the seas." Because insurance companies were reluctant to guarantee cargoes, he sought sufficient credit to allow protection. Claiming that he already possessed the power to act alone, he nonetheless asked for congressional approval: "We are jointly the servants of the people and must act together and in their spirit, so far as we can divine and interpret it." Wilson closed eloquently, saying: "We are speaking of no selfish material rights, but of rights which our hearts support and whose foundation is that of righteous passion for justice upon which all law, all structures alike of family, of state and of mankind must rest, as upon the ultimate base of our existence and our liberty. I cannot imagine any man with American principles at his heart hesitating to defend these things."[45]

A careful reading reveals that Wilson placed his request squarely on admittedly archaic international law, referring neither to Belgium's predicament nor to Zimmermann's note, much less to a moral or material interest in an Allied victory. Still, German actions on the high seas could prompt American entrance into the war. Historian William Henry Harbaugh writes of the president's stance: "In the long run this would lead to disillusionment and despair. But in the short run it was to form an issue upon which all but extremists could stand as one."[46]

Wilson believed he held the constitutional power to arm merchant ships without asking for congressional approval. He wanted to test national sentiment, having recently claimed that Americans would not support a war simply waged to protect maritime rights. Furthermore, he hoped to warn the Germans that he would not permit them to stop American commerce. He hoped to avoid a special session of Congress, a step that Lodge and other Republicans ardently desired, as he feared that heated debate would hinder administration action. Senate Republican leaders had agreed to filibuster in order to force the president's hand.

At the conclusion of Wilson's address, Democrats applauded warmly while Republicans remained silent. La Follette sat with his hands folded, afraid that the president's request marked a major step toward war. Subsequent comments reveal a partisan division. Senator Willard Saulsbury of

Delaware spoke for many Democrats when he agreed to grant Wilson "every power he needs in the premises." Representing a minority of Democrats, Vardaman found it more profitable to suspend traffic between Europe and the United States than to risk entering the war, adding that Britain was violating American rights as much as Germany was.[47]

Later that day Congressman Flood and Senator Stone, acting on behalf of their relative committees, introduced legislation that gave the president authority to arm merchant ships. The chief executive could employ "other instrumentalities and methods." He could, moreover, spend up to $100 million for these purposes. A bond issue would raise the money.

On both sides of the aisle, critics argued that Wilson had attempted to usurp congressional authority. Though most senators believed that the president either possessed or should possess the power to arm ships, they balked at the term "other instrumentalities," dreading that unlimited authority could turn a minor undeclared naval conflict into a major declared war. Charles E. Townsend attacked this "monstrous proposal," saying: "No despot could ask for more power." To Wesley L. Jones, it was "a beautifully worded request for autocratic power."[48]

Many legislators wanted Congress to remain in special session after its term expired on March 4. Representative Allen T. Treadway (R-Mass.) accused Wilson of telling the legislators: "Vote me unlimited power and go home. I will do the rest."[49] Some critics did not trust Wilson to govern alone, either fearful that he would provoke conflict or, conversely, that he would allow war fever to wane.

At the moment when Wilson was addressing Congress, word passed through the House chamber that a U-boat had sunk the armed Cunard liner *Laconia* during the previous night. Sailing from New York to Liverpool, it was torpedoed without warning 150 miles off the Irish coast. The ship carried 217 crew and 75 passengers. Of the 12 who perished, 3 were Americans. Victims included Mrs. Mary Hoy and her daughter Elizabeth, socially prominent in Chicago and friends of Mrs. Wilson, and an African American crewman who tended the coal-fired steam engines.

The *Outlook* considered the sinking the overt act to which Wilson had referred when he broke relations with Germany. The American Rights Committee considered the tragedy a "deliberate challenge to the manhood of America" and asked citizens: "Are you too timid to fight for the protection of your women and children?" To the interventionist *New York Tribune*, a declaration of war alone would suffice.[50] Popular reaction was muted, partially because it remained common knowledge that the loss of the *California* three weeks earlier had produced far more fatalities. Furthermore, the ship was British, not American.

February 28 marked the day Wilson gave the Zimmermann note to the Associated Press; it was published within twenty-four hours. The cable helped persuade the public, not to mention Congress, to back his desired policy of armed neutrality. The president had not arranged for its publication—as his anti-interventionist critics soon claimed—in order to force Congress's hand; he believed that the bill was likely to pass in some form anyhow.

No event of the war thus far, not even the invasion of Belgium or the sinking of the *Lusitania,* so jolted Americans. Shock, incredulity, outrage— these were the dominant public reactions. The press ridiculed the Zimmermann note, considering any actual threat ludicrous. The *New Republic* spoke for many: "This sense of its being absurd has prevented the ordinary American from taking the incident seriously." *Current Opinion* branded the telegram "probably the most naive document in the history of diplomacy" as it called its readers' attention to supposed German intrigues throughout the world. Among such activities were instigating an uprising in India, fostering a recent insurrection in Cuba, and replacing Mexican leader Carranza with General Álvaro Obregón.[51]

For the first time, major segments of the American press called for war, the entire nation now perceiving Germany as a hostile and untrustworthy power.[52] To much of the public, matters concerning the nation's dignity and rights remained abstract, not worth a brutal conflict. But promising entire states of the union to a foreign power, particularly one that General Pershing had invaded less than a year before, was another matter altogether. So, too, was the suggestion that Japan might join an anti-American coalition. Until now the Southwest and Pacific Coast regions saw little at stake in the Great War.

Some opinion leaders remained incredulous, others cautious. George Sylvester Viereck called the note "unquestionably a brazen forgery planted by British agents," echoing the views of William Randolph Hearst and Senator William Alden Smith. Senator Tillman deemed the document fraudulent: "The Japanese hate the Germans like the devil hates holy water."[53]

German Americans were highly embarrassed. The *New York Evening Mail* quoted the book of Joshua to them: "Choose You This Day Whom You Will Serve." The *New Yorker Staats-Zeitung* asserted: "No one could have expected such nonsense of a practical statesman."[54]

On March 3 Zimmermann publicly conceded that he had written the cable, although he stressed that its execution was contingent upon an American declaration of war. At this point even the most militant of German Americans usually accepted its validity. Viereck, however, proved an exception, remaining suspicious of the note's authenticity while repudiating any German effort to ally with America's foes. In his weekly journal, to which he gave the still newer name of *Viereck's: The American Weekly,* he alleged that the stressed Zimmermann would never have used the word "please" in reference to Mexico's "president" or deemed it necessary to label his note "confidential." ("It is contrary to the German habit to divide the bearskin before they have caught the bear.")[55]

Two days later Zimmermann revealed his motive to the Reichstag's budget committee. He wrote the cable to "set new enemies on America's neck," although he denied that Mexico could recover American territory. The committee unanimously endorsed the foreign secretary's action. The German press and public backed the foreign secretary.[56]

The Japanese embassy took pains to call Germany's action "monstrous," "impossible," "outrageous." Upon receiving the Zimmermann cable, Mexico's chargé d'affaires denied that his government was implicated in any plot. First Chief Carranza initially remained silent, his government rejecting the German proposal upon publication of the note. The Mexican leader hoped to create a diversion on America's southwest border should the United States fight overseas but later told the German ambassador that premature publication voided any possible effectiveness. Though Wilson had started to withdraw Pershing's expeditionary force in January, Carranza was remaining most apprehensive.[57]

Given the popular anger over the Zimmermann telegram, Wilson's appeal for what he called "armed neutrality" received widespread support. The great majority of urban newspaper editors endorsed Wilson's proposal, as did representatives of business, labor, and the clergy. The *New Republic,* noting that Germany was sinking ships faster than Britain could build them, feared that a starving England would surrender its fleet, submit to the dismemberment of its empire, allow Russia to plunge into the circle of German influence, and witness Japan adapt itself to the new German hegemony. "What would be the position of the United States in such a world?" Latin America would be placed in danger, while "our trade would encounter closed doors on every hand."[58]

Some pacifists supported armed neutrality, among them the leaders of the American Union Against Militarism. So, too, did several prominent German Americans, though much of the Teutonic press deplored Wilson's request. Editor Bernard Ridder of the *New Yorker Staats-Zeiting* repudiated any alliance formed to invade America. Henry Ford discontinued his Neutral Conference for Continuous Mediation and put his massive auto plant at the nation's service. He admitted that "sometimes the best thing a pacifist can do is to help get over a fight as quickly as possible." Journalist Charles Edward Russell boasted that he was an American before being a Socialist. "War between Germany and the United States," he went on, "would be a thing to rejoice and be glad about," because "ninety days after those two countries declare war, it will be all over, and the war in Europe will be over, too." The New York Peace Society endorsed "our President's action in defense of American rights and the rights of humanity."[59]

Some sought more radical action. Historian Charles Beard asked America to "align itself with the Allies and help eliminate Prussianism from the earth." Major George Haven Putnam of the American Rights Committee feared that Wilson's armed-ship scheme simply invited more German threats to American commerce and lives. The *Army and Navy Journal* favored full-scale war.[60]

Other Americans believed Wilson too belligerent. *Viereck's* accused Wilson of provoking the Germans to commit an overt act of war. Congress, commented Hearst's *New York American,* should confront British seizures of American craft with the same fervor that it opposed German U-boats. "If we insist upon forcing one belligerent to let pass American ships loaded with tons and tons of supplies and ammunition while we tamely submit to another belligerent's orders that our ships shall not even carry food to neutral countries—not even to Poland's starving millions—why, then, we must expect to go to war, and to go to war with the world's knowledge that we have not played fair." Historian Preserved Smith defended Germany: "Drowning a few thousand non-combatants is no more inhumane than trying to starve a hundred million non-combatants."[61]

Several anti-interventionists espied sheer greed at work. Congressman Charles A. Lindbergh (R-Minn.), father of the famous aviator, blamed the "greedy speculators" of "the Money Trust," as revealed in supposed Federal Reserve ties overseas, for bringing the nation to the verge of hostilities. Stone feared that Congress might arm one of J.P. Morgan's ships, "leaving the issue of peace or war with Germany to the discretion of the captain of that vessel." Socialist Meyer London warned that the United States would simply be fighting for "the right of munition makers to sell munitions." Let America remain "the one great neutral power, the one great Republic, the repository of the ideals of democracy and liberty."[62]

At first, the House Foreign Affairs Committee was deadlocked over armed neutrality, dealing with crippling amendments concerning the transport of contraband and Wilson's plea for extraordinary powers. Not until February 28 did it report a compromise bill. The legislation permitted the president to arm merchant ships but withheld authority for "other instrumentalities and methods." It forbade the War Risk Insurance Bureau, established at the beginning of the conflict, to insure ships that carried munitions.

Over fifty congressmen spoke in a seven-hour debate. Hal Flood declared, "Our duty is clear—to protect our citizens and our ships in their lawful pursuits." Ex–House speaker Joe Cannon noted Jesus's adage about turning the second cheek but remarked: "The third cheek is enough." Even such administration opponents as Claude Kitchin sustained Wilson, although confessing to severe misgivings. James R. Mann pointed to his own anti-interventionist record but stressed that patriotism demanded support of the president in times of crisis.[63] The news of Zimmerman's cable had brought the president significant backing.

Dissenters advanced several criticisms. Philip P. Campbell (R-Kan.) voiced concern about the bread riots taking place in such cites as New York, Philadelphia, and Boston, warning: "We need the food now. We may need our arms and ammunition later." If, asked Stephen G. Porter (R-Pa.), the bill's defenders denied that Wilson would arm ships bearing contraband, why was the president requesting such authority? Henry T. Helgesen (R-N.D.) remarked that authorities in Halifax refused to allow English women and children to traverse the Atlantic to Liverpool while the United States permitted its own citizens to undertake such a dangerous voyage.[64] Most opponents were progressives or radicals who came from the Midwest and represented significant German American constituencies.

Controversy intensified when Congressman Henry Allen Cooper (R-Wis.), who led the opposition, moved to recommit the bill to the House Foreign Affairs Committee, of which he was a ranking member. His motion involved an amendment prohibiting the arming of merchant ships carrying munitions. Fortifying such ships, Cooper maintained, was tantamount to a declaration of war. The motion lost, 125 to 293, although just under half of the representatives from the Midwest and almost two-thirds from the Far West voted in its favor. Seventy-two of Cooper's backers were Republicans, revealing that partisanship was as much a factor as geography. The House also defeated a proposed amendment that forbade the issue of passports to Americans intending to travel on ships carrying arms. The vote was 100-57. On March 1, the House voted 403 to 13 to approve the bill itself.[65]

A day later the Senate took up the armed-ship bill. Its version specifically added the "such other instrumentalities" clause. Under Lodge's prodding, the Senate Foreign Relations Committee recommended a bill that gave Wilson more authority than requested, a move that caused Stone, Hitchcock, O'Gorman, and Smith of Michigan to resist the amended legislation. The committee's proposal would grant ship owners and crews, not just the president, authority to protect themselves against unlawful attacks. Because U-boats struck at the bow of a ship, the legislation allowed defensive guns to be placed both "fore and aft." One amendment repealed a statute, enacted in 1819, that prohibited merchant vessels, attempting to defend themselves against pirates, from firing on nations not currently at war with the United States.

Although Stone chaired the Foreign Relations Committee and introduced the bill, he left its management to Gilbert M. Hitchcock, the next-ranking Democrat and a man who had opposed the legislation in committee. During the debate, Frank Brandegee of Connecticut pointed to an America hit by severe economic crisis as East Coast ports stagnated and the nation's merchant fleet was paralyzed. Lodge rallied many Republicans behind Hitchcock's proposal, maintaining that an American merchantman would be justified in sinking any submarine without warning, even if it was British or French. If a periscope of a German submarine appeared in the vicinity of a merchant ship, it was appropriate to presume an impending U-boat attack.[66]

As in the House, opponents expressed many anxieties. Kirby alleged that while "Wall Street and the hirelings of the press" believed that the bill would create huge profits, the American people sought no war because they knew they would be the major losers. Other critics accused the bill's defenders of promoting militarism and of betraying traditional American democracy by entering "the quarrels of Europe." In particular, dissenting senators feared that Wilson would allow the navy to escort vessels into the war zone, where they might end up exchanging shots with a German U-boat.[67]

Stone offered an amendment to withhold armed protection from ships carrying munitions. O'Gorman backed him, fearing that ship owners could disguise the contraband. Lodge accused the Missourian of refusing to trust the president concerning the arming of such vessels, while Miles Poindexter charged the Germans with planning to sink any neutral ship regardless of its cargo. Were the United States to enter the war, he continued, its participation would be "nominal," for it was far removed from the battlefront. Germany's "Brandenburg Guard was broken on the heights of Verdun."[68]

Historian Thomas W. Ryley asserts that the senators appeared ignorant as to "just what the bill was all about"; even staunch proponents seemed confused about its content. "All that they could agree upon was that it was necessary to give Wilson the power." Further tension developed on March 2, the day that the German Admiralty announced the expiration of the period of grace for neutral ships; henceforth, German U-boats would sink *all* vessels without warning, whether armed or unarmed, belligerent or neutral.[69]

On the following day, March 3, and for the next twenty-six hours, debate continued. The Senate was required to adjourn at noon on March 4, when its term expired. The Sixty-fourth Congress was not scheduled to meet until December 3, nine months later. Scarcely a senator was absent; theatergoers, arriving in evening dress, filled the galleries to witness one of the most dramatic events in congressional history. Republican Albert B. Fall (R-N.M.) favored war with Germany "within the next fifteen minutes." Frank Brandegee, too, welcomed conflict: "Do you prefer to lie down on your back and let this monstrous Frankenstein trample over you ruthlessly?"[70] Twenty-seven other Republicans concurred, indicating that they would vote for war then and there.

To prevent the armed-ship bill from coming to a vote, four Senate opponents—La Follette, Norris, Gronna, and Cummins—resorted to a filibuster. Norris led the effort. Other holdouts included Stone, O'Gorman, Works, Vardaman, Kirby, Kenyon, Lane, and Moses E. Clapp (R-Minn.). Of these twelve, seven were progressive Republicans, four Bryan Democrats. O'Gorman, an Irish American who was strongly anti-British, remained an exception, being a past Grand Sachem of New York City's Tammany Hall. Several represented states with large German American constituencies. Partisanship may have affected the alignment, for some Democrats who voted for the legislation privately told Norris they feared the consequences of breaking with the president.

Hitchcock offered to give opponents speaking time provided they would eventually allow the Senate to vote, but he was rebuffed. The bill's defenders did most of the declaiming, taking up over twenty-four hours. Foes consumed fewer than eleven hours, although Stone held the floor for four. In an effort to counter pro-Allied sentiment, he pointed to Russian atrocities against German citizens and affirmed that five American vessels had struck British mines. Cummins, who spoke for ninety minutes, opposed fighting Germany in defense of Americans who traveled on British vessels that transported munitions. Referring to the authority that the bill gave to the president, he remarked: "I am opposed to Kaisering the United States." Offering a clause-by-clause analysis of Wilson's message, Norris quoted profusely from Wilson's own *Congressional Government* (1885), a work that stressed the dominance of the legislative branch over the executive. Furthermore, he noted, British Commonwealth nations such as Canada, Australia, and India had passed laws that prevented women and children from sailing into danger zones. If the armed-ship bill was so vital to the nation's security, these critics argued, Wilson could easily call the Congress into special session. Passions became so heated that Lane, a physician, threatened to use a file as a dagger if Senator Ollie James, who was carrying a gun, threatened La Follette. The Wisconsin senator kept handy a revolver, which his son cleared from his desk.[71]

On March 4 at 1:30 A.M., Lodge, Borah, and Brandegee presented a petition that gathered seventy-five signatures. The signers proclaimed their support for the bill, blaming a small minority for preventing them from casting their votes. At noon Vice President Thomas R. Marshall, who presided over the Senate, declared an adjournment.

Opponents and supporters agreed on one matter: if armed merchant ships entered the war zone, the United States was bound to enter the conflict. In the words of Senator Kirby, a foe of the bill, "when the guns roar it will be America speaking, and the voice will be war and not peace."[72]

Parliamentary maneuvering prevented La Follette from making a speech, though he presented his case in the March edition of *La Follette's Magazine*. He called the bill unconstitutional (it gave the president unilateral authority to make war) and biased (the United States was not asserting similar rights in dealing with England). The bill's provision for "other instrumentalities and methods" bestowed dangerous power upon the chief executive. If the legislation passed, Wilson could order naval convoys for merchantmen that carried arms, ammunition, food, clothing, and shoes to the Allied armies. He could command naval patrols to hunt submarines "in the interests of the owners of our munition ships." He could land an army in Germany to destroy the Krupp works and other submarine-manufacturing plants. The senator invoked the example of the sunken liner *Laconia* and other Allied merchant ships to prove that deck armament could not deter torpedoes; military authorities, he asserted, backed his claim. The chances of hitting a periscope at two miles, he soon added, was less than one in a hundred. Agitation for armed shipping was, he claimed, spearheaded by the American Line, a subsidiary of the International Merchant Marine Company, and dominated by British and Morgan interests. Ironically, he went on, the firm owned less than 5 percent of total U.S. tonnage involved in foreign trade. Because the major belligerents faced serious deprivation, the Wilson administration was wrong to "hurl this country into the bottomless pit of the European horror." Instead, it should call a conference of neutral nations to enforce their collective rights.[73]

On the morning of Sunday, March 4, Wilson took the oath of office in private. That evening he released a statement to the press in which he described himself as facing a condition "unparalleled in the history of the country, perhaps unparalleled in the history of any modern Government." Experiencing the gravest international crisis in American history, a crippled Congress proved unable to safeguard the nation, much less vindicate the elementary rights of its citizens. Foreign governments could act with impunity, since the United States could not take action. "A little group of willful men, representing no opinion but their own, have rendered the great Government of the United States helpless and contemptible." All was not lost, however, because a change in Senate rules could "save the nation from disaster." That night Wilson issued a supplemental communiqué: the presidency enjoyed certain "general constitutional powers," although old statutes, still unrepealed, might "raise insuperable practical obstacles and may nullify his power."[74]

Link notes that Wilson made a singularly unfortunate statement. It was his delay in asking Congress for special authority that was primarily responsible for the debacle. Had he given the Senate leaders an additional week, they might have been able to wear out the dissenters; four senators could not have monopolized the floor indefinitely. In addition, the minority of obstructionists were not responsible for the failure of the armed-ship bill. Other Republican leaders would have maintained a filibuster, one that hopefully would force Wilson to call a special session, had not La Follette's band done their work for them.

Of greater consequence, notes Link, Wilson "cruelly impugned" the patriotism of senators who had the tenacity to withhold carte blanche authority for making undeclared war. The chief executive indicted all the senators who refused to sign the petition, although just four of them had blocked a vote. Cummins, Vardaman, O'Gorman, and Lane later said they would have voted for the bill if it had included Stone's amendment. Wilson did not admit that he had opposed Congress's remaining in session during the coming months, fearing that it would hinder his armed-neutrality policy and increase the danger of war. Moreover, Wilson's additional statement stretched the truth. The 1819 statute, limiting defensive action to pirates, was subject to alternative interpretation.[75]

Until this time, Devlin notes, Wilson had been unclear whether an overt act of war necessitated an attack on an American ship or included loss of American life on a belligerent ship. Devlin believes that the ambivalence was appropriate; it allowed the president the flexibility to respond to a particular submarine challenge. Now the chief executive "had placed himself on the edge of a war to defend no right more sacred than the right to travel."[76]

Wilson's attack on the dissenting senators drew strong editorial approval. The great majority of the Congress sought armed neutrality, perceiving it as the one available means of defending American commerce on the high seas. The American people, remarked Senator Henry F. Ashurst (D-Ariz.), had not been so angry at the upper house since the vote on Andrew Johnson's impeachment. At least one house in a host of state legislatures adopted resolutions condemning the filibuster or backing the president, among them those of Kentucky, Idaho, Minnesota, Missouri, Ohio, Washington, Arkansas, Oklahoma, and Tennessee. The Texas legislature accused Stone of giving "aid and comfort to the enemy," demanding his retirement as chairman of the Foreign Relations Committee. Democratic party chairman Vance McCormick started a movement to unseat him. A committee of Arkansans branded Senator Kirby the reincarnation of Judas Iscariot, sending him thirty pieces of silver. Students at the University of Illinois hung La Follette in effigy. Oregonians considered the recalling of Senator Lane. *Outlook* editor Lyman Abbott, addressing a mass meeting of the American Rights League in New York's Carnegie Hall, branded the filibustering senators "Germany's allies," while members in the audience cried "Hang them!" Senator Thomas J. Walsh remarked: "It is not inconceivable that the obstructionists—filibusters—may be actuated by traitorous sentiments."[77]

Wilson's enemies remained opposed to the president's plans. Roosevelt labeled the armed-ship bill "worthless," "nothing but timid war," and deemed the president "a thousand times" more blameworthy than the "treasonous" senators. If the chief executive "does not go to war with Germany," he wrote Lodge, "I shall skin him alive." La Follette "ought to be hung." Some took a more moderate view. The *New Republic*, although it deemed La Follette profoundly wrong and the filibuster a disgrace, denied that he was a traitor; he had a right to be heard.[78]

The dissenting senators did not lack defenders. The Emergency Peace Federation praised their "courage and devotion," telling them: "We believe you represent a vast, though unknown number of Americans whose earnest desire it is that this country should not be drawn into war, directly or indirectly." In a signed editorial, William Randolph Hearst called Wilson's censure a "diatribe," maintaining that "pure and patriotic" motives animated the resisting legislators. Socialist leader Eugene Victor Debs, endorsing a general strike at New York's Cooper Union, pledged: "I will never go to war for a capitalist government. . . . I'd rather be lined up against a wall and shot as a traitor to Wall Street than fight as a traitor to America."[79]

Wilson delivered his second inaugural address on March 5. "We stand firm in armed neutrality," he said, "since it seems that in no other way can we demonstrate what it is we insist upon and cannot forego." Using the vaguest of language, he continued, "We may even be drawn in, by circumstances, not by our own purpose or desire, to a more active assertion of our rights as we see them and a more immediate association with the great struggle itself." He listed what would later be known as Wilsonian tenets: arms reduction, freedom of the seas, "the political stability of free peoples," "the actual equality of all nations in all matters of right or privilege," and "the responsibility of all nations for the peace of the world."[80]

Three days later, the Senate, meeting as a fresh session, approved Wilson's request to limit debate. It adopted a closure rule whereby, on vote of two-thirds of the members, deliberation could be limited to a maximum of ninety-six hours, that is, one hour for each senator. For the first time in a century, it surrendered its privilege of unlimited discussion; the tally was 76 to 3. Sixteen senators cast no ballot. La Follette, Gronna, and Lawrence Y. Sherman voted no. On March 16 the Senate adjourned again.

On March 5, Attorney General Thomas W. Gregory denied that the "piracy" provision of the 1819 law handicapped the president. A day later Lansing argued that the United States could place armed guards on merchantmen. There was, he posited, no more impropriety in furnishing naval guns and gunners on merchant vessels than would exist if America landed guns and "blue jackets" on foreign soil to protect citizens against "lawless attack."[81]

Wilson waited just three more days before announcing that he would arm American ships and call Congress into special session on April 16. Within a week Daniels gave merchant crews the authority to shoot at any submarine that acted suspiciously, especially if it approached within torpedo range. The armed craft, however, must refrain from firing at any U-boat that lay over four thousand yards from the merchantman's commercial route. The merchant ship could not pursue or search out submarines or "engage in any aggressive warfare against them." Hopefully Berlin would cooperate with his arrangement. In signing the orders, Daniels confided to his diary: I might be signing what would prove the death warrant of young Americans and the arming of ships may bring us into war."[82]

Wilson believed that he had no choice. Germany attacked neutral shipping even if it had not yet committed an overt act against an American vessel. The Zimmermann cable and the sinking of the *Laconia* simply reinforced his decision, besides helping to convert congressional and public opinion to his viewpoint.

In general the American press applauded Wilson's decision. Many senators offered warm support. One of the major filibusterers, Senator Cummins, said that he upheld the arming of merchant ships. His concern centered on the provision for "other instrumentalities," as this wording authorized the president to "declare war" on his own. Myron T. Herrick, former Ohio governor and ambassador to France, told a rally of three thousand Wilson supporters in Cleveland: "One must either be a patriot or a traitor." Even Henry Weismann, president of the National German-American Alliance, defended the chief executive, saying, "We mean to insist upon our rights."[83]

Some dissent persisted. Kenyon, Cummins's ally in opposing the Senate bill, feared the arming of ships carrying munitions. Norris sounded resigned to the president's course. He opposed Wilson's move as an act of war but claimed that the president legally possessed the authority to issue the order.[84]

Despite Wilson's move, Germany did not back down. As long as it continued to wage unrestricted submarine warfare, war was only a matter of time.

10

And the War Came
March–April 1917

On March 12, at 6:00 a.m., the German *U-38* attacked the *Algonquin*, an American merchantman, sixty-five miles off the Isles of Scilly. A former lake steamer bound from New York to London, it carried $1.25 million worth of foodstuffs as well as copper, tin, machinery, and chemicals. The ship had just been transferred from British registry to the American Star Line. The vessel displayed Old Glory; the nation's colors were painted clearly on its side. When the crew asked the submarine commander to tow them toward land, he refused, saying: "I'm too busy. I expect a couple of other steamers."[1] All twenty-six members survived in lifeboats, arriving at Penzance after twenty-seven hours on the open sea. News reached the United States two days later. Hopes were dashed that Germany would modify its submarine operations.

The public remained quiet, the *Outlook* and the American Rights Committee being almost alone in advocating war.[2] Because the *Algonquin* had changed registry more than two years after war had broken out, no European naval power legally considered it a neutral. Seven other U.S. steamers had sailed since Germany's pronouncement; all arrived safely in France.

Admiral Holtzendorff soon clarified German policy. Writing to the Kaiser on March 18, he found restraint impossible. Submarines were at their stations and wireless was unreliable; it would take at least six weeks to reverse the orders for unrestricted U-boat warfare. To allow American commerce to continue unchallenged would merely undermine Germany's new tactic. Wilhelm approved the document: "Now, once and for all, an *end* to negotiations with America. If Wilson wants war, let him make it, and then let him have it."[3]

Three days later Bethmann defended the Admiralty's course before the Reichstag, declaring that Britain had forced the issue. The chancellor denied that Germany ever intended to attack the United States; if, however, the submarine assault provoked an American declaration of war, he said, "we shall not have to bear the burden of responsibility for it." Offering a dissenting view, Ambassador Bernstorff publicly expressed apprehension. While journeying back to Germany, he remarked: "If we sink an American ship we get war. If not, I suppose we avoid it."[4]

The ambassador had reason to worry. On Saturday, March 18, Americans learned that the Germans had sunk three of their ships. Two days earlier, at 10:00 A.M., a U-boat attacked the *Vigilancia*. It belonged to Gaston, Williams & Wigmore, a firm that received financial support from J.P. Morgan's subsidiary Guaranty Trust. The vessel was bound from New York to Le Havre with a cargo of iron, straw, asbestos, and dried fruits. The event took place without warning 150 miles west of Bishop, a village located on Britain's southwest coast. The submarine commander made no effort to ascertain whether the craft was carrying contraband before he torpedoed the vessel. The steamer sank in seven minutes; its captain never saw the attacking U-boat. It flew an American flag. Its name and home city were painted on port and starboard bows in letters five feet high and could be read at a distance of three miles. Of the forty-five–man crew, fifteen were drowned (six of them were Americans) while launching lifeboats. Here lay further evidence that most fatalities on merchant ships came not from torpedoes or shells but from drowning after the vessel went to the bottom. The survivors arrived in the Isles of Scilly two days later, suffering from exposure. The submarine followed the lifeboats until early the next morning but offered no assistance. The *Vigilancia* was the first American ship deliberately sunk without warning after Germany announced its new policy.

Late in the afternoon of Friday, March 17, the German *UC-66* sank the unarmed *City of Memphis*. The *City* was owned by the Savannah Line, the informal name of the Ocean Steamship Company. The young W. Averell Harriman, heir to a railroad fortune, held controlling interest. The ship had just dropped off 9,673 bales of cotton at Le Havre, France, and had begun its return voyage from Cardiff to New York. Its cargo: sheer ballast. Under traditional nautical rules, the total absence of freight would bestow immunity to the craft. The merchantman was struck thirty-five miles south of Fastnet. Like the *Algonquin,* the vessel sported on both sides the colors red, white, and blue. The ship's name was painted in six-foot letters and was illuminated at night. The U-boat skipper, Herbert Pustkuchen, was the same officer who had torpedoed the *Sussex* practically a year before. The submarine first fired two warning shots, then ordered Captain L.P. Borum to evacuate all hands. After the U-boat delivered at least ten shells, the merchantman began to sink. Borum vainly requested that the Germans tow his lifeboats to land. After a day on rough seas, the fifty-eight member crew either reached the Irish coast or were rescued by British ships.

A day later, the *Illinois,* an American oil tanker owned by the Texas Company and sailing from London to Port Arthur, Texas, met with the same fate. *UC-21* attacked it without warning twenty miles off Alderney, the northernmost of the British-ruled Channel islands off France. Like the *City of Memphis,* it carried only ballast. As the crew scurried into lifeboats, it faced continued fire. The Germans refused to pull the lifeboats toward land, the captain declaring: "I have no time."[5] One crew member was wounded.

On March 19 U-boats also sank two Belgian ships off the southwest coast of Norway. Carrying supplies for Herbert Hoover's Commission for Relief in Belgium, both vessels lost crew members. Other CRB craft soon suffered the same fate.

Some press accounts telescoped the three disasters into a single story, creating a sense that the "overt act" had indeed taken place. Each ship was built in the United States. None had ever been under foreign registration. All three were owned by major corporations, who may have assumed that their importance might persuade Germany to remain on "good behavior." None was armed. Two of the ships carried no cargo. All were torpedoed because they had sailed into Germany's proclaimed war zone. Only the *City of Memphis* received any warning. These incidents, plus similar attacks on other neutral and belligerent ships, convinced Wilson that Berlin intended to destroy all commerce and human life that ventured into its proclaimed war zones.

Editors accused Germany of "making war" and committing an "overt act" of war. Communities organized defense committees. Many labor leaders pledged their loyalty. Some Socialist intellectuals broke with the antiwar stance of their National Committee, including novelist Upton Sinclair and journalist William English Walling. The same defection held true for certain pacifists; both labor organizer Rose Pastor Stokes and suffragist leader Carrie Chapman Catt left the Woman's Peace Party. Rabbi Stephen Wise declared that he hoped to God that "it were possible for us to fight side by side with the German people for the overthrow of Hohenzollernism."[6]

Certain reactions were highly predictable. Roosevelt scorned Wilson's policy of armed neutrality: "Germany is already at war with us. The only question for us is whether we shall make war nobly or ignobly." Hughes, Root, and Lodge concurred, the Massachusetts senator writing TR: "We are doing nothing." *Viereck's* magazine, much on the defensive, observed that the three sunken ships sailed heedless of Germany's January 31 warning; he expressed gratitude that the war-making power remained with Congress, not the press.[7]

At 3:30 P.M. on March 19, the highly troubled president met with Frank Cobb, the crusading editor of the *New York World*. After confessing that he had done everything possible to avoid war, Wilson expressed deep anxiety. Once the United States entered the conflict, "the spirit of ruthless brutality will enter into the very fiber of our national life, infecting Congress, the courts, the policeman on the beat, the man in the street." The Constitution, not to mention freedom of speech and assembly, could not survive the ordeal. In short, "it required illiberalism at home to reinforce the men at the front." In addition, Germany would be so badly defeated that any peace would be a dictated one; there would be no neutral bystanders left to foster a just settlement. Cobb replied that he could see no option but war. The president was simply repeating an anxiety he had expressed to Daniels sometime in March. Claiming that war would mean the loss of every gain won since 1912, he warned the secretary of the navy: "Big business will be in the saddle."[8]

The following afternoon Wilson, recovering from illness, presided over his cabinet, asking its judgment as to whether he should call Congress into session earlier than the designated day of April 16 and, more important, what he should lay before that body. He observed that the eastern United States had become indignant, while the Midwest remained apathetic. William Gibbs McAdoo advocated war, arguing that the German government represented "every evil in history." If the administration did not act, the Treasury secretary continued, public pressure would force it to do so. Robert Lansing maintained that full-scale belligerency would have "a great moral influence on the Russians," who in mid-March had forced the czar's abdication and established a provisional parliamentary government. Entering the conflict would encourage "the democratic movement in Germany," "put new spirit in the Allies already flushed with recent military successes," end "the charges of vacillation and hesitation, which were becoming general," and "bring the people solidly behind the President." Labor secretary William B. Wilson remarked that Germany was already making war on America.

Interior Secretary Franklin K. Lane spoke of an aroused public opinion and "the principle of right." Attorney General Thomas W. Gregory stressed German intrigues within the United States. Postmaster General Albert S. Burleson read telegrams demanding hostilities. Navy Secretary Josephus Daniels, with tears in his eyes, could see no alternative to armed conflict. In summary, every cabinet member judged that war was inevitable.

The cabinet differed over the appropriate degree of American participation. McAdoo envisioned the forthcoming effort as limited to financial aid, doubting whether the United States could furnish troops. Agriculture secretary David F. Houston wanted to restrict assistance to naval involvement and supply of the Allies. William C. Redfield, secretary of commerce, spoke vaguely of bringing the Kaiser to his knees. In the event of a likely Allied defeat, argued War Secretary Newton Baker, the United States must be prepared with an army sufficiently strong to be deployed overseas; the people would demand it. After listening to the cabinet for two and a half hours, Wilson said: "I think that there is no doubt as to what your advice is. Thank you."[9]

Either during this meeting or just afterward, the president decided for war, thus ending over a week of what Link calls "the time of Wilson's Gethsemane."[10] For another several days, the chief executive kept a public silence. At the same time, he would not consider imposing conditions upon the Allies in return for American participation. On March 23 Wilson advanced the date for Congress to meet, issuing a proclamation that called Congress into extra session on April 2.

On March 21 at 8:15 P.M., the Standard Oil tanker *Healdton,* named after an oil city in Oklahoma, went down in the North Sea, news that undoubtedly emboldened Wilson. Bound from Bergen, Norway, to Rotterdam and carrying six thousand tons of petroleum, the ship sank twenty-five miles north of Terschelling Island off the Dutch coast. As in the other cases, the American ship bore clear markings, the electrically illuminated craft displaying its name and the words "New York." Although twenty of the crew reached Terschelling safely, twenty-one lives were lost, seven of them American. Causes of death included a capsized lifeboat, suffocation in bunkers, insufficient clothing in freezing waters, and the inability to jump safely from the ship. Germany denied torpedoing the craft, but Americans refused to believe Berlin's disavowal. Maritime historian Rodney Carlisle believes that the ship hit two British mines laid two days before.[11]

The president met with House on March 27. Should he should ask Congress to declare war on Germany, he queried? Or should he simply declare that a state of war already existed and then request the means to conduct the conflict? The colonel, fearing an acrimonious debate, advised the latter. (Two days earlier, House assured such pacifists as Amos Pinchot and Lillian Wald that Wilson sought to avoid conflict.) Washington observers predicted that the president would assert the existence of a state of war.[12]

By now Washington had become overtly pro-Entente. No longer did the State Department protest the blacklist, mail seizures, bunkering agreements, and other aspects of the British blockade. On March 8 the Federal Reserve Board announced that it would permit American banks to resume buying short-term Allied treasury notes. Page had just warned Lansing that Britain's gold resources were approaching exhaustion. Without further credit, continued the ambassador, Europe's finances would crumble, causing the world's commerce to collapse. "Perhaps our going to war is the only way in which our present preeminent trade position can be maintained and a panic averted."[13]

During the last week of March, Wilson recognized the new Russian government. He called the recently created Council of National Defense into session and ordered American Minister Brand Whitlock and Herbert Hoover's Commission for the Relief of Belgium to leave that nation. He instructed Daniels to coordinate plans with the British Admiralty, increased naval manpower to the statutory limit of ninety-seven thousand men, and federalized the National Guard of the eastern, midwestern, and far western states. On March 21, House wrote to Page: "As far as we are concerned, we are in the war now, even though a formal declaration may not occur until after Congress meets, April 2. All departments are preparing as rapidly as possible."[14]

As to who would win the European conflict, opinions differed radically. Certainly hope existed that the abdication of Czar Nicholas II on March 15 would bolster the Allied cause. With Russia now theoretically a republic, the Entente would be fighting alongside a reinvigorated partner while being freed of embarrassing linkage to Romanov despotism. Optimists envisioned an imminent defeat of the Central Powers, pointing to such factors as the British capture of Baghdad, the emergence of Russia as a democratic ally, China's severance of relations with Germany, unexpected Entente surges on the western front, and internal upheaval within Germany. Arguing to the contrary, *Viereck's* magazine reported that England faced a coming Irish rebellion; Italy and France lacked food and coal; and Russia, in the throes of revolution, enfeebled the Allied cause. Germany benefited, added contributor Frederick Franklin Schrader, because Poland had become a "free and independent state." Eastern European Jews could now worship without fear, and the majority of Belgians hailed Germany as a deliverer. The more neutralist *New York American* could not share the optimism of either partisan, quoting a British lord who warned two years earlier that "Europe will be little better than a wilderness, peopled by old men, women and children." A popular referendum, it continued, would show a strong U.S. majority in favor of peace.[15]

At the end of March, the *Literary Digest* reported that the press faced just one question, not whether the United States should enter the conflict, but: "Shall we wage war with Germany independently of her other foes, or shall we wage it as an ally of the Allies?" Many newspapers did not consider neutrality an option. Prowar rallies became more frequent. Former Bull Moose vice-presidential candidate Hiram Johnson joined hands with Old Guardman Boies Penrose, the new California senator assuring masses gathered in Philadelphia's Independence Square that Wilson spoke the spirit of America.[16]

Antiwar forces were far from inactive, becoming even more vocal than during the *Lusitania* and *Sussex* crises. Rallies, newspaper advertisements, demonstrations outside the Capitol and the White House—every means came into play. German-language papers begged for peace, arguing that the bankrupt Allies faced collapse and that in Japan lay the real danger. Until Congress voted hostilities, announced the *New York Call*, Socialists would oppose conflict. Bryan asked Congress to foster his peace plan: have Germany suspend its U-boat campaign pending an investigation of all disputes by an international tribunal. Stanford's chancellor emeritus David Starr Jordan and peace activist Louis Lochner made several suggestions: conduct a binding referendum on whether to enter the conflict, permit a neutral nation to mediate between the United States and Germany, convene a conference of unaligned countries to devise a common policy checking "the illegal methods of all belligerents," and establish a joint commission of inquiry and conciliation with Britain and Germany to enforce the 1909 Declaration of London. Similarly, the Women's Committee of the Emergency Peace Federation offered various options: a conference of neutrals, a joint tribunal in accordance with the Hague Convention, adoption of the 1909 Declaration of

London, and an international congress called to discuss a permanent peace. The American Union Against Militarism sought continuation of Wilson's policy of armed neutrality, which offered "a vigorous defense of American ships and American rights on the sea *without involving America in a European quarrel.*"[17]

As war drew increasingly closer, anti-interventionists faced bitter attacks and at times harassment. The Women's Preparedness Committee of the National Civic Federation compared the Emergency Peace Federation to the Tories of the American Revolution and, using a comparison earlier made by TR, the Copperheads of the Civil War. Charles A. Beard denounced pacifists for "terrorizing the President and paralyzing Congress." He headed a Columbia faculty committee that accused the EPF of being "inspired by German cunning and financed by German money." Princeton University would not allow David Starr Jordan to deliver a peace address on campus. When the Stanford chancellor spoke at Baltimore's Academy of Music, a crowd of businessmen and Johns Hopkins professors invaded the hall and disrupted the meeting. The police department of Washington, D.C., banned demonstrations, primarily to foil an EPF parade.[18]

About nine thirty on the evening of April 1, *U-46* sank the American steamer *Aztec,* bound from New York to Le Havre, off Ouessant, an island near Brest, France. The property of the Oriental Navigation Company, the *Aztec* carried foodstuffs and general supplies. The vessel was the first armed American ship to go to the bottom. Twenty-eight lives were lost, including a naval gunner; nineteen survived. By then, much of the public realized that Wilson was moving toward a war declaration.

In deciding for war, the chief executive rejected certain options. He could have adopted the "cooling-off" solution of Bryan, that is, to wait until the conflict ended and claims were adjudicated. He might have promoted legislation similar to the Gore-McLemore resolutions, thereby saving the lives of some American passengers on the Atlantic. Historian Ernest R. May believes the United States was sufficiently prosperous to forgo part of its Entente trade. Germany's U-boats had not yet made significant inroads on Allied shipping; February statistics indicated slight losses.

The president realized that American security was not in jeopardy. Historian John A. Thompson has found that few American commentators predicted German victory; most envisaged stalemate or an Allied triumph.[19] Even if the Central Powers did win the war, Wilson believed, it would take years for them to recover from the carnage. War plans of both the U.S. Army and the

U.S. Navy, as well as measures recently taken by the armed forces, concentrated on hemispheric defense rather than an overseas expeditionary force.

Several factors led to Wilson's choice. Germany's U-boat warfare was paramount. Had it not been for Berlin's announcement of January 31, the president probably would not have issued a call to arms. Only by entering the conflict, he believed, could the nation preserve its maritime rights. Historian Robert W. Tucker conveys Wilson's logic: "Once a nation's rights were abandoned through fear of the price required to defend them, its very sovereignty would be placed in jeopardy."[20] Ironically, in one sense, the chief executive was requesting war in order to preserve his nation's rights as a neutral. Connected were matters of honor, prestige, and respect, crucial in his eyes to the vitality of any great power.

The president deemed armed neutrality unworkable. By late March the chief executive had written several people to the effect that the defense of neutral rights involved shooting submarines on sight, something that was practically an act of war. He informed Washington attorney and shipping entrepreneur Matthew Hale that Germany "would treat any persons who fell into her hands from the ships that attacked her submarines as beyond the pale of law. Apparently, to make even the measures of defense legitimate, we must obtain the status of belligerents." The president's naval advisers told him that legally armed neutrality entailed a state of war; hence, if the United States was already in a de facto conflict, it should have the privileges that went with formal belligerency.[21] Furthermore, adhering to the status quo involved severe military handicaps. Submarines could submerge, but merchantmen must remain afloat. Therefore, the heavy guns on deck posed an unequal match for the torpedo.

Recent sinkings revealed that armed neutrality did not save lives and property. It merely inflamed the American public while lacking such benefits as psychological release and the opportunity to influence the postwar settlement. Add the Zimmermann cable and one possessed ample evidence that diplomatic overtures did not influence Germany's militaristic rulers. Much of Wilson's despair, writes Link, "stemmed from the fact that events beyond his control were impelling the nation blindly into a war it did not want."[22]

Conversely, continuing at peace could simply lead to Wilson's isolation and revilement. A nation already divided would have experienced deeper splits than ever, with its own internal stability threatened. Credibility was certainly an issue. If Wilson retreated, writes Ernest R. May, "he would, in effect, prove America incapable of exercising influence compatible with her population, resources, and ideals." "What weight," asks the scholar Patrick Devlin, "could anyone attach to guarantees given by a nation which quaked at the thunder of the guns?"[23]

Belligerency would also give the United States the opportunity to influence the peace. According to Link, Wilson thought the war was in its final stages. Europe was headed for stalemate, unable to suffer further agony. The president possibly thought that once Germany "shot her submarine bolt" and the Allies failed in an impending offensive, both sides would be ready to negotiate a peace. Decisive American engagement would help end the conflict and create a popular revolution within Germany. Wilson did not envision the sending of massive numbers of troops to replenish the trenches of Europe; he believed that American support would focus upon finance, war supplies, and naval action. As historian David R. Woodward writes: "The ·U.S. Army's role was largely destined to be psychological."[24]

Although possibly a less significant motive, American participation would give Wilson leverage with the Allies as well as bargaining power with Berlin. The United States could help guarantee the peace settlement, in part by fostering a postwar league. On February 28 the president told an EPF delegation that participation in the conflict would permit the United States to sit at the peace table rather than simply call "through a crack in the door."[25]

Certain reasons occasionally given for war lack credibility. Wilson did not advocate belligerency in order to rescue the Allies. By the middle of 1916, he retained little partiality toward them. According to Link, the president desired the military hegemony of Britain, France, and Russia no more than that of the Central Powers. He not only lacked any illusions concerning Allied war aims; if anything, he did not give the British adequate credit for their idealism.[26]

Wilson did not believe that the Entente stood on the verge of defeat. He was not aware of the great toll that U-boats were suddenly taking of Allied and neutral shipping. The Germans sank over 550,000 tons in March, over 850,000 tons in April. The president remained ignorant of France's manpower shortages and was unaware of the shattered morale of the French, whose army units soon engaged in open mutiny. Russia's March revolution enhanced Allied optimism, for it promised more vigorous activity on Germany's eastern front. Certainly a population liberated from an oppressive monarchy would support the war effort vigorously.

Public opinion was not determinant. The Zimmermann cable plus the news conveyed on March 18 of the three sinkings created some war sentiment within the Senate and the urban press. Nonetheless, the great majority of Americans and most journals were as hesitant as Wilson himself. No irresistible demand for entering the conflict existed. Many members of the House of Representatives remained uncommitted to military measures. Link finds lacking any "great, overwhelming, and irresistible national demand" for war. John Milton Cooper Jr., noting that ordinary citizens were not in a belligerent mood, maintains that "Wilson could have carried majorities in Congress and among the public with him in virtually any direction he chose."[27]

Economic factors were more complex. William Jennings Bryan informed his brother Charles that eastern financiers were forcing the nation into war in order to protect their war loans to the Allies. By the time the United States entered the conflict, American bankers had made over $2 billion worth of war loans. Ross Gregory notes that the provisioning of Britain and France led to the very U-boat warfare that made war appear unavoidable. Conversely, Gregory goes on, the severance of such European ties could have guaranteed peace. He nonetheless finds that this trajectory remained unacceptable to the American people, much less to the Wilson administration. By 1916, he asserts, such disengagement would have been economically disastrous.[28]

Wilson himself did not think in economic terms. Preserving Wall Street's stake in the Allied effort was far from his mind. He was no friend of big business, which had recently fought his reelection. The Federal Reserve warning of November 1916 suggests that the nation would willingly have forgone further grants of credit to the belligerents.

U.S. trade counted for comparatively little in the world economy and maritime shipping constituted at best a minor enterprise. Americans owned comparatively few oceangoing freighters. Two-thirds of Britain's imports arrived in ships that flew the Union Jack. If U.S. ships remained off the Atlantic, Britain still had the means to transport many needed goods.

Economists and public officials feared overdependence upon the war boom. Link maintains that the majority would have gladly sacrificed prosperity for peace. After the heavy casualties suffered in Europe during the latter part of 1916, a guilt-ridden American public experienced serious qualms concerning the basis of their newly acquired wealth.[29] To that end, Wilson sought no conflict, provided, that is, Germany would permit American merchantmen to travel, obey the rules of cruiser warfare, and safeguard human life on passenger vessels. But he had little hope.

On April 2, at eight thirty on a rainy evening, Wilson delivered his war message to a joint session of Congress. An unprecedented ovation lasted a full two minutes before he could·speak. In what Cooper calls the greatest address of his life, he reviewed Germany's policy of unrestricted submarine attacks, which he labeled "warfare against mankind."[30] Beginning on January 31, 1917, Germany had "set every restriction aside," ruthlessly sinking ships "of every kind, whatever their flag, their character, their cargo, their destination, their errand." Even hospital ships and those sending relief supplies to occupied Belgium were not exempt. "Property can be paid for; the lives of peaceful and innocent people cannot be." His newly adopted policy of armed neutrality could not work; it would draw the United States into war without providing for either "the rights or the effectiveness of belligerents." The Germans intimated that they would treat American armed merchantmen as pirates. With "the most sacred rights of our nation and our people" at stake, "we will not choose the path of submission."

Coming to the crux of the matter, Wilson asked Congress to recognize that a state of war—in his words, "nothing less than war"—already existed between the United States and Germany. To place the nation on a combat footing, America must levy higher taxes, increase financial support of the Allies, and outfit a fully equipped navy. Half a million men must immediately be added to the army, preferably through "universal military liability to service." The last request drew particularly great applause.

The chief executive denied that the German people were responsible for the war; rather, the conflict was rooted "in the interests of dynasties or of little groups of ambitious men who were accustomed to use their fellow men as pawns and tools." In the course of his address, he attacked "the Prussian autocracy" for filling "our unsuspecting communities and even our offices of government with spies" and setting "criminal intrigues everywhere." In an obvious reference to the Zimmermann telegram, he accused Berlin of stirring up "enemies against us at our very doors."

Wilson expressed delight to be free of the embarrassment of association with Russia's despotic regime, calling that nation "a fit partner for a League of Honour," a country always "democratic at heart, in all the vital habit of her thought, in all the intimate relationships of her people." The deposed Romanov government "was not in fact Russian in origin, character, or purpose."

In approaching the postwar settlement, Wilson spoke of "a partnership of democratic nations," "a league of honor, a partnership of opinion." The

United States was fighting "for the ultimate peace of the world and for the liberation of its peoples, the German peoples included: for the rights of nations great and small and the privilege of men everywhere to choose their way of life and of obedience. The world must be made safe for democracy. Its peace must be planted upon the tested foundations of political liberty." The president conceded that he faced "a distressing and oppressive duty. . . . It is a fearful thing to lead this great peaceful people into the most terrible and disastrous of all wars, civilization itself seeming to be in the balance." He concluded by promising that the United States would fight for what it had always treasured—"for democracy, for the right of those who submit to authority to have a voice in their own Governments, for the rights and liberties of small nations, for a universal dominion of right by such a concert of free peoples as shall bring peace and safety to all nations and make the world itself at last free." He ended with a sentence reminiscent of Martin Luther: "God helping her, she can do no other."[31]

Most of Congress reacted warmly, interrupting his speech several times with applause. Henry Cabot Lodge, who had just been physically attacked by a war opponent, told Wilson: "Mr. President, you have expressed in the loftiest manner possible the sentiments of the American people." La Follette stood motionless, chewing gum and smiling sardonically.[32]

The press supported the president. Wilson's call for war, according to the *Literary Digest,* inspired a vigorous and unanimous response. Hearst's *New York American* endorsed Wilson's speech, hoping that circumstances might permit the conquest of Mexico, a possible German ally. "War it is. So be it!" The *New Yorker Staats-Zeitung* saw in this grave hour "but one duty— America!" Many German American papers concurred with this stance. To Roosevelt, Wilson's message ranked "among the great state papers." Relief administrator Herbert Hoover foresaw "no hope for democracy or liberty unless the system which brought the world into this unfathomable misery can be stamped out once for all."[33]

Because La Follette, as was his legal prerogative, prevented the Senate from immediately considering a war resolution, it did not do so until two days later. The relevant measure, drafted by Democratic floor leader Thomas S. Martin, specified that Germany had thrust a state of belligerency upon the United States. It directed the president "to employ the entire naval and military forces of the United States and the resources of the Government to carry on war against the Imperial German Government." The Foreign

Relations Committee drafted the resolution, although its chairman, Senator Stone, remained in opposition.[34]

The debate began at 10:00 A.M. and continued until 11:11 P.M. Additional remarks were placed in the appendix of the *Congressional Record*. During the thirteen hours of debate and as revealed in appendix entries, most vocal participants favored war. Of the nineteen who spoke for Martin's resolution, the great majority stressed maritime rights. To Kentucky's Ollie James, "the blood-spattered monarch of Germany" had turned "the open sea, the gift of God to all mankind," into a death zone. Claude A. Swanson maintained that unless the nation defended its rights, "Old Glory will be sunk to low depths of shame and humiliation." To LeBaron B. Colt (R-R.I.), the United States had been drawn into a state of hostilities just "as if a German battleship had bombarded the City of New York and killed innocent non-combatants."[35]

Certain senators offered more altruistic reasons for fighting. Henry L. Myers (D-Mont.) declared that "the democracy, the civilization, the Christianization of the world are at stake." Henry Cabot Lodge argued that "the very security" of a "proud and high-spirited nation" lay at issue. Adding an ideological note, he looked toward a peace "broad-based on freedom and democracy, a world not controlled by a Prussian military autocracy, by Hohenzollerns and Hapsburgs, but by the will of the free people of the earth."[36]

Other prowar senators strongly differed. Ohioan Warren Harding denied he was voting in "the name of democracy," declaring that it was not America's business to determine the type of government preferred by a foreign power. Borah, who harbored personal misgivings, asserted that the United States was entering the conflict solely "to use force against those who use force against us."[37]

In explaining their vote, a few senators stressed the need for national unity. Lodge saw the conflict purging the nation of "national degeneracy," "national cowardice," "the division of our people into race groups." Commercial imperatives were raised. Three-fifths of America's export trade, warned Gilbert M. Hitchcock, remained in imminent danger. "At once we would be precipitated from great prosperity to acute financial and industrial distress."[38]

Other senators focused on America's destiny. In endorsing participation in the war, Henry F. Ashurst spoke of the nation's "historic position as the leader and noble pioneer in the vanguard of progress and human liberty." Strategic factors were occasionally added. Better, asserted John Sharp Williams, to fight Germany in Europe, where one had powerful allies, than face it alone later. Paul O. Husting (D-Wis.) feared that a victorious Germany would bar the United States from the oceans of the world. "Let Germany defeat Russia tomorrow," Key Pittman warned, "and the day after tomorrow it will be our turn." Others did not envision any commitment of American troops overseas. William S. Kenyon, in arguing that "patience has its limitations," denied that the resolution dictated the dispatch of any soldier abroad.[39]

The resolution's opponents made up in rhetoric what they lacked in numbers. In the course of a four-hour speech, La Follette attacked the assumptions behind Wilson's war message. The notion that a submarine campaign involved war against mankind was fantastic; certainly many neutral nations did not see the fate of the world at stake. Contrary to the president's implication that only the Germans took lives, Britain, too, killed Americans. Two U.S. ships, the *Carib* and the *Evelyn,* had fallen victim to British mines. To contend that hostilities involved no quarrel with the German people was absurd, for in any war it was the enemy's population that invariably bore the burden of suffering. The claim that the conflict advanced democracy signified a sheer denial of reality, because France and the new Russia (technically the sole republics among the Allies) alone represented any fresh political order. Britain's hereditary monarchy remained based on restricted suffrage and grinding exploitation of its laborers. Of its war aims "we know nothing." As far as the cause of domestic reform went, the municipal and social measures of Imperial Germany outstripped those of its enemies. Besides, in undertaking this crusade, the president lacked popular support. Had there been a popular referendum, the public would have voted ten to one against entering the conflict. When the Wisconsin senator finished, John Sharp Williams called the speech "pro-German, pro-Goth, pro-Vandal" as well as "anti-President, anti-Congress, and anti-American"; the address "would have better become Herr Bethmann-Hollweg."[40]

In opposing Wilson's war message, Norris accused Wall Street of fomenting American intervention. The huge loans to the Allies, he asserted, gave the United States a massive stake in the war's outcome. Millions of babies would die of hunger "because we want to preserve the commercial right of American citizens to deliver munitions of war to belligerent nations." The United States was going to war upon "the command of gold. . . . We are about to put the dollar sign on the American flag." At this point James A. Reed accused the senator of grazing "the edge of treason." Denying that the nation would enter the war to protect commercial profits, the Missouri Democrat claimed that America's honor and integrity lay at stake.[41]

Certain issues were directly joined. Key Pittman took on Asle J. Gronna's plea for a national referendum, asserting that the nation had already conducted a de facto vote; in practically every state the legislatures supported the president. He similarly challenged calls for arbitration, declaring that the invasion of Belgium proved Germany's word worthless.[42]

Senator Porter McCumber offered a substitute resolution. The United States, he thought, should insist that belligerents obey traditional rules of seizure and ensure the safety of crew and passengers. If a single American ship was henceforth sunk in violation of international law, the action would trigger the use of the nation's "entire naval and military forces." He conceded that he was giving Germany a last chance to retreat, but he preferred to enter the war with 100 percent of the population behind the effort rather than a mere 80 percent. He mustered only one vote: his own.[43]

In the end, eighty-two senators voted for the war resolution. The six opponents included Gronna, La Follette, Norris, Lane, Stone, and Vardaman. Kirby and Cummins opposed the measure but did not want to add to the nation's discord. Seven of the eight absent members avowed that they would have supported the proposal.[44]

The following day, April 5, marked the House's turn to vote on an identical resolution. Congressman Hal D. Flood, who chaired the Foreign Affairs Committee, introduced the measure. Two of the seventeen committee members were opposed. Henry Allen Cooper, the ranking Republican, held the British blockade responsible for present conditions. Dorsey Shackleford (D-Mo.), the ranking Democrat, feared participation in "intrigues and alliances with European countries whose jealousies keep them in constant conflict."[45]

The debate began at 10:00 A.M. and ended at 3:12 A.M. on the following morning. About 100 members spoke on the resolution, 78 in favor of war. Others published their views in the *Congressional Record*'s appendix, as some senators had. Almost half the resolution's defenders stressed Germany's submarine attacks. "The time for any neutrality is passed," Flood remarked: "We are at war now." Republican House leader Mann referred to Germany's deliberate affront. Scott Ferris asserted that America was fighting "only for the preservation of our modest and undoubted right to be free, to be left alone." Joe H. Eagle (D-Tex.) spoke in terms of idle ships and freight cars, leading to the closing of factories and falling farm prices. "Strikes and riots will prevail" if the United States stays aloof. Walter A. Watson (D-Va.)

feared for "the tobacco grower of Virginia, the cotton planter of Carolina, the cattle raiser of Texas, the wheat farmer of Minnesota." Clarence B. Miller (R-Minn.), quoting (quite incorrectly) from a "secret" provision of the Zimmermann cable, accused Germany of training Pancho Villa's men, supplying Mexico with arms, and planning a submarine base there. William P. Borland (D-Mo.) cited the sinking of the unarmed American steamer *Missourian* the previous day as evidence that Germany continued to disregard American rights.[46] (About four thirty the previous afternoon *U-52* had attacked the vessel, the property of the American-Hawaiian Line. Returning from Genoa to New York and carrying ballast, the ship was destroyed twenty-five miles off the Italian-French border; no one was lost.)

Fewer than one-third of those speaking referred to a better international order. Augustus P. Gardner specifically denied that he sought to sacrifice "the lives of thousands of the flower of our youth" in order to avenge the loss of two hundred Americans. At stake were nothing less than "the rights of man." Some speakers disputed certain claims of administration opponents. Flood, for example, maintained that German mines, not British ones, sank the *Evelyn* and the *Carib*.[47]

American contributions, several representatives surmised, would be limited to supplies and naval operations. Seldom was full-fledged combat on the western front anticipated. "There is no reason to believe this will be a long war," remarked Edward W. Saunders (D-Va.), as he pointed to British victories from the Marne to Mesopotamia. Former House Speaker Joe Cannon noted: "We have got our hands full on this continent, with our Monroe doctrine, taking proper care of our own defense and our own protection." Fiorello La Guardia (R-N.Y.), writing in 1948, maintained that at least 60 percent of those House members who voted for war did not think that the United States would send a single soldier abroad.[48]

Anti-interventionists challenged Flood's resolution. Charles F. Reavis (R-Neb.) contrasted "entangling alliances" with "splendid isolation." Clarence Dill (D-Wash.) refused to "send the boys to the European trenches" in order to "trade with the countries now at war." One could not spread democracy by joining such monarchical powers as Japan, Italy, and England, "whose 500 years of history has left a bloody trail on every continent of the world." William J. Cary (R-Wis.) denied that any of the Allies fought for liberty: Britain sought control of the seas, France desired Alsace and Lorraine, Russia coveted Constantinople and control of the Balkans, and smaller nations wanted "what crumbs may fall their way." Isaac Sherwood, who sought arbitration, linked the shipping of wheat and corn overseas to bread riots taking place in New York, Philadelphia, and Chicago. The newly elected Ernest Lundeen (R-Minn.) warned against America's "fixed determination . . . to thrust democracy with loving bayonets down the throats of unwilling peoples." Henry Allen Cooper argued that if prowar legislators were so concerned about the rights of American citizens, why did they not protest against the disruption of antiwar meetings in Philadelphia and Baltimore? Edward J. King (R-Ill.) opposed war on the ground that the nation was not prepared for military action. He quoted retired Major General George W. Goethals, who called the American army "a mere mob without training, clothing, or equipment, and useless for any purpose."[49]

Several members denied that the public welcomed hostilities. Lundeen cited a poll of fifty-four thousand voters in his district as revealing a ten-to-one ratio against entering the conflict. Denver S. Church (D-Calif.) alleged that 98 percent of the entire American public was opposed to intervention. To Meyer London, Wilson's call for compulsory military service offered sufficient proof that the president could not convince his people.[50]

Soon after midnight on Good Friday morning, Claude Kitchin took the floor. The United States, he contended, was confronting Germany, not Britain, simply because America honored the British war zone while challenging the legality of Germany's. Even now Berlin neither planned to invade the United States nor sought its territory. Were the United States confronted with the same blockade to which Germany was subjected, it would act no differently than the Reich. Tom Heflin (D-Ala.) told the North Carolinian to resign immediately, a suggestion that drew hisses. Known for his hot temper, Heflin snapped: "You may hiss, you who represent the Kaiser and not the President of the United States!"[51] Speculation varied widely on the number of Kitchin's supporters. Estimates ranged from twelve to fifty.

The House rejected several amendments by voice vote. Roscoe Conkling McCulloch (R-Ohio) sought special congressional approval before allowing American troops to be sent overseas. His proposal restricted participation to engagements on the high seas, thereby prohibiting involvement "in a controversy on another continent where we have no direct interest." Similarly Charles H. Sloan (R-Neb.) suggested that American involvement be limited to meeting injuries on the oceans rather than prosecuting "a foreign war for the regulation of European affairs." Fred Britten sought to continue Wilson's armed-neutrality policy; only volunteers should be sent abroad unless Congress decided otherwise. The public, he claimed, opposed war by as much as a thousand to one.[52]

Early that morning the House passed the war resolution 373-50.[53] Not since the War of 1812 had more negative votes been cast against a war resolution in either congressional chamber. If the tallies included those who were absent but who registered their sentiments, the party lineup revealed 35 Republican opponents, 18 Democrats, and 1 Socialist.

Many antiwar congressmen came from the more progressive wings of their parties, followers of La Follette or Bryan. A sectional breakdown indicates that thirty-two represented the Midwest, twelve the South, and nine the West. Meyer London alone came from the East. Opposition was rooted in such factors as hatred of Wall Street finance, the influence of a large German American constituency, and distrust of the Democratic president. Legislators representing German American communities voted on both sides of the questions. One war opponent, Missouri Democrat William Igoe, saw "abundant justification for war" but stated that he could not go against the wishes of his St. Louis constituents.[54] Dissenters represented other cities as well, including New York City, Chicago, Minneapolis, St. Paul, Denver, Los Angeles, and Milwaukee.

At least four senators and up to fifty House members voted against their personal antiwar sentiments, stressing the need for national unity. In particular, much of the South was won over not merely by party loyalty but a desire, fostered by Wilson, to demonstrate patriotism in time of crisis. Conducting a personal poll of senators, Frances M. Witherspoon, daughter of a Mississippi congressman, found that fewer than half the membership believed that circumstances necessitated war. In a similar canvass of the House, she discovered that 60 percent were decidedly opposed to war; a mere 25 percent were strongly in favor. Oswald Garrison Villard later recalled two congressional polls, one taken at the end of March, indicating that a secret ballot would have produced a large majority against intervention.[55]

At 1:18 p.m. on April 6, Wilson signed the war resolution in the lobby of the White House. The nation was now at war.

"All public reactions," Link writes, "indicated that the President had voiced the deepest thoughts and convictions and highest resolves of a united people." The Literary Digest found the press reaction vigorous and unanimous. Major economic, religious, and ethnic groups backed Wilson. Business periodicals had often feared that war would reduce profits but cited patriotism as the reason for entering the conflict. Several publications concurred with the *Journal of Commerce and Commercial Bulletin*, which said: "We have no army to send to Europe and no desire to send one." In mid-March the moderate wing of the labor movement, represented by the executive committee of the American Federation of Labor, pledged the service of 3 million members in any impending war. Protestant and Roman Catholic leaders endorsed Wilson's call. Jewish leaders, too, favored entering the conflict. The overthrow of the czar, they hoped, would end pogroms. Most Irish and German Americans rallied behind Wilson, *Viereck's* magazine proclaiming on its cover: "We are at last finally at war with Germany and we shall obtain, by force of arms, redress for the indignities we have suffered at her hands."[56]

Not everyone favored involvement, particularly in strong German American areas. The vote was 10 to 1 against war in Monroe, Wisconsin, 4,117 to 17 in Sheboygan. In one Wisconsin town, Manitowoc, the prowar side drew a mere 15 votes. A Socialist rally in New York booed upon hearing of Wilson's message; the gathering predicted class war in the nation.[57]

Despite the surface consensus, the decision for war did not engender widespread enthusiasm. The national mood reflected more resignation than eagerness, insofar as it is possible to measure such an elusive phenomenon. Most people believed that the nation sought to vindicate its rights, honor, and self-respect, not to advance the cause of humanity, preserve the balance of power, foster the aims of the Allies, or establish self-government. In neither House nor Senate did many legislators speak of making the world "safe for democracy." They focused on national honor and maritime rights. The pro-Entente *New Republic* noted either indifference or reluctance in the American majority, positing that a small but influential group of intellectuals—professors, physicians, clergymen, lawyers—took on "the effective and decisive work on behalf of war." It did warn that Germany's success would almost inevitably lead to "the defeat of the Russian Revolution, the absorption of the small nations of Central Europe, the humiliation of France, the monopolization of the road to the East, the disintegration of the British Commonwealth which is to arise out of the Empire, the terrorizing of the Americas, and a fastening upon the whole civilized world of a system of aggressive politics backed by an illiberal collectivism and a thorough conscription of human life. No league for peace could be organized, and for no great nation would fundamental democratic reform be possible."[58]

On the eve of the conflict, the United States, as John Patrick Finnegan notes, remained "a classic example of unpreparedness." The army was small, ranking seventeenth in the world. It did not have tanks, flamethrowers, mortars, grenades, gas masks, and heavy field howitzers. It possessed fewer than two thousand machine guns. The availability of 742 field pieces and forty-three heavier guns could not fill the gap. Its field artillery lacked sufficient rounds to sustain bombardment on the western front for more than a few minutes. Its air arm consisted of a few ill-assorted flying machines. The small National Guard was woefully inadequate, despite its recent service on the Mexican border. Most ships needed repair; 90 percent were not fully manned. The navy needed experience in the very antisubmarine warfare that would be its primary task. Relatively speaking, the United States had been better prepared in the American Revolution and the War of 1812. Compounding America's problems were incredibly unrealistic war plans. The first, designed for an American expeditionary force and drafted in late March 1917, provided for an invasion of Bulgaria through Greece and of France through the Netherlands. The president could perhaps have taken some comfort in House's claim, made on March 19, that neither the French nor the British as yet desired an American army in Europe.[59]

Historians still debate the focus and wisdom of Wilson's war message. Ernest R. May praises the president for emphasizing the immediate needs of his nation. Rather than calling upon the United States to prevent a German victory, overturn authoritarian and militarist ideologies, and preserve Anglo-American control of the seas, the president wisely focused on fending off threats to America's economic power and international prestige. Wilson's government, writes Edward H. Buehrig, realized that Congress would offer significant support only over the issue of neutral rights: "The Administration had been caught in the unenviable position where the larger purpose," that is, the universal aspirations of democracy, "depended on the smaller."[60]

Other historians are more critical. John W. Coogan first notes Wilson's claim that the United States was forced into the conflict because, in the president's words, "there are no other means of defending our rights," but he indicts the chief executive for undermining the system of international law he claimed to defend. At best his war message "indicates Wilson's capacity for self-delusion; at worst it indicates his capacity for hypocrisy." After all, for two years the nation's leader had failed to maintain a genuine neutrality.[61]

Robert Endicott Osgood finds possible merit in American entry because German U-boats might have rendered the British Isles helpless. Certainly the Treaty of Brest Litovsk (1918), which transferred huge amounts of Russian territory to other governments, showed that a victorious Germany would embody an infinitely greater threat to American ideals and interests than would any Allied settlement. He accuses the president, however, of linking American rights to those of mankind, even resorting to motifs of holy war as a rationale for entering the struggle. Wilson should have focused on national self-interest rather than bringing up any mission to help rescue the world.[62]

Lloyd E. Ambrosius faults Wilson for ignoring Europe's balance of power, which had been the traditional system for preserving peace on the Continent. During the period of neutrality, the president showed little interest in the belligerents' war aims and remained indifferent to possible victory by the Central Powers, simply entering the struggle after Germany attacked American ships. He failed to coordinate political goals and military strategy, neglecting to prepare American armed forces to fight overseas while simply stressing a postwar association of nations and a new era of peace.[63]

John A. Thompson views Wilson's legacy with ambivalence. Had the United States not declared war on Germany, hopes of an Allied victory could hardly have survived the combination of Britain's financial difficulties, Italy's military failure, the abysmal morale of the French army, and the continued collapse of the Russian front in early 1918. Either a negotiated peace would have resulted or the Central Powers would have been able to dictate terms. "It is inconceivable that Germany would have suffered the kind of defeat she did in 1918 or the kind of terms imposed by the Treaty of Versailles. Since these experiences and the resentments they bred contributed so largely to Hitler's rise to power, it is almost certain that Europe would have been spared at least some of the horrors of the 1930s and 1940s."[64]

To help resolve such views, further reflections are necessary.

11

Conclusion

To EVALUATE AMERICAN POLICY during the first half of World War I, one must focus on the leadership of Woodrow Wilson. As president he held responsibility for the individuals he chose to advise him and execute his policies. Here, far too often, the chief executive made poor choices. Secretary of State Bryan remained an inept moralist, for whom every broad problem could be solved by a dogmatic form of neutrality and every narrow one by cooling-off treaties. Colonel House, although far more cosmopolitan, was equally inexperienced at diplomacy. Given the sensitive nature of his missions, his capacity for self-deception made him much more dangerous than Bryan. Robert Lansing revealed himself a disloyal subordinate, undercutting the president when Wilson undertook his December 1916 peace initiative to end the war. The president retained two major ambassadors at major posts despite their pronounced drawbacks. Page was so pro-British that he could not properly represent his nation; Gerard was so inept that Joseph Grew handled many significant matters. Except for House, Wilson was aware of the many defects of his subordinates, but he retained them in places of trust.

As far as European policies were concerned, Wilson compiled a mixed record. His prewar writings stressed the need for markets and an Open Door global economy. In 1914, with his nation in recession, he realized that the need to sell overseas was greater than ever. Given this outlook, he understandably found it difficult to see what the United States could gain by challenging the British blockade, a policy that would force confrontation with the world's greatest sea power. Admittedly, the president's acquiescence bolstered German accusations of rank partiality, particularly given the huge quantities of armament shipped to the Allies. Britain stood in flagrant violation of international law, a matter that did not go unnoticed in Washington. American diplomats devoted countless man hours to such matters as contraband, continuous voyage, and stop-and-search proceedings.

In 1936 historian Charles A. Beard wrote *The Devil Theory of War,* based on a series of articles he had written for the *New Republic.* The Columbia historian, prowar in 1917, showed himself fiercely anti-interventionist two decades later. He aptly argued that only radical changes in America's economic system, centering on the necessity of absorbing industrial and agricultural surpluses at home, could have served as an alternative policy. Rather than blame bankers, "politicians," and munitions-makers, as many opinion leaders of his time were doing, Beard found the American public, focused on the desire to export its products, bearing ultimate responsibility.[1] He titled one chapter "War Is Our Own Work."

Had the United States resisted the British blockade, it would have needed some means of enforcing its policies. Could Wilson have ordered warships to escort American merchantmen? With pacifistic-minded Bryanites dominating in the House of Representatives, would the legislators have acquiesced in such a costly and brazen military move? Could the president have carried the public with him? Such suppositions are at best problematic.

None of this is to argue that Wilson practiced the most astute diplomacy. Consider the outcome of the president's three major aims: to keep the United States out of war, to uphold the right to sell American goods without hindrance, and to negotiate a conflict that he realized was becoming increasingly fratricidal. At certain crucial junctures, his policies proved counterproductive to these goals.

In the American note of February 10, 1915, the president held the Germans to "strict accountability" concerning the destruction of "an American vessel or the lives of American citizens on the high seas."[2] Yet, as John Milton Cooper Jr. shows, the missive did not specify precisely what this strict accountability might mean or how one could hold the Germans to proper behavior. Had counselor Lansing, who drafted the message, limited his concern to protecting American citizens on American ships, rather than on those of the belligerent nations, the United States would not have been in the quandary it soon found itself in. As it was, a single American traveler journeying on a British vessel appeared to confer immunity from attack by German U-boats. Lansing purposely and irresponsibly obscured the issue. In a personal letter dated just over two weeks later, he admitted as much, calling this particular matter "open to interpretation."[3]

Wilson's first *Lusitania* note, of May 13, 1915, reveals the baneful consequences of "strict accountability," the policy he specifically evoked in this communication. Not only did the president demand an apology and reparations; he required that all U-boat warfare be abandoned. Wilson insisted that Germany give up its only potentially effective weapon against the British blockade, by invoking rules that had been obsolete since the invention of the submarine. Furthermore, as Thomas A. Bailey and Paul B. Ryan cogently observe, the president claimed an immunity for his countrymen that British subjects sailing on the same vessels, if these ships were offensively armed or resisting attack, could not demand for themselves.[4]

The House-Grey memorandum of February 16, 1915, manifests diplomatic amateurism at its worst. Wilson sent the colonel to Britain primarily to persuade its leaders to lift its blockade. Secretly defying the president, House uncritically supported England's war effort. More significantly, he committed his nation, under certain conditions, to enter the conflict on the Allied side. Admittedly, Wilson qualified any pledge of American intervention by inserting the word "probably." But why, upon House's return, did Wilson express profuse gratitude to him? Here is a president of the United States entrusting to a rank novice the most sensitive of negotiations, focusing on an agreement that might lead to dispatching millions of American troops overseas and drastically altering the world's balance of power. Of course, no commitment could occur without congressional approval, but House was playing a most dangerous game. The fact that the American people knew nothing of parlays that could radically affect their lives appears particularly haunting in the days of "the imperial presidency."

Also disturbing is Wilson's reaction to the sinking of the Italian passenger liner *Ancona* in early November 1915, a disaster that took nine American lives. According to Link, the president unintentionally permitted Lansing to send a virtual ultimatum to Vienna.[5] Although more temperate policies soon prevailed, Wilson had irresponsibly permitted a pro-Entente secretary of state to engage in brinkmanship.

Lansing and Wilson again revealed their ineptitude when they proposed the modus vivendi of January 1916. This proposal provided for the disarmament of Allied merchantmen, which would mount no guns. In return, the Central Powers would observe traditional rules of cruiser warfare, that is, submarines would fire only after giving previous warning and assuring the safety of all people on board. Washington soon had to backtrack because of House's sensitive negotiations in London and the sudden exposure of unarmed merchantmen to German U-boats, for Berlin was undoubtedly much encouraged by Lansing's overture. The episode left the British with the decided impression that the United States was at best confused, at worst hostile.

In his public letter to William J. Stone of February 24, 1916, Wilson revealed a dangerous rigidity. The Missouri senator argued that those Americans "recklessly risking their lives on armed belligerent ships" were committing "a sort of moral treason against the Republic." Wilson replied the same day, declaring that he could not abridge any right of Americans without sacrificing the nation's honor and self-respect. Referring to "many other humiliations" and "the whole fine fabric of international law," he saw at issue "the very essence of the things that have made America a sovereign nation."[6] The president did not recognize that this "fine fabric" was already outmoded, stubbornly insisting upon immunity for British ships that transported Americans.

On April 2, 1917, when Wilson asked Congress to recognize that a state of war existed between the United States and Imperial Germany, he combined the need to uphold American neutral rights with the advancement of universalistic goals. The United States, he said, would fight "for the ultimate peace of the world and the liberation of its peoples"; it would enter the conflict to establish "the rights of nations great and small and the privilege of men everywhere to choose their way of life and of obedience." The president did not suggest any specific military threat to the nation, or even to the Western Hemisphere, much less convey what concrete power relationships should replace the global equilibrium as it had existed before 1914. Although Wilson vaguely hinted at conscription, he gave no indication of what role the American military would play in the European war. Would Congress commit the nation to transporting doughboys overseas, who would be engaged in ground fighting, or would the nation limit its contribution to supplying money and material goods to the Allies? If, as he maintained, civilization itself appeared to lie "in the balance," he should have offered far greater clarification. He simply spoke of an end to Germany's U-boat "warfare against mankind" and advanced vague and utopian war aims that bore little relationship to his eloquent rationale for a "peace without victory."[7]

In August 1919, at a meeting between Wilson and the Senate Foreign Relations Committee, Senator McCumber asked him if "the unrighteousness of the German war would have brought us into this war even if Germany had not committed any acts against us." The president responded: "I hope it would eventually, Senator, as things developed." The Dakota senator pressed this point, asking, "You think we would have gotten in anyway?" to which the president responded, "I do."[8] Unfortunately for the historian, Senator Brandegee interrupted this colloquy and the questioning took a different turn. Hence we do not know why Wilson foresaw the United States as ultimately a full-scale participant in the Great War.

Wilson might well have been speaking in the wake of wartime passions. Certainly, without Germany's submarine activity, it would have been most difficult for him to have taken America into the conflict. Even had he so desired (a proposition that remains highly dubious), he would have experienced extreme difficulty had not the Germans kept sinking U.S. merchant ships while making no provision for their crews. If, by many indications, the public in early 1917 was not anxious to enter the conflict, it was the continued U-boat warfare that brought about American participation.

Although Wilson privately voiced strong pro-Entente views early in the conflict, expressing outrage at Germany's conquest of Belgium, by 1916 British activities made him far more neutral in sentiment. Yet he never revealed a genuine knowledge of what had caused the Great War. During the presidential campaign of that year, he told a Cincinnati audience that "nothing in particular" had started it but "everything in general." He then spoke vaguely about "a mutual suspicion," "an interlacing of alliances and understandings, a complex web of intrigue and spying, that presently was sure to entangle the whole of the family of mankind on that side of the water in its meshes." Wilson's private remarks indicate even less sophistication than his public ones, something particularly telling as they came from the mouth of a man who had been one of America's leading political scientists. In speaking privately to Ambassador Page that August, he referred to "England's having the earth and Germany's wanting it" and called the conflict "a quarrel to settle economic rivalries."[9] He did little to address the fundamental dislocations that caused this catastrophic event. Nor did he wrestle with alternative outcomes.

As historian David S. Patterson notes, not all of Wilson's failures were his fault. The United States lacked an intelligence agency that might have reported systematically on opinion in the belligerent nations. The president had no national security team to present sophisticated analyses and policy alternatives. Public opinion polls had not yet emerged, and throughout Europe there were no wartime elections. Little wonder the president was so "poorly informed and was largely acting in the shadows of reality."[10] Besides, there were few, if any, sophisticated advisers whom he could consult.

Wilson's leadership did have some positive aspects. He realized that his nation could not remain rooted in its isolationist past or continue to act uni-laterally on the world scene. He saw that membership in what he called in 1916 "any feasible association of nations" could benefit the United States, not injure it. At same time, he possessed an almost uncanny ability to sense the general sentiment of the American public and articulate it most eloquently. Although the more fervent pro-German and pro-Allied elements attacked him bitterly, he was able to maximize support for his policies. Be the mat-ter "the rape of Belgium" or revelations over German sabotage or disputes surrounding the *Falaba,* the *Lusitania,* and the *Arabic,* the president refused to exploit national anxieties. Rather, he kept calm and thereby effectively defused numerous crises. During the fall of 1916, when Germany flagrantly violated the *Sussex* pledge, he did not protest. Even when Germany declared unrestricted submarine warfare in January 1917, Wilson exercised caution. He severed diplomatic relations but would have accepted a limited form of submarine warfare if American ships had remained relatively immune. He decided for war only after U.S. ships were sunk and armed neutrality ap-peared futile.

In general, throughout several years of crisis, Wilson realized that the public sought both to remain at peace and to protect the nation's rights. He said in the wake of the *Lusitania* sinking: "I wish with all my heart I saw a way to carry out the double wish of our people, to maintain a firm front in respect of what we demand of Germany and yet do nothing that might by any possibility involve us in the war."[11]

No other political leader would have been half as skillful in this regard. Roosevelt, Bryan, Root, Lodge, La Follette, Taft—each possessed severe limitations. TR revealed himself to be blustery and bitter, alienating many erstwhile followers because he made no secret of his personal disdain for the president. Bryan sought to personify "the Christian statesman," but public manifestations of his simplistic approach revealed that he was singularly out of his depth. Root and Lodge exhibited so much pro-British partisanship that they distanced themselves from the broad populace. La Follette pos-sessed a Rooseveltian temperament, although he assumed just the opposite stance on foreign policy. His militancy on such matters as an arms embargo made him appear pro-German; his conspiratorial view of "predatory" business interests failed to impress a public suddenly benefiting from an economic boom. Taft had been soundly repudiated in the 1912 election and projected a negative charisma. Although he disliked the president personally, his views were surprisingly close to those of Wilson.

Unfortunately for the nation, the debate over preparedness did little to inform the public of the role America should play in international relations. Far too often arguments centered on absurd scenarios concerning invasion of the United States. At times Roosevelt raised serious issues about the relationship between force and statecraft, deeming powerful armed forces as essential to statecraft as effective diplomatic strategy. Far too often, however, TR and his disciples articulated a narrow nationalism, moralized about such matters as Belgium, narrowly emphasized maritime rights, and voiced suspicion of plans for postwar international organization. His volatile personality and bitter personal hatred of Wilson so skewed his judgment as to eliminate him from serious dialogue.

Arthur S. Link argues that a German victory would have seriously threatened U.S. security: "At the very least, Americans would have lived in a dangerous world if they had to deal with a militaristic and imperialistic Germany—triumphant, strident, and in effective control of Europe from the English Channel to the Urals."[12] In late August 1914, Wilson warned Colonel House that a German victory "would change the course of our civilization and make the United States a military nation."[13] In the succeeding two and a half years, the president seldom if ever pursued such reasoning, instead focusing on abstract rights. In the words of historian Norman A. Graebner: "Wilson did not inform the American people of their deep historic interest in the world equilibrium; instead, he made himself the prophet of a world free of power politics, in which the old balance of power would recede before a community of power."[14]

Wilson came belatedly to the preparedness cause, manifesting a studied vagueness during his midwestern tour early in 1916 and acting expediently in firing Secretary of War Garrison. Certainly he found it difficult to think in terms of force, strategy, and power relations. To the very eve of American entry into the conflict, few in his administration considered the possibility of fighting on European soil in order to frustrate potential hegemonic powers. Admittedly, given the nature of the Congress as reflected in such powerful leaders as James Hay, it remains doubtful whether any other leader could have been more effective in rearming the nation. In short, even had Wilson possessed a more perceptive strategic vision, he lacked political leverage.

In the end, it was Germany that forced the administration's hand, doing so at a moment when relations with Berlin were improving and those with London were growing worse. When U-boats began sinking American vessels without rescuing their crews, Wilson had run out of options. He could only hope that the conflict would justify the required sacrifice.

Notes

Abbreviations

CASR	Cecil Arthur Spring Rice
CO	*Current Opinion*
CR	*Congressional Record*
EBG	Edith Bolling Galt
EG	Edward Grey
EMH	Edward M. House
F	*Fatherland*
FCP	Frederic C. Penfield
FR	*Foreign Relations of the United States*
HCL	Henry Cabot Lodge
JCG	Joseph C. Grew
JvB	Johann von Bernstorff
JWG	James W. Gerard
LD	*Literary Digest*
LMG	Lindley M. Garrison
LP	*The Lansing Papers, 1914–1920*, 2 vols. (Washington, DC: Government Printing Office, 1939–40)
LTR	Elting E. Morison, ed., *The Letters of Theodore Roosevelt*, 8 vols. (Cambridge, MA: Harvard Univ. Press, 1951–54)
N	*Nation*
NAR	*North American Review*
NR	*New Republic*
NYA	*New York American*
NYT	*New York Times*
O	*Outlook*
OGD	Reichstag Commission of Inquiry, *Official German Documents Relating to the World War*, 2 vols. (New York: Oxford Univ. Press, 1923)
PWW	Woodrow Wilson, *The Papers of Woodrow Wilson*, ed. Arthur S. Link, 69 vols. (Princeton, NJ: Princeton Univ. Press, 1966–93)

RL   Robert Lansing
TR   Theodore Roosevelt
WGM   William Gibbs McAdoo
WHP   Walter Hines Page
WHT   William Howard Taft
WJB   William Jennings Bryan
WW   Woodrow Wilson

1. Setting the Stage

1. WW to Lucy Marshall Smith, Sept. 15, 1915, *PWW,* 34:474; George F. Kennan, *The Decline of Bismarck's European Order: Franco-Russian Relations, 1875–1890* (Princeton, NJ: Princeton Univ. Press, 1979), 3 (emphasis Kennan's).

2. Mexican war in Woodrow Wilson, *Division and Reunion* (New York: Longmans, Green, 1893), 152; Hawaiian revolution, "Mr. Cleveland as President," Jan. 15, 1897, *PWW,* 10:116; Spanish-American War, "What Ought We to Do?" c. Aug. 1, 1898, *PWW,* 10:574; American founding, speech of Oct. 28, 1910, *PWW,* 21:462; moral example, "Democracy and Efficiency," c. Oct. 1, 1900, *PWW,* 12:10–11; *NYT,* July 5, 1914, 3.

3. Wilson, New York address, Nov. 20, 1905, *PWW,* 16:228.

4. Wilson, speech, New York, Jan. 30, 1904, *PWW,* 15:149; Wilson, *Princeton University Bulletin* 12 (Oct. 20, 1900): 12.

5. Wilson, "Democracy and Efficiency," c. Oct. 1, 1900, *PWW,* 12:13; "The Theory of Organization," Nov. 2, 1898, *PWW,* 11:66; speech at Mobile, *NYT,* Oct. 28, 1913, 1.

6. Wilson, "Education and Democracy," c. May 4, 1907, *PWW,* 17:135.

7. Wilson in John Milton Cooper Jr., *Woodrow Wilson: A Biography* (New York: Knopf, 2009), 182; WW in *NYT,* Dec. 11, 1915, 4.

8. Robert W. Tucker, *Woodrow Wilson and the Great War: Reconsidering America's Neutrality, 1914–1917* (Charlottesville: Univ. of Virginia Press, 2007), 19; Stockton Axson, *"Brother Woodrow": A Memoir of Woodrow Wilson* (Princeton, NJ: Princeton Univ. Press, 1993), 231.

9. Wilson, *Constitutional Government in the United States* (New York: Columbia Univ. Press, 1908), 77; Patrick Devlin, *Too Proud to Fight: Woodrow Wilson's Neutrality* (New York: Oxford Univ. Press, 1975), 468.

10. John Milton Cooper Jr., *Walter Hines Page: The Southerner as American* (Chapel Hill: Univ. of North Carolina Press, 1977), 314; House diary, Nov. 6, 1914, *PWW,* 31:275.

11. Wilson in Arthur S. Link, *Wilson,* vol. 2, *The New Freedom* (Princeton, NJ: Princeton Univ. Press, 1956), 68.

12. Johann von Bernstorff, *My Three Years in America* (London: Skeffington and Son, 1920), 193.

13. WW in Charles Seymour, ed., *The Intimate Papers of Colonel House,* 4 vols. (Boston: Houghton Mifflin, 1926), 1:114; Tucker, *Wilson and the Great War,* 39.

14. EBG to WW, Aug. 26, 1915, *PWW,* 34:338; WW to EBG, Aug. 28, 1915, *PWW,* 34:352.

15. Jonathan Daniels, *The End of Innocence* (Philadelphia: Lippincott, 1954), 89.

16. Spoilsman, diary of Nancy Saunders Toy, Jan. 3, 1915, *PWW,* 32:10; Wilson on cooling-off, *NYT,* Sept. 5, 1919, 2.

17. John Milton Cooper Jr., *The Vanity of Power: American Isolationism and World War I, 1914–1917* (Westport, CT: Greenwood, 1969), 57; House diary, Nov. 26, 1916, *PWW,* 40:87n1.

18. Cooper, *Wilson,* 295; Lansing quoted in Daniel M. Smith, "Robert Lansing and the Formulation of American Neutrality Policies, 1914–1915," *Mississippi Valley Historical Review* 43 (June 1956): 62.

19. *War Memoirs of Robert Lansing, Secretary of State* (Indianapolis: Bobbs-Merrill, 1935), 128.

20. WW to EMH, Mar. 28, 1917, *PWW,* 41:497.

21. WW in Burton J. Hendrick, ed., *The Life and Letters of Walter H. Page,* 3 vols. (New York: Doubleday, Page, 1922–26), 2:23; WHP to Edwin A. Alderman, June 22, 1916, ibid., 2:144; WHP to Henry A. Page, n.d., ibid., 2:154.

22. Viscount Grey of Falladon, *Twenty-Five Years, 1892–1916,* 2 vols. (New York: Frederick A. Stokes, 1925), 2:110.

23. Arthur S. Link, *Wilson,* vol. 3, *The Struggle for Neutrality, 1914–1915* (Princeton, NJ : Princeton Univ. Press, 1960), 311.

24. Unidentified scholar cited in Gordon A. Craig, *Europe since 1815,* 3rd ed. (New York: Holt, Rinehart, and Winston, 1971), 356.

25. On Germany, TR to Stewart Edward White, Aug. 31, 1914, in Russell Buchanan, "Theodore Roosevelt and American Neutrality, 1914–1917," *American Historical Review* 43 (July 1938): 777; on league of nations, Kathleen Dalton, *Theodore Roosevelt: A Strenuous Life* (New York: Knopf, 2002), 446; on Wilson, TR to Kermit Roosevelt, Aug. 28, 1915, in *LTR,* vol. 8, *The Days of Armageddon, 1914–1919* (Cambridge, MA: Harvard Univ. Press, 1954), 963.

26. Roosevelt, "The World War: Its Tragedies and Its Lessons," *O* 108 (Sept. 23, 1914): 176; "Books on the War," *N* 100 (Feb. 11, 1915): 175; *NYT,* Feb. 1, 1916, 10.

27. Philip C. Jessup, *Elihu Root,* 2 vols. (New York: Dodd, Mead, 1932), 2:322–23.

28. HCL to TR, Mar. 1, 1915, in John A. Garraty, *Henry Cabot Lodge: A Biography* (New York: Knopf, 1953), 312.

29. Viereck poem, *F* 1 (Aug. 10, 1914): 3; *F* 3 (Dec. 29, 1915): cover.

30. Resolutions, "What the German-Americans Are Organizing For," *LD* 50 (Feb. 13, 1915): 300.

31. Hexamer in Reinhard R. Doerries, "Promoting *Kaiser* and *Reich*: Imperial German Propaganda in the United States during World War I," in *Confrontation and Cooperation in the Era of World War I, 1900–1924,* ed. Hans-Jürgen Schröder (Providence, RI: Berg, 1993), 146.

32. Arthur S. Link in John A. Garraty, *Interpreting American History: Conversations with Historians,* 2 vols. (New York: Macmillan, 1970), 2:127; David Wayne Hirst, "German Propaganda in the United States, 1914–1917" (Ph.D. diss., Northwestern Univ., 1962), 148.

33. James K. McGuire, *The King, the Kaiser, and Irish Freedom* (New York: Devin-Adair, 1915), 285; rally, *NYT,* Oct. 10, 1914, 11.

34. CASR to Lord Newton, Oct. 21, 1914; to Valentine Chirol, Nov. 27, 1914; to

EG, Aug. 19, 1915; to Lord Newton, n.d., all in Stephen Gwynn, ed., *The Letters and Friendships of Sir Cecil Spring Rice: A Record,* 2 vols. (Boston: Houghton Mifflin, 1929), 2:239, 249, 278, 321.

2. The Earliest Debates

1. Wilson in Arthur Walworth, *Woodrow Wilson,* 2nd ed., rev., 2 vols. in 1 (Baltimore: Penguin, 1969), 1:400; WW to Mary Allen Peck, Aug. 23, 1914, *PWW,* 30:437; Stockton Axson in Ray Stannard Baker, *Woodrow Wilson: Life and Letters,* vol. 5, *Neutrality, 1914–1915* (New York: Doubleday, Doran, 1935), 51.

2. House diary, Nov. 14, 1914, *PWW,* 31:320; Nov. 6, 1914, *PWW,* 31:274.

3. Wilson, press conference, July 27, 1914, *PWW,* 30:307.

4. David F. Houston in Mark Sullivan, *Our Times,* vol. 5, *Over Here, 1914–1918,* 6 vols. (New York: Scribner, 1926–35), 49n3.

5. David F. Houston, *Eight Years with Wilson's Cabinet, 1913 to 1920,* 2 vols. (New York: Doubleday, Page, 1926), 1:120; Roosevelt in Geoffrey C. Ward, *A First-Class Temperament: The Emergence of Franklin Roosevelt* (New York: Harper and Row, 1989), 244; Taft, *Independent,* Aug. 10, 1914, 198–99; James in John Milton Cooper Jr., *Pivotal Decades: The United States, 1900–1920* (New York: Norton, 1990), 221.

6. WHP to WW, July 29, 1914, *PWW,* 30:316; WHP to WW, Aug. 2, 1914, *PWW,* 30:331.

7. Press citations in Sullivan, *Our Times,* 5:59.

8. "American Sympathies in the War," *LD* 49 (Nov. 14, 1914): 939–41, 974–78.

9. Ernest R. May, *The World War and American Isolation, 1914–1917* (Cambridge, MA: Harvard Univ. Press, 1958), 36, 172; Sullivan, *Our Times,* 5:59; newsboy, Robert Endicott Osgood, *Ideals and Self-Interest in America's Foreign Relations: The Great Transformation of the Twentieth Century* (Chicago: Univ. of Chicago Press, 1953), 114; CASR to EG, Apr. 16, 1915, in Gwynn, *Letters of Spring Rice,* 2:262.

10. Wilson, *NYT,* Aug. 5, 1914, 7; "Appeal to the American People," Aug. 18, 1914, *PWW,* 30:394.

11. *F* 1 (Aug. 24, 1914): 5; *O* 107 (Aug. 15, 1914): 894; Lodge, *New York Sun,* Aug. 23, 1914, in Henry Cabot Lodge, *The Senate and the League of Nations* (New York: Scribner, 1925), 26.

12. WW to EG, Aug. 19, 1914, *PWW,* 30:403; CASR to EG, Sept. 3, 1914, *PWW,* 30:472; House diary, Aug. 30, 1914, *PWW,* 30:462; WW to JWG, Oct. 19, 1914, *PWW,* 31:181; Joseph P. Tumulty, *Woodrow Wilson as I Know Him* (Garden City, NY: Doubleday, Page, 1921), 230–31.

13. Link, *Wilson,* 3:51–52; Devlin, *Too Proud to Fight,* 231; Reinhard R. Doerries, *Imperial Challenge: Ambassador Count Bernstorff and German-American Relations, 1908–1917* (Chapel Hill: Univ. of North Carolina Press, 1989), 91–92.

14. House diary, Sept. 28, 1914, *PWW,* 31:95; WW to WHP, Nov. 10, 1914, *PWW,* 31:294; House diary, Nov. 4, 1914, *PWW,* 31:265.

15. House diary, Nov. 25, 1914, *PWW,* 31:355; Daniels in Baker, *Wilson,* 5:77.

16. H.B. Brougham, "Memorandum of Interview with the President," Dec. 14, 1914, *PWW,* 31:458–59; Axson in Cooper, *Wilson,* 276.

17. WJB to WHP, July 28, 1914, *FR, 1914, Supplement* (Washington, DC: Gov-

ernment Printing Office, 1928), 19; WHP to WJB, July 31, 1914, *PWW,* 30:325; "A Press Release," Aug. 4, 1914, *PWW,* 30:342; "Appeal to the American People," Aug. 18, 1914, *PWW,* 30:394; WHP to WJB, Nov. 18, 1914, *FR, 1914, Supplement,* 132.

18. British aims in Hendrick, *Life and Letters of Page,* 1:340.

19. German aims in Doerries, *Imperial Challenge,* 88.

20. *NAR* 200 (Sept. 1914): 334–37; James M. Beck, *The Evidence in the Case* (New York: Grosset and Dunlap, 1915), 189; [Rollo Ogden], "Belated War Documents," *N* 100 (Feb. 25, 1915): 213.

21. Henry F. Pringle, *The Life and Times of William Howard Taft,* 2 vols. (New York: Farrar and Rinehart, 1939), 2:872; Eliot, *NYT,* Jan. 10, 1915, 21.

22. *New York World* cited in Clifton James Child, *The German-Americans in Politics, 1914–1917* (Madison: Univ. of Wisconsin Press, 1939), 24; WHP to EMH, Sept. 22, 1914, Hendrick, *Life and Letters of Page,* 1:327–28.

23. Friedrich von Bernhardi, *Germany and the Next War* (1911; New York: Chas. A. Eron, 1914), 14, 105.

24. *NYA,* Oct. 18, 1914, E3.

25. Sanborn, "Why the Teuton Fights: I," *F* 1 (Aug. 24, 1914): 7; Burgess in Hirst, "German Propaganda," 104–5.

26. German newspaper in Carl Wittke, *German-Americans and the World War* (Columbus: Ohio State Archeological and Historical Society, 1936), 11; "Where the Blame Rests," *F* 1 (Aug. 31, 1914): 3; "The Truth about Pan-Germanism," *F* 1 (Sept. 30, 1914): 3; Viereck, "Causes of the War," *F* 1 (Jan. 27, 1915): 11.

27. "The Truth Coming Out," *F* 1 (Aug. 10, 1914): 2; Francke, *NYT,* Aug. 6, 1914, 10; Japan in Wittke, *German-Americans,* 15; "Germany's Defensive Aggression," *F* 1 (Aug. 10, 1914): 7.

28. Münsterberg, "Blaming Germany for the War," *LD* 49 (Aug. 22, 1914): 293; Patten, *NR* 1 (Nov. 14, 1914): 22; Villard, "The United States and the Peace Treaty," *NAR* 201 (Mar. 1915): 382.

29. John Keegan, *The First World War* (New York: Knopf, 1999), 29.

30. Larry Zuckerman, *The Rape of Belgium: The Untold Story of World War I* (New York: New York Univ. Press, 2004), 13, 42.

31. Bethmann, *NYT,* Aug. 5, 1914, 2; *NYT,* Aug. 28, 1914, 2.

32. Davis and Irwin in Sullivan, *Our Times,* 5:22, 26.

33. Wilhelm to WW, Sept. 7, 1914, *PWW,* 31:17.

34. Sullivan, *Our Times,* 5:51; [Rollo Ogden], "The Responsibility for War," *N* 99 (Aug. 6, 1914): 151; RL to WJB, Aug. 28, 1914, *LP,* 1:29; Mary Bryan in William Jennings Bryan, *Memoirs* (Chicago: John C. Winston, 1925), 415–16.

35. TR to Arthur Hamilton Lee, Aug. 22, 1914, *LTR,* 7:810–12; Roosevelt, "The World War: Its Tragedies and Its Lessons," *O* 108 (Sept. 23, 1914): 171, 173.

36. TR to Hugo Münsterberg, Oct. 3, 1914, *LTR,* 8:824; TR to Bernhard Dernburg, Dec. 4, 1914, *LTR,* 8:859; daughter, Dalton, *Roosevelt,* 444–45.

37. Patten, "Timid Neutrality," *NR* 1 (Nov. 28, 1914): 22; McClure in entry of Apr. 27, 1916, Allan Nevins, ed., *The Letters and Journal of Brand Whitlock* (New York: Appleton-Century, 1936), 257.

38. Burgess, *NYT,* Oct. 28, 1914, 12; Sanborn, "The Violation of Belgian Neutrality," *F* 1 (Sept. 30, 1914): 5.

39. Viereck, "'German Brutality,'" *F* 1 (Sept. 6, 1914): 3; Ridder, *New Yorker Staats-Zeitung,* Sept. 2, 1914, in *NYT,* same day, p. 2; Ridder in Russell Buchanan, "European Propaganda and American Public Opinion, 1914–1917" (Ph.D. diss., Stanford Univ., 1938), 96–97; journalists, *NYT,* Sept. 7, 1914, 1; Antwerp, *F* 1 (Sept. 6, 1914): 11.

40. WW to Belgian Commission, Sept. 16, 1914, *FR, 1914, Supplement,* 796–97; WJB to JWG, enclosing WW response, Sept. 16, 1914, ibid., 797.

41. Belgian documents, *NYT,* Dec. 20, 1914, C4; Usher, "Was Belgium Neutral?" *NR* 1 (Nov. 28, 1914): 18.

42. Zuckerman, *Rape of Belgium,* 86.

43. Roosevelt, "The International Posse Comitatus," *NYT,* Nov. 8, 1914, SM1; TR to HCL, Dec. 8, 1914, *Selections from the Correspondence of Theodore Roosevelt and Henry Cabot Lodge,* 2 vols. (New York: Scribner, 1925), 2:450.

44. RL to WW, Nov. 23, 1914, *LP,* 1:35–37; WW to RL, Nov. 26, 1914, *LP,* 1:37.

45. WHP to WW, Jan. 12, 1915, in Hendrick, *Life and Letters of Page,* 3:210.

46. Harvey, "Europe at Armageddon," *NAR* 200 (Sept. 1914): 331–32.

47. Naval officials, Holger H. Herwig, *Politics of Frustration: The United States in German Naval Planning, 1889–1941* (Boston: Little, Brown, 1976), 98, 101–3; Stimson, *NYT,* Jan. 17, 1915, 12.

48. For invasion, see Osgood, *Ideals and Self-Interest,* 136; and William Henry Harbaugh, *Power and Responsibility: The Life and Times of Theodore Roosevelt* (New York: Farrar and Straus, 1961), 475 (emphasis Roosevelt's); *NYT,* Oct. 31, 1914, 4. For terrorizing cities, see "The International Posse Comitatus," *NYT,* Nov. 8, 1914, SM1. For fear of Russia, see TR to Hugo Münsterburg, Nov. 2, 1914, *LTR,* 8:826.

49. *NYA,* Jan 16, 1915, 16; von Edelsheim, *NYT,* Dec. 27, 1914, BR585; House diary, Nov. 4, 1914, *PWW,* 31:265–66.

50. 1903 plan in Herwig, *Politics of Frustration,* 150, 90–91.

51. Roosevelt, *NYT,* Oct. 22, 1914, 4.

52. Blue, *NYT,* Dec. 13, 1914, 1; *Army and Navy Journal* in "Should We Prepare for Attack?" *LD* 49 (Dec. 12, 1914): 1159–61; Roosevelt, *NYT,* Dec. 17, 1914, 9; Sterling, "Turning the Search-Light on the Navy's Flaws," *LD* 50 (Jan. 2, 1915): 2; Chadwick in Herwig, *Politics of Frustration,* 157.

53. Fiske in John Patrick Finnegan, *Against the Specter of a Dragon: The Campaign for American Military Preparedness, 1914–1917* (Westport, CT: Greenwood, 1974), 26; NYT, Dec. 18, 1914, 2.

54. Badger, *NYT,* Dec. 9, 1914, 7; Ronald Spector, *Admiral of the New Empire: The Life and Career of George Dewey* (Baton Rouge: Louisiana State Univ. Press, 1974), 198; Fletcher, *NYT,* Dec. 10, 1914, 1.

55. Daniels, *NYT,* Dec. 11, 1914, 1; and *CO* 58 (Jan. 1915): 1; annual report, *NYT,* Dec. 12, 1914, 1.

56. FDR role, John A.S. Grenville and George Berkeley Young, *Politics, Strategy, and American Diplomacy: Studies in Foreign Policy, 1873–1917* (New Haven, CT: Yale Univ. Press, 1966), 328; resolution, *NYT,* Oct. 16, 1914, 5.

57. Gardner, *NYT,* Oct. 17, 1914, 6; *CR,* Oct. 16, 1914, 16694.

58. Gardner, *NYT,* Dec. 19, 1914, 2; and "Should We Prepare for Attack?" *LD* 49 (Dec. 12, 1914): 1160; Frank Freidel, *Franklin D. Roosevelt: The Apprenticeship* (Boston: Little, Brown, 1952), 245–46.

59. [Oswald Garrison Villard], "The 'Preparedness' Flurry," *N* 99 (Dec. 3, 1914): 647; *NR* 1 (Dec. 5, 1914): 3.

60. Wilson, *NYT,* Oct. 20, 1914, 1; Gardner, *NYT,* Dec. 8, 1914, 1.

61. Dies, *CR,* Dec. 10, 1914, 105; Lodge, *CR,* Jan. 15, 1915, 1610; *NYT,* Sept. 24, 1914, 5.

62. Wood in John Garry Clifford, *The Citizen Soldiers: The Plattsburg Training Camp Movement, 1913–1920* (Lexington: Univ. Press of Kentucky, 1972), 39; *NYT,* Dec. 16, 1914, 5.

63. Roosevelt, *NYT,* Sept. 27, 1914, SM1; *NYT,* Nov. 15, 1914, SM1; *NYT,* Oct. 18, 1914, SM1.

64. Roosevelt, *NYT,* Aug. 16, 1914, 10; Wood in Dalton, *Roosevelt,* 448.

65. Daniels, *End of Innocence,* 116; Armin Rappaport, *The Navy League of the United States* (Detroit: Wayne State Univ. Press, 1962), 24, 35, 9.

66. Putnam, *NYT,* Dec. 2, 1914, 1.

67. *NYT,* Dec. 10, 1914, 4; *NYT,* Dec. 19, 1914, 4; "The Week," *O* 108 (Dec. 30, 1914): 977.

68. Wilson, "An Annual Message to Congress," Dec. 8, 1914, *PWW,* 31:422–23.

69. Taft, *NYT,* Dec. 10, 1914, 4.

70. Garrison, *NYT,* Dec. 10, 1914, 4.

71. *Banker's Magazine* in C. Hartley Grattan, *Why We Fought* (New York: Vanguard, 1929), 129.

72. New York Chamber of Commerce in Alexander D. Noyes, *The War Period of American Finance, 1908–1925* (New York: Putnam, 1926), 63.

73. Baker, *Wilson,* 5:98.

74. Colquitt, *NYT,* Dec. 27, 1914, 7; John Sharp Williams to WW, June 29, 1915, *PWW,* 33:457–58.

75. WJB to WW, Aug. 10, 1914, *PWW,* 30:372–73; *NYT,* Aug. 16, 1914, 1; Bryan, *Commoner* 14 (Sept. 1914): 2; "The Week," *N* 99 (Dec. 3, 1914): 644.

76. Cooper, *Wilson,* 264.

77. Arthur S. Link, *Woodrow Wilson: Revolution, War, and Peace* (Wheeling, IL: Harlan Davidson, 1979), 28; Link, *Wilson,* 3:64 plus n28.

78. Link, *Wilson,* 3:64; Daniel M. Smith, *The Great Departure: The United States and World War I* (New York: John Wiley, 1965), 38; Kendrick A. Clements, *The Presidency of Woodrow Wilson* (Lawrence: Univ. Press of Kansas, 1992), 117.

79. Lansing, "Memorandum," Oct. 23, 1914, *PWW,* 31:219–20; Cooper, *Wilson,* 265.

80. WJB to WW, Mar. 29, 1915, *PWW,* 32:451.

81. Noyes, *War Period,* 92.

82. Grey, *Twenty-Five Years,* 2:107.

83. WJB to WHP, Aug. 6, 1914, *FR, 1914, Supplement,* 216; JWG to WJB, Aug. 22, 1914, ibid., 218; WHP to WJB, Aug. 26, 1914, ibid., 219.

84. RL to WHP, Sept. 26, 1914, ibid., 231; RL to WHP, Oct. 22, 1914, ibid., 257–58.

85. WHP, "Memoranda" [Sept. 23, 1916], *PWW,* 38:243; Link, *Wilson,* 3:107; May, *World War,* 20.

86. Devlin, *Too Proud to Fight,* 191; WHP to WJB, undated, with attached note

dated Aug. 22, 1914, *FR, 1914, Supplement,* 219; WHP to WJB, Nov. 3, 1914, ibid., 260–63, including Order in Council, Oct. 29, 1914.

87. CASR to WJB, Nov. 3, 1914, *FR, 1914, Supplement,* 463–64.

88. TR to CASR, Nov. 11, 1914, *LTR,* 8:840.

89. RL to WHP, Sept. 28, 1914, *FR, 1914, Supplement,* 232; Thomas A. Bailey and Paul B. Ryan, *The Lusitania Disaster: An Episode in Modern Warfare and Diplomacy* (New York: Free Press, 1975), 31; May, *World War,* 52.

90. WJB to WHP, Dec. 26, 1914, *FR, 1914, Supplement,* 372–75.

91. Buchanan, "European Propaganda," 143; *NR* 1 (Jan. 2, 1915): 3.

92. Chandler Parsons Anderson, diary, Jan. 8, 1915, *PWW,* 32:47–48.

93. EG to WHP, Jan. 7, 1915, *FR, 1915, Supplement,* 299–302.

94. "How Our Press Take the British Reply," *LD* 50 (Jan. 23, 1915): 131; "The Rights of Neutral Nations and Our Protest to Great Britain," *CO* 58 (Feb. 1915): 73.

95. Link, *Revolution,* 34.

96. Baker, *Wilson,* 5:152.

97. WW to WJB, Mar. 24, 1915, *PWW,* 32:424–25 (emphasis Wilson's); Ross Gregory, *The Origins of American Intervention in the First World War* (New York: Norton, 1971), 44.

98. Arthur S. Link, *The Higher Realism of Woodrow Wilson* (Nashville: Vanderbilt Univ. Press, 1971), 90; Link, *Wilson,* 3:127–29.

99. EMH to WW, July 22, 1915, *PWW,* 34:12; John Callan O'Laughlin, *Imperiled America: A Discussion of the Complications Forced upon the United States by the World War* (Chicago: Reilly and Britton, 1916), 228; Gregory, *Origins,* 4–5.

100. Link, *Revolution,* 34.

101. Link, *Wilson,* 3:129.

102. Baker, Wilson, 5:196; Tucker, *Wilson and the Great War,* 86.

103. John W. Coogan, *The End of Neutrality: The United States, Britain, and Maritime Rights, 1899–1915* (Ithaca, NY: Cornell Univ. Press, 1981), 209, 216, 16.

104. Coogan, *End of Neutrality,* 214–15; Bailey and Ryan, *Lusitania,* 46.

105. *NYT,* Apr. 5, 1915, 2.

106. Bryan, public circular, Oct. 15, 1914, *FR, 1914, Supplement,* 574.

107. Albert J. Beveridge, *What Is Back of the War* (Indianapolis: Bobbs-Merrill, 1915), 70.

108. Vollmer cited in Edmund von Mach, "Who Kills the Germans?" *F* 2 (Feb. 17, 1915): 11; Hugo Münsterberg to WW, Nov. 19, 1914, *PWW,* 31:336–37; Vollmer, *NYT,* Dec. 31, 1914, 4; Bartholdt, *CR,* Dec. 16, 1914, 268.

109. Charles C. Tansill, *America Goes to War* (Boston: Little Brown, 1938), 64; Walter Millis, *Road to War, 1914–1917* (Boston: Houghton Mifflin, 1935), 101.

110. Vollmer cited in Mach, "Who Kills the Germans?" 11; Mach, "Humaneness," *F* 2 (Mar. 10, 1915): 9; Tavenner in Buchanan, "European Propaganda," 195.

111. "An Unneutral Embargo," *NYT,* Dec. 10, 1914, 12; RL to WW, Dec. 10, 1914, *LP,* 1:180; WJB to WW, Jan. 6, 1915, *PWW,* 32:24; WW to WJB, Jan. 7, 1915, *PWW,* 32:25; *NR* 2 (Feb. 6, 1915): 1.

112. JWG to EMH, Dec. 29, 1914, forwarded in EMH to WW, Jan. 15, 1915, *PWW,* 32:75; Lansing, "Confidential for the President: Memorandum on Professor Hugo Münsterberg's Letter to the President," Dec. 9, 1914, *PWW,* 31:441–42.

113. Bernstorff cited in WJB to Sen. William J. Stone, Jan. 20, 1915, *FR, 1914, Supplement,* x–xi; Francke, *NYT,* Feb. 3, 1915, 10.

114. House diary, Nov. 25, 1914, *PWW,* 31:355; JWG to EMH, Dec. 29, 1914, Seymour, *Intimate Papers of Colonel House,* 1:345; *Chicago Tribune,* Jan. 6, 1915, in Buchanan, "European Propaganda," 192; *Nashville Banner* in "Press Poll on Prohibiting the Export of Arms," *LD* 50 (Feb. 6, 1915): 275.

115. O'Laughlin, *Imperiled America,* 218–19.

116. White, "The Move to Keep Our Guns Out of Europe," *LD* 49 (Dec. 26, 1914): 1259–60; *NR* 1 (Jan. 9, 1915): 1.

117. WJB to Sen. William J. Stone, Jan. 20, 1915, *FR, 1914, Supplement,* vi–vii.

118. Press reaction, Buchanan, "European Propaganda," 17; "Contraband and Common Sense," *NR* 1 (Jan. 30, 1915): 7–8; *F* 1 (Feb. 3, 1915): 5; *F* 2 (Feb. 10, 1915): 5; "England Can Do No Wrong," *F* 2 (Feb. 24, 1915): 10; "Our Secretary of State as Defender of Britain," *NYA,* Jan. 25, 1915, 16.

119. *CR,* Feb. 12, 1915, 3633.

120. "Press Poll on Prohibiting the Export of Arms," *LD* 50 (Feb. 6, 1915): 225–26, 274–81.

121. WJB to WW, Nov. 12, 1914, *PWW,* 31:310; WW to Jacob Schiff, Dec. 8, 1914, *PWW,* 31:425.

3. In Peril on the Sea

1. Lamar Cecil, *Wilhelm II,* 2 vols. (Chapel Hill: Univ. of North Carolina Press, 1989–96), 2:221.

2. JWG to WJB, Feb. 4, 1915, *FR, 1915, Supplement* (Washington, DC: Government Printing Office, 1928), 94; JvB to WJB, Feb. 7, 1915, ibid., 95–97.

3. Pohl in May, *World War,* 120; Tirpitz in Tansill, *America Goes to War,* 227.

4. Bethmann in May, *World War,* 121.

5. Haldane in Coogan, *End of Neutrality,* 222.

6. "The Week," *N* 100 (Feb. 11, 1915): 156.

7. WJB to JWG, Feb. 10, 1915, *PWW,* 32:208–10; WJB to WHP, Feb. 10, 1915, *FR, 1915, Supplement,* 100–101.

8. "England Can Do No Wrong," *F* 2 (Feb. 24, 1915): 10; TR to Hiram Johnson, Feb. 22, 1915, *LTR,* 8:894; TR to EG, Jan. 22, 1915, in Grey, *Twenty-Five Years,* 2:153.

9. Link, *Revolution,* 40; May, *World War,* 140.

10. Bailey and Ryan, *Lusitania,* 38; Tucker, *Wilson and the Great War,* 99 (includes Lansing).

11. WW to EMH, Feb. 13, 1915, *PWW,* 32:231; John A. Thompson, *Woodrow Wilson* (London: Longman, 2002), 107.

12. Churchill in Bailey and Ryan, *Lusitania,* 10.

13. Ibid., 47–48, 52–53, 255; Admiralty orders, Feb. 25, 1915, in *FR, 1916, Supplement* (Washington, DC: Government Printing Office, 1929), 196.

14. Bernstorff in May, *World War,* 123 (emphasis Bernstorff's).

15. JWG to WJB, Feb. 17, 1915, *FR, 1915, Supplement,* 112–15.

16. WW to Mary Allen Hulbert, Feb. 14, 1915, *PWW,* 32:232; WJB to WHP and JWG, Feb. 20, 1915, *FR, 1915, Supplement,* 119–20.

17. Jones, Townsend, and Lewis in *NYT,* Feb. 27, 1915, 4.

18. CASR to RL, Mar. 1, 1915, *FR, 1915, Supplement,* 127–28; Asquith, *NYT,* Mar. 2, 1915, 1; WHP to WJB, Mar. 15, 1915, *FR, 1915, Supplement,* 144–45.

19. Grey in Devlin, *Too Proud to Fight,* 210; British rejection, *NYT,* Mar. 16, 1915, 1.

20. WW to WJB, Mar. 24, 1915, *PWW,* 32:424–25; WJB to WHP, Mar. 30, 1915, *FR, 1915, Supplement,* 152–56.

21. WHP to RL, July 24, 1915, *FR, 1915, Supplement,* 168–71.

22. Ross A. Kennedy, *The Will to Believe: Woodrow Wilson, World War I, and America's Strategy for Peace and Security* (Kent, Ohio: Kent State Univ. Press, 2009), 79, 81; Thompson, *Wilson,* 105 (which cites Churchill); Tucker, *Wilson and the Great War,* 105.

23. *New York Tribune* in *LD* 50 (Mar. 13, 1915): 530; *Chicago Tribune* in Buchanan, "European Propaganda," 186; *NYA,* Mar. 18, 1915, 18; Walsh, *NYT,* Mar. 17, 1915, 1; Smith, *NYT,* Mar. 27, 1915, 4.

24. Breitung in Link, *Wilson,* 3:179.

25. WHP to WJB, Jan. 18, 1915, *FR, 1915, Supplement,* 683; WJB to WHP, Jan. 23, 1915, ibid., 684–87.

26. Root, *CR,* Jan. 25, 1915, 2217; Lodge, *NYT,* Jan. 23, 1915, 5; HCL to TR, Jan. 15, 1915, *Correspondence of Roosevelt and Lodge,* 2:451; TR to Miles Poindexter, Jan. 30, 1915, *LTR,* 8:887; Stone, *CR,* Feb. 8, 1915, 3376.

27. Link, *Wilson,* 3:149–50; Cooper, *Wilson,* 270; voting, *CR,* Feb. 18, 1915, 4016.

28. Wood in William Henry Harbaugh, "Wilson, Roosevelt, and Interventionism, 1914–1917: A Study of Domestic Influences on the Formulation of American Foreign Policy" (Ph.D. diss., Northwestern Univ., 1974), 49.

29. "When the Torpedo Kills Non-Combatants," *LD* 50 (Apr. 10, 1915): 789–90; *NYT,* Mar. 31, 1915, 10; "The Week," *N* 100 (Apr. 1, 1915): 344; *NYA,* Apr. 3, 1915, 16.

30. *Deutsches Journal* in *LD* 50 (Apr. 10, 1915): 790; "The Lesson of the *Falaba,*" *F* 2 (Apr. 7, 1915): 16; Ridder, *New Yorker Staats-Zeitung,* Apr. 3, 1915, in *NYT,* Apr. 3, 1915, 3.

31. WJB to WW, Apr. 6, 1915, *LP,* 1:372; WJB to WW, Apr. 7, 1915, *LP,* 1:374–76; Lansing, "Comments on Mr. Anderson's Memorandum of April 5, 1915," Apr. 7, 1915, *PWW,* 33:492–93.

32. WW to WJB, Apr. 3, 1915, *LP,* 1:368; WW to WJB, Apr. 28, 1915, *LP,* 1:380.

33. [Rollo Ogden], "Our Relations with Germany," *N* 100 (May 6, 1915): 484; Roosevelt, *NYT,* May 5, 1915, 1; "The Incident of the 'Gulflight,'" *F* 2 (May 12, 1915): 10.

34. Examples of the notice in *NYT,* May 1, 1915, 19; and in *NYA,* May 1, 1915, 4; Cunard agent, *NYT,* May 1, 1915, 3; RL to WJB, May 1, 1915, *LP,* 1:381–82; Bryan in Link, *Wilson,* 3:369.

35. Cooper, *Wilson,* 285.

36. See, for example, *NYT,* May 2, 1915, 1; *NYA,* May 2, 1915, 1.

37. For the circumstances of the *Lusitania* sinking, see Bailey and Ryan, *Lusitania,* chap. 9.

38. Schwieger in Rodney Carlisle, *Sovereignty at Sea: U.S. Merchant Ships and American Entry into World War I* (Gainesville: Univ. Press of Florida, 2009), 23.

39. Devlin, *Too Proud to Fight,* 284, 287.

40. Public reaction, including *Chicago Tribune,* in "The 'Lusitania' Torpedoed,"

LD 50 (May 15, 1915): 1133–34; Presbyterian journal in Frederick C. Luebke, *Bonds of Loyalty: German- Americans and World War I* (De Kalb: Northern Illinois Univ. Press, 1974), 131; [Rollo Ogden], "The Outlaw German Government," *N* 100 (May 13, 1915): 527; Sullivan, *Our Times,* 5:120.

41. House in Hendrick, *Life and Letters of Page,* 2:2; EMH to WW, [May 9, 1915], *PWW,* 33:134; Roosevelt, *NYT,* May 12, 1915, 3; WHT to WW, May 10, 1915, *PWW,* 33:151; Garraty, *Lodge,* 317.

42. George H. Nash, *The Life of Herbert Hoover,* vol. 2, *The Humanitarian, 1914–1917* (New York: Norton, 1988), 283, 289; *NR* 3 (May 15, 1915): 24.

43. German and Irish press in "The 'Lusitania' Torpedoed," *LD* 50 (June 15, 1915): 1134; "Where the German-Americans Stand," *LD* 50 (May 22, 1915): 1200; Joseph Edward Cuddy, *Irish-America and National Isolationism, 1914–1920* (New York: Arno Press, 1976), 89–90. For Henderson, see "Ourselves as Germans See Us," *NYT,* May 21, 1915, 12.

44. Frank Koester, "The 'Lusitania's' Armament of Twelve Six-Inch Guns," *F* 2 (June 30, 1915): 3–5; "'English Murder,' Says Hobson," *F* 2 (May 26, 1915): 10.

45. Public opinion, Spring Rice, Martin, Flood in Link, *Wilson,* 3:375–76, 416–17; editorials and polls, Cooper, *Wilson,* 285: and David Lawrence, *The True Story of Woodrow Wilson* (New York: George H. Doran, 1924); Wood in Bailey and Ryan, *Lusitania,* 235.

46. Stone and Palmer, *NYT,* May 9, 1915, 2, 7; Works, *NYT,* June 1, 1915, 5; Hitchcock, *F* 2 (May 26, 1915): 11; JWG to RL, July 5, 1915, *FR, 1915, Supplement,* 461; Wood in H.C. Peterson, *Propaganda for War: The Campaign against American Neutrality* (Norman: Univ. of Oklahoma Press, 1939), 129.

47. Bailey and Ryan, *Lusitania,* 87, 330–31, 63; Gregory, *Origins,* 58–59.

48. Wilson, Philadelphia address, May 10, 1915, *NYT,* May 11, 1915, 1; Oswald Garrison Villard, *Fighting Years: Memoirs of a Liberal Editor* (New York: Harcourt, Brace, 1939), 257.

49. For Wilson to press, see Bailey and Ryan, *Lusitania,* 238; John Milton Cooper Jr., *The Warrior and the Priest: Woodrow Wilson and Theodore Roosevelt* (Cambridge, MA: Harvard Univ. Press, 1983), 289.

50. Cooper, *Wilson,* 287; WW to WJB, June 7, 1915, *PWW,* 33:349.

51. JWG to WJB, May 10, 1915, *FR, 1915, Supplement,* 389.

52. Philadelphia newspaper cited in Bailey and Ryan, *Lusitania,* 239.

53. Zuckerman, *Rape of Belgium,* 133, 136.

54. Link, *Wilson,* 3:387; WW to WJB, May 13, 1915, *LP,* 1:403.

55. WJB to WW, May 9, 1915, *LP,* 1:386; RL to WJB, May 9, 1915, *LP,* 1:387–88; WW to WJB, May 11, 1915, *PWW,* 33:154; WW to WJB, May 14, 1915, *LP,* 1:406.

56. Link in Garraty, *Interpreting,* 2:131.

57. WW to WJB, May 12, 1915 (enclosing final draft of note), *PWW,* 33:174–78.

58. WJB to WW, May 12, 1915, *PWW,* 33:165–66.

59. Cooper, *Wilson,* 289.

60. "Are We on the Verge of a War with Germany?" *CO* 58 (June 1915): 380; Pittman, *NYT,* May 15, 1915, 3; Root in Edward H. Buehrig, *Woodrow Wilson and the Balance of Power* (Bloomington: Indiana Univ. Press, 1955), 122; Gardner, *NYT,* May 15, 1915, 3; Ridder, *NYT,* May 15, 1915, 5.

61. *Vital Issue* 2 (May 22, 1915): 11; TR to Archibald Roosevelt, May 19, 1915, *LTR,* 8:922.

62. Gregory, *Origins,* 64; Thompson, *Wilson,* 113.

63. Tucker, *Wilson and the Great War,* 112; Bailey and Ryan, *Lusitania,* 246, 39, 62–63. See also Devlin, *Too Proud to Fight,* 341.

64. JWG to WJB, May 9, 1915, *FR, 1915, Supplement,* 387–88.

65. JWG to WJB, May 29, 1915, ibid., 419–21.

66. Press opinion, *NYT,* June 1, 1915, 4; and "Why America Rejects Germany's Argument," *LD* 50 (June 12, 1915): 1383–84; "The German Note and America's Duty," *O* 110 (June 9, 1915): 297; [Rollo Ogden], "Germany Still 'In the Dark,'" *N* 100 (June 3, 1915): 615; Viereck, "The German Answer," *F* 2 (June 9, 1915): 5; Hearst, *NYA,* June 6, 1915, 2.

67. WJB to WW, June 3, 1915, *PWW,* 33:321–26; WJB to WW, June 5, 1915, *PWW,* 33:342–43.

68. Bryan, *Memoirs,* 423; WW to WJB, June 9, 1915, *PWW,* 33:376; WW to EBG, June 9, 1915, *PWW,* 33:377; House diary, June 24, 1915, *PWW,* 33:449; Bryan in Houston, *Eight Years,* 1:146.

69. Lawrence W. Levine, *Defender of the Faith—William Jennings Bryan: The Last Decade, 1915–1925* (New York: Oxford Univ. Press, 1965), 22.

70. Press opinion in Link, *Wilson,* 3:425–26; and in "Mr. Bryan's Split with the President, *LD* 50 (June 19, 1915): 1449–52; Roosevelt in Harbaugh, *Power,* 478; Robert Page in Cooper, *Vanity,* 89; Walter Hines Page and Watterson in Michael Kazin, *A Godly Hero: The Life of William Jennings Bryan* (New York: Knopf, 2006), 239; Harding, *NYA* (June 10, 1915): 2.

71. "Colonel Bryan's War for Peace," *LD* 50 (June 16, 1915): 1517; *NYA,* June 10, 1915, 20; Works in Cooper, *Vanity,* 99; "The Inner Significance of Mr. Bryan's Action," *F* 2 (June 23, 1915): 11.

72. Millis, *Road to War,* 189; Gregory, *Origins,* 61, quotation on 134; May, *World War,* 156–57, 436.

73. RL to JWG, June 9, 1915, *FR, 1915, Supplement,* 436–38.

74. RL to JWG, June 7, 1915 (final version sent on June 9), *PWW,* 33:355–60.

75. Press reaction in Link, *Wilson,* 3:429–31; and in "The President's Latest Note to Germany: A Poll of the International Press," *O* 110 (June 23, 1915): 413–17; *NYA,* June 11, 1915, 18; "The Burden of Presidential Office," *NR* 3 (June 19, 1915): 162; college presidents, *NYT,* June 14, 1915, 4.

76. TR to Arthur Hamilton Lee, June 17, 1915, *LTR,* 8:937; TR to HCL, *Correspondence of Roosevelt and Lodge,* 2:459; Viereck, "Humanity—American Style," *F* 2 (June 23, 1915): 3; Mann, *NYT,* June 28, 1915, 4; Mann in Gerald D. McKnight, "A Party against Itself: The Grand Old Party in the New Freedom Era, 1913–1916" (Ph.D. diss., Univ. of Maryland, 1972), 241.

77. Link, *Wilson,* 3:427–28; Houston, *Eight Years,* 1:141; EMH to WW, June 16, 1915, *PWW,* 33:409; House diary, June 24, 1915, *PWW,* 33:450.

78. Lansing in Buehrig, *Wilson,* 135–36.

79. Vardaman, *NYT,* July 26, 1915, 5; Franklin K. Lane to John Crawford Burns, May 29, 1915, in Anne Wintermute Lane and Louise Herrick Wall, eds. *The Letters of Franklin K. Lane: Personal and Political* (Boston: Houghton Mifflin, 1922), 173; RL to WHP, July 16, 1915, *FR, 1915, Supplement,* 473–74; Link, *Wilson,* 3:597.

80. WW to RL, July 13, 1915, *LP,* 1:456; *O* 110 (July 7, 1915): 533–34; "The Ocean Travelers' Suicide Club," *F* 2 (July 14, 1915): 12.

81. JWG to RL, July 8, 1915, *FR, 1915, Supplement,* 463–66.

82. EMH to WW, July 10, 1915, *PWW,* 33:491; Lansing, memorandum of July 11, 1915, as in Smith, "Robert Lansing," 80–81; JWG to EMH, July 20, 1915, in Seymour, *Intimate Papers of Colonel House,* 2:23.

83. WW to Melancthon W. Jacobus, July 20, 1915, *PWW,* 33:535.

84. JvB to Foreign Office, June 2, 1915, *PWW,* 33:319; WW to EMH, July 14, 1915, *PWW,* 33:505 (emphasis Wilson's).

85. Congress, *NYA,* July 11, 1915, 7; public reaction in Buchanan, "European Propaganda," 321; Link, *Wilson,* 3:438–39; and "Trying to Solve the Deadlock with Germany," *LD* 51 (July 24, 1915): 142; "The New German Note," *O* 110 (July 21, 1915): 647; Roosevelt, *CO* 59 (Aug. 1915): 76; Harvey, *NAR* 202 (Aug. 1915): 169–70; *NYA,* July 14, 1915, 16; German American press, *NYT,* July 11, 1915, 2; "Germany's Generous Concessions," *F* 2 (July 21, 1915): 12; Bailey and Ryan, *Lusitania,* 262.

86. RL to JWG, July 19, 1915 (includes Wilson draft), *PWW,* 33:545–48.

87. Wilhelm in Link, *Wilson,* 3:449.

88. Public opinion in ibid., 3:448n22; and in "Our 'Last Word' on the 'Lusitania,'" *LD* 51 (Aug. 7, 1915): 234–36; "The Next Step," *NR* 3 (July 31, 1915): 322–23.

89. South Carolina newspaper and Roosevelt in Bailey and Ryan, *Lusitania,* 245; "The Next Step," *F* 2 (Aug. 4, 1915): 3–4; *NYA,* July 26, 1915, 16.

90. Alvin Adee to JWG, July 24, 1915, *FR, 1915, Supplement,* 485.

91. RL to JWG, July 31, 1915, ibid., 492.

92. JWG to WJB, Feb. 14, 1915, ibid., 104; EMH to WW, Apr. 11, 1915, *PWW,* 32:505; JvB to WJB, Apr. 4, 1915, *FR, 1915, Supplement,* 157–58.

93. Press opinion in Link, *Wilson,* 3:352–53; and in "Germany Challenges Our Neutrality," *LD* 50 (Apr. 24, 1915): 937–39; "The Week," *N* 100 (Apr. 15, 1915): 402; Williams in Timothy Gregory McDonald, "Southern Democratic Congressmen and the First World War, August 1914–April 1917: The Public Record of Their Support for or Opposition to Wilson's Policies" (Ph.D. diss., Univ. of Washington, 1962), 87.

94. WJB to JvB, Apr. 21, 1915, *FR, 1915, Supplement,* 160–62; Viereck, "The Work of the Grape Juice," *F* 2 (May 5, 1915): 3; *NR* 2 (Apr. 24, 1915): 289.

95. See, for example, *NYA,* Apr. 5, 1915, 10. For German financing, see Buchanan, "European Propaganda," 196.

96. *NYA,* Apr. 7, 1915, 18; *NR* 2 (Apr. 10, 1915): 245.

97. *New York Call* and *Evening Post* in Buchanan, "European Propaganda," 196–97.

98. Advertisement discussed in *CO* 59 (Aug. 1915): 79–80.

99. *Toledo Blade* in ibid., 80; *NYT,* July 1, 1915, 10.

100. *NYT,* July 4, 1915, 1–2; *NYT,* July 7, 1915, 1; "The Attack on Mr. Morgan," *F* 2 (July 14, 1915): 12.

101. Burke, *NYA,* July 19, 1915, 2; Walsh, *NYA,* July 18, 1915, 6.

102. Lane in Link, *Wilson,* 3:390; Seymour, *Intimate Papers of Colonel House,* 2:50.

103. Stephan Burián to FCP, June 29, 1915, *FR, 1915, Supplement,* 791–93; RL to FCP, Aug. 12, 1915, ibid., 794–98; EMH to WW, July 22, 1915, *PWW,* 34:12.

104. "The Export of Munitions," *O* 110 (Aug. 11, 1915): 843; "The Reply to Austria," *N* 101 (Aug. 19, 1915): 220; Frederick Franklin Schrader, "Mr. Lansing Missed One Point," *F* 3 (Sept. 1, 1915): 69; Louis Viereck, "News from Germany," *F* 3 (Sept. 8, 1915): 88–90.

4. Toward the Arabic Crisis

1. [Edward M. House], *Philip Dru: Administrator—A Story of Tomorrow, 1920–1925* (New York: B.W. Huebsch, 1919).

2. Godfrey Hodgson, *Woodrow Wilson's Right Hand: The Life of Colonel Edward M. House* (New Haven, CT: Yale Univ. Press, 2006), 139.

3. Seymour, *Intimate Papers of Colonel House,* 1:192; entry of Apr. 9, 1914, 1:246.

4. Wilhelm interview in Hodgson, *Wilson's Right Hand,* 98, 100; Tirpitz interview, EMH to WW, May 29, 1914, *PWW,* 30:109; French aims, EMH to WW, June 17, 1914, *PWW,* 30:190; Grey interview, EMH to WW, Aug. 1, 1914, *PWW,* 30:327.

5. EMH to WW, Aug. 22, 1914, *PWW,* 30:432–33; EMH to WW, Oct. 24, 1914, *PWW,* 31:228; House diary, Nov. 25, 1914, *PWW,* 31:355.

6. WW to EMH, Jan. 29, 1915, *PWW,* 32:158; Bernstorff meeting noted in CASR to EG, Dec. 24, 1914, *PWW,* 31:522; Spring Rice meeting, House diary, Dec. 18, 1914, *PWW,* 31:490; EMH to WW, Dec. 26, 1914, *PWW,* 31:535.

7. Link, *Wilson,* 3:212–13.

8. WHP to WW, Feb. 10, 1915, *PWW,* 32:214; House diary, Feb. 10, 1915, Seymour, *Intimate Papers of Colonel House,* 1:368–69.

9. Link, *Wilson,* 3:219.

10. EMH to WW, Feb. 23, 1915, *PWW,* 32:277–78; Arthur Zimmermann to EMH, Seymour, Feb. 4, 1915, *Intimate Papers of Colonel House,* 1:371.

11. Link, *Wilson,* 3:228; House diary, Mar. 24, 1915, Seymour, *Intimate Papers of Colonel House,* 1:403.

12. EMH to WW, Apr. 30, 1915, *PWW,* 33:88–89; Link, *Wilson,* 3:230.

13. EMH to WW, May 25, 1915, *PWW,* 33:254; House diary, June 1, 1915, Seymour, *Intimate Papers of Colonel House,* 1:454.

14. EMH to WW, June 16, 1915, *PWW,* 33:406; WW to EBG, Aug. 9, 1915, *PWW,* 34:151.

15. RL to WW, Aug. 18, 1915, *PWW,* 34:236–37.

16. Mercedes M. Randall, *Improper Bostonian: Emily Greene Balch* (New York: Twayne, 1964), 140.

17. Balch, "The Time for Making Peace," in *Women at the Hague: The International Congress of Women and Its Results,* by Jane Addams, Emily G. Balch, and Alice Hamilton, ed. Harriet Hyman Alonso (1915; reprint, Urbana: Univ. of Illinois Press, 2003), 54–56.

18. RL to WW, Sept. 1, 1915, *PWW,* 34:397–99; WW to RL, Aug. 31, 1915 [Sept. 1, 1915], *PWW,* 34:399; Balch in David S. Patterson, *The Search for Negotiated Peace: Women's Activism and Citizen Diplomacy in World War I* (New York: Routledge, 2008), 133. For full accounts of the Woman's Peace Party, the Hague Congress, and its aftermath, see Addams, Balch, and Hamilton, *Women at the Hague;* Randall, *Improper Bostonian,* chaps. 5–9; and Jane Addams, *Peace and Bread in Time of War,* ed. Katherine Joslin (1929; reprint, Urbana: Univ. of Illinois Press, 2002).

19. WW to EBG, Aug. 18, 1915, *PWW,* 34:242–43.

20. Roosevelt, *NYT,* Apr. 16, 1915, 1; and Patterson, *Search,* 115; TR to Raymond Robins, June 3, 1915, *LTR,* 8:928; women's response, *NYT,* Apr. 17, 1915, 6.

21. *NYA,* June 19, 1915, 16; *NYT,* Feb. 22, 1916, 2; "The League to Enforce Peace,"

O 102 (Apr. 12, 1916): 831–32; Warren F. Kuehl, *Hamilton Holt: Journalist, Internationalist, and Educator* (Gainesville: Univ. of Florida Press, 1960), 129.

22. Program, *NYT,* June 17, 1915, 4; William C. Widenor, *Henry Cabot Lodge and the Search for an American Foreign Policy* (Berkeley: Univ. of California Press, 1980), 229; Berger and Kirchwey, *NYT,* June 18, 1915, 4; Taft, *NYT,* June 17, 1915, 3.

23. Bryan, *NYT,* June 20, 1915, 1; Root in Ruhl J. Bartlett, *The League to Enforce Peace* (Chapel Hill: Univ. of North Carolina Press, 1944), 43–44; Penrose in Cooper, *Vanity,* 59.

24. Roosevelt in Cooper, *Vanity,* 60; and in *The Works of Theodore Roosevelt: National Edition,* 20 vols. (New York: Scribner's, 1926), 18:158–60.

25. Hay in Finnegan, *Specter of a Dragon,* 33, and in George C. Herring Jr., "James Hay and the Preparedness Controversy, 1915–1916," *Journal of Southern History* 30 (Nov. 1964): 386.

26. *NR* 1 (Jan. 20, 1915): 3.

27. Voting tally, *CR,* Feb. 5, 1915, 3152; Manahan, *CR,* Jan. 29, 1915, 2734; Witherspoon, *CR,* 2671–78.

28. Gerry, *CR,* Jan. 29, 1915, 2717; Hobson, *CR,* 2701–3; Roosevelt and Satterlee, *NYT,* Jan. 31, 1915, C4.

29. Taggart, *CR,* Jan. 29, 1915, 2726; Swanson, *CR,* Feb. 26, 1915, 4701; Thomas, 4696; Smoot, 4695.

30. *NYT,* Mar. 3, 1915, 5; Daniels, *CO* 58 (Apr. 1915): 227.

31. "Nation-Wide Press Poll on Army and Navy Increase," *LD* 50 (Jan. 23, 1915): 137–38, 162–69.

32. Finnegan, *Specter of a Dragon,* including Strunsky, 92, 94.

33. Benson, *NYT,* June 6, 1915, 3; Wood, *NYT,* May 21, 1915, 7; *NYA,* Jan. 19, 1916, 20.

34. Hanna, *NYT,* April 9, 1915, 3; "Numbers in National Defense," *NAR* 202 (Aug. 1915): 181; NSL, *NYT,* July 26, 1915, 5.

35. Gardner in Finnegan, *Specter of a Dragon,* 35; Stimson, "The Attack on New York," *Harper's Weekly* 59 (Dec. 12, 1914): 556–59; Captain J.P. Drouillard, *NYA,* Aug. 22, 1915, 6; F.V. Greene, *The Present Military Situation in the United States* (New York: Scribner, 1915); Julius W. Muller, *The Invasion of America: A Fact Story Based on the Inexorable Mathematics of War* (New York: Dutton, 1916); White in John A. Thompson, *Reformers and War: American Progressive Publicists and the First World War* (New York: Cambridge Univ. Press, 1967), 132.

36. J. Bernard Walker [George Dyson], *America Fallen! The Sequel to the European War* (New York: Dodd, Mead, 1915), preface by Dewey, iii–iv.

37. George Lauferti, *The United States and the Next War* (London: Athenaeum, 1915); Hobson, *NYT,* Jan. 30, 1915, 11; editorial, *NYA,* Feb. 26, 1915, 18.

38. Finnegan, *Specter of a Dragon,* 49–50.

39. Hudson Maxim, *Defenseless America* (New York: Hearst's International Library, 1915), 90.

40. McCormick, *NYT,* July 21, 1915, 3.

41. *F* 3 (Oct. 27, 1915): 205.

42. Kitchin, *NYT,* Sept. 2, 1915, 4; "The Week," *N* 99 (Dec. 10, 1914): 676; "Why Do We Arm?" *NR* 4 (Oct. 30, 1915): 323–34; Sherwood, "The Threatening Danger of a Military Autocracy," *Commoner* 15 (Nov. 1915): 8.

43. Herwig, *Politics of Frustration,* 156.

44. Finnegan, *Specter of a Dragon,* 48–51; John Whiteclay Chambers II, *To Raise an Army: The Draft Comes to Modern America* (New York: Free Press, 1987), 86.

45. *NYT,* Mar. 1, 1915, 1.

46. *NYT,* Mar. 12, 1915, 9.

47. *NYT,* May 11, 1915, 4.

48. *NYT,* May 12, 1915, 1; *NYT,* Oct. 3, 1915, 32; Harbaugh, "Wilson," 82; Thompson in Bryan, "The Navy League's Demands," *Commoner* 15 (Nov. 1915): 4; and in *NYT,* Aug. 31, 1915, 3.

49. For the ADS, see John Carver Edwards, *Patriots in Pinstripe: Men of the National Security League* (Washington, DC: Univ. Press of America, 1982), 24–26.

50. Harold T. Pulsifer, "The Security League Conference," *O* 111 (Dec. 8, 1915): 853; Finnegan, *Specter of a Dragon,* 98.

51. Dalton, *Roosevelt,* 448.

52. Clifford, *Citizen Soldiers,* 76; Wilson, *NYT,* Aug. 19, 1915, 5.

53. Finnegan, *Specter of a Dragon,* 108.

54. *NYT,* Aug. 26, 1915, 1; Clifford, *Citizen Soldiers,* 84–85.

55. *NYT,* Aug. 27, 1915, 1; *NYT,* Aug. 28, 1915, 1; TR to Kermit Roosevelt, Aug. 28, 1915, *LTR,* 8:963.

56. *Chicago Tribune* in "The Ex-Presidential War on the War Department," *LD* 51 (Sept. 11, 1915): 514.

57. Bryan and Tavenner in Cooper, *Vanity,* 90; La Follette, "Take the Profit Out of War," *La Follette's Magazine* 7 (Feb. 1915): 2.

58. *New York World,* other newspapers, "Light on German Propaganda," *LD* 51 (Aug. 28, 1915): 388; TR to Arthur Hamilton Lee, Sept. 2, 1915, *LTR,* 8:967; "The German Exposures," *N* 101 (Aug. 19, 1915): 219.

59. "Dr. Albert Demolishes 'World' Charges," *F* 3 (Sept. 1, 1915): 62–63; George Sylvester Viereck, *Spreading Germs of Hate* (New York: Horace Liveright, 1930), 74.

60. Konstantin Dumba to Stephan Burián, Aug. 20, 1915, enclosure forwarded by WHP to RL, Sept. 1, 1915, *PWW,* 34:404.

61. Link, *Wilson,* 3:645–47; Papen, *NYT,* Sept. 22, 1915, 1.

62. *NYT,* Sept. 6, 1915, 1, 3.

63. RL to WW, Sept. 7, 1915, *PWW,* 34:429; RL to FCP, Sept. 8, 1915, *FR, 1915, Supplement,* 933–34; Dumba in Link, *Wilson,* 3:650.

64. Press opinion in "Dismissal of the Austrian Ambassador," *LD* 51 (Sept. 18, 1915): 573–74; and *CO* 59 (Oct. 1915): 218; "Dishonorable Warfare," *O* 111 (Sept. 15, 1915): 113; *NR* 4 (Sept. 11, 1915): 136; Bryan, *Commoner* 15 (Sept. 1915): 6.

65. Viereck, "Danger Ahoy!" *F* 3 (Sept. 22, 1915): 118–19; Schrader, "Recall Van Dyke and Page," *F* 3 (Oct. 13, 1915): 174.

66. JWG to RL, July 29, 1915, *FR, 1915, Supplement,* 491.

67. WHP to RL, July 24, 1915, ibid., 168–71; Lansing in Link, *Wilson,* 3:597.

68. JWG to RL, Sept. 7, 1915, *FR, 1915, Supplement,* 539–40; Bernstorff, *My Three Years,* 142, 147.

69. Press opinion, "The Attack on the 'Arabic,'" *LD* 51 (Aug. 28, 1915): 387–88; *N* 101 (Aug. 26, 1915): 249; "The German Attitude: 'Anything' for America!" *NAR* 202 (Oct. 1915): 487–88; "Snipers of the Sea," *F* 3 (Sept. 1, 1915): 68.

70. EMH to WW, Aug. 22, 1915, *PWW,* 34:299; House diary, Aug. 21, 1915, Seymour, *Intimate Papers of Colonel House,* 2:31; RL to WW, Aug. 24, 1915, *PWW,* 34:319; WW to RL, Aug. 26, 1915, *PWW,* 34:329.

71. Link, *Wilson,* 3:569; WW to EBG, Aug. 19, 1915, *PWW,* 34:260–61 (emphasis Wilson's).

72. *NYT,* Aug. 23, 1915, 1; WW to EBG, Aug. 22, 1915, *PWW,* 34:288.

73. *War Memoirs of Lansing,* 47; Tucker, *Wilson and the Great War,* 37; Walworth, *Wilson,* 2:23.

74. JWG to RL, Aug. 24, 1915, *FR, 1915, Supplement,* 525–26; Link, *Wilson,* 3:574–75; Bethmann, *NYT,* Aug. 26, 1915, 1.

75. JvB to RL, Sept. 1, 1915, *PWW,* 34:400; *NYT,* Sept. 2, 1915, 1–2; Doerries, *Imperial Challenge,* 114.

76. May, *World War,* 223 (emphasis Wilhelm's).

77. Press and Roosevelt, *NYT,* Sept. 2, 1915, 1, 2; and "Germany Yields to Wilson," *LD* 51 (Sept. 11, 1915): 509–11; Bryan, *NYT,* Sept. 7, 1915, 4; "Breaking with Germany?" *NR* 4 (Sept. 18, 1915): 166–67; "President Wilson's Hour of Destiny," *F* 3 (Sept. 8, 1915): 86.

78. WW to EBG, Sept. 3, 1915, *PWW,* 34:407.

79. JWG to RL, Sept. 7, 1915, *FR, 1915, Supplement,* 539–40; Devlin, *Too Proud to Fight,* 327.

80. Press reaction, *NYT,* Sept. 11, 1915, 2; Wilson in House diary, Sept. 22, 1915, *PWW,* 34:506; RL to WW, Sept. 11, 1915, *PWW,* 34:451.

81. JWG to RL, Sept. 10, 1915, *FR, 1915, Supplement,* 545.

82. WW to EMH, Sept. 7, 1915, *PWW,* 34:426; House diary, Sept. 22, 1915, *PWW,* 34:506.

83. "The Submarine Not Yet Tamed," *LD* 51 (Sept. 18, 1915): 575–76; *NR* 4 (Sept. 11, 1915): 137; "The Hesperian," *F* 3 (Sept. 15, 1915): 102–3.

84. Link, *Wilson,* 3:673, 680–81; JvB to RL, Oct. 5, 1915, *PWW,* 35:26–27; Doerries, *Imperial Challenge,* 116.

85. "America's Diplomatic Victory," *LD* 51 (Oct. 16, 1915): 821–24; *N* 101 (Oct. 14, 1915): 451; House in Devlin, *Too Proud to Fight,* 337; Link, *Wilson,* 3:669.

86. Link, *Wilson,* 3:691–92; Devlin, *Too Proud to Fight,* 338; Tucker, *Wilson and the Great War,* 38.

5. Frustrating Times

1. For material on the *Baralong,* see Link, *Wilson,* 3:669n72; Bailey and Ryan, *Lusitania,* 51; Devlin, *Too Proud to Fight,* 413–14.

2. Lansing and Wilson in Link, *Wilson,* 3:669n72; State Department, *NYT,* Oct. 19, 1915, 1.

3. Grey, *NYA,* Jan. 12, 1916, 20; *NYT,* Jan. 6, 1916, 3; *NYT,* Mar. 8, 1916, 3.

4. Crewe, *NYT,* Dec. 21, 1915, 2.

5. *NYA,* Oct. 2, 1915, 2; *New York World* advertisement, Sept. 17, 1915, cited in Buchanan, "European Propaganda," 391.

6. RL to WHP, Oct. 21, 1915, *FR, 1915, Supplement,* 578–89.

7. Cooper, *Page,* 321; Link, *Wilson,* 3:687, 691.

8. Press opinion, "Our Case against Great Britain," *LD* 51 (Nov. 20, 1915): 1141–42; and *NYT*, Nov. 8, 1915, 5; "Another American Protest," *O* 111 (Nov. 17, 1915): 651; Bryan, "The Note to Great Britain," *Commoner* 15 (Nov. 1, 1915): 7; Hendrick, *Life and Letters of Page*, 2:78; Lansing in Gregory, *Origins*, 75.

9. WGM to WW, Aug. 21, 1915, *PWW*, 34:275, 279; RL to WW, Sept. 6, 1915, *LP*, 1:144–47.

10. Reading in John Milton Cooper Jr., "The Command of Gold Reversed: American Loans to Britain, 1915–1917," *Pacific Historical Review* 45 (May 1976): 213.

11. "Summing Up a Year of Slaughter," *LD* 51 (Aug. 14, 1915): 281–84.

12. Richard W. Van Alstyne, "Private American Loans to the Allies, 1914–1916," *Pacific Historical Review* 2 (June 1933): 186–88; "Misdirected Energy," *NYT*, Sept. 29, 1915, 12.

13. Press reaction (including Ridder), *NYT*, Oct. 23, 1915, 3; "The Case of Miss Cavell," *N* 101 (Oct. 28, 1915): 509; Frederick Franklin Schrader, *Handbook Political, Statistical, and Sociological for German Americans* (New York: Frederick Franklin Schrader, 1916), 18–19; Viereck to Everett V. Abbot, Feb. 9, 1916, *F* 4 (Feb. 23, 1916): 43.

14. *NYT*, Sept. 27, 1915, 5; *NYT*, Oct. 4, 1915, 1.

15. *NR* 4 (Oct. 9, 1915): 245; *NYA*, Sept. 25, 1915, 16; "How About the Jews?" *F* 3 (Oct. 20, 1915): 191.

16. FCP to State Department, Nov. 16, 1915, *PWW*, 35:208–9.

17. "Another 'Lusitania' Case in the Mediterranean," *LD* 51 (Nov. 20, 1915): 1139–40; *O* 111 (Nov. 17, 1915): 638; "The Ancona," *F* 3 (Nov. 24, 1915): 278.

18. Report of conversation, RL to WW, Nov. 19, 1915, *PWW*, 35:219; EMH to WW, Nov. 21, 1915, *PWW*, 35:234.

19. Link, *Wilson*, vol. 4, *Confusions and Crises, 1915–1916* (Princeton, NJ: Princeton Univ. Press, 1964), 69; RL, draft note dated Dec. 3, 1915, *PWW*, 35:287; House in Link, *Wilson*, 4:66; Stephan Burián to RL, Dec. 15, 1915, *PWW*, 35:365–66; RL to WW, Dec. 19, 1915, *PWW*, 35:368–70; Dec. 21 meeting, *War Memoirs of Lansing*, 92; RL to WW, Dec. 28, 1915, *PWW*, 35:403–4.

20. FCP to WW, Dec. 29, 1915, *PWW*, 35:410; "Summary of the News," *N* 102 (Jan. 6, 1916): 1.

21. *NYT*, Jan. 5, 1916, 1; Tumulty memorandum, Jan. 4, 1916, *PWW*, 35:424; JvB to RL, Jan. 7, 1916, *FR, 1916, Supplement*, 144–45; *NYT*, Jan. 8, 1916, 1.

22. JvB to RL, Oct. 2, 1915, *LP*, 1:484–85; RL to WW, Nov. 2, 1915, *LP*, 1:488–89; Memorandum of Lansing interview with Bernstorff, Nov. 17, 1915, *LP*, 1:490–91; WW to RL, Nov. 21, 1915, *LP*, 1:493.

23. "The Second *Lusitania* Crisis," Link, *Wilson*, vol. 4, chapter 3; Bailey and Ryan, *Lusitania*, 267–68.

24. RL to JvB, Dec. 20, 1915, *LP*, 1:502; Falkenhayn in Link, *Wilson*, 4:86–87.

25. *War Memoirs of Lansing*, 103; *NYT*, Jan. 30, 1916, 1.

26. Link, *Wilson*, 4:93.

27. JvB to RL, Feb. 4, 1916, *FR, 1916, Supplement*, 157; RL to WW, Feb. 4, 1916, *LP*, 1:531; *NYT*, Feb. 9, 1916, 1.

28. Doerries, *Imperial Challenge*, 180; Bernstorff, *My Three Years*, 105.

29. Papen statement, Apr. 16, 1920, Reichstag Commission of Inquiry, *OGD*, 2:1313.

30. "Still Conspiring," *F* 3 (Nov. 10, 1915): 244; *New York Journal of Commerce* in "Bringing the War to the United States," *LD* 51 (Nov. 27, 1915): 1207; Millis, *Road to War,* 240; Peterson, *Propaganda,* 148.

31. Okie, review in *NYT,* Oct. 10, 1915, 69.

32. WW to EMH, Aug. 4, 1915, *PWW,* 34:79; EMH to WW, Aug. 23, 1915, *PWW,* 34:309; WW to EMH, Aug. 25, 1915, *PWW,* 34:315; EMH to WW, Aug. 26, 1915, Seymour, *Intimate Papers of Colonel House,* 2:34–35; WGM to WW, Aug. 16, 1915, *PWW,* 34:218.

33. Thomas H. Hartig, *Robert Lansing: An Interpretive Biography* (New York: Arno Press, 1982), 241.

34. "German Sympathizers, Roosevelt and Others," *F* 3 (Sept. 8, 1915): 84–85; "Mr. Wilson's 'Frightfulness,'" *F* 3 (Dec. 15, 1915): 334–35; "Are We Secretly Pledged to England?" *F* 3 (Dec. 22, 1915): 343–45; *F* 3 (Dec. 29, 1915): 367; *Irish World* in John Patrick Buckley, "The New York Irish: Their View of American Foreign Policy, 1914–1981" (Ph.D. diss., New York Univ., 1974), 40.

35. Two memoranda by Louis Lochner, Nov. 12, 1915, *PWW,* 35:195–200; Jordan on results of meeting, House diary, Nov. 18, 1915, *PWW,* 35:218; House diary, Nov. 21, 1915, Seymour, *Intimate Papers of Colonel House,* 2:96.

36. Ford, *NYT,* Apr. 11, 1915, SM14; Nov. 25, 1915, 1, 2; *NYT,* Nov. 30, 1915, 1.

37. Barbara S. Kraft, *The Peace Ship: Henry Ford's Pacifist Adventure in the First World War* (New York: Macmillan, 1978), 51, 33, 49.

38. Ibid., 50–51, 55; Sullivan, *Our Times,* 5:168.

39. Kraft, *Peace Ship,* 66–67.

40. Ibid., 86–87; "Henry Ford in Search of Peace," *LD* (Dec. 11, 1915): 1333; *NR* 5 (Dec. 4, 1915): 112.

41. Kraft, *Peace Ship,* 47, 221–22; *NYT,* Jan. 3, 1916, 1.

42. Kraft, *Peace Ship,* 297.

43. David S. Patterson, "Woodrow Wilson and the Mediation Movement," *Historian* 33 (Aug. 1971): 554.

44. Link, *Wilson,* 4:102; EG to EMH, Sept. 22, 1915, in EMH to WW, Nov. 10, 1915, *PWW,* 35:187; Lloyd E. Ambrosius, *Wilsonian Statecraft: Theory and Practice of Liberal Internationalism during World War I* (Wilmington, DE: Scholarly Resources, 1991): 43–44.

45. House diary, Sept. 22, 1915, *PWW,* 34:506; Oct. 8, 1915, 35:43–44.

46. WW to EMH, Oct. 18, 1915, enclosing an altered draft of EMH to EG, Oct. 17, 1915, *PWW,* 35:80–82.

47. EG to EMH, Nov. 11, 1915, *PWW,* 35:255.

48. House diary, Dec. 15, 1915, *PWW,* 35:356.

49. WW to EMH, Dec. 24, 1915, *PWW,* 35:387–88.

50. House, Dec. 25, 1915, in Tucker, *Wilson and the Great War,* 155; EMH to WW, Dec. 26, 1915, *PWW,* 35:391; WW to EMH, Dec. 17, 1915, *PWW,* 35:364.

51. Link, *Wilson,* 4:111, 116–17; Tucker, *Wilson and the Great War,* 157.

52. House diary, Jan. 11, 1915, in Link, *Wilson,* 4:116; EMH to WW, Jan. 13, 1916, *PWW,* 35:472.

53. EMH to WW, Jan. 16, 1916, *PWW,* 35:488.

54. EMH to WW, Jan. 11, 1916, *PWW,* 35:466; House diary, Jan. 14, 1916, Seymour, *Intimate Papers of Colonel House,* 2:129.

55. EMH to WW, Feb. 3, 1916, *PWW,* 36:123; House diary, Jan. 27, 1916, Seymour, *Intimate Papers of Colonel House,* 2:139.

56. EMH to WW, Jan. 30, 1916, *PWW,* 36:52; EMH to WW, Feb. 3, 1916, *PWW,* 36:123.

57. EMH to WW, Feb. 3, 1916, *PWW,* 36:125–26.

58. Cambon memo, Feb. 7, 1916, *PWW,* 36:148–49.

59. EMH to WW, Feb. 7, 1916, *PWW,* 36:138; EMH to WW, Feb. 9, 1916, *PWW,* 36:147–48.

60. Link, *Wilson,* 4:126–27, 138.

61. EMH to WW, Feb. 9, 1916, *PWW,* 36:150.

62. Link, *Wilson,* 4:131.

63. Turkey, Seymour, *Intimate Papers of Colonel House,* 2:181; peace terms, Asquith query, Link, *Wilson,* 4:132.

64. Grey memorandum, Feb. 22, 1916 (the date Grey initialed the document), *PWW,* 36:180n1.

65. WHP, memorandum, Feb. 9, 1916, in Hendrick, *Life and Letters of Page,* 3:281–82 (emphasis Page's); Page comment, ibid., 3:285.

66. David M. Esposito, "Imagined Power: The Secret Life of Colonel House," *Historian* 60 (Summer 1968): 748.

67. Arthur S. Link, *Woodrow Wilson and the Progressive Era, 1910–1917* (New York: Harper, 1954), 205n20; Link, *Wilson,* 4:133–34, 141; Link, *Higher Realism,* 102; Ray Stannard Baker, *Woodrow Wilson: Life and Letters,* vol. 6, *Facing War, 1915–1917* (New York: Doubleday, Doran, 1940), 147.

68. Cooper, *Warrior,* 294; Cooper, "Wilson's Courier," *Weekly Standard,* Sept. 25, 2006, 33.

69. Devlin, *Too Proud to Fight,* 461.

70. Hodgson, *Wilson's Right Hand,* 120; Clements, *Presidency of Wilson,* 130; House diary, Feb. 17, 1916, Seymour, *Intimate Papers of Colonel House,* 2:194–95; Joyce Grigsby Williams, *Colonel House and Sir Edward Grey: A Study in Anglo-American Diplomacy* (Lanham, MD: Univ. Press of America, 1984), 90, 113.

71. House diary, Mar. 6, 1916, *PWW,* 36:262; Tucker, *Wilson and the Great War,* 49; House diary, Mar. 12, 1916, Seymour, *Intimate Papers of Colonel House,* 2:224.

72. House diary, July 10, 1915, Seymour, *Intimate Papers of Colonel House,* 2:18; EMH to WW, July 14, 1915, ibid., 2:19; Clifford, *Citizen Soldiers,* 37–38.

73. *NYT,* July 24, 1915, 1; WW speech, Oct. 6, 1915, *PWW,* 35:29; Link, *Wilson,* 4:15.

74. *NYT,* Nov. 6, 1915, 3.

75. Scott in Herring, "James Hay," 389; Finnegan, *Specter of a Dragon,* 55.

76. Jane Addams et al., Oct. 29, 1915, *PWW,* 35:134–35; Stephen Samuel Wise to WW, Nov. 12, 1915, *PWW,* 35:195; Oswald Garrison Villard to WW, Oct. 30, 1915, *PWW,* 35:141–42; Michael Wreszin, *Oswald Garrison Villard: Pacifist at War* (Bloomington: Indiana Univ. Press, 1965), 57.

77. Wilson, address to Manhattan Club, Nov. 4, 1915, *PWW,* 35:167–73.

78. Harbaugh, "Wilson," 129; "Evasions by Mr. Wilson," *NR* 5 (Nov. 13, 1915): 29; *NR* 5 (Nov. 20, 1915): 55.

79. WW to RL, Mar. 1, 1916, *LP,* 2:516.

80. "National Defense," *O* 111 (Oct. 27, 1915): 459; public opinion in *CO* 59 (Dec. 1915): 378; and Link, *Wilson,* 4:22–23; NSL poll, *NYT,* Nov. 14, 1915, 4.

81. Kitchin, *NYT,* Nov. 19, 1915, 4.

82. Viereck, "Preparedness and the German American," *F* 3 (Dec. 18, 1915): 307–8; "The Hand That Pulls the Strings," *F* 3 (Sept. 8, 1915): 86; "Correcting Our Contemporaries," *F* 3 (Sept. 29, 1915): 136.

83. ARC, *NYT,* Dec. 19, 1915, 2.

84. General opposition, Link, *Wilson,* 4:26–27; WJB, interview of Nov. 5, 1915, *Commoner* 15 (Nov. 1915): 4; WJB, "Preparedness a Republican Plan," ibid., 6; Villard, *NYT,* Nov. 9, 1915, 4.

85. *NYT,* Dec. 22, 1915, 12; "Suggestions from the Anti-Militarism Committee," *O* 112 (Jan. 5, 1916): 4.

86. Annual message, Dec. 7, 1915, *PWW,* 35:293–310.

87. Link, *Wilson,* 4:37; Harbaugh, "Wilson," 35–37.

88. General press, Bryan, Ford ship, Roosevelt, German Americans in "A Presidential Peace-Message in War-Time," *LD* 51 (Dec. 18, 1915): 1411; Gordon Jerome Goldberg, "Meyer London: A Political Biography" (Ph.D. diss., Lehigh Univ., 1971), 234.

89. La Follette, "Patriots," *La Follette's Magazine* 7 (Nov. 1915): 1; Kitchin, "Another Democratic Split on Preparedness," *LD* 51 (Dec. 4, 1915): 1268.

90. New York, Jan. 27, 1916, *PWW,* 36:11; Pittsburgh, Jan. 29, 1916, *PWW,* 36:37; Cleveland, Jan. 29, 1916, *PWW,* 36:47.

91. Kansas City, Feb. 2, 1916, *PWW,* 36:103, 108; Topeka, Feb. 2, 1916, *PWW,* 36:92, 93; St. Louis, Feb. 3, 1916, *PWW,* 36:116, 120.

92. WJB, *Commoner,* 16 (Feb. 1916): 2; NSL, *NYT,* Jan. 23, 1916, 1; Viereck, "No *Lusitania* Crisis," *F* 4 (Feb. 9, 1916): 10; Baker in Thompson, *Reformers and War,* 135 (emphasis Baker's).

93. James Hay to WW, Feb. 5, 1916, *PWW,* 36:135.

94. Garrison, *NYT,* Jan. 7, 1916, 6; Hay in Finnegan, *Specter of a Dragon,* 85.

95. Miles, *NYT,* Feb. 9, 1916, 1.

96. Wood, *NYT,* Jan. 20, 1916, 1; Jan. 27, 1916, 1; Scott, *NYT,* Feb. 5, 1916, 6; Roosevelt, *NYT,* Oct. 13, 1915, 1; Jan. 6, 1916, 3; *CO* 59 (Dec. 1915): 382.

97. LMG to WW, Jan. 12, 1915, *PWW,* 35:468–71; WW to LMG, Jan. 15, 1916 (sent on Jan. 17), *PWW,* 35:482; WW to LMG, Feb. 9, 1916, *PWW,* 36:145; LMG to WW, Feb. 9, 1916, *PWW,* 36:144; LMG on WW in Link, *Progressive Era,* 186.

98. Press, *NYT,* Feb. 12, 1916, 2; "A Costly Resignation," *NR* 6 (Feb. 19, 1916): 56; Oswald Garrison Villard, "The Shifting Administration," *N* 102 (Feb. 17, 1916): 189–90.

99. Baker, *NYT,* Mar. 18, 1916, 1; *NYT,* Mar. 19, 1916, 6.

100. "The Naval-Increase Programs," *LD* 52 (Jan. 8, 1916): 54; *NYA,* Feb. 25, 1916, 6.

6. Tensions with Germany and Britain

1. RL to WW, Sept. 12, 1915, *PWW,* 34:454–55.

2. WW to EMH, Oct. 4, 1915, *PWW,* 35:19; RL to WW, Jan. 2, 1916, *LP,* 1:332–33; Gerard in Seymour, *Intimate Papers of Colonel House,* 2:210.

3. RL to WW, Jan. 7, 1916, *PWW,* 35:448–49.

4. WW to RL, Jan. 31, 1916, *LP,* 1:581; WW to EMH, Feb. 16, 1916, *PWW,* 36:185.

5. RL to CASR, Jan. 18, 1916, *FR, 1916, Supplement,* 146–48.

6. Grey in Link, *Wilson,* 4:160.

7. Schrader, "Behind the Scenes at the Capital," *F* 4 (Feb. 23, 1916): 40; *NYA,* Feb. 15, 1916, 22; [Rollo Ogden], "The Question of Armed Merchantmen," *N* 102 (Feb. 17, 1916): 183; *O* 112 (Feb. 9, 1916): 290; "Guns on the Merchant Ship," *NR* 6 (Feb. 19, 1916): 57–59; "The Way of the Neutral," *NR* 6 (Mar. 18, 1916): 167–68.

8. Devlin, *Too Proud to Fight,* 418; Gregory, *Origins,* 84.

9. Link, *Progressive Era,* 206; Link, *Revolution,* 43.

10. RL, memorandum, Feb. 9, 1916, citing meeting of Jan. 26, 1916, *LP,* 1:341; Bethmann in Link, *Wilson,* 4:158.

11. *War Memoirs of Lansing,* 113; May, 186.

12. Tirpitz quoted in Bethmann report, Jan. 4, 1916, *OGD,* 2:1117; Holtzendorff to Bethmann, Jan. 7, 1916, *OGD,* 2:1120; enclosure, Tirpitz to Bethmann, Feb. 13, 1916, *OGD,* 2:1127.

13. JWG to RL, Feb. 10, 1916, *FR, 1916, Supplement,* 163–66; submarine order, *NYT,* Feb. 11, 1916, 1; memorial of Bethmann, Feb. 29, 1916, *OGD,* 2:1130; Wilhelm noted in Bethmann to Jagow, Mar. 5, 1916, *OGD,* 1142; Walter Görlitz, ed., *The Kaiser and His Court: The Diaries, Note Books, and Letters of Admiral Georg von Müller, Chief of the Naval Cabinet, 1914–1918* (New York: Harcourt, Brace, and World, 1964), 138.

14. Link, *Wilson,* 4:162–63; *NYT,* Feb. 16, 1916, 1; RL to WW, Feb. 16, 1916, *LP,* 1:531–32; *NYT,* Feb. 17, 1916, 1.

15. *NYT,* Apr. 27, 1916, 1.

16. Kitchin in Robert Hoyt Block, "Southern Opinion of Woodrow Wilson's Foreign Policies, 1913–1917" (Ph.D. diss., Duke Univ., 1968), 158–59; McLemore, *CR,* Feb. 17, 1916, 2756.

17. Sterling and Lodge in *CR,* Feb. 18, 1916, 2759–62, 2766.

18. Gore bill, *CR,* Jan. 5, 1916, 495.

19. Stone in Link, *Wilson,* 4:168.

20. Jagow, ibid., 4:169; canvass, *NYT,* Feb. 24, 1916, 2; Gore in Tansill, *America Goes to War,* 472.

21. William J. Stone to WW, Feb. 24, 1916, *PWW,* 36:210; WW to William J. Stone, Feb. 24, 1916, *PWW,* 36:214.

22. Root, *NYT,* Feb. 16, 1916, 1, 4.

23. "Our Right to Travel on Armed Merchantmen," *LD* 52 (Mar. 11, 1916): 625; *CO* 60 (Apr. 1916): 237; "The Week," *N* 102 (Mar. 2, 1916): 238; *NR* 6 (Mar. 4, 1916): 114.

24. Tucker, *Wilson and the Great War,* 201–2; Buehrig, *Wilson,* 46; Bailey and Ryan, *Lusitania,* 310; Link, *Wilson,* 4:174–75; Thompson, *Wilson,* 120–21.

25. Link, *Wilson,* 4:175–76.

26. Gore resolution, *CR,* Feb. 25, 1916, 3120; poll, Link, *Wilson,* 4:177; pessimism, *NYT,* Feb. 25, 1916, 2.

27. Lansing, *NYT,* Feb. 27, 1916, 1, 3; Link, *Wilson,* 4:177.

28. WW to Pou, *NYT,* Mar. 1, 1916, 1.

29. *New York World* and Alliance view in Buchanan, "European Propaganda," 419–20; Viereck, *Spreading Germs,* 104–5.

30. JvB to RL, Feb. 28, 1916, *FR, 1916, Supplement,* 181–82.

31. Lodge, *CR,* Mar. 2, 1916, 3406; Borah, 3409; Williams, 3407; Gore and Stone, 3410; Link, *Wilson,* 4:190–91.

32. Link, *Wilson,* 4:190; RL to Henry D. Flood, "Memorandum on House Resolution 147," *LP,* 1:343–47.

33. *NYT,* Mar. 4, 1916, 1.

34. Clarke, *CR,* Mar. 3, 1916, 3470; Smoot in Thomas W. Ryley, *A Little Group of Willful Men: A Study of Congressional Authority* (Port Washington, NY: Kennikat, 1975), 49; Jones in Tansill, *America Goes to War,* 478; Borah, *NYT,* Mar. 4, 1916, 2; Cooper, *Vanity,* 113.

35. Norris, *CR,* Mar. 3, 1916, 3485; Abbot, *NYA,* Mar. 4, 1916, 1; Lawrence in Tansill, *America Goes to War,* 478; "Disintegrated America," *NR* 6 (Mar. 11, 1916): 141; "The Flag on the Capitol," *NYT,* Mar. 5, 1916, 20.

36. Vote, *CR,* Mar. 7, 1916, 3720; Mann in Buchanan, "European Propaganda," 420.

37. Bryan in Link, *Wilson,* 4:193; Harbaugh, "Wilson," 103.

38. Cline, *CR,* Mar. 7, 1916, 3706.

39. *CO* 60 (Apr. 1916): 237; "Our Right to Travel on Armed Merchantmen," *LD* 52 (Mar. 11, 1916): 625; Bernstorff to Foreign Office, Mar. 10, 1916, *OGD,* 2:1289.

40. Link, *Wilson,* 4:182–83.

41. Ibid., 4:185–86.

42. Bernstorff, *My Three Years,* 203.

43. RL to WW, Mar. 27, 1916, *PWW,* 36:372; Cooper, *Wilson,* 323.

44. House diary, Mar. 30, 1916, *PWW,* 36:388.

45. EMH to WW, Apr. 3, 1916, *PWW,* 36:405; WW to EG, Apr. 6, 1916, *PWW,* 36:421.

46. Lane in House diary, Apr. 6, 1916, *PWW,* 36:424; Josephus Daniels, *The Wilson Era: Years of Peace—1910–1917* (Chapel Hill: Univ. of North Carolina Press, 1944), 439; House in Link, *Wilson,* 4:238; EG to EMH, Apr. 8, 1916, *PWW,* 36:444–45; EMH to WW regarding Bernstorff, Apr. 8, 1916, *PWW,* 36:446.

47. JWG to RL, Apr. 11, 1916, *FR, 1916, Supplement,* 227–29; *NYT,* Apr. 13, 1916, 1; Müller entry in Görlitz, *Kaiser,* Apr. 28, 1916, 153.

48. Press, including *New York Evening Post,* in "Germany's 'Denial' in the Sussex Case," *LD* 52 (Apr. 22, 1916): 1129–34; Bernstorff, *My Three Years,* 211.

49. "With Malice Aforethought," *F* 4 (Apr. 12, 1916): 154; O'Leary, "War Is Inevitable," *F* (Apr. 19, 1916): 165; Schrader, "Behind the Scenes at the Capital," *F* 4 (Apr. 26, 1916): 184.

50. WW to RL, draft of Apr. 12, 1916, *PWW,* 36:496.

51. RL to WW, Apr. 17, 1915, enclosing Gottfried von Jagow to HvB, Apr. 15, 1916, *PWW,* 36:498–99; Link, *Wilson,* 4:252.

52. Wilson, address to Congress, Apr. 19, 1916, *PWW,* 36:510.

53. Pomerene and Lodge, *NYT,* Apr. 20, 1916, 4; survey, *NYA,* Apr. 22, 1916, 3.

54. Kenyon in Buchanan, "European Propaganda," 429; Herbert F. Margulies, *Reconciliation and Revival: James R. Mann and the House Republicans of the Wilson Era* (Westport, CT: Greenwood, 1966), 140; William F. Holmes, *The White Chief: James Kimble Vardaman* (Baton Rouge: Louisiana State Univ. Press, 1970), 312.

55. Press reaction in Link, *Wilson,* 4:254–55; "Our Final Word to Germany," *LD* 52 (Apr. 29, 1916): 1201–4; and *CO* 60 (May 1916): 301–2; *N* 102 (Apr. 27, 1916): 446; "The President and Germany," *O* 112 (Apr. 26, 1916): 932; *NR* 6 (Apr. 22, 1916): 304.

56. Bryan in *NYT,* Apr. 20, 1916, 3; Ford in Link, *Wilson,* 4:254; Roosevelt in Buchanan, "European Propaganda," 46.

57. RL to JWG, Apr. 28, 1916, *FR, 1916, Supplement,* 252; Link, *Wilson,* 4:263–68 (emphasis Holtzendorff's).

58. Link, *Wilson,* 4:257 (emphasis Wilhelm's); James W. Gerard, *My Four Years in Germany* (New York: George H. Doran, 1917), 341.

59. RL to WW, May 6, 1916, with enclosure Jagow to JWG, May 4, 1916, *PWW,* 36:621–26, quotation 625; Jagow to JWG, May 8, 1916, *FR, 1916, Supplement,* 265–66.

60. RL to WW, May 6, 1916, *PWW,* 36:620; EMH to WW, May 6, 1916, *PWW,* 36:629.

61. *NYT,* May 6, 1916, 2; Viereck, "President Wilson's Opportunity," *F* 4 (May 17, 1916): 234.

62. *NYT,* May 9, 1916, 1; Bailey and Ryan, *Lusitania,* 313.

63. *NYA,* May 6, 1916, 3; *New York Tribune* in Ralph O. Nafziger, "The American Press and Public Opinion during the World War, 1914 to April 1917" (Ph.D. diss., Univ. of Wisconsin, 1936), 182; "After the Ultimatum," *O* 113 (May 17, 1916): 119–20.

64. Millis, *Road to War,* 300; Tucker, *Wilson and the Great War,* 143; May, *World War,* 194; Link, *Revolution,* 45–46; August Heckscher, *Woodrow Wilson: A Biography* (New York: Scribner, 1991), 387.

65. Jules Witcover, *Sabotage at Black Tom: Imperial Germany's Secret War in America, 1914–1917* (Chapel Hill: Algonquin Books, 1989); "The Hand of God," *F* 5 (Aug. 9, 1916): 10.

66. Goff in Francis Hackett, "A Policy for Ireland," *NR* 6 (Mar. 25, 1916): 209; societies in Buchanan, "European Propaganda," 441.

67. Cohalan in unknown person to JvB, Apr. 17, 1916, *PWW,* 36:503; Papen, Bernstorff in Doerries, *Imperial Challenge,* 73, 155–65.

68. Buchanan, "European Propaganda," 441; Doerries, *Imperial Challenge,* 161, 175.

69. *F* 5 (Aug. 16, 1916): 27; *NYA,* July 30, 1916, 5; "America to Europe, August, 1916," *NR* 7 (July 29, 1916): 321; Howells, *N* 102 (May 18, 1916): 541.

70. *NYA,* Feb. 3, 1916, 22.

71. Circular of Oct. 1915 in CASR to RL, Oct. 16, 1916, *FR, 1916, Supplement,* 457–59.

72. CASR to RL, Apr. 24, 1916, *FR, 1916, Supplement,* 368–82; *NYT,* Sept. 17, 1916, E3.

73. RL to Jules Jusserand, May 24, 1916, *FR, 1916, Supplement,* 604–8; WHP to RL, July 22, 1916, ibid., 613–14; Jusserand to RL, Oct. 12, 1916, ibid., 624.

74. *LD* 52 (June 10, 1916): 1686; *NR* 7 (June 3, 1916): 99; *NYA,* June 6, 1916, 22.

75. Robert P. Skinner, consul general at London, to RL, Sept. 15, 1916, *FR, 1916, Supplement,* 623; *War Memoirs of Lansing,* 127.

76. William Graves Sharp to RL, June 22, 1916, *FR, 1916, Supplement,* 974–77.

77. RL to WW, June 23, 1916, *PWW,* 37:287–88; Stone, *NYT,* July 11, 1916, 12; Harvey, NFTC in *CO* 61 (Nov. 1916): 300; "The Allies' Economic Combine," *NR* (July 8, 1916): 239.

78. Burgess, "John Bull's Blackmail," *F* 4 (Aug. 2, 1916): 411; Collman, "Congress Strikes Back at England," *F* 4 (July 12, 1916): 355; Koester, "America's Perilous Position," *F* 357.

79. Asquith, *NYT,* Aug. 3, 1916, 4; Simon in [Simeon Strunsky], "World Trade after the War," *N* 203 (Aug. 10, 1916): 122.

80. EG to EMH, Mar. 24, 1916, Seymour, *Intimate Papers of Colonel House,* 2:273–74; EMH to EG, Apr. 7, 1916, in May, *World War,* 357; EMH to EG, May 10, 1916, *PWW,* 37:7; May 11, 1916, 37:21; EG to EMH, May 12, 1916, *PWW,* 37:43; British meeting, Link, *Wilson,* vol. 5, *Campaigns for Progressivism and Peace, 1916–1917* (Princeton, NJ: Princeton Univ. Press, 1965), 33; Grey speech, *Current History* 4 (July 1916), 730–31; army council in Devlin, *Too Proud to Fight,* 492.

81. JWG to RL, Apr. 5, 1916, *FR, 1916, Supplement,* 23; Apr. 25, 1916, 243–44; May 11, 1916, 267.

82. WW to EMH, May 16, 1916, *PWW,* 37:57; EMH to WW, May 17, 1916, *PWW,* 37:63.

83. Address to League to Enforce Peace, May 27, 1916, *PWW,* 37:113–16.

84. Allied reaction in Laurence W. Martin, *Peace without Victory: Woodrow Wilson and the British Liberals* (New Haven, CT: Yale Univ. Press, 1958), 108–11; "President Wilson's Peace-Plan," *LD* 52 (June 10, 1916): 1684–85; Drummond in CASR to EG, Sept. 4, 1916, Gwynn, *Letters of Spring Rice,* 2:347.

85. JWG to RL, May 31, 1916, *FR, 1916, Supplement,* 33; Link, *Wilson,* 5:29; FCP to EMH, June 5, 1916, Seymour, *Intimate Papers of Colonel House,* 2:254.

86. Press reaction in *LD* 52 (June 10, 1916): 1683–85; [Rollo Ogden], "Not Mediation but Definition," *N* 102 (June 1, 1916): 583; "Mr. Wilson's Great Utterance," *NR* 7 (June 3, 1916): 102–4; "America to Europe, August, 1916," *NR* 7 (July 29, 1916): 322; Harding and Curtis, *NYA,* May 29, 1916, 1.

87. Gore, *NYA,* May 29, 1916, 1; Gardner, *CR,* June 1, 1916, 9141; TR to Arthur Hamilton Lee, June 7, 1916, *LTR,* 8:1053–54.

88. RL to WW, May 25, 1916, *PWW,* 37:107–8.

89. "President Wilson as a Leader," *O* 113 (June 7, 1916): 303–4; Schrader, "Behind the Scenes at the Capital," *F* 4 (June 7, 1916): 280–81; Viereck, "The New Woodrow Wilson," ibid., 282.

90. Wilson, Memorial Day Address, May 30, 1916, *PWW,* 37:126.

91. EMH to EG, June 9, 1916, *PWW,* 37:179; House diary, June 23, 1916, in Link, *Wilson,* 5:37; Grey in ibid., 5:35.

92. WW to EMH, May 9, 1916, *PWW,* 37:3; EMH to WW, July 5, 1916, *PWW,* 37:365.

93. E.S. Montagu, Mar. 18, 1916, in Link, *Wilson,* 4:140.

94. Link, *Revolution,* 49.

95. Lloyd George, *NYT,* Sept. 29, 1916, 3; Grey in Sterling J. Kernek, "Distractions of Peace during War: The Lloyd George Government's Reactions to Woodrow Wilson: December 1916–November 1918," *Transactions of the American Philosophical Society* 65, n.s. (Apr. 1975), 9; Briand, *NYT,* Sept. 20, 1916, 1.

96. Frank L. Polk to EMH, July 22, 1916, Seymour, *Intimate Papers of Colonel House,* 2:312–13.

97. "Britain's Black List of Firms in America," *LD* 53 (July 29, 1916): 325 (includes *New York Tribune*); Hendrick, *Life and Letters of Page,* 2:184; EMH to WW, July 25, 1916, *PWW,* 37:475; *NR* 7 (July 29, 1916): 314.

98. Bennet, *CR,* Aug. 8, 1916, 12331, 12333; Gallivan, *CR,* Aug. 2, 1916, 12013.

99. Jones, *NYA,* July 24, 1916, 2; Vardaman, *NYA,* July 22, 1916, 2; *Marion Star* in Wittke, *German-Americans,* 86.

100. WW to EMH, July 23, 1916, *PWW,* 37:467.

101. WW to British Foreign Office [July 26, 1916], *PWW,* 37:476–79.

102. Cecil in WHP to RL, July 26, 1916, *FR, 1916, Supplement,* 420; British accusations, *NYT,* July 23, 1916, 1; Devlin, *Too Proud to Fight,* 514.

103. Thomas A. Bailey, "The United States and the Blacklist during the Great War," *Journal of Modern History* 6 (Mar. 1934): 21–22.

104. *NYT,* May 21, 1916, 7; *NYT,* Aug. 19, 1916, 1; Link, *Wilson,* 4:339–40.

105. Thomas amendment, Phelan, *NYT,* Sept. 11, 1916, 12; voting and signing, *NYT,* Sept. 8, 1916, 1, 5.

106. *NR* 8 (Sept. 9, 1916): 126; Bailey, "Blacklist," 16–28.

107. *War Memoirs of Lansing,* 171–72; Ross Gregory, *Walter Hines Page: Ambassador to the Court of St. James's* (Lexington: Univ. Press of Kentucky, 1970), 167–68.

108. Hendrick, *Life and Letters of Page,* 2:178, 185–86; Cooper, *Page,* 346; Link, *Wilson,* 5:72.

109. CASR to EG, Dec. 23, 1915, in Gwynn, *Letters of Spring Rice,* 2:305.

7. Preparedness Debates and the Presidential Election

1. Hay, *CR,* Mar. 20, 1916, 4480; Greene, *CR,* Mar. 17, 1916, 4337–38; Hay, *CR,* May 8, 1916, 7599; London, *CR,* Mar. 17, 1916, 4355.

2. Davis, *CR,* appendix, Mar. 9, 1916, 511; London, *CR,* Mar. 17, 1916, 4354.

3. *New York Tribune* in "The Democratic Plan for Strengthening the Army," *LD* 52 (Mar. 4, 1916): 548; "Nation-Wide Press-Poll on Size of the Army and Navy," *LD* 52 (Mar. 11, 1916): 617; Gardner, *CR,* Mar. 17, 1916, 4342; Finnegan, *Specter of a Dragon,* 141.

4. Bliss in Finnegan, *Specter of a Dragon,* 142; JWG to EMH, May 10, 1916, Seymour, *Intimate Papers of Colonel House,* 2:246.

5. Kahn, *CR,* Mar. 18, 1916, 4406; Hay, *CR,* Mar. 20, 1916, 4490; Finnegan, *Specter of a Dragon,* 144.

6. Voting tally on Kahn amendment and full bill, *CR,* Mar. 23, 1916, 4729–30.

7. Kitchin in Link, *Wilson,* 4:329; *O* 112 (Mar. 29, 1916): 723.

8. Chamberlain, *NYT,* Nov. 16, 1915, 9; *NYT,* Jan. 9, 1916, 4; Finnegan, *Specter of a Dragon,* 146.

9. McCumber, *CR,* Mar. 17, 1916, 4280–82, 4286; Vardaman, *CR,* Apr. 4, 1916, 5418; Sherman, *CR,* Apr. 17, 1916, 6293.

10. Works, *CR,* Dec. 16, 1915, 322–25; Wilson address, New York, [Jan. 27, 1916], *PWW,* 36:13.

11. Chamberlain, O'Ryan, *CO* 60 (May 1916): 309–10; Finnegan, *Specter of a Dragon,* 148.

12. Brandegee, *CR,* Apr. 18, 1916, 6356; vote on Brandegee amendment, *CR,* Apr. 18, 1916, 6359; volunteer system, *NYT,* Apr. 19, 1916, 1; WW to James Hay, Apr. 19, 1916, in Baker, *Wilson,* 6:305; press survey in Buchanan, "European Propaganda," 451.

13. *CR,* May 8, 1916, 7599–7601.

14. Press in Finnegan, *Specter of a Dragon,* 153; TR noted in *NR* 7 (May 6, 1916):

2; Taft in Pringle, *Taft,* 880; "The German American and Preparedness," *F* 4 (May 10, 1916): 219.

15. Mann and Gardner, *CR,* May 20, 1916, 8399–8400; Ferris, 8402; Hay, *NYT,* May 21, 1916, 1; House voting tally, *CR,* May 20, 1916, 8406.

16. NSL, Roosevelt, Scott in Link, *Wilson,* 4:332; "The Week," *O* 113 (June 7, 1916): 289–90.

17. Wood in Link, *Wilson,* 4:332; *NYT,* Jan. 28, 1916, 1.

18. *NR* 7 (May 20, 1916): 49–50; [Oswald Garrison Villard], "The Army Bill," *N* 102 (June 1, 1916): 584–85.

19. Finnegan, *Specter of a Dragon,* 155–56; Harbaugh, "Wilson," 145–46.

20. Finnegan, *Specter of a Dragon,* 165–72.

21. Wilson, *NYT,* June 15, 1916, 1.

22. Wilson, speech, Feb. 3, 1916, *PWW,* 36:120; Charles Chatfield, *For Peace and Justice: Pacifism in America, 1914–1941* (Knoxville: Univ. of Tennessee Press, 1971), 23.

23. Blanche Wiesen Cook, "Woodrow Wilson and the Anti-Militarists, 1914–1917" (Ph.D. diss., Johns Hopkins Univ., 1970), chaps. 1–3; Patterson, *Search,* 189; Chambers, *Army,* 116.

24. Colloquy with antipreparedness leaders, [May 8, 1916], *PWW,* 36:632–48.

25. Bryan, "The Munitions-Militarist Conspiracy," *Commoner* 16 (May 1916): 3; AFL in Finnegan, *Specter of a Dragon,* 125.

26. Villard in Finnegan, *Specter of a Dragon,* 122; "Paper Soldiers," *Saturday Evening Post* 188 (Apr. 22, 1916): 26.

27. EMH to WW, May 17, 1916, *PWW,* 37:64; House diary, Sept. 24, 1916, *PWW,* 38:258–59.

28. Meyer, *NYA,* May 28, 1916, part 4, p. 4; "Expert Opinion on the Naval Bill," *O* 113 (June 21, 1916): 402–3; *New York Tribune* in "Is Our Navy Ready?" *LD* 52 (Apr. 15, 1916): 1046; Reuterdahl, June 2, 1916, 3.

29. *NYA,* June 5, 1915, 18; O'Laughlin, *Imperiled America,* 27, 155.

30. Sims, Glenn in "Is Our Navy Ready?" *LD* 52 (Apr. 15, 1916): 1046; Dewey, *NYT,* Feb. 6, 1916, 8.

31. Ford advertisement, *NYA,* May 7, 1916, 13; Callaway in Millis, *Road to War,* 326.

32. *NYT,* May 19, 1916, 1.

33. *CR,* June 2, 1916, 9189–90.

34. Finnegan, *Specter of a Dragon,* 162.

35. Swanson, *CR,* July 13, 1916, 10923–24.

36. Borah, ibid., 11171, 11174.

37. Norris, ibid., 11185–92.

38. La Follette, *CR,* July 20, 1916, 11330–32.

39. *NYT,* July 22, 1916, 1.

40. Link, *Wilson,* 4:337.

41. Voting tally, *CR,* Aug. 15, 1916, 12700.

42. Harbaugh, "Wilson," 147; Kitchin in Link, *Wilson,* 4:337; Villard, "The Navy Bill," *N* 103 (July 20, 1916): 51–52.

43. Link in Garraty, *Interpreting,* 2:132; Osgood, *Ideals and Self-Interest,* 220; Finnegan, *Specter of a Dragon,* 154, 194.

44. Root, *NYT,* Feb. 16, 1916, 1, 4.

45. "Republican Forecast of the Presidential Campaign," *LD* 51 (Dec. 18, 1915): 1403; Harvey, "On Republican Candidates," *NAR* 203 (Mar. 1916): 336–37; *NR* 6 (Feb. 19, 1916): 53.

46. White in S.D. Lovell, *The Presidential Election of 1916* (Carbondale: Southern Illinois Univ. Press, 1980), 192n52; Taft in Harbaugh, "Wilson," 155; Hearst, *NYA*, June 6, 1916, p. 1.

47. *NYT,* May 20, 1916, 1, 4; Harbaugh, "Wilson," 174–75.

48. TR to George W. Perkins, Apr. 16, 1916, *LTR,* 8:1030.

49. *NYT,* Mar. 10, 1916, 20; May 12, 1916, 1, 5; Cooper, *Warrior,* 305.

50. TR to Raymond Robins, Mar. 6, 1915, *LTR,* 8:932; TR to John J. Pershing, June 6, 1916, 8:1051.

51. HCL to TR, Feb. 1, 1916, *Correspondence of Roosevelt and Lodge,* 2:474; Taft in Link, *Wilson,* 5:3.

52. William Allen White, *Autobiography* (New York: Macmillan, 1946), 513.

53. Lovell, *Election of 1916,* 32; Jack C. Lane, *Armed Progressive: General Leonard Wood* (San Rafael, CA: Presidio, 1978), 207.

54. Schrader, "Behind the Scenes at the Capital," and Viereck, "A Word with the Republicans," *F* 3 (Dec. 29, 1915): 366, 370; *F* 3 (Jan. 26, 1916): 431.

55. Bacon in Buchanan, "European Propaganda," 484.

56. Progressive platform in *NYT,* June 9, 1916, 2; "The Progressive Party—an Obituary," *NR* 7 (June 17, 1916): 160.

57. Republican platform in Donald Bruce Johnson, *National Party Platforms,* 2 vols. (Urbana: Univ. of Illinois Press, 1978), 1:204–5; Lodge, Borah in Link, *Wilson,* 5:5; La Follette, *NYT,* June 9, 1915, 3.

58. TR to the conferees of the Progressive Party, June 10, 1916, *LTR,* 8:1061–62.

59. Hughes, *NYT,* June 11, 1916, 1.

60. Harbaugh, "Wilson," 191.

61. Lippmann, "At the Chicago Conventions," *NR* 7 (June 17, 1916): 165; TR to Progressive National Convention, undated, *LTR,* 8:1062–63; June 22, 1916, 8:1069, 1071.

62. Democratic platform in Johnson, *Party Platforms,* 1:194–200.

63. Glynn, *NYT,* June 15, 1916, 2; James and Bryan, *NYT,* June 16, 1916, 2.

64. Wilson in Lovell, *Election of 1916,* 212; Thompson, *Wilson,* 130.

65. Colloquy, American Neutral Conference Committee, Aug. 30, 1916, *PWW,* 38:115–17.

66. Wilson, speech, Sept. 2, 1916, *PWW,* 38:132–36.

67. General press reaction, "The President's Defense of His Record," *LD* 53 (Sept. 16, 1916): 654–56; *Evening Post* in Buchanan, "European Propaganda," 487; "The Field of Politics," *O* 114 (Sept. 13, 1916): 61–62; Viereck, "Mr. Wilson Accepts," *F* 5 (Sept. 13, 1916): 90.

68. Wilson address, *NYT,* Oct. 1, 1916, 2; Walsh in Link, *Wilson,* 5:109.

69. Jeremiah A. O'Leary to WW, Sept. 29, [1916], *PWW,* 38:285; WW to Jeremiah A. O'Leary, [Sept. 29, 1916], *PWW,* 38:286.

70. Press reaction, "The President and the Hyphen," *LD* 53 (Oct. 14, 1916): 935; *NYA,* Oct. 1, 1916, 1; Collman, "Behind the Scenes at the Capital," *F* 5 (Oct. 11, 1916): 152; O'Leary in Buchanan, "European Propaganda," 490.

71. Omaha speech, Oct. 5, 1916, *PWW,* 38:347; Cincinnati speech, Oct. 26, 1916, *PWW,* 38:531–32; endorsements in Cook, "Wilson," 156, 166–68.

72. TR as secretary of war in Wittke, *German-Americans,* 109; as secretary of state in Luebke, *Loyalty,* 190; Stone, *NYT,* Oct. 12, 1916, 1, 5; Bernstorff in Link, *Wilson,* 5:139.

73. "Why Hughes Finds Wilson Wanting," *LD* 53 (Aug. 12, 1916): 336.

74. "The Week," *N* 103 (Aug. 3, 1916): 96; "The Hughes Acceptance," *NR* 8 (Aug. 5, 1916): 4; Hughes, *NYT,* Nov. 5, 1916, 2.

75. *NYT,* Oct. 13, 1916, 1, 2; Nov. 1, 1916, 1, 7.

76. Harding, *NYT,* June 8, 1916, 4; Hughes, *NYT,* Oct. 23, 1916, 1; Fairbanks in Wittke, *German-Americans,* 98; Alliance and general praise in Child, *German-Americans,* 133, 137; press in "Sizing Up Mr. Hughes's Chances," *LD* 52 (June 24, 1916): 1830–31; Viereck, "Before the Verdict," *F* 5 (Nov. 8, 1916): 218; "The Neutral Vote and the Socialist Party," ibid., 219.

77. Milwaukee, *NYT,* Sept. 21, 1916, 2; Philadelphia, Oct. 10, 1916, 1; "Mr. Hughes Finds an Issue," *NR* 9 (Nov. 4, 1916): 6–7; New York speeches, *NYT,* Oct. 25, 1916, 1; Nov. 1, 1916, 1.

78. TR to Robert Perkins Bass, June 28, 1916, *LTR,* 8:1095; TR to William Austin Wadsworth, June 23, 1916, 8:1078; Harbaugh, *Power,* 488, 492; Patricia O'Toole, *When Trumpets Call: Theodore Roosevelt after the White House* (New York: Simon and Schuster, 2005), 293; endorsement, *NYT,* June 29, 1916, 1, 22.

79. Lewiston, *NYT,* Sept. 1, 1916, 6; Hughes, *NYT,* Sept. 3, 1916, 1.

80. Battle Creek, *NYT,* Oct. 1, 1916, 1, 3; Denver, *NYT,* Oct. 25, 1916, 6; slogan, *NYT,* Oct. 11, 1916, 6; Cooper Union, *NYT,* Nov. 4, 1916, 4.

81. *Commoner* and Hughes failure cited in Harbaugh, "Wilson," 248; *F* 5 (Oct. 11, 1916): 154.

82. Harbaugh, "Wilson," 230; McKnight, "Party," 356.

83. "'Yes' or 'No,' Mr. Hughes?" *Commoner* 16 (Aug. 1916): 26.

84. WW to Bernard Baruch, Aug. 19, 1916, *PWW,* 38:51; WW to RL, Oct. 2, 1916, *PWW,* 38:319.

85. Lodge controversy, *NYT,* Oct. 27, 29, 30, 31, 1916, all p. 1; Walworth, *Wilson,* 2:63n37.

86. *NYT,* Feb. 11, 1916, 3.

87. Allan L. Benson, *Inviting War to America* (New York: B.W. Huebsch, 1916), 7.

88. Socialist platform in Johnson, *Party Platforms,* 1:209–10; "The Neutral Vote and the Socialist Party," *F* 5 (Nov. 5, 1916): 219; Meyer Jonah Nathan, "The Presidential Election of 1916 in the Middle West" (Ph.D. diss., Princeton Univ., 1965), 203, 268.

89. TR to John St. Leo Strachey, Jan. 1, 1917, *LTR,* 8:1139; TR to William Allen White, ibid.; Taft in Pringle, *Taft,* 2:899.

90. *NYA,* Nov. 10, 1916, 18; "The Election," *NR* 9 (Nov. 11, 1916): 34.

91. Link, *Progressive Era,* 250; Nathan, "Election of 1916," 272–74; Cooper, *Wilson,* 359.

8. To End a Conflict

1. Conference at Pless Castle, Aug. 31, 1916, *OGD,* 2:1155–56; Link, *Wilson,* 5:168–69, 186; entry of Sept. 29, 1916, Müller in Görlitz, *Kaiser,* 206.

2. Business panic, *NYT,* Oct. 10, 1916, 4; Wilson, *NYT,* Oct. 10, 1916, 1; JvB to Foreign Office, Oct. 14, 1916, *OGD,* 2:988; naval reports, *NYT,* Oct. 11, 1916, 1; WHP to RL, Oct. 18, 1916, *FR, 1916, Supplement,* 779.

3. Roosevelt, *NYT,* Oct. 11, 1916, 6; [Rollo Ogden], "Renewing the Submarine Peril," *N* 103 (Oct. 12, 1916): 337; Viereck, "U-53," *F* 5 (Oct. 18, 1916): 170.

4. WHP to RL, Oct. 11, 1916, *FR, 1916, Supplement,* 773–74.

5. Entry of Dec. 12, 1916, in Görlitz, *Kaiser,* 221; RL to JCG, Oct. 30 and 31, 1916, *FR, 1916, Supplement,* 298–99.

6. House diary, Nov. 2, 1916, *PWW,* 38:607–8; Link, *Wilson,* 5:187; WW to EMH, Nov. 24, 1916, *PWW,* 40:62–63.

7. EMH to WW, Dec. 7, 1916, with enclosure of EMH to David Lloyd George, Dec. 7, 1916, *PWW,* 40:184–86; Gregory, *Origins,* 113; Lansing diary, Dec. 21, 1916, *PWW,* 40:310n1 (emphasis Lansing's); RL to WW, Dec. 8, 1916, *PWW,* 40:190.

8. JCG to EMH, Oct. 17, 1916, in Seymour, *Intimate Papers of Colonel House,* 2:387; JCG to RL, Nov. 7, 1916, *PWW,* 40:141–42.

9. Ludendorff in Herwig, *Politics of Frustration,* 121; Bethmann to Werner Freiheer von Grünau, Oct. 1, 1916, *OGD,* 2:1169–70; Helfferich testimony, Nov. 12, 1919, *OGD,* 1:659.

10. Link, *Wilson,* 5:241–42; Herwig, *Politics of Frustration,* 122.

11. Tumulty, *Wilson,* 248.

12. Bernstorff to German Foreign Office, Sept. 8, 1916, in Bernstorff, *My Three Years,* 245; Bernstorff, Oct. 5, 1916, *OGD,* 2:986; Nov. 12, 1916, *OGD,* 2:1304; Nov. 24, 1916, *OGD,* 2:993.

13. Karl E. Birnbaum, *Peace Moves and U-Boat Warfare: A Study of Germany's Policy towards the United States, April 18, 1916—January 7, 1917* (Stockholm: Almquist & Wiksell, 1958), 185.

14. Link, *Wilson,* 5:170–71.

15. JvB to EMH, Oct. 18, 1916, *PWW,* 38:495–96; EMH to WW, Oct. 20, 1916, *PWW,* 38:494; Arthur Zimmermann to JvB, Nov. 26, 1916, *OGD,* 2:995; EMH to WW, Nov. 20, 1916, *PWW,* 40:5.

16. House diary, Nov. 14, 1916, *PWW,* 38:646–47.

17. House diary, Nov. 15, 1916, *PWW,* 38:658; Doerries, *Imperial Challenge,* 199.

18. House diary, Nov. 15, 1916, *PWW,* 38:658; Link, *Revolution,* 27.

19. Interdepartmental conference, Keynes in Gregory, *Page,* 174–75; McKenna in Link, *Wilson,* 5:184; and in extracts from letters of Norman Hapgood, Dec. 30, 1916; Jan. 4, 1917, *PWW,* 40:497.

20. Committee warning in Link, *Wilson,* 5:183.

21. Link, *PWW,* 40:20n1.

22. Statement, Federal Reserve Board, Nov. 27, 1916, *PWW,* 40:80; Statement for the Press, Nov. 27, 1916, *PWW,* 40:87–88.

23. Spring Rice in Thompson, *Wilson,* 131; Harding in Cooper, "Command of Gold," 222.

24. Stuart in Tansill, *America Goes to War,* 119.

25. *NYT,* Nov. 5, 1916, 2.

26. WHP to RL, Oct. 11, 1916, *FR, 1916, Supplement,* 455–56.

27. "Memorandum," enclosed with Jules Jusserand to RL, Oct. 12, 1916, *FR, 1916, Supplement,* 626, 628.

28. "Why Britain Reads Our Letters," *LD* 53 (Oct. 28, 1916): 1096; *NR* 8 (Oct. 21, 1916): 279; *O* 114 (Oct. 25, 1916): 393.

29. "British-American Irritation," *NR* 9 (Dec. 9, 1916): 137–38; House diary, Nov. 17, 1916, Seymour, *Intimate Papers of Colonel House,* 2:327.

30. "Memorandum on the Means of Combating Foreign Restrictions on American Commerce," attached to Redfield to Lansing, Oct. 23, 1916, *FR, 1916, Supplement,* 466–77.

31. Gregory, *Origins,* 109–10.

32. Wilson, "An Unpublished Prolegomenon to a Peace Note," c. Nov. 25, 1916, *PWW,* 40:68–69.

33. RL to JCG, Nov. 29, 1916, *FR, 1916, Supplement,* 70–71; JCG to RL, Dec. 11, 1916, ibid., 869; Root, *NYT,* Dec. 16, 1916, 1; "Those Belgian Deportations," *F* 5 (Nov. 29, 1916): 266–67.

34. Bethmann address, *NYT,* Dec. 13, 1916, 1; Bethmann to JCG, *FR, 1916, Supplement,* Dec. 12, 1916, 87.

35. Link, *Wilson,* 5:211.

36. Fritz Fischer, *Germany's Aims in the First World War* (New York: Norton, 1967), 297; May, *World War,* 395; Patterson, *Search,* 267.

37. Press opinion, "Germany's Peace-Proposals," *LD* 53 (Dec. 23, 1916): 1643; Viereck, "Red Christmas or White?" *F* 5 (Dec. 20, 1916): 320; *NYA,* Dec. 13, 1916, 18; *NR* 9 (Dec. 16, 1916): 166; Stone, *NYA,* Dec. 15, 1916, 2; Bryan, *NYT,* Dec. 16, 1916, 1.

38. Czar and Duma, *NYT,* Dec. 16, 1916, 1; Briand, *NYT,* Dec. 15, 1916, 2; French Senate, *NYT,* Dec. 25, 1916, 2; Sonnino, *NYT,* Dec. 15, 1916, 2.

39. Lloyd George, *NYT,* Dec. 20, 1916, 1, 2; Link, *Wilson,* 5:230–31.

40. "Summary of the News," *N* 103 (Dec. 21, 1916): 575; Harding in Buchanan, "European Propaganda," 537.

41. *War Memoirs of Lansing,* 182; Bernstorff to Foreign Office, Nov. 21, 1916, *OGD,* 2:993.

42. Wilson, "An Appeal for a Statement of War Aims," Dec. 18, 1916, *PWW,* 40:273–76.

43. RL to WW, Dec. 10, 1916, *PWW,* 40:209–10; House diary, Dec. 14, 1916, *PWW,* 40:238; Dec. 20, 1916, *PWW,* 40:304–5.

44. Walworth, *Wilson,* 2:74; Devlin, *Too Proud to Fight,* 580, 631; Clements, *Presidency of Wilson,* 136.

45. *NYA,* Dec. 21, 1916, 18; WJB to WW, Dec. 21, 1916, *PWW,* 40:314; Stone, *NYT,* Dec. 21, 1916, 1; Viereck, "Gentlemen, State Your Terms," *F* 5 (Jan. 3, 1917): 362; Bernstorff, *NYT,* Dec. 21, 1916, 1.

46. ANCC in Buchanan, "European Propaganda," 548; *NYT,* Nov. 26, 1916, 1; Nov. 28, 1916, 4; Balch, *NYT,* Dec. 24, 1916, X8.

47. Weeks and *New York Tribune* in *LD* 53 (Dec. 30, 1916): 1694; Roosevelt in Tansill, *America Goes to War,* 624; Lodge in Widenor, *Lodge,* 251; "The President's Unasked Advice," *O* 115 (Jan. 3, 1917): 13; Wood in Millis, *Road to War,* 624.

48. *NYT,* Dec. 31, 1916, 2.

49. Neutral sentiment, *NYT,* Dec. 26, 1916, 1; German policy in Link, *Wilson,* 5:233–35.

50. George V and Cambon in Link, *Wilson,* 5:230; Kerr in Widenor, *Lodge,* 249; James Bryce to WW, Dec. 22, 1916, *PWW,* 40:317; *Manchester Guardian* in *NYA,* Dec. 22, 1916, 16.

51. RL to WW, Dec. 10, 1916, *PWW,* 40:209.

52. *NYT,* Dec. 22, 1916, 1.

53. "The Autocrat of American Policy," *NAR* 205 (Feb. 1917): 164; Lansing, *NYT,* Dec. 22, 1916, 1.

54. Devlin, *Too Proud to Fight,* 583; Cooper, *Wilson,* 367.

55. Link, *Wilson,* 5:224–25.

56. House meeting, Dec. 22, 1916, *PWW,* 40:308–9n1; and Cooper, *Pivotal Decades,* 256.

57. EMH to WW, Dec. 20, 1916, *PWW,* 40:294.

58. JWG to RL, Dec. 26, 1916, *PWW,* 40:331; Zimmermann to Bernstorff, Dec. 26, 1916, *OGD,* 2:1005; Zimmermann, Jan. 7, 1917, in Doerries, *Imperial Challenge,* 207 (emphasis Zimmermann's); Bernstorff testimony, Oct. 22, 1919, *OGD,* 1:265.

59. Press opinion, including *New York World,* in "Germany's Request for a Peace-Conference," *LD* 54 (Jan. 6, 1917): 1–3.

60. House in Link, *Wilson,* 5:250; House diary, Jan. 3, 1917, *PWW,* 40:404.

61. House diary, Jan. 4, 1917, *PWW,* 40:409.

62. William Graves Sharp to RL, Dec. 29, 1916, *FR, 1916, Supplement,* 123–25.

63. Hitchcock, *NYT,* Dec. 22, 1916, 1; Lodge, *CR,* Jan. 3, 1917, 792–97; Lewis and Borah, *NYT,* Jan. 6, 1917, 1–2.

64. Voting, *CR,* Jan. 5, 1917, 897.

65. *NYT,* Jan. 4, 1917, 1; Roosevelt cited in "Roosevelt and Righteousness," *NR* 9 (Jan. 13, 1917): 281.

66. Link, *Revolution,* 60; JCG to RL, Jan. 10, 1917, *PWW,* 40:435.

67. Fischer, *Germany's Aims,* 285; Link, *Wilson,* 5:245–46.

68. Helfferich to Arnold Wahnschaffe, Jan. 9, 1917, *OGD,* 1:643–45; report of Pless conference, Jan. 9, 1917, *OGD,* 2:1321; Wilhelm in Cecil, *Wilhelm II,* 2:242–43.

69. Both orders in Link, *Wilson,* 5:247.

70. Bernstorff to Foreign Office, Jan. 10, 1917, *OGD,* 2:1017; Foreign Office to Bernstorff, Jan. 19, 1917, in Bernstorff, *My Three Years,* 306.

71. Link, *Wilson,* 5:289.

72. Millis, *Road to War,* 373.

73. Jellicoe in Correlli Barnett, *The Great War* (London: BBC, 2003), 125.

74. Cooper, "Command of Gold," 228.

75. EMH to WW, Jan. 15, 1917, *PWW,* 40:477–78; Jan. 18, 1917, *PWW,* 40:516–17; WW to EMH, Jan. 19, 1917, *PWW,* 40:524.

76. Bethmann terms, Link, *Wilson,* 5:255.

77. JvB to EMH, Jan. 18, 1917, *PWW,* 40:525–26; JvB to EMH, Jan. 20, 1917, *PWW,* 40:529; Devlin, *Too Proud to Fight,* 616.

78. EMH to WW, Jan. 20, 1917, *PWW,* 40:526–27.

79. Allied terms, William G. Sharp to RL, Jan. 10, 1917, *PWW,* 40:439–42; *NYT,* Jan. 12, 1917, 1.

80. Link, *Wilson,* 5:254.

81. [Rollo Ogden], "The Allied Step Forward," *N* 104 (Jan. 18, 1917): 64; "A Masterpiece in Diplomacy," *NR* 9 (Jan. 20, 1917): 311–13; *NYA,* Jan. 12, 1917, 20; Viereck, "The Ten Four-Flushers," *F* 5 (Jan. 24, 1917): 403.

82. Wilson, address to the Senate, Jan. 22, 1917, *PWW,* 40:533–39.

83. WW to John Palmer Gavit, Jan. 29, 1917, *PWW,* 41:55 (emphasis Wilson's); WW to Charles William Eliot, ibid.

84. Tansill, *America Goes to War,* 631; Millis, *Road to War,* 375; Walworth, *Wilson,* 2:80; Cooper, *Wilson,* 371; Kennedy, *Wilson,* 51.

85. Gregory, *Origins,* 116; Link, *Progressive Era,* 266; Devlin, *Too Proud to Fight,* 623.

86. Benedict and French Socialists, *NYT,* Jan. 26, 1917, 2; liberals in Link, *Wilson,* 5:271–75; Russia, *NYT,* Jan. 27, 1917, 1.

87. Clemenceau, *NYT,* Jan. 26, 1917, 2; Bonar Law, *NYT,* Jan. 25, 1917, 1; Helfferich, testimony, Nov. 12, 1919, *OGD,* 1:683.

88. Press summary, *NYT,* Jan. 23, 1917, 2; and "Feasibility of the President's Peace-Program," *LD* 54 (Feb. 3, 1917), 229–32; [Rollo Ogden], "Wilson the Idealist," *N* 104 (Jan. 25, 1917): 94; "Peace Without Victory," *NR* 9 (Dec. 23, 1916): 201; WW to Herbert Croly, Jan. 25, 1917, *PWW,* 41:13; clergy, *NYT,* Jan. 25, 1917, 3; Lillian D. Wald et al., Jan. 24, 1917, *PWW,* 41:8.

89. La Follette, Pittman in *NYT,* Jan. 23, 1917, 2; Tillman in *NYA,* Jan. 23, 1917, 3.

90. Thomas, *CR,* Feb. 1, 1917, 2372; Taft, *NYT,* Jan. 26, 1917, 2; Gillett in Cooper, *Vanity,* 157; Croly, "The Structure of Peace," *NR* 9 (Jan. 13, 1917): 287–91.

91. Viereck, "Mr. Wilson's Sermon on the Mount," *F* 5 (Jan. 31, 1917): 419; O'Leary, *NYA,* Jan. 23, 1917, 2; editorial, *NYA,* Jan. 25, 1917, 18; Bryan, *NYT,* Jan. 26, 1917, 2.

92. Warren in Cooper, *Vanity,* 156–57; Smoot, *NYA,* Jan. 23, 1917, 3; Cummins, *NYT,* Jan. 24, 1917, 1.

93. *Herald* cited in Harbaugh, "Wilson," 277; TR in *NYT,* Jan. 29, 1917, 6; ARC, *NYT,* Jan. 30, 1917, 8; Root, *NYT,* Jan. 26, 1917, 1; Depew in Buchanan, "European Propaganda," 576 (emphasis mine); Beck, *NYT,* Jan. 25, 1917, 3; *Irish World* in Cuddy, *Irish-America,* 131.

94. Gallinger, Sherman, *NYA,* Jan. 23, 1917, 2; Thomas, *CR,* Feb. 1, 1917, 2373; Beard, *NYA,* Jan. 23, 1917, 3.

95. Watson and Poindexter, *NYA,* Jan. 23, 1917, 3; Benson in *LD* 54 (Feb. 3, 1917): 231; Gardner, *CR,* Feb. 15, 1917, 3358; Cummins, *NYT,* Jan. 31, 1917, 1; Reed, *NYT,* Jan. 23, 1917, 2.

96. Borah, *NYT,* Jan. 27, 1917, 2.

97. Lodge, *CR,* Feb. 1, 1917, 2365–68.

98. Harbaugh, "Wilson," 278.

99. Jusserand to Foreign Ministry, Mar. 7, 1917, *PWW,* 41:356–57.

100. EMH to WW, Jan. 26, 1917, *PWW,* 41:26–27.

101. WW to EMH, Jan. 24, 1917, *PWW,* 41:3 (emphasis Wilson's).

102. Warning in Link, *Wilson,* 5:278; JvB to Foreign Office, Jan. 27, 1917, and Stumm to JvB, Jan. 29, 1917, *OGD,* 2:1048.

103. Memorandum, *War Memoirs of Lansing,* 208.

9. The Break with Germany

1. JvB to RL, Jan. 31, 1917, *FR, 1917, Supplement* (Washington, DC: Government Printing Office, 1931), 1:97–102.

2. Press opinion in *NYT,* Feb. 1, 1917, 4; "Our Break with Germany," *LD* 54

(Feb. 10, 1917), 321–23 (including *New York Evening Post*); and Link, *Wilson,* 5:292–93; *Brooklyn Eagle* in Bailey and Ryan, *Lusitania,* 317; [Rollo Ogden], "Germany's Worst Blunder," *N* 104 (Feb. 8, 1917): 150; *O* 115 (Feb. 7, 1917): 217; Sherman in *NYT,* Feb. 8, 1917, 5; "Postscript," Feb. 1, 1917, *NR* 10 (Feb. 3, 1917): end cover; "America's Part in the War," *NR* 10 (Feb. 10, 1917): 33–34; TR to Newton D. Baker, Feb. 2, 1917, *LTR,* 8:1149.

3. *NYA,* Feb. 1, 1917, 20; Feb. 3, 1917, 16.

4. Hale, *NYA,* Feb. 2, 1917, 1; Viereck, "Great Britain's New Reign of Terror," *F* 6 (Feb. 7, 1917): 18; journals, Wittke, *German-Americans,* 119–20; Jones in Buchanan, "European Propaganda," 584.

5. Bryan, *NYT,* Feb. 3, 1917, 11; pacifists and socialists in *NYT,* Feb. 2, 1917, 8; and Link, *Wilson,* 5:293.

6. Link, *Wilson,* 5:299.

7. Lansing, memorandum of Feb. 4, 1917, *PWW,* 41:118–25.

8. House diary, Feb. 1, 1917, *PWW,* 41:87.

9. Lane to George W. Lane, Feb. 9, 1917, in Lane and Wall, *Letters of Lane,* 234; Houston, *Eight Years,* 1:229.

10. Senators, *NYT,* Feb. 3, 1917, 2; Link, *Wilson,* 5:297–98.

11. Wilson, address to joint session of Congress, Feb. 3, 1917, *PWW,* 41:108–12.

12. Gardner, *NYA,* Feb. 4, 1917, 6-L; Harding, Tillman, Kitchin, Mann, *NYT,* Feb. 4, 1917, 2; Taft, *NYT,* Feb. 6, 1917, 8; Vardaman, *NYT,* Feb. 8, 1917, 5.

13. General press reaction, Link, *Wilson,* 5:301–2; "An Ally or a Hindrance?" *NAR* 205 (Mar. 1917): 322, 326; "America's Duty," *O* 115 (Feb. 14, 1917): 263.

14. German American press reaction, *NYT,* Feb. 4, 1917, 5; "Where German-Americans Stand," *LD* 54 (Mar. 17, 1917): 388; and *CO* 62 (Mar. 1917): 156; "Yet Time to Consider," *New World* 6 (Feb. 14, 1917): 25; Alliance, *NYT,* Feb. 9, 1917, 3; *New York Evening Mail* in "Our Break with Germany," *LD* 54 (Feb. 10, 1917): 321.

15. Socialists in Buchanan, "European Propaganda," 593.

16. Slogan, *NYT,* Feb. 7, 1917, 8; EPF in C. Roland Marchand, *The American Peace Movement and Social Reform, 1898–1918* (Princeton, NJ: Princeton Univ. Press, 1972), 250; Hearst to S.S. Carvalho, Mar. 2, 1917, in *NYT,* Dec. 11, 1918, 3; Bryan, *NYT,* Feb. 5, 1917, 4; Addams in *La Follette's Magazine* 9 (Feb. 1917): 4.

17. CDC, advertisement, *NR* 10 (Feb. 17, 1917): 82.

18. Senate vote, *CR,* Feb. 7, 1917, 2750; Stone, 2731; Lodge, Borah in *NYT,* Feb. 8, 1917, 5; Ruth Warner Towne, *Senator William J. Stone and the Politics of Compromise* (Port Washington, NY: Kennikat, 1979), 209.

19. Vardaman, *CR,* Feb. 7, 1917, 2734; Works, 2731; La Follette in Cooper, *Vanity,* 171–72.

20. Callaway, *NYT,* Feb. 10, 1917, 2; other resolutions, *NYT,* Feb. 11, 1917, 2; Sherwood, *NYT,* Feb. 14, 1917, 8; Stone, *NYT,* Feb. 17, 1917, 3; Hearst, *NYA,* Feb. 22, 1917, 18; Feb. 19, 1917, 18.

21. Maurer, *NYT,* Feb. 5, 1917, 2; Villard, "'Limited-Liability' War," *LD* 54 (Mar. 3, 1917): 538.

22. ARC, *NYT,* Feb. 17, 1917, 2; Lodge in Harbaugh, "Wilson," 281; TR to HCL, Feb. 20, 1917, *LTR,* 8:1156; TR to HCL, Feb. 12, 1917, *Correspondence of Roosevelt and Lodge,* 2:494.

23. Gregory, *Origins,* 122.

24. CASR to Arthur Balfour, Feb. 23, 1917, Gwynn, *Letters of Spring Rice,* 2:381; *NR* 10 (Feb. 17, 1917): 56–57; Ludendorff in Cecil, *Wilhelm II,* 2:243.

25. Carleton J.H. Hayes, "Which? War without a Purpose?" *Survey* 37 (Feb. 10, 1917): 535–38.

26. Peace groups in Harbaugh, "Wilson," 286; and Link, *Wilson,* 5:307; [Oswald Garrison Villard], "A League of Armed Neutrals," *N* 104 (Feb. 15, 1917): 179; Lenroot, *CR,* Feb. 17, 1917, 3529.

27. Ira Nelson Morris to RL, *FR, 1917, Supplement,* 1:124; Devlin, *Too Proud to Fight,* 642.

28. Bergson conversation, Link, *Wilson,* 5:340–41.

29. Houston, *Eight Years,* 1:236; Franklin K. Lane to George W. Lane, Feb. 25, 1917, in Lane and Wall, *Letters of Lane,* 240; Daniels, *Wilson Era,* 504.

30. Consul General R.P. Skinner to RL, Feb. 22, 1917, *FR, 1917, Supplement,* 1:493; Devlin, *Too Proud to Fight,* 646.

31. Maryland League, *NYT,* Jan. 26, 1917, 1; cabinet, Franklin K. Lane to George W. Lane, Feb. 16, 1917, in Lane and Wall, *Letters of Lane,* 236; Link, *Wilson,* 5:309; demonstrations, WW to Charles S. Hamlin, Feb. 15, 1917, *PWW,* 41:233.

32. Dent, Crago in Finnegan, *Specter of a Dragon,* 186.

33. Fiske, *NYT,* Feb. 11, 1917, 5; Peary, *NYT,* Feb. 27, 1917, 10.

34. NSL, *NYT,* Jan. 28, 1917, 11; Rockefeller in Buchanan, "Wilson," 296–97.

35. Finnegan, *Specter of a Dragon,* 182; Bliss, ibid., 183; Baker in Daniel R. Beaver, *Newton D. Baker and the American War Effort, 1917–1919* (Lincoln: Univ. of Nebraska Press, 1966), 30.

36. *NYT,* Feb. 14, 1917, 8; Mar. 4, 1917, 1.

37. Czernin to RL, Feb. 6, 1917, *FR, 1917, Supplement,* 1:38–39; FCP to RL, ibid., 1:39.

38. RL to WHP, Feb. 8, 1917, ibid., 1:40.

39. WHP to RL, Feb. 11, 1917, ibid. 1:42–44.

40. Bernstorff, *NYT,* Feb. 13, 1917, 1.

41. Zimmermann to Botho von Wedel, Feb. 6, 1917, *OGD,* 2:1325; Zimmermann in Link, *Wilson,* 5:320, 325; Lansing, *NYT,* Feb. 13, 1917, 1; House, Gerard in Devlin, *Too Proud to Fight,* 237; Jagow in Holger H. Herwig and Neil M. Heyman, *Biographical Dictionary of World War I* (Westport, CT: Greenwood, 1982), 365.

42. Zimmermann cable in Link, *Wilson,* 5:343.

43. Hull exchange, ibid., 5:346; EMH to WW, Feb. 27, 1917, *PWW,* 41:296–97.

44. Doerries, *Imperial Challenge,* 174.

45. Wilson, address to joint session of Congress, Feb. 26, 1917, *PWW,* 41:286–87.

46. Harbaugh, "Wilson," 290–91.

47. Saulsbury in Buchanan, "European Propaganda," 604; Vardaman, *CR,* Mar. 2, 1917, 4778.

48. Townsend, *NYA,* Feb. 27, 1917, 2; Jones, *NYT,* Feb. 27, 1917, 1.

49. Treadway, *NYT,* Feb. 27, 1917, 1.

50. *O* 115 (Mar. 7, 1917): 397; ARC, *NYT,* Mar. 1, 1917, 9; *New York Tribune* in Buchanan, "European Propaganda," 610.

51. Press reaction, *NYT,* Mar. 2, 1917, 5; and *CO* 62 (Apr. 1917): 232–35; "A Lesson in Diplomacy," *NR* 10 (Mar. 10, 1917): 151.

52. War sentiment, Link, *Wilson,* 5:357.

53. Viereck in *NYT,* Mar. 2, 1917, 3; Hearst to S.S. Carvalho, Mar. 2, 1917, as in *NYT,* Dec. 11, 1918, 3; Smith and Tillman in Ryley, *Willful Men,* 90, 92.

54. *Evening Mail* in "How Zimmermann United the United States," *LD* 54 (Mar. 17, 1917): 688; *New Yorker Staats-Zeitung* in *CO* 62 (Apr. 1917): 234.

55. Zimmermann, *NYT,* Mar. 4, 1917, 1; Viereck, *NYT,* 2; Viereck to Everett V. Abbott, Mar. 6, 1917, *Viereck's* 6 (Apr. 4, 1917): 139.

56. Link, *Wilson,* 5:344; *NYT,* Mar. 5, 1917, 7; Mar. 7, 1917, 2.

57. Link, *Wilson,* 5:359; *NYT,* Mar. 3, 1917, 1; Mar. 4, 1917, E2; Mar. 6, 1917, 6; Eckhardt to Zimmermann, Apr. 14, 1917, in Hendrick, *Life and Letters of Page,* 3:354.

58. Public opinion, Link, *Wilson,* 5:349–50; Harbaugh, "Wilson," 291; and *NYT,* Feb. 27, 1917, 4; "To Defeat the Submarine," *NR* 10 (Mar. 3, 1917): 121–22; "If the Submarine Succeeds," *NR* (Feb. 24, 1917): 89–90.

59. AUAM and German Americans, *NYT,* Feb. 27, 1917, 2; and Wittke, *German-Americans,* 124; Ridder, *NYT,* Mar. 4, 1917, 2; Ford, Russell, New York society in "Efforts of American Pacifists to Avert War," *LD* 54 (Feb. 24, 1917): 452–53.

60. Beard, Putnam, *NYT,* Feb. 27, 1917, 2; *Army and Navy Journal* in Harbaugh, "Wilson," 291n69.

61. "The President's Message," *Viereck's* 6 (Mar. 7, 1917): 74; *NYA,* Feb. 20, 1917, 20; Smith in *N* 104 (Mar. 1, 1917): 238.

62. Lindbergh, *CR,* Feb. 24, 1917, 4202; Stone, *CR,* Mar. 3, 1917, 4892; London, *CR,* Feb. 17, 1917, 3528.

63. *NYT,* Mar. 2, 1917, 1, 4.

64. Campbell, *CR,* Mar. 1, 1917, 4638; Porter, 4641; Helgesen, 4657.

65. Cooper and voting, *NYT,* Mar. 2, 1917, 1.

66. Brandegee, *CR,* Mar. 2, 1917, 4767; Lodge, 4753.

67. Kirby, *NYT,* Mar. 3, 1917, 2; Cooper, *Vanity,* 181–82; Ryley, *Willful Men,* 99.

68. Stone, O'Gorman, Lodge, *CR,* Mar. 2, 1917, 4751; Poindexter, 4765, 4768.

69. Ryley, *Willful Men,* 101; German Admiralty, Link, *Wilson,* 5:372.

70. Fall, *CR,* Mar. 3, 1917, 4870; Brandegee, 4868.

71. Stone, *CR,* Mar. 3, 1917, 4888; Cummins, 4912; Norris, 5008; revolver matter in Belle Case La Follette and Fola La Follette, *Robert M. La Follette,* 2 vols. (New York: Macmillan, 1953), 1:620–23; and Cooper, *Pivotal Decades,* 263.

72. Kirby, *CR,* Mar. 2, 1917, 4771.

73. La Follette, "The Armed Ship Bill Means War," *La Follette's Magazine* 9 (Mar. 1917): 3.

74. Wilson statements, *NYT,* Mar. 5, 1917, 1.

75. Link, *Wilson,* 5:363–65.

76. Devlin, *Too Proud to Fight,* 658.

77. Opinion, including legislatures, in Link, *Wilson,* 5:365, 372; Harbaugh, "Wilson," 297; *CO* 62 (Apr. 1917): 231; "The Last Senatorial Filibuster," *LD* 54 (Mar. 17, 1917): 691–92; *NYT,* Mar. 6, 1917, 1, 2; entry, Mar. 9, 1917, in George F. Sparks, ed., *A Many-Colored Toga: The Diary of Henry Fountain Ashurst* (Tucson: Univ. of Arizona Press, 1962), 59.

78. TR to John Callan O'Laughlin, Mar. 8, 1917, *LTR,* 8:1161; TR to HCL, *Correspondence of Roosevelt and Lodge,* 2:503; TR to HCL, Feb. 20, 1917, *LTR,* 8:1157; *NR* 10 (Mar. 10, 1917): 148.

79. EPF in *LD* 54 (Mar. 17, 1917): 692; Hearst, *NYA,* Mar. 6, 1917, 20; Debs, *NYT,* Mar. 8, 1917, 3.

80. Wilson inaugural, *NYT,* Mar. 6, 1917, 3.

81. Gregory, *NYT,* Mar. 10, 1917, 1–2; RL to WW, Mar. 6, 1917, *LP,* 1:615.

82. "Attached memorandum," Daniels to RL, Mar. 11, 1917, *LP,* 1:623–26; entry of Mar. 13, 1917, E. David Cronon, ed., *The Cabinet Diaries of Josephus Daniels* (Lincoln: Univ. of Nebraska Press, 1963), 113.

83. "Nation-Wide Approval of Arming Our Ships," *LD* 54 (Mar. 24, 1917): 801–2; Cummins, Herrick, Weismann, *NYT,* Mar. 10, 1917, 2; Mar. 13, 1917, 2.

84. Kenyon, *NYA,* Mar. 10, 1917, 2; Norris, *NYT,* Mar. 19, 1917, 2.

10. And the War Came

1. Commander in *NYT,* Mar 15, 1917, 1, 2.

2. *O* 115 (Mar. 21, 1917): 493; ARC in Link, *Wilson,* 5:391.

3. Holtzendorff to Wilhelm (with Wilhelm comment on margin), Mar. 18, 1917, *OGD,* 2:1335–36 (emphasis Wilhelm's).

4. Bethmann, *NYT,* Mar. 30, 1917, 1; Bernstorff, *NYT,* Mar. 14, 1917, 1.

5. Captain in Carlisle, *Sovereignty,* 116.

6. Editors, *NYT,* Mar. 19, 1917, 2; "A 'State of War' with Germany," *LD* 54 (Mar. 31, 1917): 882–83; pacifist defection in Link, *Wilson,* 5:416; Stokes, Catt, *NYT,* Mar. 18, 1917, 4; Wise, *NYT,* Mar. 24, 1917, 1; Socialists, *NYT,* Mar. 25, 1917, 2.

7. Roosevelt, *NYT,* Mar. 20, 1917, 2; Hughes, Root, *NYT,* Mar. 21, 1917, 1, 2; Lodge in Harbaugh, "Wilson," 298; "The Barred Zone," *Viereck's* 6 (Mar. 28, 1917): 122.

8. Cobb, "A Recollection," in *Cobb of "The World": A Leader in Liberalism,* ed. John L. Heaton (New York: Dutton, 1924), 267–70; Daniels, *Wilson Era,* 582.

9. Robert Lansing, "Memorandum of the Cabinet Meeting," Mar. 20, 1917, *PWW,* 41:436–44.

10. Link, *Progressive Era,* 275.

11. Carlisle, *Sovereignty,* 129, 141.

12. House diary, Mar. 27, 1917, *PWW,* 41:483; House diary, Mar. 25, 1917, Seymour, *Intimate Papers of Colonel House,* 2:445; observers, *NYT,* Mar. 22, 1917, 1.

13. WHP to RL, Mar. 5, 1917, *FR, 1917, Supplement,* 2:516–18.

14. EMH to WHP, Mar. 21, 1917, Seymour, *Intimate Papers of Colonel House,* 2:462.

15. "Their Crumbling House of Cards," *Viereck's* 6 (Mar. 28, 1917): 123; Frederick Franklin Schrader, "In the Clutch of the Vampire," ibid., 116; *NYA,* Mar. 31, 1917, 16.

16. "Shall We Join the Entente?" *LD* 54 (Apr. 7, 1917): 965; Johnson, Penrose, *NYT,* Apr. 1, 1917, 1.

17. German press, Wittke, *German-Americans,* 127; *Call* and EPF in Buchanan, "European Propaganda," 635–37; Bryan, *NYT,* Mar. 30, 1917, 2; Jordan and Lochner, "Plea for Clarification of the Issues; An Open Letter," *CR,* appendix, Apr. 5, 1917, 6; AUAM advertisement, *NR* 10 (Mar. 31, 1917): 275 (emphasis in original).

18. NCF, *NYT,* Apr. 1, 1917, 2; Beard, *Columbia* [Univ.] *Spectator,* Apr. 2, 1917, 1; Jordan, *NYT,* Mar. 27, 1917, 11; Apr. 2, 1917, 1; Washington police, *NYT,* Mar. 30, 1917, 4.

19. Thompson, *Wilson,* 143.

20. Tucker, *Wilson and the Great War,* 201, 204.

21. Hale, naval advisers in Link, *Wilson,* 5:412–13.

22. Link, *Progressive Era,* 278.

23. May, *World War,* 427; Devlin, *Too Proud to Fight,* 680.

24. Link, *Wilson,* 5:414; David R. Woodward, *Trial by Friendship: Anglo-American Relations, 1917–1918* (Lexington: Univ. Press of Kentucky, 1993), 37.

25. Addams, *Peace and Bread,* 38.

26. Link, *Wilson,* 5:411.

27. Ibid.; Cooper, *Pivotal Decades,* 266.

28. Paolo E. Coletta, *William Jennings Bryan: Political Puritan, 1915–1925* (Lincoln: Univ. of Nebraska Press, 1969), 53; Gregory, *Origins,* 133, 139.

29. Link in Garraty, *Interpreting,* 2:128.

30. Cooper, *Wilson,* 387.

31. WW, address to joint session of Congress, Apr. 1, 1917, *PWW,* 41:519–27.

32. Lodge, La Follette, *NYT,* Apr. 3, 1917, 2.

33. Press reaction, *NYT,* Apr. 3, 1917, 2; "War for Democracy" (includes *New Yorker Staats-Zeitung*) and "German-American Thoughts on America at War," *LD* 54 (Apr. 14, 1917): 1043–46, 1051–52; *NYA,* Apr. 4, 1917, 18; Roosevelt, *NYT,* Apr. 4, 1917, 14; Hoover, *NYT,* 9.

34. Martin, *CR,* Apr. 4, 1917, 200.

35. James, *CR,* appendix, Apr. 4, 1917, 104; Swanson, *NYT,* Apr. 5, 1917, 2; Colt, *CR,* Apr. 4, 1917, 223.

36. Myers, *CR,* Apr. 4, 1917, 223; Lodge, 208.

37. Harding and Borah, ibid., 253.

38. Lodge, ibid., 208; Hitchcock, 205.

39. Ashurst, ibid., 222; Williams, 236; Husting, 242; Pittman, 252; Kenyon, 219.

40. La Follette, ibid., 223–34; Williams, 235.

41. Norris, ibid., 214; Reed, 215.

42. Gronna, ibid., 220; Pittman, 250.

43. McCumber, ibid., 210, 212, 258.

44. Voting, ibid., 261; Kirby, 221; Cummins, 250.

45. Cooper and Shackleford, *NYT,* Apr. 5, 1917, 3.

46. Flood, *CR,* Apr. 5, 1917, 310; Mann, 377; Ferris, 393; Eagle, 357; Watson, *CR,* appendix, Apr. 4, 1917, 93A; Miller, *CR,* Apr. 5, 1917, 328–29; Borland, 340.

47. Gardner, *CR,* Apr. 5, 1917, 378–79; Flood, 311.

48. Saunders, ibid., 346; Cannon, 344; Fiorello H. La Guardia, *The Making of an Insurgent—An Autobiography, 1882–1919* (Philadelphia: Lippincott, 1948), 140.

49. Reavis, *CR,* Apr. 5, 1917, 357; Dill, 344–45; Cary, *CR,* appendix, Apr. 5, 1917, A5; Sherwood, *CR,* Apr. 5, 1917, 336; Lundeen, 364; Cooper, 312; King, 341.

50. Lundeen, *CR,* Apr. 5, 1917, 362; Church, *CR,* appendix, Apr. 5, 1917, A89; London, *CR,* Apr. 5, 1917, 329.

51. Kitchin, *CR,* Apr. 5, 1917, 332–33; Heflin, 349.

52. McCulloch, ibid., 398; Sloan, 412; Britten, 317, 397.

53. Voting, ibid., 412–13.

54. Igoe, ibid., 322.

55. Southern sentiment, Anthony Gaughan, "Woodrow Wilson and the Rise of

Militant Interventionism in the South," *Journal of Southern History* 65 (Nov. 1999): 787–88; Witherspoon survey, David Starr Jordan, *The Days of a Man: Being Memories of a Naturalist, Teacher, and Minor Prophet of Democracy,* 2 vols. (New York: World Book, 1922), 2:733n1; Villard, *Fighting Years,* 322.

56. Link, *Wilson,* 5:427; "War for Democracy," *LD* 54 (Apr. 14, 1917): 1043–45; Harold C. Syrett, "The Business Press and American Neutrality, 1914–1917," *Mississippi Valley Historical Review* 32 (Sept. 1945): 223–30, quotation on 228; AFL, *NYT,* Mar. 13, 1917, 1; religious and ethnic leaders, Harbaugh, "Wilson," 301–4; "A Plea to the Press," *Viereck's* 6 (Apr. 18, 1917): cover.

57. Wisconsin towns, *NYT,* Apr. 4, 1917, 19; Socialist rally, *NYT,* Apr. 3, 1917, 3.

58. "Who Willed American Participation," *NR* 10 (Apr. 14, 1917): 308; "The Great Decision," *NR* 10 (Apr. 7, 1917): 280.

59. Finnegan, *Specter of a Dragon,* 189–90; EMH to WW, Mar. 19, 1917, *PWW,* 41:429.

60. May, *World War,* 437; Buehrig, *Wilson,* 149.

61. Coogan, *End of Neutrality,* 236.

62. Osgood, *Ideals and Self-Interest,* 252–53, 262, 192–93.

63. Ambrosius, *Wilsonian Statecraft,* 87–88.

64. Thompson, *Wilson,* 141.

Conclusion

1. Charles A. Beard, *The Devil Theory of War: An Inquiry into the Nature of History and the Possibility of Keeping Out of War* (New York: Vanguard, 1936), 105, 121.

2. WJB to JWG, Feb. 10, 1915, *PWW,* 32:208–10.

3. Cooper, *Wilson,* 275; Lansing in Tucker, *Wilson and the Great War,* 99.

4. WJB to JWG, May 12, 1915, *PWW,* 33:174–78; Bailey and Ryan, *Lusitania,* 39.

5. Link, *Wilson,* 4:69.

6. William J. Stone to WW, Feb. 24, 1916, *PWW,* 36:210; WW to William J. Stone, Feb. 24, 1916, *PWW,* 36:214.

7. Wilson, address to a joint session of Congress, Apr. 2, 1917, *PWW,* 41:519–27.

8. "Conference at the White House," Aug. 19, 1919, *PWW,* 62:390.

9. Cincinnati speech, Oct. 26, 1916, *PWW,* 38:531; Hendrick, *Life and Letters of Page,* 2:185; Cooper, *Page,* 346.

10. Patterson, *Search,* 302.

11. WW to WJB, June 7, 1915, *PWW,* 33:349.

12. Link, *Revolution,* 36.

13. House diary, Aug. 30, 1914, *PWW,* 30:462.

14. Norman A. Graebner, *America as a World Power: A Realistic Appraisal from Wilson to Reagan* (Wilmington, DE: Scholarly Resources, 1984), xix–xx.

Bibliographic Essay

By far the most extensive bibliography is Thomas J. Knock's "The United States, World War I, and the Peace Settlement, 1914–1920," in *American Foreign Relations since 1600: A Guide to the Literature,* 2 vols., ed. Robert L. Beisner (Santa Barbara, CA: ABC Clio, 2003), 1:665–735.

Superior accounts of World War I include Martin Gilbert, *The First World War: A Complete History* (New York: Henry Holt, 1994); John Keegan, *The First World War* (New York: Knopf, 1999); Correlli Barnett, *The Great War* (London: BBC, 2003); and David Stevenson, *Cataclysm: The First World War as Political Tragedy* (New York: Basic Books, 2004). *To Arms* (New York: Oxford Univ. Press, 2001), volume 1 of Hew Strachan's extremely detailed *The First World War,* focuses on the year 1914 but covers topics (e.g., Africa, East Asia, the Near East) that go beyond it. Among the able treatments of America during this time are John Whiteclay Chambers II, *The Tyranny of Change: America in the Progressive Era, 1900–1917* (New York: St. Martin's, 1980); John Milton Cooper Jr., *Pivotal Decades: The United States, 1900–1920* (New York: Norton, 1990); and David Traxel, *Crusader Nation: The United States in Peace and the Great War, 1898–1920* (New York: Knopf, 2006). *Over Here, 1914–1918,* volume 5 of journalist Mark Sullivan's *Our Times,* 6 vols. (New York: Scribner, 1926–35), is impressionistic but effectively captures contemporary moods. Deftly drawn portraits of major figures are found in Holger H. Herwig and Neil M. Heyman, *Biographical Dictionary of World War I* (Westport, CT: Greenwood, 1982).

Scholars dealing with the Wilson presidency during the neutrality period must begin with volumes 30–41 of Arthur S. Link, ed., *The Papers of Woodrow Wilson,* 69 vols. (Princeton, NJ: Princeton Univ. Press, 1966–93). Wilson gives his prepresidential views on policymaking in *Constitutional Government in the United States* (New York: Columbia Univ. Press, 1908). Also crucial are Department of State, *Papers Relating to the Foreign Relations of the United States, 1914–1917,* all titled *Supplement: The World War* (Washington, DC: Government Printing Office, 1928–31); and volume 1 of *The Lansing Papers,* 2 vols. (Washington, DC: Government Printing Office, 1939–40) in the Foreign Relations series.

Arthur S. Link offers by far the most thorough account of the president's actions in volumes 3–5 of his *Wilson,* 5 vols. (Princeton, NJ: Princeton Univ. Press, 1947–65): *The*

Struggle for Neutrality, 1914–1915; Confusions and Crises, 1915–1916; and *Campaigns for Progressivism and Peace, 1916–1917.* See as well Link's *The Higher Realism of Woodrow Wilson* (Nashville: Vanderbilt Univ. Press, 1971), a series of previously published essays; and *Woodrow Wilson: Revolution, War, and Peace* (Wheeling, IL: Harlan Davidson, 1979), a rewriting of his *Wilson the Diplomatist: A Look at His Major Foreign Policies* (Baltimore: Johns Hopkins Press, 1957). A comprehensive narrative is offered in Link's *Woodrow Wilson and the Progressive Era, 1910–1917* (New York: Harper, 1954). Link's informal reflections are found in an interview in volume 2 of John A. Garraty, *Interpreting American History: Conversations with Historians* (New York: Macmillan, 1970), 121–44. Link is usually sympathetic to Wilson, though he makes some negative observations. His interpretation is critiqued in Robert D. Accinelli, "Confronting the Modern World: Woodrow Wilson and Harry S. Truman—Link's Case for Wilson the Diplomatist," *Reviews in American History* 9 (September 1981): 285–94.

There are several one-volume lives of the twenty-eighth president. John Milton Cooper Jr.'s *Woodrow Wilson: A Biography* (New York: Knopf, 2009) is generally in accord with his subject; it promises to be definitive. Volumes 5–6 of Ray Stannard Baker's *Woodrow Wilson: Life and Letters,* 8 vols. (New York: Doubleday, Doran, 1927–39), titled *Neutrality, 1914–1915* and *Facing War, 1915–1917,* offer a far more critical view. The chief executive finds support in such able works as Arthur Walworth's *Woodrow Wilson,* 2nd ed., rev. (Baltimore: Penguin, 1969); August Heckscher, *Woodrow Wilson: A Biography* (New York: Scribner, 1991); Kendrick A. Clements, *Woodrow Wilson: World Statesman,* rev. ed. (Chicago: Ivan R. Dee, 1999); and John A. Thompson, *Woodrow Wilson* (London: Longman, 2002). Alexander L. George and Juliette L. George, *Woodrow Wilson and Colonel House: A Personality Study* (New York: John Day, 1956), attempt a psychoanalytical study, with mixed results. Ray Stannard Baker's autobiography, *American Chronicle* (New York: Scribner, 1945), covers his encounters as a journalist with Wilson and is supplemented by Merrill D. Peterson, *The President and His Biographer: Woodrow Wilson and Ray Stannard Baker* (Charlottesville: Univ. of Virginia Press, 2007). John Morton Blum, in *Woodrow Wilson and the Politics of Morality* (Boston: Little, Brown, 1956), finds his subject much too rigid to be a discerning leader.

Certain accounts are more specialized. Harley Notter, *The Origins of the Foreign Policy of Woodrow Wilson* (Baltimore: Johns Hopkins Press, 1937); and John M. Mulder, *Woodrow Wilson: The Years of Preparation* (Princeton, NJ: Princeton Univ. Press, 1978), contain rich material on intellectual development. The brother of Wilson's first wife, Stockton Axson, contributes a perceptive personality sketch in his *"Brother Woodrow": A Memoir of Woodrow Wilson* (Princeton, NJ: Princeton Univ. Press, 1993). Kendrick A. Clements's *The Presidency of Woodrow Wilson* (Lawrence: Univ. Press of Kansas, 1992) admires Wilson's intelligence while conceding his rigidity and self-righteousness. Frederick S. Calhoun, *Power and Principle: Armed Intervention in Wilsonian Foreign Policy* (Kent, OH: Kent State Univ. Press, 1986), stresses the role of international law in the president's thinking. Phyllis Lee Levin, *Edith and Woodrow: The Wilson White House* (New York: Scribner, 2001), offers a particularly critical account of the president's second wife, Edith Bolling Galt. Personal memoirs include journalist David Lawrence's *The True Story of Woodrow Wilson* (New York: George H. Doran, 1924); and press secretary Joseph P. Tumulty's *Woodrow Wilson as I Know Him* (Garden City, N.Y.: Doubleday,

Page, 1921), the latter work somewhat corrected by John M. Blum, *Joe Tumulty and the Wilson Era* (Boston: Houghton Mifflin, 1951).

Some works emphasize the president's role in World War I. Edward H. Buehrig's *Woodrow Wilson and the Balance of Power* (Bloomington: Indiana Univ. Press, 1955) defends the chief executive against charges of naïveté. Robert Endicott Osgood, *Ideals and Self-Interest in America's Foreign Relations: The Great Transformation of the Twentieth Century* (Chicago: Univ. of Chicago Press, 1953); and Lloyd E. Ambrosius, *Wilsonian Statecraft: Theory and Practice of Liberal Internationalism during World War I* (Wilmington, DE: Scholarly Resources, 1991), maintain that their subject lacked the necessary realism. So, too, does Norman A. Graebner, *America as a World Power: A Realistic Appraisal from Wilson to Reagan* (Wilmington, DE: Scholarly Resources, 1984). British jurist Patrick Devlin, *Too Proud to Fight: Woodrow Wilson's Neutrality* (New York: Oxford Univ. Press, 1975), emphasizes German initiative in creating conflict with the United States, although Devlin is by no means uncritical of the American leader. Robert W. Tucker, *Woodrow Wilson and the Great War: Reconsidering America's Neutrality, 1914–1917* (Charlottesville: Univ. of Virginia Press, 2007), claims that the flaws in the president's neutrality policy were so extensive that he drew the nation into the very war he hoped to avoid. Ross A. Kennedy, *The Will to Believe: Woodrow Wilson, World War I, and America's Strategy for Peace and Security* (Kent, OH: Kent State Univ. Press, 2009), faults not only the chief executive but also his critics among pacifists and such "Atlanticists" as Theodore Roosevelt and Henry Cabot Lodge. Kennedy offers a strong critique of the president in his "Woodrow Wilson, World War I, and an American Conception of National Security," *Diplomatic History* 25 (Winter 2001): 1–31. John A. Thompson, "Wilsonianism: The Dynamics of a Conflicted Concept," *International Affairs* 86 (2010): 1–22, notes that only when the United States became a belligerent did Wilson argue that a peaceful world order required the extension of democracy. In "More Tactics than Strategy: Woodrow Wilson and World War I, 1914–1919," in *Artists of Power: Theodore Roosevelt, Woodrow Wilson, and Their Enduring Impact on U.S. Foreign Policy,* ed. William N. Tilchin and Charles E. Neu (Westport, CT: Praeger Security International, 2006), 96–16, Thompson notes that after the *Lusitania* sinking, the president shifted his focus from avoiding war to preparedness and collective security.

Within a decade after the Great War ended, historians sought to explain American involvement. A revisionist school stressed the influence of American business and an Anglophile administration. The most notable examples include John Kenneth Turner, *Shall It Be Again?* (New York: B.W. Huebsch, 1922); C. Hartley Grattan, *Why We Fought* (New York: Vanguard, 1929); Walter Millis, *Road to War, 1914–1917* (Boston: Houghton Mifflin, 1935); and Charles C. Tansill, *America Goes to War* (Boston: Little Brown, 1938). Charles A. Beard, *The Devil Theory of War: An Inquiry into the Nature of History and the Possibility of Keeping Out of War* (New York: Vanguard, 1936), views the export-conscious American people as ultimately responsible for U.S. entry into the conflict. Warren I. Cohen offers a fine account of the entire revisionist movement in *The American Revisionists: The Lessons of Intervention in World War I* (Chicago: Univ. of Chicago Press, 1967). Robert E. Hannigan, *The New World Order: American Foreign Policy, 1898–1917* (Philadelphia: Univ. of Pennsylvania Press, 2002), presents a different kind of revisionism, one that perceives the 1914–17 crisis in terms of U.S. efforts to create a global framework that would guarantee its wealth and power.

Wilson never lacked defenders. Charles Seymour backs him in *American Diplomacy during the World War* (Baltimore: Johns Hopkins Press, 1934) and *American Neutrality, 1914–1917* (New Haven, CT: Yale Univ. Press, 1935), the latter a volume of essays. The same viewpoint is found in Newton D. Baker, *Why We Went to War* (New York: Harper, 1936), in which Wilson's secretary of war includes some personal recollections. Ernest R. May covers internal decision-making in Britain, Germany, and the United States in his highly significant *The World War and American Isolation, 1914–1917* (Cambridge, MA: Harvard Univ. Press, 1958). Like Seymour, May stresses Berlin's role in triggering confrontation with the United States, as do Daniel M. Smith, *The Great Departure: The United States and World War I* (New York: John Wiley, 1965); Ross Gregory, *The Origins of American Intervention in the First World War* (New York: Norton, 1971); and Richard F. Hamilton and Holger H. Herwig, *Decisions for War: 1914–1917* (New York: Cambridge Univ. Press, 2004).

For biographies of Wilson's first secretary of state, see Lawrence W. Levine, *Defender of the Faith—William Jennings Bryan: The Last Decade, 1915–1925* (New York: Oxford Univ. Press, 1965); volumes 2 and 3 of Paolo E. Coletta's *William Jennings Bryan,* 3 vols. (Lincoln: Univ. of Nebraska Press, 1964–69), titled *Progressive Politician and Moral Statesman, 1909–1915* and *Political Puritan, 1915–1925;* Louis W. Koenig, *Bryan: A Political Biography of William Jennings Bryan* (New York: Putnam, 1971); Kendrick A. Clements, *William Jennings Bryan: Missionary Isolationist* (Knoxville: Univ. of Tennessee Press, 1982); and Michael Kazin, *A Godly Hero: The Life of William Jennings Bryan* (New York: Knopf, 2006). The secretary's pacifism is the subject of Merle Curti, *Bryan and World Peace* (Northampton, MA: Smith College Studies in History, 1931). *The Memoirs of William Jennings Bryan* (Chicago: John C. Winston, 1925) offers little. Bryan's contemporary views are found in his monthly, the *Commoner.*

Bryan's successor contributed his own account, *War Memoirs of Robert Lansing, Secretary of State* (Indianapolis: Bobbs-Merrill, 1935), most noteworthy for its confirmation that Lansing was always strongly pro-Entente. Daniel M. Smith presents major research on Lansing in "Robert Lansing and the Formulation of American Neutrality Policies, 1914–1915," *Mississippi Valley Historical Review* 43 (June 1956): 59–81; and *Robert Lansing and American Neutrality, 1914–1917* (Berkeley: Univ. of California Press, 1958), both of which stress the secretary's influence on Wilson. Thomas H. Hartig, *Robert Lansing: An Interpretive Biography* (New York: Arno Press, 1982), maintains that Lansing well understood America's global interests.

Aside from the study by George and George (see page 350), there exists only one biography of Edward M. House, the president's leading confidant: Godfrey Hodgson, *Woodrow Wilson's Right Hand: The Life of Colonel Edward M. House* (New Haven, CT: Yale Univ. Press, 2006), a work that often internalizes House's perspectives. Joyce Grigsby Williams, *Colonel House and Sir Edward Grey: A Study in Anglo-American Diplomacy* (Lanham, NY: Univ. Press of America, 1984), claims that both nations ultimately benefited from their relationship. For research proving that the British never took House's machinations seriously, consult John Milton Cooper Jr., "The British Response to the House-Grey Memorandum: New Evidence and New Questions," *Journal of American History* 59 (March 1973): 958–71. Despite these efforts, one awaits Charles E. Neu's thorough study. Volumes 1–2 of Charles Seymour, ed., *The Intimate Papers of Colonel House,* 4 vols. (Boston: Houghton Mifflin, 1926–28), must be used with caution because House's diary is heavily edited to indicate that Wilson's adviser was wiser than the president. For House's novel, see *Philip Dru: Administrator—A Story of Tomorrow, 1920–1925* (New York: B.W. Huebsch, 1919). Billie Barnes Jensen offers the background of House's novel in "*Philip Dru,* the Blueprint of a Presidential Adviser," *American Studies* 12 (Spring 1971): 49–58. Wilson's intimate is strongly criticized in David M. Esposito, "Imagined Power: The Secret Life of Colonel House," *Historian* 60 (Summer 1968): 741–55.

Similarly, much more work is needed on Wilson's often-maligned naval secretary. Josephus Daniels presents his recollections in *The Wilson Era: Years of Peace—1910–1917* (Chapel Hill: Univ. of North Carolina Press, 1944); and E. David Cronon edited *The Cabinet Diaries of Josephus Daniels* (Lincoln: Univ. of Nebraska Press, 1963). Both works are disappointing on the 1914–17 period. Daniels's son Jonathan's account of wartime Washington, *The End of Innocence* (Philadelphia: Lippincott, 1954), supplements these sources. Joseph L. Morrison's *Josephus Daniels—The Small-d Democrat* (Chapel Hill: Univ. of North Carolina Press, 1966) is a laudatory account. Daniels's assistant secretary is covered in volume 1 of Frank Freidel, *Franklin D. Roosevelt,* titled *The Apprenticeship* (Boston: Little, Brown, 1952); and Geoffrey C. Ward, *A First-Class Temperament: The Emergence of Franklin Roosevelt* (New York: Harper and Row, 1989).

Certain other members of Wilson's cabinet have been studied. For material on Wilson's best-known secretary of war, see C.H. Cramer, *Newton D. Baker: A Biography* (Cleveland: World, 1961); and Daniel R. Beaver, *Newton D. Baker and the American War Effort, 1917–1919* (Lincoln: Univ. of Nebraska Press, 1966). One should note Anne Wintermute Lane and Louise Herrick Wall, eds., *The Letters of Franklin K. Lane: Personal and Political* (Boston: Houghton Mifflin, 1922), dealing with Wilson's Interior secretary; Keith W. Olson, *Biography of a Progressive: Franklin K. Lane* (Westport, CT: Greenwood, 1979); and David F. Houston, *Eight Years with Wilson's Cabinet, 1913 to 1920* (New York: Doubleday, Page, 1926), a memoir of the president's secretary of agriculture. For the secretary of the Treasury, consult *Crowded Years: The Reminiscences of William G. McAdoo* (Boston: Houghton Mifflin, 1931); and John J. Broesamle, *William Gibbs McAdoo: A Passion for Change, 1863–1917* (Port Washington, NY: Kennikat, 1973). Needed is scholarly treatment of Wilson's first war secretary, Lindley M. Garrison.

Wilson's emissary to Britain is the subject of several works, all of which criticize their subject: Ross Gregory, *Walter Hines Page: Ambassador to the Court of St. James's* (Lexington: Univ. of Kentucky Press, 1970); Mary R. Kihl, "A Failure of Ambassadorial Diplomacy," *Journal of American History* 57 (December 1970): 636–53; and John Milton Cooper Jr., *Walter Hines Page: The Southerner as American, 1855–1918* (Chapel Hill: Univ. of North Carolina Press, 1977). Burton J. Hendrick, ed., *The Life and Letters of Walter H. Page,* 3 vols. (New York: Doubleday, Page, 1922–26), presents material from the standpoint of the ambassador. Wilson's ambassador to Berlin, James W. Gerard, wrote two accounts: *My Four Years in Germany* (New York: George H. Doran, 1917); and *Face to Face with Kaiserism* (New York: George H. Doran, 1918). Walter Johnson's edition of Joseph C. Grew, *Turbulent Era: A Diplomatic Record of Forty Years, 1904–1945* (Boston: Houghton Mifflin, 1952); and Waldo H. Heinrichs Jr., *American Ambassador: Joseph C. Grew and the Development of the United States Diplomatic Tradition* (Boston: Little Brown, 1966), offer accounts of the man whose labors kept the

Berlin embassy functioning amid incompetent leadership. *Ambassador Morgenthau's Story* (Garden City, NY: Doubleday Page, 1918), presents the memoir of Henry Morgenthau, Wilson's representative to the Ottoman Empire. It should be supplemented by Henry Morgenthau III, *Mostly Morgenthaus: A Family History* (New York: Ticknor and Fields, 1991). Full-scale studies are needed of such ambassadors as Gerard, Frederic C. Penfield (Austria-Hungary), Thomas Nelson Page (Italy), and David R. Francis (Russia). Charles E. Neu presents an overview of the president's diplomats in "Woodrow Wilson and His Foreign Policy Advisers," in Tilchin and Neu, *Artists of Power* (see page 351), pp. 77–94.

Certain works are particularly helpful on German policy. Underlying economic rivalries are stressed in Ragnhild Fiebig–von Hase, "The United States and Germany in the World Arena, 1900–1917," in *Confrontation and Cooperation in the Era of World War I, 1900–1924,* ed. Hans-Jürgen Schröder (Providence, RI: Berg, 1993), 33–68. For decisions concerning submarine warfare, see the Reichstag Commission of Inquiry, *Official German Documents Relating to the World War,* 2 vols. (New York: Oxford Univ. Press, 1923). Based upon testimony of leading civilian and military leaders, the hearings present material in a somewhat eclectic fashion. Fritz Fischer, *Germany's Aims in the First World War* (New York: Norton, 1967), remains controversial but offers rich detail. Volume 2 of Lamar Cecil, *Wilhelm II,* 2 vols. (Chapel Hill: Univ. of North Carolina Press, 1989–96), titled *Emperor and Exile, 1900–1941,* is superior on the Kaiser. Holger H. Herwig's *Politics of Frustration: The United States in German Naval Planning, 1889–1941* (Boston: Little Brown, 1976) offers excellent history, as does the older work by Karl E. Birnbaum, *Peace Moves and U-Boat Warfare: A Study of Germany's Policy towards the United States, April 18, 1916–January 7, 1917* (Stockholm: Almquist & Wiksell, 1958). For an unmatched view of Admiralty politics, see Walter Görlitz, ed., *The Kaiser and His Court: The Diaries, Note Books, and Letters of Admiral Georg von Müller, Chief of the Naval Cabinet, 1914–1918* (New York: Harcourt, Brace, and World, 1964). Debates among naval authorities are described in Philip K. Lundeberg, "The German Naval Critique of the U-Boat Campaign, 1915–1918," *Military Affairs* 27 (January 1964): 105–18. R.H. Gibson, *The German Submarine War, 1914–1918* (New York: Richard R. Smith, 1931), is a thorough account, if occasionally marred by wartime polemics. Friedrich von Bernhardi's *Germany and the Next War* (1911; New York: Chas. A. Eron, 1914), written by a German cavalry general, served as ammunition for Allied sympathizers who sought to portray the Reich as a ruthlessly imperialistic regime.

Count Johann von Bernstorff, Berlin's ambassador to the United States, tells his story in *My Three Years in America* (London: Skeffington and Son, 1920) and in *Memoirs of Count Bernstorff* (New York: Random House, 1936). Reinhard R. Doerries, *Imperial Challenge: Ambassador Count Bernstorff and German-American Relations, 1908–1917* (Chapel Hill: Univ. of North Carolina Press, 1989), supplies much more information than the title suggests. For a brief but succinct treatment of its subject, see Doerries, "From Neutrality to War: Woodrow Wilson and the German Challenge," in Tilchin and Neu, *Artists of Power* (see page 351), 117–35. See also Ethel Mary Tinneman, "Count Johann von Bernstorff and German-American Relations, 1908–1917" (Ph.D. diss., Univ. of California at Berkeley, 1960). Franz von Papen, *Memoirs* (New York: Dutton, 1953), includes some description of Papen's role as Berlin's military attaché in Washington.

Greater research is needed on Britain's policy toward America during the neutrality period. The memoirs of the first British wartime foreign secretary are offered in Viscount Grey of Fallodon, *Twenty-Five Years, 1892–1916,* 2 vols. (New York: Frederick A. Stokes, 1925), although Sir Edward needs a modern biographer. Also note Williams, *Colonel House and Sir Edward Grey* (see page 352). John Grigg offers a definitive biography in his *Lloyd George: From Peace to War, 1912–1916* (London: Eyre Methuen, 1985) and in *War Leader, 1916–1918* (London: Allen Lane, 2002). Sterling J. Kernek uses hitherto classified materials in his "The British Government's Reaction to President Wilson's 'Peace' Note of December 1916," *Historical Journal* 13 (December 1970): 721–66 and in "Distractions of Peace during War: The Lloyd George Government's Reactions to Woodrow Wilson: December 1916–November 1918," *Transactions of the American Philosophical Society* 65, n.s. (April 1975): 1–117.

For Britain's ambassador to Washington, see volume 2 of Stephen Gwynn, ed., *The Letters and Friendships of Sir Cecil Spring Rice: A Record,* 2 vols. (Boston: Houghton Mifflin, 1929); and the critical treatment of Kihl (see page 353). David R. Woodward covers such matters as the House-Grey memorandum in his *Trial by Friendship: Anglo-American Relations, 1917–1918* (Lexington: Univ. Press of Kentucky, 1993). Marion C. Siney, *The Allied Blockade of Germany, 1914–1916* (Ann Arbor: Univ. of Michigan Press, 1957); and C. Paul Vincent, *The Politics of Hunger: The Allied Blockade of Germany, 1915–1919* (Athens: Ohio Univ. Press, 1985) present the British effort as increasingly effective. Armin Rappaport, *The British Press and Wilsonian Neutrality* (Stanford, CA: Stanford Univ. Press, 1951), draws upon thirty-seven British and Scottish journals to show increasing impatience with American policy. Laurence W. Martin, *Peace without Victory: Woodrow Wilson and the British Liberals* (New Haven, CT: Yale Univ. Press, 1958), delves into more than the title indicates.

Not surprisingly, Theodore Roosevelt has been the subject of considerable scholarship. One might begin with volumes 7–8, the latter titled *The Days of Armageddon, 1914–1919,* of Elting E. Morison's edition of *The Letters of Theodore Roosevelt,* 8 vols. (Cambridge, MA: Harvard Univ. Press, 1951–54). Roosevelt's books during this period include *America and the World War* and *Fear God and Take Your Own Part,* both in volume 18 of *The Works of Theodore Roosevelt: National Edition* (New York: Scribner's, 1926). Superior work is manifested in William Henry Harbaugh, "Wilson, Roosevelt, and Interventionism, 1914–1917: A Study of Domestic Influences on the Formulation of American Foreign Policy" (Ph.D. diss., Northwestern Univ., 1954); Harbaugh presents TR as the greater realist. Modifying Harbaugh's claim, John Milton Cooper Jr.'s *The Warrior and the Priest: Woodrow Wilson and Theodore Roosevelt* (Cambridge, MA: Harvard Univ. Press, 1983) finds Wilson as hardheaded as TR. Among the strong biographies of the twenty-sixth president, one must note William Henry Harbaugh, *Power and Responsibility: The Life and Times of Theodore Roosevelt* (New York: Farrar and Straus, 1961); H.W. Brands, *T.R.: The Last Romantic* (New York: Basic, 1997); and Kathleen Dalton, *Theodore Roosevelt: A Strenuous Life* (New York: Knopf, 2002). Patricia O'Toole covers TR's later years in *When Trumpets Call: Theodore Roosevelt after the White House* (New York: Simon and Schuster, 2005), as does Edmund Morris in *Colonel Roosevelt* (New York: Random House, 2010). Russell Buchanan, "Theodore Roosevelt and American Neutrality, 1914–1917," *American Historical Review* 43 (July 1938): 775–90, shows early work in the Roosevelt papers. For the rationale behind

Roosevelt's thinking, see David H. Burton, "Theodore Roosevelt and His English Correspondents: The Intellectual Roots of the Anglo-American Alliance," *Mid-America* 53 (January 1971): 13–34.

William C. Widenor, *Henry Cabot Lodge and the Search for an American Foreign Policy* (Berkeley: Univ. of California Press, 1980), remains the best work on the thought of the Massachusetts senator, although John A. Garraty, *Henry Cabot Lodge: A Biography* (New York: Knopf, 1953), is still most helpful. For various speeches, see Lodge, *War Addresses, 1915–1917* (Boston: Houghton Mifflin, 1917). Lodge's *The Senate and the League of Nations* (New York: Scribner, 1925) covers parts of earlier periods as well. *Selections from the Correspondence of Theodore Roosevelt and Henry Cabot Lodge,* 2 vols. (New York: Scribner, 1925) reveals the strong friendship between the two men.

Certain material exists on Democratic congressional leaders. Timothy Gregory McDonald offers a thorough account in his "Southern Democratic Congressmen and the First World War, August 1914–April 1917: The Public Record of Their Support for or Opposition to Wilson's Policies" (Ph.D. diss., Univ. of Washington, 1962). In *Claude Kitchin and the Wilson War Policies* (Boston: Little Brown, 1937), Alex Mathews Arnett offers a eulogistic treatment of the prominent North Carolina representative who strongly criticized Wilson's foreign policy. For a corrective to Arnett, see the more dispassionate Homer Larry Ingle, "Pilgrimage to Reform: A Life of Claude Kitchin" (Ph.D. diss., Univ. of Wisconsin, 1967). Studies of other southern legislators include George Coleman Osborn, *John Sharp Williams: Planter-Statesman of the Deep South* (Baton Rouge: Louisiana State Univ. Press, 1943); Dewey W. Grantham Jr., *Hoke Smith and the Politics of the New South* (Baton Rouge: Louisiana State Univ. Press, 1958); and William F. Holmes, *The White Chief: James Kimble Vardaman* (Baton Rouge: Louisiana State Univ. Press, 1970). Thomas W. Ryley, *Gilbert Hitchcock of Nebraska—Wilson's Floor Leader in the Fight for the Versailles Treaty* (Lewiston, NY: Edwin Mellen, 1998), traces the evolution of a strong anti-interventionist. Monroe Billington, *Thomas P. Gore: The Blind Senator from Oklahoma* (Lawrence: Univ. of Kansas Press, 1967), is helpful on the Gore-McLemore proposals. Ruth Warner Towne, *Senator William J. Stone and the Politics of Compromise* (Port Washington, NY: Kennikat, 1979), shows how a loyal backer of Wilson's domestic legislation fought his overseas measures.

Republican insurgent congressional leaders have received much attention. Belle Case La Follette and Fola La Follette, the wife and the daughter of the prominent Wisconsin dissenter, offer a sympathetic biography, *Robert M. La Follette* (New York: Macmillan, 1953). Nancy C. Unger, *Fighting Bob La Follette: The Righteous Reformer* (Chapel Hill: Univ. of North Carolina Press, 2000), presents a more analytical treatment. Volume 2 of Richard Lowitt, *George W. Norris,* subtitled *The Persistence of a Progressive, 1913–1933* (Urbana: Univ. of Illinois Press, 1971), supplies needed background to *Fighting Liberal: The Autobiography of George W. Norris* (New York: Macmillan, 1945). Robert James Maddox, *William E. Borah and American Foreign Policy* (Baton Rouge: Louisiana State Univ. Press, 1969), gives the best treatment of a major Wilson critic. John Braeman's *Albert J. Beveridge: American Nationalist* (Chicago: Univ. of Chicago Press, 1971), is far less thorough on the role of the Indiana Progressive during the neutrality period than is Claude G. Bowers, *Beveridge and the Progressive Era* (Boston: Houghton Mifflin, 1932). Beveridge's own view of the war, based on a trip to Europe, is found in his *What Is Back of the War* (Indianapolis: Bobbs-Merrill, 1915).

For overall views of the Republican and Progressive parties, note Howard Scott Greenlee, "The Republican Party in Division and Reunion" (Ph.D. diss., Univ. of Chicago, 1950); James Holt, *Congressional Insurgents and the Party System, 1909–1916* (Cambridge, MA: Harvard Univ. Press, 1967); Gerald D. McKnight, "A Party Against Itself: The Grand Old Party in the New Freedom Era, 1913–1916" (Ph.D. diss., Univ. of Maryland, 1972); and James Oliver Robertson, *No Third Choice: Progressives in Republican Politics, 1916–1921* (New York: Garland, 1983). The best work on Roosevelt's predecessor remains volume 2 of Henry F. Pringle, *The Life and Times of William Howard Taft: A Biography,* 2 vols. (New York: Farrar and Rinehart, 1939).

William E. Leuchtenburg, "Progressivism and Imperialism: The Progressive Movement and American Foreign Policy, 1898–1916," *Mississippi Valley Historical Review* 39 (December 1952): 483–504, started a lengthy debate; at issue in part was the World War I era. The article drew responses in Howard W. Allen, "Republican Reformers and Foreign Policy, 1913–1917," *Mid-America* 44 (October 1962): 222–29; Walter A. Sutton, "Progressive Republican Senators and the Submarine Crisis, 1915–1916," *Mid-America* 47 (April 1965): 75–88; Barton J. Bernstein and Franklin A. Lieb, "Progressive Republican Senators and American Imperialism, 1898–1916: A Reappraisal," *Mid-America* 50 (July 1968): 163–205; and John Milton Cooper Jr., "Progressivism and American Foreign Policy," *Mid-America* 51 (October 1969): 260–77.

Robert Seager II communicates much of the richness of a highly complex movement in his "The Progressives and American Foreign Policy, 1898–1917: An Analysis of the Attitudes of the Leaders of the Progressive Movement toward External Affairs" (Ph.D. diss., Ohio State Univ., 1958). Similarly, Walter Trattner, "Progressivism and World War I: A Re-appraisal," *Historian* 44 (July 1962): 131–44; and John A. Thompson, *Reformers and War: American Progressive Publicists and the First World War* (New York: Cambridge Univ. Press, 1967), warn against traditional stereotypes.

There are several biographies of leading Republicans. For a detailed study of New York's most prominent senator, see volume 2, *1905–1937,* of Philip C. Jessup, *Elihu Root,* 2 vols. (New York: Dodd, Mead, 1938). A briefer treatment is found in Richard W. Leopold, *Elihu Root and the Conservative Tradition* (Boston: Little, Brown, 1954). Herbert F. Margulies, *Reconciliation and Revival: James R. Mann and the House Republicans of the Wilson Era* (Westport, CT; Greenwood, 1966), ably covers the minority leader. Howard W. Allen's *Poindexter of Washington: A Study of Progressive Politics* (Carbondale: Southern Illinois Univ. Press, 1981) reveals the hawkishness of an ardent Bull Mooser. Other studies include Robert P. Wilkins, "Porter J. McCumber and World War I," *North Dakota History* 34 (Summer 1967): 192–207; Bruce L. Larson, [Charles A.] *Lindbergh of Minnesota: A Political Biography* (New York: Harcourt Brace Jovanovich, 1973); Hannah Josephson, *Jeannette Rankin: First Lady in Congress—A Biography* (Indianapolis: Bobbs-Merrill, 1974); and Alan Boxerman, "[Julius] Kahn of California," *California Historical Quarterly* 55 (Winter 1976): 340–51.

There are several congressional memoirs, among them Henry Lee Myers, *The United States Senate: What Kind of Body?* (Philadelphia: Dorrance, 1939); Fiorello La Guardia, *The Making of an Insurgent—An Autobiography: 1882–1919* (Philadelphia: Lippincott, 1948); and George F. Sparks, ed., *A Many-Colored Toga: The Diary of Henry Fountain Ashurst* (Tucson: Univ. of Arizona Press, 1962). Some figures merit more intense investigation, among them Champ Clark, Clyde H. Tavenner, Jacob Gallinger,

Richard Bartholdt, J. Hamilton Lewis, James Harvey ("Cyclone") Davis, Augustus Gardner, Jeff: McLemore, George E. Chamberlain, Fred A. Britten, Philander C. Knox, Frank Brandegee, John W. Weeks, James A. O'Gorman, John D. Works, and Albert B. Cummins.

Various topics, themes, and events have their own narrators. Larry Zuckerman indicts the Germans in *The Rape of Belgium: The Untold Story of World War I* (New York: New York Univ. Press, 2004). For the activities of the Commission for Relief in Belgium, see volume 1 of *The Memoirs of Herbert Hoover* (3 vols; New York: Macmillan, 1951), titled *Years of Adventure, 1874–1920;* volume 1 of Hoover's *An American Epic,* 4 vols. (Chicago: Henry Regnery, 1961–64), titled *Introduction: The Relief of Belgium and Northern France, 1914–1930;* and volume 2 of George H. Nash, *The Life of Herbert Hoover* (3 vols.; New York: Norton, 1983–96), titled *The Humanitarian, 1914–1917.* John W. Coogan, *The End of Neutrality: The United States, Britain, and Maritime Rights, 1899–1915* (Ithaca, NY: Cornell Univ. Press, 1981), supersedes much of Edwin Borchard and William Potter Lage, *Neutrality for the United States* (New Haven, CT: Yale Univ. Press, 1937), while being equally critical of the Wilson administration. Alice M. Morrissey, *The American Defense of Neutral Rights, 1914–1917* (Cambridge, MA: Harvard Univ. Press, 1939); and volume 2 of Carlton Savage, *Policy of the United States toward Maritime Commerce in War* (Washington, DC: Government Printing Office, 1934), reveal the complexity of this issue. The Reich's rejection of Wilson's peace bid is found in Reinhard R. Doerries, "Imperial Berlin and Washington: New Light on Germany's Foreign Policy and America's Entry into World War I," *Central European History* 11 (March 1978): 23–49.

Major ship incidents receive special coverage. Ross Gregory, "A New Look at the Case of the *Dacia,*" *Journal of American History* 55 (September 1968): 292–96, shows why France, not Britain, decided to tackle a highly controversial matter. Thomas A. Bailey and Paul B. Ryan, *The Lusitania Disaster: An Episode in Modern Warfare and Diplomacy* (New York: Free Press, 1975), questions the president's judgment while avoiding the conspiratorial overtones of Colin Simpson, *The Lusitania* (Boston: Little, Brown, 1973). Rodney Carlisle, *Sovereignty at Sea: U.S. Merchant Ships and American Entry into World War I* (Gainesville: Univ. Press of Florida, 2009), describes in detail the sinkings that in 1917 led the United States into the conflict. See also James P. Duffy, *The Sinking of the Laconia and the U-Boat War: Disaster in the Mid-Atlantic* (Santa Barbara, CA: Praeger, ABC-Clio, 2009).

For background and debate over Wilson's interview with the editor of the *New York World,* see John L. Heaton, ed., *Cobb of "The World": A Leader in Liberalism* (New York: Dutton, 1924); Jerold S. Auerbach, "Woodrow Wilson's 'Prediction' to Frank Cobb: Words Historians Should Doubt Ever Got Spoken," *Journal of American History* 54 (December 1967): 608–17; Arthur S. Link and Jerold S. Auerbach, "That Cobb Interview," *Journal of American History* 55 (June 1968): 7–17; and Brian J. Dalton, "Wilson's Prediction to Cobb: Notes on the Auerbach-Link Debate," *Historian* 32 (August 1970): 545–63.

Congressional debates have been given special attention. Timothy G. McDonald, "The Gore-McLemore Resolutions: Democratic Revolt against Wilson's Submarine Policy," *Historian* 26 (November 1963): 50–74, reveals Wilson's backers as governed by more than political expediency. Thomas W. Ryley, *A Little Group of Willful Men: A Study of Congressional Authority* (Port Washington, NY: Kennikat, 1975); and Richard Lowitt, "The Armed-Ship Controversy: A Legislative View," *Historian* 46 (January 1964): 38–47, cover senatorial opposition to Wilson's proposal of February 1917. Paul Holbo, "They Voted against War: A Study of Motivations" (Ph.D. diss., Univ. of Chicago, 1961), focuses on the fifty-six senators and representatives who opposed the war resolution of 1917, finding them at the core of opposition to interventionist policies from 1914 to 1917. Arthur Wallace Dunn presents a journalist's perspective in *From Harrison to Harding: A Personal Narrative, Covering a Third of a Century, 1888–1921* (New York: Putnam, 1922). A full-scale treatment of Congress during the neutrality period has long been needed, possibly modeled on David L. Porter, *The Seventy-sixth Congress and World War II, 1939–1940* (Columbia: Univ. of Missouri Press, 1979); and his *Congress and the Waning of the New Deal* (Port Washington, NY: Kennikat, 1980).

Anti-interventionism is skillfully examined in John Milton Cooper Jr., *The Vanity of Power: American Isolationism and World War I, 1914–1917* (Westport, CT: Greenwood, 1969). For a debate over the proclivities of the central states, see Ray Allen Billington, "The Origins of Middle Western Isolationism," *Political Science Quarterly* 60 (March 1945): 44–64; and William G. Carleton, "Isolationism and the Middle West," *Mississippi Valley Historical Review* 33 (December 1946): 377–90. Arthur S. Link deals with a major source of anti-interventionism in his "The Middle West and the Coming of World War I," *Ohio State Archeological and Historical Quarterly* 62 (1953): 109–21. Robert Hoyt Block, "Southern Opinion of Woodrow Wilson's Foreign Policies, 1913–1917" (Ph.D. diss., Duke Univ., 1968), covers manuscripts, journals, and legislative proceedings to reveal a majority of articulate southerners backing the president. Anthony Gaughan, "Woodrow Wilson and the Rise of Militant Interventionism in the South," *Journal of Southern History* 65 (November 1999): 771–808, notes that the region's belligerency developed after the United States entered the conflict.

For an able treatment of the 1916 election, see S.D. Lovell, *The Presidential Election of 1916* (Carbondale: Southern Illinois Univ. Press, 1980). Meyer Jonah Nathan, "The Presidential Election of 1916 in the Middle West" (Ph.D. diss., Princeton Univ., 1965), offers more than the title indicates; Nathan emphasizes the peace issue. Thomas J. Kerr IV, "German-Americans and Neutrality in the 1916 Election," *Mid-America* 43 (April 1961): 95–105, claims that Berlin's propaganda efforts backfired because the German element often supported Wilson. The same holds true for the Emerald Isle, as William M. Leary Jr. indicates in his "Woodrow Wilson, Irish Americans, and the Election of 1916," *Journal of American History* 54 (June 1967): 57–72. For background on the Republican presidential candidate, note volume 1 of Merlo J. Pusey, *Charles Evans Hughes,* 2 vols. (New York: Macmillan, 1952); and Betty Glad, *Charles Evans Hughes and the Illusions of Innocence: A Study in American Diplomacy* (Urbana: Univ. of Illinois Press, 1966), the latter faulting her subject for failing to see the integral relationship between policy and power.

Several works deal with German undercover activity, though much more study is needed. Contemporary writing, designed to evoke fear, includes William Henry Skaggs, *German Conspiracies in America* (London: T.F. Unwin, 1915); Howard Pitcher Okie, *America and the German Peril* (London: W. Heinemann, 1915); Frederic William Wile, *The German-American Plot: The Record of a Great Failure* (London: C.A. Pearson, 1915); and John Price Jones, *The German Secret Service in America, 1914–1918* (Boston: Small, Maynard, 1918). For one effort at stopping munition flows to the Allies, see Jules Witcover, *Sabotage at Black Tom: Imperial Germany's Secret War in America, 1914–1917* (Chapel Hill, NC: Algonquin Books, 1989). Martin Kitchen, "The German Invasion in the First World War," *International History Review* 7 (May 1985): 245–60, shows how Berlin sought to use the United States as an informal base to launch raids on Canada. German efforts to trigger war between the United States and Mexico are described in Barbara W. Tuchman, *The Zimmermann Telegram* (New York: Viking, 1958); and Friedrich Katz, *The Secret War in Mexico: Europe, the United States, and the Mexican Revolution* (Chicago: Univ. of Chicago Press, 1981). Laura Garcés, "The German Challenge to the Monroe Doctrine in Mexico, 1917," in Schröder, *Confrontation and Cooperation* (see page 354), 281–313, offers a wider context.

Literature on the preparedness movement is rich. William Waring Tinsley, "The American Preparedness Movement, 1913–1916" (Ph.D. diss., Stanford Univ., 1939), combines thorough research with a pacifist-leaning perspective. John Patrick Finnegan, *Against the Specter of a Dragon: The Campaign for American Military Preparedness, 1914–1917* (Westport, CT: Greenwood, 1974), finds intelligence, patriotism, and wisdom on both sides of the debate but asserts that presidential leadership and clear understanding were lacking. John A.S. Grenville and George Berkeley Young, *Politics, Strategy, and American Diplomacy: Studies in Foreign Policy, 1873–1917* (New Haven, CT: Yale Univ. Press, 1966), indicts Wilson and Daniels for ignoring the advice of naval planners; both leaders underestimated America's role in any overseas conflict. John Whiteclay Chambers II, *To Raise an Army: The Draft Comes to Modern America* (New York: Free Press, 1987), has a surprising amount of material on the neutrality period. In *The Citizen Soldiers: The Plattsburg Training Camp Movement, 1913–1920* (Lexington: Univ. of Kentucky Press, 1972), John Garry Clifford reveals why the efforts of Leonard Wood and attorney Grenville Clark became so successful. Michael Perlman, *To Make Democracy Safe for America: Patricians and Preparedness in the Progressive Era* (Urbana: Univ. of Illinois Press, 1984), offers insightful profiles of preparedness leaders. Chase C. Mooney and Martha E. Layman, "Some Phases of the Compulsory Military Training Movement, 1914–1920," *Mississippi Valley Historical Review* 38 (March 1952): 633–56, indicates continued popular suspicion of this crusade. George C. Herring Jr., "James Hay and the Preparedness Controversy, 1915–1916," *Journal of Southern History* 30 (November 1964): 383–404, shows the agility of the powerful chairman of the House Committee on Military Affairs. For biographies of the general most outspoken in the preparedness crusade, see the hostile account by Jack C. Lane, *Armed Progressive: General Leonard Wood* (San Rafeal, CA: Presidio, 1978); and the somewhat more friendly one by Jack McCallum, *Leonard Wood: Rough Rider, Surgeon, Architect of American Imperialism* (New York: New York Univ. Press, 2006). For Wood's less powerful naval counterpart, consult Paolo E. Coletta, *Admiral Bradley A. Fiske and the American Navy* (Lawrence: Regents Press of Kansas, 1979). Ronald Spector's *Admiral of the New Empire: The Life and Career of George Dewey* (Baton Rouge: Louisiana State Univ. Press, 1974), can serve as a model for full-scale studies on other leading naval figures.

Several preparedness organizations have found their historian. The nation's leading group is covered in Robert D. Ward, "The Origin and Activities of the National Security League, 1914–1919," *Mississippi Valley Historical Review* 47 (June 1960): 51–65; and John Carver Edwards, *Patriots in Pinstripe: Men of the National Security League* (Washington, DC: Univ. Press of America, 1982). Armin Rappaport, *The Navy League of the United States* (Detroit: Wayne State Univ. Press, 1962), denies that business and financial elites used the organization for selfish interests. Needed are studies of the American Defense Society, the American Legion (of 1915), the Viglilantes, and the American Rights Committee.

General propreparedness tracts include Hudson Maxim, *Defenseless America* (New York: Hearst's International Library, 1915); F.V. Greene, *The Present Military Situation in the United States* (New York: Scribner, 1915); William R. Castle Jr., *Wake Up, America: A Plea for the Recognition of Our Individual and National Responsibilities* (New York: Dodd, Mead, 1916); John Callan O'Laughlin, *Imperiled America: A Discussion of the Complications Forced upon the United States by the World War* (Chicago: Reilly and Britton, 1916); and Frederick A. Huidekoper, *The Military Unpreparedness of the United States* (New York: Macmillan, 1916). Invasion scenarios, often centering on Germany, are found in J. Bernard Walker [George Dyson], *America Fallen! The Sequel to the European War* (New York: Dodd, Mead, 1915); Greene, *The Present Military Situation in the United States;* George Lauferti, *The United States and the Next War* (London: Athenaeum, 1915); Cleveland Moffett, *The Conquest of America: A Romance of Disaster and Victory, U.S.A., 1921, A.D.* (New York: George H. Doran, 1916); and Julius W. Muller, *The Invasion of America: A Fact Story Based on the Inexorable Mathematics of War* (New York: Dutton, 1916). Edward S. Martin's *The Diary of a Nation: The War and How We Got Into It* (Garden City, NY: Doubleday, Page, 1917), is a compilation of interventionist editorials written for the weekly *Life* magazine, a journal quite different in focus from the picture periodical launched by Henry Luce in 1936. Preparedness advocate Hudson Maxim offers *Leading Opinions Both For and Against National Defense* (New York: Hearst's International Library, 1916).

Several books condemn Germany's role in the conflict. Former solicitor general James M. Beck contributed *The Evidence in the Case* (New York: Grosset and Dunlap, 1915) and *The War and Humanity* (New York: Putnam, 1916). Beck's background is discussed in Morton Keller, *In Defense of Yesterday: James M. Beck and the Politics of Conservatism* (New York: Coward-McCann, 1958). Other anti-German works include Owen Wister, *The Pentecost of Calamity* (New York: Macmillan, 1915); and William Roscoe Thayer, *Germany vs. Civilization: Notes on the Atrocious War* (Boston: Houghton Mifflin, 1916). Pro-Entente presses also published books revealing Germany's supposedly aggressive war aims, among them Friedrich von Bernhardi, *Germany and the Next War* (New York: Chas. A Eron, 1914); *Germany's War Mania: The Teutonic Point of View as Officially Stated by Her Leaders* (New York: Dodd, Mead, 1915); and *I Accuse (J'Accuse) by a German* (New York: George H. Doran, 1915). Frederic L. Paxson, Edward S. Corwin, and Samuel B. Hardin, eds., *War Cyclopedia: A Handbook for Ready Reference on the Great War* (Washington, DC: Government Printing Office, 1918), covers issues of the 1914–17 period as colored by wartime passions.

Certain works treat the American economy. Although obviously dated, Alexander D. Noyes, *The War Period of American Finance, 1908–1925* (New York: Putnam, 1926), remains a good starting place. Joseph V. Fuller reflects the view of the interwar revisionists in his "The Genesis of the Munitions Traffic," *Journal of Modern History* 6 (March 1934): 280–93. Richard W. Van Alstyne, "Private American Loans to the Allies, 1914–1916," *Pacific Historical Review* 2 (June 1933): 180–93, presents contemporary arguments concerning such investment. John Milton Cooper Jr., "The Command of Gold Reversed: American Loans to Britain, 1915–1917," *Pacific Historical Review* 45 (May 1976): 209–30, shows England's strong financial dependence upon the United States, as does Kathleen Burk, *Britain, America, and the Sinews of War, 1914–1918* (Winchester, MA: Allen and Unwin, 1985). Roberta Allbert Dayer, "Strange Bedfellows: J.P. Morgan & Co., Whitehall, and the Wilson Administration during World War I," *Business History* 18 (July 1976): 127–51, finds the president's advisers suspicious of Wall Street. Thomas A. Bailey, "The United States and the Blacklist during the Great War," *Journal of Modern History* 6 (March 1934): 14–35, reveals that the British ban affected few Americans. In "The Business Press and American Neutrality, 1914–1917," *Mississippi Valley Historical Review* 32 (September 1945): 215–30, Harold C. Syrett denies that the nation's commercial leaders sought to maneuver the nation into war. Ron Chernow traces major financiers over the generations in *The House of Morgan: An American Banking Dynasty and the Rise of Modern Finance* (New York: Atlantic Monthly Press, 1990) and *The Warburgs: The Twentieth-Century Odyssey of a Remarkable Jewish Family* (New York: Random House, 1993). For testimony of leading banking figures concerning loans to the Entente, see U.S. Senate, *Hearings before the Special Committee Investigating the Munitions Industry,* 74th Cong., 2nd sess., 1934. Chaired by Senator Gerald P. Nye (R-N.D.), it was informally called the "Nye Committee."

Much writing has been done on the peace movement. Blanche Wiesen Cook, "Woodrow Wilson and the Anti-Militarists, 1914–1917" (Ph.D. diss., Johns Hopkins Univ., 1970), focuses on the American Union Against Militarism and the "Henry Street group" from which it emerged. Wilson, she claims, was able to co-opt the organization while foolishly ignoring its pleas. James P. Martin casts a wider net in his "The American Peace Movement and the Progressive Era, 1910–1917" (Ph.D. diss., Rice Univ., 1975). Charles Chatfield, *For Peace and Justice: Pacifism in America, 1914–1941* (Knoxville: Univ. of Tennessee Press, 1971; rev. ed., Beacon, 1973), and his "World War I and the Liberal Pacifist in the United States," *American Historical Review* 75 (December 1970): 1920–37, combine organizational and ideological history. C. Roland Marchand, *The American Peace Movement and Social Reform, 1898–1918* (Princeton, NJ: Princeton Univ. Press, 1972), an almost encyclopedic work, is organized topically (e.g., women, labor, the churches). David S. Patterson, "Woodrow Wilson and the Mediation Movement," *Historian* 33 (August 1971): 535–56, portrays the pacifists as sustaining the president in his mediation hopes; at the same time, Patterson finds the chief executive wise in avoiding premature moves. Ernst A. McKay covers a series of opinion leaders in his *Against Wilson and War, 1914–1917* (Malabar, FL: Krieger, 1996). Chapters are devoted to Bryan, Kitchin, New York congressman Meyer London, Missouri senator William J. Stone, publisher William Randolph Hearst, Ohio congressman Isaac Sherwood, Socialist leader Norman Thomas, and the women who participated in the 1915 Hague conference. A favorite cause of peace leaders is effectively treated in Ernest C. Bolt Jr., *Ballots before Bullets: The War Referendum Approach to Peace in America, 1914–1941* (Charlottesville: Univ. Press of Virginia, 1977).

Work by prominent pacifists includes Oswald Garrison Villard, *Preparedness* (Washington, DC: Anti-Preparedness Committee, 1915); Charles E. Jefferson, *Christianity and International Peace* (New York: Thomas Y. Crowell, 1915); William Isaac Hull, *Preparedness: The American versus Military Programme* (Chicago: F.H. Revell, 1916); Washington Gladden, *Forks in the Road* (New York: Macmillan, 1916); John

Haynes Holmes, *New Wars for Old* (New York: Dodd, Mead, 1916); and Frederic C. Howe, *Why War?* (New York: Scribner, 1916). Such pacifists as Hull, Holmes, and Amos Pinchot deserve further study.

The International Congress of Women, which met at The Hague in 1915, has received much attention. One might start with Katherine Joslin's edition of Jane Addams, *Peace and Bread in Time of War* (1929; reprint, Urbana: Univ. of Illinois Press, 2002); and Harriet Hyman Alonso's edition of Jane Addams, Emily G. Balch, and Alice Hamilton, *Women at the Hague: The International Congress of Women and Its Results* (1915; reprint, Urbana: Univ. of Illinois Press, 2003). For able treatments of Addams's life and thought, see John C. Farrell, *Beloved Lady: A History of Jane Addams' Ideas on Reform and Peace* (Baltimore: Johns Hopkins Press, 1967); Allen F. Davis, *American Heroine: The Life and Legend of Jane Addams* (New York: Oxford Univ. Press, 1973); and Jean Bethke Elshtain, *Jane Adams and the Dream of American Democracy* (New York: Basic Books, 2002). Also significant are Mercedes M. Randall, *Improper Bostonian: Emily Greene Balch* (New York: Twayne, 1964); and Marie Louise Degen, *The History of the Woman's Peace Party* (Baltimore: Johns Hopkins Press, 1939). David S. Patterson's extremely comprehensive *The Search for Negotiated Peace: Women's Activism and Citizen Diplomacy in World War I* (New York: Routledge, 2008) covers far more than the title would indicate. Barbara S. Kraft's *The Peace Ship: Henry Ford's Pacifist Adventure in the First World War* (New York: Macmillan, 1978) reveals surprising merit in a venture often dismissed as quixotic.

Autobiographies of peace activists include volume 2 of David Starr Jordan, *The Days of a Man: Being Memories of a Naturalist, Teacher, and Minor Prophet of Democracy*, 2 vols. (New York: World Book, 1922); Louis P. Lochner, *Always the Unexpected: A Book of Reminiscences* (New York: Macmillan, 1956); and Lillian D. Wald, *Windows on Henry Street* (Boston: Little, Brown, 1934). For Jordan, see also Edward McNall Burns, *David Starr Jordan: Prophet of Freedom* (Stanford, CA: Stanford Univ. Press, 1953); and Luther William Spoehr, "Progress' Pilgrim: David Starr Jordan and the Circle of Reform" (Ph.D. diss., Stanford Univ., 1975).

The very titles of Ray H. Abrams, *Preachers Present Arms* (New York: Round Table, 1933); and Richard M. Gamble, *The War for Righteousness: Progressive Christianity, the Great War, and the Rise of the Messianic Nation* (Wilmington, DE: ISI Books, 2003), betray their perspective. An in-depth look at American Protestantism, with special attention to denominational journals, is still much needed.

Connected is the matter of internationalism. Warren F. Kuehl has contributed two major works: *Seeking World Order: The United States and World Organization* (Nashville: Vanderbilt Univ. Press, 1969); and *Hamilton Holt: Journalist, Internationalist, and Educator* (Gainesville: Univ. of Florida Press, 1960), the latter an account of the editor of the *Independent* magazine. Ruhl J. Bartlett, *The League to Enforce Peace* (Chapel Hill: Univ. of North Carolina Press, 1944), remains definitive on its topic.

Several scholars have studied press opinion. According to Ralph O. Nafziger's massive study, "The American Press and Public Opinion during the World War, 1914 to April 1917" (Ph.D. diss., Univ. of Wisconsin, 1936), newspapers did not create sentiment; rather, they served as "middle men," simply reflecting already existing views. Russell Buchanan, "European Propaganda and American Public Opinion, 1914–1917" (Ph.D. diss., Stanford Univ., 1938), an extremely thorough work, argues that even in late 1916, the public might have favored peace although it remained strongly pro-Entente. Kevin O'Keefe's *A Thousand Deadlines: The New York Press and American Neutrality, 1914–17* (The Hague: Martinus Nijhoff, 1972), concedes that most of the city's newspapers showed an initial sympathy for the Allies but always within a neutralist framework. There is no substitute for perusing issues of the *Literary Digest* and *Current Opinion*. Selected newspapers are worth studying, the *New York World,* because of its closeness to the Wilson administration, being foremost among them. So, too, are certain journalists, and here one might mention Will Irwin, Richard Harding Davis, John Callan O'Laughlin, David Lawrence, and Frederick Palmer.

Studies of public opinion are always somewhat elusive, particularly those written before the era of polling. Hence, if examining events before 1935, one is forced to focus on opinion-makers. For example, examination of the reactions of university faculty to Wilsonian policy could prove fruitful. A focus on selected periods, such as the last few months of peace, would be most helpful. Justus D. Doenecke, *When the Wicked Rise: American Opinion-Makers and the Manchurian Crisis of 1931–1933* (Lewisburg, PA: Bucknell Univ. Press, 1984), might serve as a model.

Propaganda has received more than its share of research. German American propagandist George Sylvester Viereck presents a colorful account of propaganda from all belligerents, in the process covering his own role in such efforts, in *Spreading Germs of Hate* (New York: Horace Liveright, 1930). In a study highly influenced by the revisionist school, H.C. Peterson, *Propaganda for War: The Campaign against American Neutrality* (Norman: Univ. of Oklahoma Press, 1939), contrasts British effectiveness to German incompetence, although he greatly exaggerates the former's influence.

David Wayne Hirst, "German Propaganda in the United States, 1914–1917" (Ph.D. diss., Northwestern Univ., 1962), asserts that Teutonic defenders succeeded far better than they realized. Felice A. Bonadio, "The Failure of German Propaganda in the United States, 1914–1917," *Mid-America* 41 (January 1959): 40–57, sees ultimate defeat lying in the influence of the "melting pot." Reinhard R. Doerries argues that Teutonic apologia was ineffective. See his "Promoting *Kaiser* and *Reich:* Imperial German Propaganda in the United States during World War I," in Schröder, *Confrontation and Cooperation,* 235–65. Frank Trommler presents similar conclusions in "Inventing the Enemy: German-American Cultural Relations, 1900–1917," also in Schröder, *Confrontation and Cooperation,* 99–125.

The German case is also presented in such works as *The Truth about Germany* (New York: Trow Press, 1914); Hugh Münsterberg, *The War and America* (New York: D. Appleton, 1914); Hugh Münsterberg, *The Peace and America* (New York: Appleton, 1915); Edmund von Mach, *What Germany Wants* (Boston: Little, Brown, 1914); Herman Ridder, *Hyphenations* (New York: Max Schmetterling, 1915), a volume of editorials that appeared in the *New Yorker Staats-Zeitung;* Frank Harris, *England or Germany?* (New York: Wilmarch, 1915); Karl H. von Wiegand, *Current Misconceptions about the War* (New York: Fatherland, 1915); John W. Burgess, *Germany's Just Cause* (New York: Fatherland, 1915); Kuno Francke, *A German-American's Confession of Faith* (New York: H. Holt, 1916); George B. McClellan, *The Heel of War* (New York: Dillingham, 1916); Gustavus Ohlinger, *Their True Faith and Allegiance* (New York: Macmillan, 1916); Roland Hugins, *Germany Misjudged: An Appeal to International Good Will and the Interest of a Lasting Peace* (Chicago: Open Court, 1916); Frederick Franklin Schrader, *Hand-*

book *Political, Statistical, and Sociological for German Americans* (New York: Frederick Franklin Schrader, 1916); and the New York weekly *Vital Issue,* which in October 1915 became *Issues and Events.*

British efforts have been the subject of several studies: James Duane Squires, *British Propaganda at Home and in the United States from 1914 to 1917* (Cambridge, MA: Harvard Univ. Press 1935); Cate Haste, *Keeping the Home Fires Burning: Propaganda in the First World War* (London: Allen Lane, 1977); and M.L. Sanders and Philip M. Taylor, *British Propaganda during the First World War, 1914–18* (London: Macmillan, 1982). Stewart Halsey Ross, *Propaganda for War: How the United States was Conditioned to Fight the Great War of 1914–1918* (Joshua Tree, CA: Progressive Press, 2009), mars its extensive research by its implications of conspiracy.

As an ethnic group, German Americans have been subject to much examination. Frederick C. Luebke offers the most sensitive and thorough analysis in his *Bonds of Loyalty: German-Americans and World War I* (De Kalb: Northern Illinois Univ. Press, 1974). Clifton James Child, *The German-Americans in Politics, 1914–1917* (Madison: Univ. of Wisconsin Press, 1939), denies any domination from Berlin. See also Child's "German-American Attempts to Prevent the Exportation of Munitions of War, 1914–1915," *Mississippi Valley Historical Review* 25 (December 1938): 351–68. Carl Wittke, *German-Americans and the World War* (Columbus: Ohio State Archeological and Historical Society, 1936), stresses the Ohio press. Karl J.R. Arndt and May E. Olsen, *German-American Newspapers and Periodicals, 1732–1955: History and Bibliography* (Heidelberg: Quelle & Myer, 1961), presents an extremely thorough listing. Dean R. Esslinger, "American German and Irish Attitudes toward Neutrality, 1914–1917: A Study of Catholic Minorities," *Catholic Historical Review* 53 (July 1967): 194–216, reveals that a greater percentage of Roman Catholics than of the general population favored the Central Powers. In December 1918 and January 1919, a subcommittee of the Senate Judiciary Committee held hearings, reported in *Brewing and Liquor Interests and German Propaganda* (Washington, DC: Government Printing Office, 1919), which combined serious investigation with sensationalist findings.

In *States of Belonging: German-American Intellectuals and the First World War* (Cambridge, MA: Harvard Univ. Press, 1979), Phyllis Keller presents shrewd intellectual portraits of Hugo Münsterberg, George Sylvester Viereck, and the Roosevelt partisan Hermann Hagedorn. Viereck is treated most responsibly in Neil M. Johnson, *George Sylvester Viereck: German-American Propagandist* (Urbana: Univ. of Illinois Press, 1972). For a personal memoir, see Elmer Gertz, *Odyssey of a Barbarian: The Biography of George Sylvester Viereck* (Buffalo, NY: Prometheus Books, 1978). There is, of course, no substitute for Viereck's *Fatherland, Viereck's New World,* and *Viereck's: The American Weekly.*

Irish Americans, too, have been covered extensively. Joseph Edward Cuddy, in *Irish-America and National Isolationism, 1914–1920* (New York: Arno Press, 1976) and in "Irish-American Propagandists and Neutrality, 1914–1917," *Mid-America* 49 (October 1967): 252–75, stresses anti-interventionist feeling, as does John Patrick Buckley, "The New York Irish: Their View of American Foreign Policy, 1914–1981" (Ph.D. diss., New York Univ., 1974): 605–18. In "Some American Responses to the Easter Rebellion," *Historian* 29 (August 1967): 205–18, David M. Tucker shows surprising sympathies for the Irish among Anglophiles. Charles Callan Tansill, *America and the*

Fight for Irish Freedom: 1866–1922—An Old Story Based upon New Data (New York: Devin-Adair, 1987), presents Irish-American relations from the point of view of editor John Devoy, leader of Clan na Gael, and Tammany judge Daniel Cohalan. Jeremiah O'Leary, *My Political Trial and Experiences* (New York: Jefferson, 1919), is the memoir of a self-confessed firebrand. Equally impassioned is *The King, the Kaiser, and Irish Freedom* (New York: Devin-Adair, 1915), by James K. McGuire, former mayor of Syracuse. Other ethnic groups should be researched, including Italians, Americans stemming from the British Isles, and the nationalities of the German, Russian, and Austro-Hungarian empires. Joseph Rappaport, "Jewish Immigrants and World War I: A Study of American Jewish Press Reactions" (Ph.D. diss., Columbia Univ., 1951), offers a start on a fruitful topic.

Certain opinion leaders have received special attention. Of the many biographies of America's leading press czar, Ben Proctor's *William Randolph Hearst: The Later Years, 1911–1951* (New York: Oxford Univ. Press, 2007) is outstanding, although there is no substitute for reading firsthand the *New York American.* For material on the *New Republic,* see Charles Forcey, *The Crossroads of Liberalism: Croly, Weyl, Lippmann, and the Progressive Era, 1900–1925* (New York: Oxford Univ. Press, 1961); Ronald Steel, *Walter Lippmann and the American Century* (Boston: Little, Brown, 1980); and David W. Levy, *Herbert Croly of the New Republic: The Life and Thought of an American Progressive* (Princeton, NJ: Princeton Univ. Press, 1985). The publisher of the *Nation* and the *New York Evening Post* is the subject of Michael Wreszin, *Oswald Garrison Villard: Pacifist at War* (Bloomington: Indiana Univ. Press, 1965); and Villard's own *Fighting Years: Memoirs of a Liberal Editor* (New York: Harcourt, Brace, 1939). Villard's *Germany Embattled: An American Interpretation* (New York: Scribner, 1915) shows why the noted German American pacifist did not desire Berlin's victory. Daniel C. Haskell performed an invaluable service by compiling *The Nation, Volumes 1–105: Indexes of Titles and Contributors* (New York: New York Public Library, 1951). Willis Fletcher Johnson, *George Harvey: "A Passionate Patriot"* (Boston: Houghton Mifflin, 1929), is the sole work on the publisher of the *North American Review;* a far stronger biography is needed. For the *Outlook*'s editor, see Ira V. Brown, *Lyman Abbott, Christian Evolutionist: A Study in Religious Liberalism* (Cambridge, MA: Harvard Univ. Press, 1953).

American socialism is subject to intense and often sympathetic study. Norman Binder presents the most extensive general treatment in his "American Socialism and the First World War" (Ph.D. diss., New York Univ., 1970). Socialist presidential candidate Allan L. Benson attacks preparedness in *Inviting War to America* (New York: B.W. Huebsch, 1916), but far more is needed on Benson and his 1916 campaign. Frederick C. Giffin, *Six Who Protested: Radical Opposition to the First World War* (Port Washington, NY: Kennikat, 1977), deals with Emma Goldman, John Reed, Max Eastman, Morris Hillquit, William Haywood, and Eugene V. Debs.

Studies of certain Socialists are most helpful. For work on the prominent congressman from New York's lower East Side, see Gordon Jerome Goldberg, "Meyer London: A Political Biography" (Ph.D. diss., Lehigh Univ., 1971); and William Frieburger, "The Lone Socialist Vote: A Political Study of Meyer London" (Ph.D. diss., Univ. of Cincinnati, 1980).

New York party leader Morris Hillquit has written an autobiography, *Loose Leaves from a Busy Life* (New York: Macmillan, 1934), although one should also consult

Norma Fain Pratt, *Morris Hillquit: A Political History of an American Jewish Socialist* (Westport, CT: Greenwood, 1979). For information about the editor of the *Masses*, note Max Eastman's autobiographical *Enjoyment of Living* (New York: Harper, 1948); and William L. O'Neill, *The Last Romantic: A Life of Max Eastman* (New York: Oxford Univ. Press, 1978).

Index

Devil Theory of War, The (Beard), 301
Devlin, Patrick: on Wilson's leadership style, 5; on Britain's "starvation policy," 47; on *Lusitania* crisis, 72, 79; on *Arabic* crisis, 119, 121; on House-Grey memorandum, 144; on Lansing's modus vivendi plan, 157; on British blacklist, 185; on Wilson's peace bid (Dec. 18, 1916), 231; on Lansing's sabotage of Wilson's peace bid, 234; on Bernstorff's response (Jan. 18, 1917), 241; on Wilson's "peace without victory" speech, 244; on U.S. armed neutrality, 259; on British neutrality order (Feb. 16, 1917), 260; on Wilson's "willful men" statement, 275; on entering the war, 287
Dewey, George H., 33, 36, 106, 146, 197
Diennes, Martin, 115
Dies, Martin, Sr., 37
Dill, Clarence, 294
Dodge, Cleveland H., 127
Doerries, Reinhard R., 223, 264
Dominican Republic, 133
Drummond, Eric, 180
Dumba, Konstantin Theodor, 114–16, 133
Du Pont, Henry A., 192
Du Pont, T. Coleman, 204
Du Pont Company, 133, 196
Dutton, Samuel Train, 127

Eagle, Joe H., 293
Easter Rebellion. *See* Ireland, rebellion of 1916
Eastman, Crystal. *See* Crystal Eastman Benedict
Eastman, Max, 149, 195, 215, 254–55
Eavestone (ship), 257
Eckhardt, Heinrich von, 263
Edelsheim, Franz, 33
Edison, Thomas A., 194
economy, U.S.: depression of 1914, 41–43; begins to rebound, 45, 61; observers on, 51; McAdoo on, 124–25; Lansing on, 125; experiences boom (1916), 215; dependence on Allied trade, 227; stock market plummets, 234; Page on, 283; and entrance into war, 288
elections: of 1914, 13, 42; of 1916, 201–16
Eliot, Charles W., 25
Emergency Peace Federation (EPF): organized, 254; proposes German-American High Commission, 254; meets with Wilson, 264, 287; opposes armed-ship bill, 276; proposes options to war, 284
Europe (ship), 66
Evelyn (ship), 67–68, 292, 294

Fairbanks, Charles W., 214
Falaba (ship), 68–69, 77, 80, 83, 305
Falkenhayn, Erich von: background of, 12; and *Arabic* crisis, 118; favors U-boat use, 129–30, 158, 171, 180
Fall, Albert B., 272
Fatherland: background of, x, 16; German subsidies of, 16, 114; early anti-interventionist stance of, 21; defends Wilhelm II, 26; denounces Allies, 26; defends Germany in Belgium, 30; on Bryan, 56, 82; opposes Wilson's "strict accountability" policy, 60; defends *Falaba* sinking, 68–69; defends *Gulflight* sinking, 70; and *Lusitania* crisis, 73, 87, 88; defends *Armenian* sinking, 85; on attempted Morgan assassination, 91; presents invasion scenario, 107; on *Arabic* crisis, 117, 119, 120; on *Hesperian* sinking, 120; defends Turks in Armenia, 127; defends *Ancona* sinking, 127–28; on German sabotage accusations, 132, 133, 174; on preparedness, 148, 192; on *Sussex* crisis, 169; reveres Irish rebels, 175; condemn Paris economic conference (1916), 177; role in 1916 election, 211, 213, 214; defends Belgian deportations, 228; changes name to *New World,* 254; favors breaking relations with Germany, 254; changes name to *Viereck's: The American Weekly,* 268. *See also* Collman, Charles A.; O'Sheel, Shaemus; Schrader, Frederick Franklin; Viereck, George Sylvester; Viereck, Louis
Federal Reserve Board: and 1914 financial panic, 41; and "cotton loan" funds, 42; warns against investing in Allied notes, 224–25, 288; attacked by Lindbergh, 269; approves resuming foreign loans, 283
Ferris, Scott, 193, 293
Finnegan, John Patrick: on preparedness sentiment, 105; on invasion scenarios, 108; on Roosevelt's preparedness stance, 112; on U.S. defense needs, 146; on Hay-Chamberlain Act, 189, 194; on National Guard debate, 191; on 1916 naval bill,